German Poetry
A Critical Anthology

German Poetry

A Critical Anthology

Robert M. Browning
Hamilton College

and

Thomas Kerth
State University of New York
at Stony Brook

Editors

BRANDYWINE PRESS • St. James, New York

ISBN: 1-881-089-40-1

1st Printing 1995

Telephone Orders: 1-800-345-1776

Printed in the United States of America

Acknowledgments

We should like to take this opportunity to thank Professors Edwin H. Zeydel and Stuart Pratt Atkins for their extremely valuable help and advice and for their careful perusal of an earlier version of this manuscript. To the libraries of Hamilton College and the State University of New York at Stony Brook, we are grateful for adding to their collections the books we needed and, when that was impossible, to facilitate our use of interlibrary loan. The Herzog August Bibliothek, Wolfenbüttel, and the Schiller Nationalmuseum, Marbach am Neckar, generously provided us with many illustrations for this textbook. To Professors Ulrich K. Goldsmith, Otto K. Leidke, Richard Exner, and John R. Russell we are grateful for a number of suggestions and much encouragement. We also thank Patricia O'Brien and her assistants, especially Debbie Debellis, for their invaluable help in preparing this manuscript for publication, and Kevin Meagher for his help in compiling bibliography. We particularly wish to remember Helene Ulmer Browning, wife to one of us and wonderful friend to the other, for listening to Robert read hundreds of poems aloud and for giving him her "on the spot" reaction to them. And, last but far from least, we are thankful to all our students throughout the years for showing us what needs to be clarified if they are to understand a poem.

Hamilton College and SUNY Stony Brook   R.M.B. and T. K.
March, 1995

Table of Contents

---

*Starred poems are discussed as they occur in the text, sometimes in considerable detail, sometimes only in general or in part. Footnotes provide helpful commentary on a number of poems not starred.

Preface

To the Student,

After two years of college-level German you should be able to read and enjoy the greater number of the poems in this anthology. A good many of them you could easily have read even earlier, while some, even with the assistance provided by the notes, will still take a good deal of thought and study. Your anthologists hope that they have not included any poems that are not worth this effort. Since this text does not contain a vocabulary, you will probably need to consult your dictionary to understand everything. But much help is provided here in the form of explanations of allusions that may be unfamiliar to you, glosses of many words whose meaning you might mistake (or might not find in the ordinary desk dictionary), and assistance with difficult constructions and unusual grammatical forms.

This anthology contains a number of interpretive essays, most but not all of them in English. You are not necessarily expected to agree with all these interpretations. Remember that every work of art can be seen from many different points of view, and the greater that work is, the more points of view. *The* interpretation of *Hamlet*, for example, is still to be found. In our view, there is perhaps only one "rule" for analyzing a poem: the analysis must be derived from and consistent with the work itself, not imposed from without, though of course outside information can be of great assistance.

This anthology also contains quite a number of questions, usually on the poem you have just read, which are meant to help you along the way towards an understanding of the poem; occasionally, interpretations by German critics have been placed under the questions. The purpose of these questions is to make you read the poems more closely and think, perhaps even dream, about them more intensely. "On rêve sur un poème comme on rêve sur un être," a French poet (Paul Valéry) has said: one can dream over a poem as over a living form. A poem we have read only once we have hardly read at all. Poetry is the most concentrated — though not necessarily the most involved — form of verbal expression we know. Thus, quite unlike the way one reads a newspaper, one must always read a poem *slowly*. And, because it possesses compact and multiple layers of feeling and meaning, one should read, and even dream, a poem again and again. Some may want to know where to find further material on German lyric poetry. A great deal of excellent work has been done in this field.

1.   Blume, Bernhard, and Adolf E. Schroeder. "Interpretations of German Poetry (1939-1956): A Bibliography." *Monatshefte* 49 (1957): 241-263. [Lists single independent interpretations of individual poems.]

2.   Friedmann, Hermann, Otto Mann, and Wolfgang Rothe, ed. *Deutsche Literatur im zwanzigsten Jahrhundert: Gestalten und Strukturen: Dreiundzwanzig Darstellungen.* Bern: Francke, ⁵1967. [Critical essays on poets and movements; not limited to lyric poetry.]

3.   Friedmann, Hermann, and Otto Mann, ed. *Expressionismus: Gestalten einer Bewegung.* Heidelberg: Rother, 1956. [Another compilation; studies on German lyricists and dramatists of the Expressionist movement.]

4.   Heselhaus, Clemens. *Deutsche Lyrik der Moderne von Nietzsche bis Yvan Goll,* Düsseldorf: Bagel, ²1962. [History, interpretation and evaluation of the work of 38 lyric poets. For advanced students.]

5.   Hinderer, Walter, ed. *Geschichte der deutschen Lyrik vom Mittelalter bis zur Gegenwart.* Stuttgart: Reclam, 1983. [Separate essays by different authors for periods and literary movements; useful bibliography.]

6.   Hirschenauer, Rupert, and Albrecht Weber, ed. *Wege zum Gedicht.* München and Zürich: Schnell & Schneider, ⁸1972. [Contains, besides interpretations of 58 poems from the 12th to the middle of the 20th century, a detailed bibliography on the interpretation of German lyric poetry.]

7.   Hock, Erich, ed. *Motivgleiche Gedichte.* Am Born der Literatur A7L. Bamberg: Bayerischer Verlagsanstalt, ⁷1964. Also: *Motivgleiche Gedichte: Lehrerband,* ⁷1963. [Hock's analyses, written in clear, though not simple, German, can hardly be too highly recommended. These volumes were prepared for use in German Gymnasien.]

8.   Kayser, Wolfgang. *Das sprachliche Kunstwerk: Eine Einführung in die Literaturwissenschaft.* Bern: Francke, ¹⁸1978. [One of the best critical works of its day. Not confined to lyric poetry. Useful bibliography.]

9.   Klein, Johannes. *Geschichte der deutschen Lyrik von Luther bis zum Ausgang des Zweiten Weltkrieges.* Zweite, erweiterte Ausgabe. Wiesbaden: F. Steiner, 1960. [Exhaustive history of German lyrical poetry with bibliography.]

10.   Kohlschmidt, Werner, and Herbert Lehnert, ed. *Geschichte der deutschen Literatur von den Anfängen bis zur Gegenwart,* ed. Reclams Universal Bibliothek. 5 vols. Stuttgart: Reclam, 1974-80. [Good overview, not just poetry; useful bibliography.]

11.   Pfeiffer, Johannes. *Wege zur Dichtung: Eine Einführung in die Kunst des Lesens.* Hamburg: Wittig, ⁷1969. [Pfeiffer is one of the most perceptive readers of poetry as poetry.]

12. Schneider, Wilhelm. *Liebe zum deutschen Gedicht. Ein Begleiter für alle Freunde der Lyrik*. Freiburg: Herder, ⁵1963. [Essays on 36 poems.]

13. Wiese, Benno von, ed. *Die deutsche Lyrik: Form und Geschichte*. 2 vols. Düsseldorf: Bagel, 1956; Schwann-Bagel, 1981. [Detailed analysis by different hands of 94 poems from the Middle Ages to the middle 20th century. Informative and stimulating, but often difficult. Bibliographical references.]

14. Echtermeyer, Theodor, ed. *Deutshe Gedichte von den Anfängen bis zur Gegenwart*, neugestaltet von Benno von Wiese, 20 Jh. von E. K Paefgen. Bielefeld: Cornelsen, ¹⁸1990. [A standard anthology twice refurbished. Bibliographical aids.]

15. Hohoff, Curt, ed. *Flügel der Zeit: Deutshe Gedichte 1900-1950*. Fischer-Bücherei 113. Frankfurt a.M.: Fischer, 1956. [Good selection of modern poetry.]

16. Holthusen, Hans Egon, and Friedhelm Kemp, ed. *Ergriffenes Dasein: Deutsche Lyrik des zwanzigsten Jahrhunderts*. Ebenhausen bei München: Hartfrid Voss, ¹³1972. [Probably the best selection of modern German poetry available; seldom overlaps with 14.]

17. *Killy, Walter, ed. Epochen der deutschen Lyrik*. DTV Wissenschaftliche Reihe 4015-4024, 4162-63, 4184. 10 vols in 12. München: DTV, 1977-84. [Comprehensive, though idiosyncratic selection of poems from the Middle Ages to 1960. Original orthography in earlier poems can be difficult for students.]

18. *The Penguin Book of German Verse*, intro. and ed. by Leonard Forster. Baltimore: Penguin, ²1972. [This interesting anthology contains prose translations of each poem.]

19. Kayser, Wolfgang. *Kleine deutsche Versschule*. Dalp Taschenbücher 306. Bern: Francke, ²¹1982. [An indispensable vademecum for anyone interested in German verse. Treats questions of form in a delightfully clear fashion.]

20. Paul, Otto, and Ingeborg Glier. *Deutsche Metrik*. München: Hueber, ⁹1974. [The standard reference for metrics; used by students in German universities.]

To the Teacher,

It may come as a surprise that an anthology arranged chronologically — and not thematically — should contain no historical introduction. Insofar as this text pretends to instruct in literary history, it seeks to do so by means of actual example, that is through examination of the poems as they occur in the body of the book, or by means of introductory remarks to selections from poets whose work forms an historically important articulation in the development of German literature. One will thus find material on the Baroque under Opitz, on Pietism under Tersteegen, on Romanticism under Novalis, on Symbolism under C. F. Meyer, and so on. But this is not an anthology to illustrate the history of a literature. It is an anthology to introduce the English-speaking student to some of the greatest poems in the German language. In making the selections, therefore, literary excellence was the first criterion; historical importance was a distinctly secondary, though not entirely neglected, consideration. This will account both for certain omissions and certain inclusions.

As we are all aware, literary criticism in Europe, as in America and Britain, has taken a new direction in the last two decades. Critics have turned to an intensive examination of literary texts primarily as examples of sociological power discourse and intertextuality rather than literary structures or, following an earlier trend, historical and biographical documents. While critical theory can be a fascinating way for the initiated to reexamine and reinterpret texts, it can also be an added interpretive hurdle for the student who is just beginning to study a foreign literature. For this reason, we have chosen to refer, in the text of this introduction to German poetry, almost exclusively to "classic" interpretations from the justly renowned practitioners of "the art of interpretation," among them, Heinrich Henel, Erich Hock, Wolfgang Kayser, Johannes Pfeiffer, Emil Staiger, Erich Trunz, and Elizabeth Wilkinson. Those who are fortunate enough to have more theoretically sophisticated students who can profit from the newest trends in critical theory will, we hope, find it easy to supplement our interpretive framework with additional material. For us, it is not a question of presenting more "modern" or "up-to-date" theories; it is one of presenting the great poetry in the German language in a way that is most easily accessible to the American student of German.

While compiled and annotated with the needs of the American undergraduate clearly in mind, and thereby offering more aids to first-level comprehension than any available large anthology of German verse, *German Poetry* also treats the reader as an intelligent person, interested in — or capable of becoming interested in — questions beyond a bare and initial comprehension of the text. It tries to involve the student deeply in poetry.

As stimulants to class discussion and as a means of encouraging closer reading, a fairly large number of questions have been included, some rather elementary in nature, others more difficult. These questions are meant to lead to, not to dictate, an interpretation. Occasionally an analysis by a German critic has been placed under the questions to provide further stimulus.

The questions, as starting points for class discussion, naturally do not pretend to "exhaust" the poems; neither do the interpretations, not even the more detailed ones. Some interpretative passages are by the compilers. Some are entirely by other hands or are based upon analyses by several critics. Here, especially, we have tried to exploit the gratifyingly rich critical material available on German lyric poetry. Undoubtedly there will be far from universal agreement on some of these analyses. This is not necessarily to the bad; for even if they arouse decided argument, the analyses will serve their purpose if they arouse thoughtful discussion. The goal is involvement. The compilers are clearly aware that a poem can be interpreted or analyzed meaningfully more than one way.

With three exceptions, the poems included in this anthology are meant to be complete and unabridged. (The exceptions are: the 31 lines taken from Klaj's *Der Engel- und Drachen-Streit*, Zäunemann's *Ode auf die ... Herren*

Hussaren, and the omission of the final *Hymne an die Nacht*.) We have not included some famous poems from novels when the context of the larger work seemed essential to the proper understanding of it.

A word concerning the chronological limits of this book. Luther's German, and only some of it, is the earliest the student can read with relative ease; hence the anthology begins with Luther. *Minnesang*, as we all know, requires special study. Had it been included, it would have had to be in translation, which seemed rather pointless in a book of this kind. The birth date 1900 was chosen as the extreme limit in the modern direction. This date permits the inclusion of the most important poets writing in the first half of this century, while relieving the compilers of the fear of anthologizing that which could soon prove ephemeral. It is, of course, in selections from poets after Rilke that one feels most uncertain. Here we have gratefully accepted guidance from other lovers of German poetry, though never against personal conviction.

Martin Luther (1483–1546)

Der 46. Psalm
Deus noster refugium et virtus

Ein feste Burg ist unser Gott,
Ein gute Wehr und Waffen,
Er hilft uns frei aus aller Not,
Die uns itzt[1] hat betroffen.
Der alt böse Feind   5
Mit Ernst er's itzt meint,
Groß Macht und viel List
Sein grausam[2] Rüstung ist,
Auf Erd ist nicht seins gleichen.[3]

Mit unser Macht ist nichts getan,   10
Wir sind gar bald verloren,
Es streit[4] für uns der rechte Mann,
Den Gott selbst hat erkoren.[5]
Fragstu,[6] wer der ist?
Er heißt Jesu Christ,   15
Der Herr Zebaoth,[7]
Und ist kein ander Gott,
Das Feld muß er behalten.[8]

---

[1] =*jetzt*   [2] =*schreckenerregend*   [3] 'equal'   [4] 'there fights'   [5] =*erwählt*   [6] =*fragst du*
[7] 'Lord of hosts' (Hebrew)   [8] 'gain'

Und wenn die Welt voll Teufel wär
Und wollt uns gar[9] verschlingen,   20
So fürchten wir uns nicht zu sehr,
Es soll uns doch gelingen.
Der Fürst dieser Welt,
Wie saur er sich stellt,[10]
Tut er uns doch nicht,[11]   25
Das macht, er ist gericht,[12]
Ein Wörtlein[13] kann ihn fällen.

Das Wort[14] sie sollen lassen stahn,[15]
Und kein Dank dazu haben.[16]
Er[17] ist bei uns wohl auf dem Plan[18]   30
Mit seinem Geist und Gaben.
Nehmen sie[19] den Leib,
Gut, Ehr', Kind und Weib,
Laß fahren dahin,
Sie haben's[20] kein Gewinn,   35
Das Reich[21] muß uns doch bleiben.

"Ein feste Burg" has been called "the marching song of the Reformation." It first appeared in the hymnals in 1529, the year of the Augsburg Confession. Its tone is militantly confident. A comparison with the 46th Psalm shows us at once that Luther has not merely translated "a song for the children of Korah" into German, but written a new song for the children of the new faith, the "youth" of the Reformation.

As a community of laymen, the evangelical church expects *all* its members to take part in the divine service. Hymns for congregational singing are therefore of central importance in creating a sense of union and participation. In this hymn the sense of union — the first person plural is used throughout — is especially strong. So is the sense of imminent danger, and this reflects the historical situation of the new faith. Like all hymns, "Ein feste Burg" is poetry for daily use. This does not keep it from being good, perhaps even great. That it eminently fulfills the purpose for which it was written is proved by its continued use in Protestant churches everywhere.

---

[9]=*gänzlich* [10]'acts' [11]=*nichts* [12]'That's because he's judged' [13]i.e., *ein Gotteswort*
[14]*the Scriptures* [15]=*stehen* [16]=*ob sie wollen oder nicht* [17]Christ [18]'field' (of battle)
[19]'though they take' [20]*es* (genitive) 'therefrom' [21]the Kingdom of Heaven

Let us examine the stanza structure of "Ein feste Burg," marking the stresses, counting the syllables, and noting the rime scheme:

Ein féste Búrg ist únser Gótt,	*a*	8 syllables /4 stresses / masc. rime*
Ein gúte Wéhr und Wáffen,	*b*	7 syllables / 3 stresses / fem. rime
Er hílft uns freí aus áller Nót,	*a*	
Die úns itzt hát betróffen.	*b*	
Der ált böse Feínd	*c*	5 syllables / 3 stresses / masc. rime
Mit Érnst èr's itzt meínt,	*c*	
Groß Mácht ùnd viel Líst	*d*	(like c)
Sein graúsam Rüstung íst.	*d*	6 syllables / 3 stresses/ masc. rime
Auf Érd ist nícht seins gleíchen.	*x*	7 syllables / 3 stresses / fem. rimeless

The structure of "Ein feste Burg" is clearly evident: the first four verses (*Aufgesang*) are strongly set off against the second four (*Abgesang*), and each group is bound within itself by rime. Moreover, the first group is sub-divided into two sets of verses with identical rime and stress patterns. The last verse of the stanza, which does not rime (*Waise*) and which contrasts in form with the verses immediately preceding, seems to stand isolated. To note all this might be mere pedantry — if, that is, it led no further. But it is not difficult to show that it does lead further. In a *formal* sense each stanza presents a dichotomy, or cutting-in-two, plus a third element. Our problem is to try to discover how the formal structure of the poem reflects the content or "message."

One can easily ascertain what is reflected by the division between the first four verses and the second four. In the first stanza, it is the conflict between God and the devil, in their struggle for man's soul. In the second, it is the contrast between man's weakness and Christ's strength. In the third, it is the contrast between the strength of the Christian, for whom Christ, *der rechte Mann*, is fighting, and the impotence of the devil. In the fourth stanza, it is the contrast between spiritual victory and material defeat, for that which gains us the Kingdom of Heaven may well lose us the goods of this world. All this accounts very well for the meaning of the form of the first eight verses of each stanza. But what about the ninth verse?

"Ein feste Burg" concerns itself with the struggle between God and the devil for the soul of man. With Christ's help, that is with the help of the Word made flesh (*der rechte Mann*), God wins the victory and man gains salvation. The struggle is ended. It is this cessation of strife or final victory over Satan that is symbolically expressed in the last verse of each stanza. If we read the final *Waisen* (unrimed lines) in sequence by themselves, we see that they sum up the meaning of the poem.

---

*The terms "masculine rime" and "feminine rime" are used in both German and English to denote verses that end on accented syllables (*getán*) or unaccented syllables (*bleíben*), respectively.

Johannes Heermann (1585–1647)

In Krieges- und Verfolgungsgefahr

Groß ist, o großer Gott,
Die Not, so[1] uns betroffen.
Das Unrecht haben wir
Wie Wasser eingesoffen,
Doch das ist unser Trost: 5
Du bist voll Gütigkeit,
Du nimmst die Strafe hin,[2]
Wann uns die Sünd' ist leid.[3]

Wir liegen hier für[4] dir,
Betrauern[5] unsre Sünden.   10
Ach, laß uns Gnade doch
Für[4] deinen Augen finden!
Treib ab die Kriegsgefahr
Durch deine starke Hand;
Gib uns den lieben Fried,[6]   15
Schütz unser Vaterland.

Erhalte deine Kirch'
In diesen letzten Zeiten,
Da Teufel, Hell[7] und Welt
Sie plagt auf allen Seiten.   20
Dein ist die Sach,[8] o Gott;
Drum wach und mach dich auf,[9]
Schlag eine Wagenburg[10]
Um deinen kleinen Hauf,[11]

Der sich auf dich verläßt,   25
Der sich dir ganz ergibet,
Der dich im Herzen trägt,
Der dich von Herzen liebet,
Der dein Wort höher acht[12]
Denn alles Gut und Geld   30
Und was die Welt sonst mehr
Für ihre Freude hält.

---

[1] =*die* (*so* for the relative pronoun is very common in older German) [2] =*weg* [3] =*wenn wir unsere Sünden bereuen* [4] =*vor* (*für* for *vor* is common in the older language) [5] =*bereuen* [6] =*Frieden* [7] =*Hölle* [8] 'cause' [9] 'bestir yourself' [10] 'ring of wagons' (for protection) [11] =*Haufen* (body of soldiers) [12] =*achtet*

Laß sehen jedermann,
Laß jedermann erfahren,
Du eben seist der Gott,   35
Der sein Volk kann bewahren,
Der Hülfe senden kann,
Wann niemand Hülfe weiß.
Dafür wird alles Volk
Dir singen Lob und Preis.   40

Not Luther's century, the 16th, but the 17th, the century of the Thirty Years' War, is the age of the classical Protestant *Kirchenlied*. The hymns of Johannes Heermann are noted for the vigor of their language, the aptness of their imagery, their warmth of feeling and virtuosity of form. All these are well exemplified in our present poem, a hymn in the form of a prayer uttered in "Krieges- und Verfolgungsgefahr."

The situation that dictates the form of the first three stanzas is typical: the plight of the worshiper is called to the attention of the deity in the first four lines, help is prayed for in the last four. In the last two stanzas this form is elegantly varied: the *whole* of the fourth stanza performs the office of the first four lines of stanzas 1-3 (depicts the state of the worshiper), while the first six lines of the last stanza take over the function performed in stanzas 1-3 by the last four lines (asking for help). The last two verses, promising *Lob und Preis* for the help God is to grant, bring the hymn to a noble close.

This elegant and subtle variation is achieved with complete naturalness. In lines 21ff., the poem reaches its intensest pitch, so intense that stanza 3 "spills over" into 4, as though the worshiper could not restrain himself now that he has begun to enumerate the virtues of God's *kleinen Hauf* — note the five *der*'s in a row and that the whole stanza is nothing but a series of dependent clauses. This gives an effect of uncontrollable feeling. In reality, however, all is perfectly controlled, and it is precisely this that constitutes the charm of this poem as of so many others: emotion subjected to formal control.

Towards Interpretation
1. Why is the metaphor of the *Wagenburg* (23f.) especially apt?
2. Does the God addressed here seem to be more the God of the Old or the New Testament? With what people is *der kleine Hauf* implicitly compared?
3. Point out what seems to you a good example of Heermann's vigorous language.
4. What kinds of verbs are associated with God and what with humankind? What do these say about Heermann's view of their relationship?
5. Note the rime and meter of the poem. Do these contribute significantly to its meaning? How? (Hint: think of Luther's "Ein feste Burg.")

Paul Gerhardt (1607–1676)

Abendlied

Nun ruhen alle Wälder,
Vieh, Menschen, Stadt und Felder,
Es schläft die ganze Welt:
Ihr aber, meine Sinnen,[1]
Auf, auf, ihr sollt beginnen,   5
Was eurem Schöpfer wohlgefällt.

Wo bist du, Sonne, blieben?[2]
Die Nacht hat dich vertrieben,
Die Nacht, des Tages Feind:
Fahr hin, ein' ander' Sonne,   10
Mein Jesus, meine Wonne,
Gar hell in meinem Herzen scheint.

Der Tag ist nun vergangen,
Die güldnen Sterne prangen
Am blauen Himmelsaal: 15
Also werd ich auch stehen,
Wenn mich wird heißen[3] gehen
Mein Gott aus diesem Jammertal.

Der Leib eilt nun zur Ruhe,
Legt ab das Kleid und Schuhe,   20
Das Bild der Sterblichkeit,[4]
Die ich zieh aus:[5] dagegen
Wird Christus mir anlegen
Den Rock der Ehr' und Herrlichkeit.

Das Häupt, die Füß', die Hände   25
Sind froh, daß nun zu Ende
Die Arbeit kommen[6] sei:
Herz freu dich, du sollst werden
Vom Elend dieser Erden[7]
Und von der Sünden Arbeit frei.[8]   30

Nun geht, ihr matten Glieder,
Geht hin und legt euch nieder,

---

[1]'thoughts' (and senses)   [2]=*geblieben*   [3]'bid'   [4]'image of mortality'   [5]=*die ziehe ich aus*   [6]=*gekommen*   [7]singular   [8]=*von der Arbeit der Sünden* (*Arbeit* 'affliction')

Der Betten[9] ihr begehrt:
Es kommen Stund' und Zeiten,
Da wird man euch bereiten   35
Zur Ruh ein Bettlein in der Erd.

Mein' Augen stehn verdrossen,[10]
Im Hui[11] sind sie geschlossen,
Wo bleibt denn Leib und Seel?
Nimm sie zu deinen Gnaden,   40
Sei gut für allem Schaden[12]
Du Aug und Wächter Israel.[13]

Breit aus die Flügel beide,
O Jesu, meine Freude,
Und nimm dein Küchlein[14] ein,   45
Will Satan mich verschlingen,[15]
So laß die Englein singen:
Dies Kind soll unverletzet sein.

Auch euch, ihr meine Lieben,
Soll heinte[16] nicht betrüben   50
Ein Unfall noch Gefahr.
Gott laß euch selig schlafen,
Stell euch die güldne Waffen
Ums Bett und seiner Engel Schar.[17]

The songs of Paul Gerhardt are considered the crown jewels of Lutheran devotional poetry. Wilhelm Wackernagel (1806-1869), an authority on the *Kirchenlied*, says of Gerhardt:

> Vielleicht ist keines [seiner Lieder] mit der Absicht kirchlichen Gebrauches gedichtet; alle geben den unmittelbaren Ausdruck eigener und augenblicklicher Empfindung und Erfahrung: das hat aber ihren dichterischen Wert nur erhöht, weil es ihnen den Ton der reinen Lyrik gab, und die kirchliche Brauchbarkeit nicht verkürzt; denn des Dichters Denken und Empfinden ist eben ein rein evangelisches und deshalb auch ein kirchliches, ist allen Gliedern der Kirche verständlich, für alle so wie für ihn selbst erweckend und erhebend, tröstend und kräftigend. Paul Gerhardt ist ein zum zweitenmal dichtender Luther. . . .*

Gerhardt's songs are, however, much more polished than those of Luther, for Gerhardt had the benefit of the reform in German poetry initiated by Martin

---

[9]genitive with *begehren* [10]'weary' [11]=*im Nu* [12]'protect them from all harm' [13]Cf. Psalms 33:18. [14]'chick,' cf. Matthew 23:37 [15]Cf. "Ein feste Burg," lines 19f. [16]=*heute nacht* [17]=*die Schar seiner Engel*

*Wilhelm Wackernagel, *Geschichte der deutschen Literatur*, ed. Ernst Martin, 2nd ed. (Basel: Schwabe, 1894), 2:241.

Optiz (see page 28f.). Wackernagel means that Gerhardt possessed the Reformer's fervor and simplicity. He did not, to be sure, possess his belligerency.

Towards Interpretation

1. What contrast or dichotomy is the subject of this "Abendlied" and how is it expressed in the *form* of the song? (You can easily find the answer to this question by explaining the reason for the full stops at the end of the third line of each stanza with the exception of the fourth.)
2. Work out the rime scheme, assigning a letter to each rime. How is the second half of each stanza connected with the first half? What would you say is expressed by this connection of disparates?
3. Does Gerhardt speak in the first person singular or plural? Does your answer support what Wackernagel says of him?
4. Compare the images of protection in Luther's hymn, Heermann's prayer, and Gerhardt's "Abendlied". Which of the three seems on most intimate terms with the deity?

Adventgesang

Wie soll ich dich empfangen
Und wie begegn' ich dir?
O aller Welt Verlangen,
O meiner Seelen[1] Zier!
    O Jesu, Jesu, setze   5
Mir selbst die Fackel bei,[2]
Damit, was dich ergetze,[3]
Mir kund und wissend sei.[4]

Dein Zion[5] streut dir Palmen
Und grüne Zweige hin,   10
Und ich will dir in Psalmen
Ermuntern meinen Sinn.[6]
    Mein Herze soll dir grünen
In stetem Lob und Preis
Und deinem Namen dienen,   15
So gut es kann und weiß.

Was hast du unterlassen[7]
Zu meinem Trost und Freud?

---

[1]singular [2]*setze ... bei* 'enlighten me' [3]'gives joy' [4]'be known to me' [5]Jerusalem, i.e., the faithful [6]i.e., *dir zeigen, wie ich fühle und denke* [7]'neglected to do'

Als Leib und Seele saßen
In ihrem größten Leid,   20
    Als mir das Reich[8] genommen,
Da[9] Fried und Freude lacht:
Da bist du, mein Heil, kommen
Und hast mich frei gemacht.

Ich lag in schweren Banden,   25
Du kömmst und machst mich los;
Ich stund in Spott und Schanden,
Du kömmst und machst mich groß
    Und hebst mich hoch zu Ehren
Und schenkst mir großes Gut,   30
Das sich nicht läßt verzehren,[10]
Wie irdisch Reichtum tut.

Nichts, nichts hat dich getrieben
Zu mir vom Himmels Zelt
Als das geliebte Lieben,   35
Damit[11] du alle Welt
    In ihren tausend Plagen
Und großen Jammerlast,[12]
Die kein Mund kann aussagen,
So fest umfangen hast.   40

Das schreib dir in dein Herze,
Du hochbetrübtes Heer,[13]
Bei denen[14] Gram und Schmerze
Sich häuft je mehr und mehr.
    Seid unverzagt! Ihr habet   45
Die Hülfe für[15] der Tür;
Der[16] eure Herzen labet
Und tröstet, steht allhier.

Ihr dürft[17] euch nicht bemühen
Und sorgen Tag und Nacht,   50
Wie ihr Ihn wollet ziehen
Mit eures Armes Macht.
    Er kömmt, Er kömmt mit Willen,
Ist voller Lieb und Lust,

---

[8]Kingdom of God, taken away at man's Fall. [9]=*wo* [10]'cannot be consumed' [11]=*womit* [12]accusative masculine (archaic) [13]'army,' 'host' of believers [14]=*dem* (plural because an army contains many members) [15]=*vor* [16]'the one who' [17]=*braucht*

All Angst und Not zu stillen,   55
Die Ihm an[17] euch bewußt.

Auch dürft ihr nicht erschrecken
Für euer Sünden Schuld;[18]
Nein, Jesus will sie decken
Mit seiner Lieb und Huld.[19]   60
   Er kömmt, Er kömmt den Sündern
Zum Trost und wahren Heil,
Schafft, daß[20] bei Gottes Kindern
Verbleib' ihr Erb und Teil.[21]

Was fragt ihr nach dem Schreien   65
Der Feind' und ihrer Tück'?
Der Herr wird sie zerstreuen
In einem Augenblick.
   Er kömmt, Er kömmt, ein König,
Dem wahrlich alle Feind'   70
Auf Erden viel zu wenig
Zum Widerstande seind.[22]

Er kömmt zum Weltgerichte,[23]
Zum Fluch dem, der Ihm flucht,[24]
Mit Gnad' und süßem Lichte   75
Dem, der Ihn liebt und sucht.
   Ach komm, ach komm, o Sonne,
Und hol uns allzumal
Zum ew'gen Licht und Wonne
In deinen Freudensaal.   80

"Advent" means a coming. The four Sundays that precede Christmas, when Christ came to earth, are called in German *Adventszeit*. The present song may have been written for this season, though it does not specifically refer to it. It does, however, refer to other comings with such insistency and mounting fervor that it becomes a song interpreting the essential meaning of Advent to all Christians.

In the first stanza the hymnist asks how he shall receive, how he shall meet Christ: one can only receive someone who is indeed coming. In the second, he tells of Jesus' coming to Jerusalem for the Feast of Passover (John 12:12-13) and how the faithful came to meet him with palm leaves. The poet's song shall be *his* palm leaves:

---

[17]'in regard to' [18]=*wegen der Schuld eurer Sünden* [19]'mercy' [20]'sees to it that' [21]*Erb und Teil =Erbteil* 'heritage' [22]=*sind* [23]Last Judgment [24]'to the curse of him who curses Him'

> Mein Herze soll dir grünen
> In stetem Lob und Preis.

Stanzas 3-4 tell how the Savior came to the hymnist in his hour of direst need. Stanza 5, the pivot of the poem, speaks of the great mystery of the Christian religion, Christ's coming to *all* men, "driven" by nothing but *das geliebte Lieben* to embrace and so redeem all human suffering. Stanzas 6-9 assure the *hochbetrübtes Heer* of believers (Gerhardt no doubt means oppressed Protestant Christians) that Christ's coming is imminent, *für der Tür*. With each *Er kömmt, Er kömmt* the certainty of the coming grows. Stanzas 6-9 are marked by a definite division between the first four and the last four verses. In the first half of each stanza: waiting in fear and trembling; in the second half: assurance of succor. (The Lutheran doctrine of salvation not through works but by faith is stressed in 7 and 8 — the Lutheran *can* do nothing but wait!) The poem ends with a vision of the Last Judgment, that is, the Second Coming, and now *Er kömmt, Er kömmt* is transformed into a cry of yearning: *Ach komm, ach komm*. Stanza 10 balances stanza 5: in the middle of the poem the coming that is for all time: at the end, the coming when time shall be no more.

We can summarize the argument as follows: Christ came physically to earth to redeem all mankind. He came to me spiritually in my time of need (when I was granted the inner conviction of His saving power); therefore, He will also come to you. When He comes again physically, it will be to sit in judgment. There are three "comings": past, present, and future. In this hymn we can see with all clarity that Gerhardt feels his own experience to be representative — the "I" of his hymn is very nearly the equivalent of Luther's "we."

Paul Gerhardt   *Friedrich von Spee*

Friedrich von Spee (1591–1635)

Vom Ochs und Eselein bei der Krippen

Der Wind auf leeren Straßen
Streckt aus die Flügel sein,
Streicht hin gar scharf ohn Maßen[1]
Zur Bethlems Krippen[2] ein;
Er brummelt[3] hin und wieder,   5
Der fliegend Winterbot',
Greift an die Gleich[4] und Glieder
Dem frisch vermenschten Gott.[5]

Ach, ach, laß ab von Brausen,
Laß ab, du schnöder Wind,   10
Laß ab von kaltem Sausen
Und schon[6] dem schönen Kind!
Vielmehr du deine Schwingen
Zerschlag[7] im wilden Meer,
Allda dich satt magst ringen   15
Kehr nur nit[8] wieder her.

Mit dir nun muß ich kosen,[9]
Mit dir, o Joseph mein!
Das Futter misch mit Rosen[10]
Dem Ochs und Eselein,   20
Mach deinen frommen Tieren
So lieblichs Mischgemüß,[11]
Bald, bald, ohn Zeit verlieren
Mach ihn[12] den Atem süß.

Drauf blaset her, ihr beiden,   25
Mit süßem Rosenwind,
Ochs, Esel, wohl bescheiden,[13]
Und wärmet 's[14] nacket Kind.
Ach, blaset her und hauchet:
Aha, aha, aha!   30

---

[1]'beyond measure' [2]dative singular [3]'mutters, grumbles' [4]=*Gelenke* [5]'the god who has just assumed human form' [6]'spare' [7]*Vielmehr ... zerschlag* 'Rather go and beat your wings to pieces ...' [8]=*nicht* [9]=*verhandeln* 'talk business' [10]Trees reputedly put forth blossoms and fruit on the first Christmas [11]'mixed fodder' [12]=*ihnen* [13]=*gut Bescheid wissend* [14]=*das*

Fort, fort, euch weidlich brauchet.[15]
Aha, aha, aha!

Friedrich von Spee, the author of this Christmas song, was a Jesuit priest and one of the great preachers of the Counter-Reformation. Independently of the Protestant poets, Spee deduced his own rules for writing good German verse, rules that, except for the admission of dialect forms (the Catholic lands had no "standard" German), scarcely differ from those of Opitz and his school (see p. 28f.). Spee is fond of giving his poems the form of miniature dramas, thus exploiting the dialectic inherent in all poetry. Charming as this poem undoubtedly is, it is perhaps just a bit too obvious that the author is mainly interested in the conceit of warming the Christ Child with the beasts' rosy breath and that he arranged everything to lead up to this. But some delightful realistic touches make up for this fault, if it is a fault. For instance the *aha*'s in the final stanza, which must be uttered with the mouth wide open, just as an ox or donkey (but not a man!) would have to blow. The element of gesture is, in fact, very marked throughout and always charmingly natural. One can see the poet taking Joseph aside by the arm to reveal his little scheme to him. The personification of the wind is also very successful; the wind becomes an actor in the drama.

Trauergesang von der Not Christi am Ölberg in dem Garten

Bei stiller Nacht zur ersten Wacht[1]
Ein' Stimm sich gund[2] zu klagen;
Ich nahm in Acht, was die dann sagt',
Tat hin mit Augen schlagen.[3]

Ein junges Blut,[4] von Sitten gut,   5
Alleinig, ohn Gefährten,
In großer Not, fast halber tot,
Im Garten lag auf Erden.

Es war der liebe Gottessohn,
Sein Haupt er hat in Armen,   10
Viel weißer und bleicher als der Mon,[5]
Ein' Stein es möcht erbarmen.[6]

„Ach, Vater, liebster Vater mein,
Und muß den Kelch ich trinken?

---

[15]'Come on, blow hard!'

[1]'watch' (of the night) [2]=*begann* [3]'cast my eyes thither' [4]'thing' [5]=*Mond* [6]'it would move a stone to pity'

Und mag's dann ja nit anders sein,   15
Mein' Seel nit laß versinken!"

„Ach, liebes Kind, trink aus geschwind,
Dir's laß in Treuen[7] sagen.
Sei wohl gesinnt, bald überwind,[8]
Den Handel mußtu wagen."   20

„Ach, Vater mein, und kann's nit sein,
Und muß ich's je[9] dann wagen,
Will trinken rein[10] den Kelch allein,
kann dir's ja nit versagen.

Doch Sinn und Mut erschrecken tut,[11]   25
soll ich mein Leben lassen.
O bitter Tod, mein' Angst und Not
Ist über alle Maßen.

Maria zart, jungfräulich Art,[12]
Sollt du[13] mein' Schmerzen wissen,   30
Mein Leiden hart zu dieser Fahrt,
Dein Herz wär schon gerissen.

Ach, Mutter mein, bin ja kein Stein,
Das Herz mir dörft[14] zerspringen;
Sehr große Pein muß[15] nehmen ein,   35
Mit Tod und Marter ringen.

Ade, ade zu guter Nacht,
Maria, Mutter milde.
Ist niemand, der dann mit mir wacht
In dieser Wüsten wilde?[16]   40

Ein Kreuz mir vor den Augen schwebt.
O weh der Pein und Schmerzen!
Dran soll ich morgen wern[17] erhebt,
Das greifet mir zum Herzen.

Viel Ruten, Geißel, Skorpion[18]   45
In meinen Ohren sausen.
Auch kommt mir vor ein dörnen Kron:[19]
O Gott, wen wollt nit grausen?

---

[7]'in good faith' [8]'be of good cheer, overcome (your weakness)' [9]=*immerhin* [10]=*leer*
[11]=*erschreckt* [12]'of virgin nature' [13]=*solltest du* [14]=*dürfte* 'is about to' [15]Supply *ich*
[16]=*in dieser wilden Wüste* [17]=*werden* [18]'switches, scourges, nailed whips' [19]=*auch
sehe ich eine Dornenkrone*

Zu Gott ich hab gerufen zwar   50
Aus tiefen Todesbanden;
Dennoch ich bleib verlassen gar,[20]
Ist Hilf noch Trost verhanden.[21]

Der schöne Mon will untergohn,
Für[22] Leid nit mehr mag scheinen;   55
Die Sternen lan ihr Glitzen stahn,[23]
Mit mir sie wollen weinen.

Kein Vogelsang noch Freudenklang
Man höret in den Luften,
Die wilden Tier auch trauern mit mir   60
In Steinen und in Kluften."

Towards Interpretation

    1. Where does this scene take place? Find the passage in the New Testament on which this poem is based and determine how much Spee has borrowed from his source.

    2. The pathos of this poem arises from the central mystery of the Christian faith: God becomes man. How does the poem depict this mystery?

    3. Imagine this poem in non-dramatic form. Would it gain or lose?

Christian Knorr von Rosenroth (1636–1689)

Morgenlied

Morgenglanz der Ewigkeit,
Licht vom unerschöpften Lichte,
Schick uns diese Morgenzeit[1]
Deine Strahlen zu Gesichte[2]
Und vertreib durch deine Macht   5
Unsre Nacht.

Die bewölkte Finsternis
Müsse deinem Glanz entfliegen,
Die durch Adams Apfelbiß

---

[20] = *gänzlich* [21] = *weder Hilfe noch Trost ist vorhanden* [22] = *Vor* [23] 'leave off their glittering'

[1] accusative of definite time [2] 'sight'

Uns, die kleine Welt,[3] bestiegen,   10
Daß wir, Herr, durch deinen Schein
Selig sein.

Deiner Güte Morgentau
Fall'[4] auf unser matt Gewissen:
Laß die dürre Lebensau[5]   15
Lauter[6] süßen Trost genießen
Und erquick uns, deine Schar,
Immerdar.

Gib, daß deiner Liebe Glut
Unsre kalten Werke töte   20
Und erweck uns Herz und Mut[7]
Bei entstandner Morgenröte,[8]
Daß wir, eh wir gar[9] vergehn,
Recht aufstehn.

Laß uns ja das Sündenkleid   25
Durch des Bundes Blut[10] vermeiden,
Daß uns die Gerechtigkeit
Mög' als wie ein Rock bekleiden
Und wir so vor aller Pein
Sicher sein.   30

Ach, du Aufgang aus der Höh',
Gib, daß auch am Jüngsten Tage[11]
Unser Leichnam aufersteh'
Und, entfernt von aller Plage,
Sich auf jener Freudenbahn   35
Freuen kann.

Leucht uns selbst in jener Welt,
Du verklärte Gnadensonne;
Führ uns durch das Tränenfeld
In das Land der süßen Wonne,   40
Da die Lust, die uns erhöht,
Nie vergeht.

Knorr von Rosenroth was a mystic, famous in his own day as an alchemist rather than as a poet. His "Morgenlied" is a prayer addressed to the Savior,

---

[3]The microcosm, i.e., man, who corresponds on a small scale to the macrocosm or universe. [4]'May the morning dew of thy goodness fall ...' [5]'meadow of life' [6]'pure, nothing but' [7]=*Sinn* 'mind' [8]'when the dawn breaks' [9]=*ganz* [10]'blood of the (New) Covenant' [11]Last Judgment

the "dawn of eternity," and "light of the inexhaustible light." The whole poem is an extended metaphor. Everything in it has to do with the dawn: the dispersal of darkness, the morning dew, the first hot rays of the sun, rising and dressing; all have a clearly stated figurative meaning.

Towards Interpretation
1. Compare the last stanza of "Morgenlied" with the last stanza of Gerhardt's "Adventgesang." What same image is used in both?
2. Reread the last two lines of each stanza of "Morgenlied." What state of being is always referred to here? What is the effect of the final two-stress line of each stanza? Might one say that this prayer "answers" itself?

Johannes Scheffler, "Angelus Silesius"
(1624-1677)

From: *Der Cherubinische Wandersmann*

1.
Blüh auf, gefrorner Christ,[1] der Mai ist für der Tür:
Du bleibest ewig tot, blühst du nicht jetzt und hier.

2.
Zwei Wörtlein lieb ich sehr: sie heißen aus und ein:
aus Babel,[2] und aus mir, in Gott und Jesum ein.

3.
Die Rose, welche hier dein äußeres Auge sieht,
Die hat von Ewigkeit in Gott also geblüht.

4.
Die Ros' ist ohn Warum, sie blühet, weil sie blühet;
Sie acht[3] nicht ihrer selbst, fragt nicht, ob man sie siehet.

5.
Gott ist ein lauter[4] Nichts, Ihn rührt kein Nun noch Hier:
Je mehr du nach Ihm greifst, je mehr entwird[5] Er dir.

[1]'Christian' [2]'Babylon,' i.e., the sinful, unredeemed world; *Jesum*, accusative (Latin) [3]=*achtet* [4]'pure,' 'nothing but' [5]'unbecomes,' i.e., 'eludes'

6.

Ich weiß, daß ohne mich Gott nicht ein Nu kann leben;
Werd ich zu nicht, Er muß vor Not den Geist aufgeben.

7.

Ich selbst muß Sonne sein, ich muß mit meinen Strahlen
Das farbenlose Meer der ganzen Gottheit malen.

8.

Ich sterb und lebe Gott:[6] will ich Ihm ewig leben,
So muß ich ewig auch für Ihn den Geist aufgeben.

9.

Die Gottheit ist ein Brunn,[7] aus ihr kommt alles her:
Und läuft auch wieder hin, drum ist sie auch ein Meer.

10.

Hier fließ ich noch in Gott, als eine Bach der Zeit:
Dort bin ich selbst das Meer der ew'gen Seligkeit.

11.

Man sagt die Zeit ist schnell: wer hat sie sehen fliegen?
Sie bleibt ja unverrückt[8] im Weltbegriffe liegen.

12.

Du selber machst die Zeit: das Uhrwerk sind die Sinnen;
Hemmst du die Unruh nur, so ist die Zeit von hinnen.[9]

13.

Zeit ist wie Ewigkeit, und Ewigkeit wie Zeit,
So du nur selber nicht machst einen Unterscheid.

14.

Mensch, werde wesentlich: denn wenn die Welt vergeht,
So fällt der Zufall weg, das Wesen, das besteht.

15.

Mensch, allererst wenn du bist alle Dinge worden,
So stehst du in dem Wort[10] und in der Götter Orden.

16.

Tod ist ein selig Ding: je kräftiger er ist,
Je herrlicher daraus das Leben wird erkiest.[11]

Like most of the 17th century German mystics, Johannes Scheffler, called
Angelus Silesius — "the Silesian messenger" — was a follower of Jakob

---

[6]*Gott* is adverbial accusative [7]=*Brunnen* 'fountain' [8]'unmoved' [9]'gone' [10]Cf. John
1:1 [11]=*erwählt*

Böhme (1575-1624), probably the greatest creative genius of his time in Germany. "Der cherubinische Wandersmann" is one of the most successful attempts in European literature to put into words the mystical view of creation. The mystic turn of mind, no matter where we meet it, is always characterized by a passion for speculation combined with deep religiosity. One feeds the other: the mystic tries to express religious feeling through speculative thought, and this speculation confirms his religiosity. But what the mystic tries to express must by its own nature remain inexpressible. All that can be expressed is its inexpressibleness, and this only by means of a paradox. A paradox is precisely what each of Scheffler's *Sprüche* is.

Scheffler uses the alexandrine, a favorite meter of his age, as the form best suited to his purpose. This meter normally has a heavy pause (called the "caesura" or "cutting") after the third foot, so that one half of the verse is weighed against the other half:

Die Góttheit íst ein Brúnn, | aus íhr kommt álles hér

In "Der cherubinische Wandersmann" this system of balances comes to symbolize the balancing and combining of opposites that constitutes the "message" of many couplets: transitoriness vs. infinite duration, creator vs. creature, nothingness vs. somethingness, here vs. there, life vs. death, and so on and so on.

It would be impossible to discuss Scheffler's thought adequately without going into the history of mysticism. We call attention only to a few points in the epigrams quoted. No. 9 deals with the neo-Platonic doctrine that all emanates from God and returns to Him: being is circulatory. Nos. 11-13 clearly state that time is a category of human perception, as Kant later maintained. Nos. 6-7 affirm that God the creator is dependent upon His creature, man. Man is God's life and death, and since one cannot be without the other, man's dying is also God's life (no. 8). Though this world is scorned (no. 2), it must nevertheless be experienced in all its parts before man can return to God (no. 15), for otherwise creation would be soulless. Man's task is to give creation a soul, and thus raise it to the realm of the spirit. The rose is "without why" only within itself, not in the eye and mind of man. This idea, important in the philosophy of Hegel and Fichte, we will also meet again in Novalis. No. 16 summarizes in two lines the theme of Rilke's 10th Duino Elegy. Naturally this does not imply that these poets and thinkers derived their ideas from Scheffler, or that they had even necessarily read him. Is it not so much the originality of his thought as the felicity of his form that has made his poetry live.

Volkslieder

The folk song is first of all a song, rather than a poem. Nonetheless, an anthology that does not include at least a sampling of the folk song is not really representative of German poetry.

Volkslieder seldom, perhaps never, stem directly from the *Volk*, but from individual poets. They are songs the people have taken over, often changing them almost beyond recognition; the name of the author has been forgotten. Typical of this kind of poetry are a fondness for stock epithets and stereotyped situations (*Formelhaftigkeit*), a tendency to jump from one situation to another without apparent motivation (*Sprunghaftigkeit*), and direct, vivid imagery (*Anschaulichkeit*).

The folk song was at its height in 15th century Germany, though we also find appealing examples of later date. A true folk song of really recent date, however, is rare indeed, since it prospers only in a culture with an active oral tradition. Thus Gutenberg (died 1467) is largely responsible for the decline of the *Volkslied*.

Goethe, in a review of a famous collection of folk songs dedicated to him, characterizes this type of poetry in these words:

Diese Art Gedichte, die wir seit Jahren Volkslieder zu nennen pflegen, ob sie gleich eigentlich weder vom Volk noch fürs Volk gedichtet sind, sondern weil sie so etwas Stämmiges, Tüchtiges in sich haben und begreifen, daß der kern- und stammhafte Teil der Nationen dergleichen Dinge faßt, behält, sich zueignet und mitunter fortpflanzt — dergleichen Gedichte sind so wahre Poesie, als sie irgend nur sein kann; sie haben einen unglaublichen Reiz, selbst für uns, die wir auf einer höheren Stufe der Bildung stehen, wie der Anblick und die Erinnerung der Jugend fürs Alter hat. Hier ist die Kunst mit der Natur im Konflikt, und eben dieses Werden, dieses wechselseitige Wirken, dieses Streben scheint ein Ziel zu suchen, und hat sein Ziel schon erreicht. Das wahre dichterische Genie, wo es auftritt, ist in sich vollendet; mag ihm Unvollkommenheit der Sprache, der äußeren Technik, oder was sonst will entgegenstehen, es besitzt die höhere innere Form, der doch am Ende alles zu Gebote steht, und wirkt selbst im dunkeln und trüben Elemente oft herrlicher, als es später im klaren vermag. Das lebhafte poetische Anschauen eines beschränkten Zustandes erhebt ein Einzelnes zum begrenzten, doch unumschränkten All, so daß wir im kleinen Raume die ganze Welt zu sehen glauben.*

Des Knaben Wunderhorn: Alte deutsche Lieder, gesammelt von L. Achim von Arnim und Clemens Brentano (Heidelberg: Mohr und Zimmer, 1806). Goethe's review is reprinted in his *Werke, Hamburger Ausgabe*, ed. Erich Trunz *et al.*, 14 vols. (München: Beck, ⁷1973), 12:270-284.

„Es ist ein Reis entsprungen"

Es ist ein Reis[1] entsprungen
Aus einer Wurzel zart,
Als uns die Alten sungen,
Aus Jesse kam die Art[2]
Und hat ein Blümlein bracht   5
Mitten im kalten Winter
Wohl zu der halben Nacht.

Das Reislein, das ich meine,
Davon Jesaias[3] sagt,
Ist Maria, die reine,   10
Die uns das Blümlein bracht:
Aus Gottes ew'gem Rat[4]
Hat sie ein Kind geboren
Und blieb doch reine Magd.

„Innsbruck, ich muß dich lassen"

Innsbruck,[1] ich muß dich lassen,
Ich fahr dahin mein Straßen,
In fremde Land dahin,
Mein Freud ist mir genommen,
Die weiß ich nicht bekommen,   5
Wo ich im Elend[2] bin.

Groß Leid muß ich jetzt tragen,
Das ich allein tu klagen
Dem liebsten Buhlen[3] mein.
Ach Lieb, nun laß mich Armen   10
Im Herzen dein erbarmen,
Daß ich muß dannen[4] sein.

Mein Trost ob allen Weiben,[5]
Dein tu ich ewig bleiben,
Stet, treu, der Ehren fromm,
Nun müß' dich Gott bewahren,   15
In aller Tugend sparen,[6]
Bis daß ich weiderkomm.

---

[1]'stock, branch' [2]'family' (tree) [3]Isaiah [4]'will'

[1]town in Tirol (Austria) [2]'foreign land' [3]'lover' [4]'away' [5]'My comfort above all women' [6]'keep'

„Dat du min Leevsten büst"

Dat du min Leevsten büst,[1]
  dat du woll weest.
Kumm bi de Nacht, kumm bi de Nacht,
  segg, wo du heest.

Kumm du üm Middernacht,   5
  kumm du Klock een;
Vader slöppt, Moder slöppt,
  ick slaap alleen.

Klopp an de Kammerdör,
  klopp an de Klink;   10
Vader meent,[2] Moder meent,
  dat deit de Wind.

Twe Künigeskinner[1]

Et wassen twee Künigeskinner,
De hadden eenander so leef,
De konnen ton anner nich kummen:
Dat Water was vil to breed.

„Leef Herte, kanst du der nich swemmen?   5
Leef Herte, so swemme to mi!
Ick will di twe Keskes upsteken,
Un de söllt löchten to di!"

Dat horde ne falske Nunne
Up ere Slopkammer, o we!   10
Se dey de Keskes utdömpen:
Leef Herte bleef in de See.

---

[1]This poem is in Low German. With a bit of imagination you can easily read it.
[2]=meint

---

[1]The ballad of the two royal children, of which there are several versions (the one given here is in the dialect of Westphalia), ultimately derives from the story of Hero and Leander. *Es waren zwei Königskinder, / Die hatten einander so lieb, / Die konnten zu einander nicht kommen, / Das Wasser war viel zu tief (breit). // „Lieb Herze, kannst du denn nicht schwimmen? / Lieb Herze, so schwimme zu mir! / Ich will dir zwei Kerzen aufstecken / Und die sollen leuchten zu dir." // Das hörte eine falsche Nonne / Auf ihrer Schlafkammer, o weh! / Sie tat die Kerzen auslöschen / Lieb Herze blieb in dem See.*

Et was up en Sundage Morgen,
De Lüde[2] wören alle so fro;
Nich so de Künigesdochter,   15
De Augen de seten ehr to.[3]

„O Moder", säd se,[4] „Moder!
Min Augen doht mi der so we;[5]
Mag ick der nich gohn spatzeren
An de Kant von de ruskende See?"[6]   20

„O Dochter", säde se, „Dochter!
Allene kanst du der nich gohn;
Weck up dine jüngste Süster,
Un de sall met di gohn." —

„Mine allerjüngste Süster   25
Is noch so'n[7] unnüsel[8] Kind,
Se plücket wol alle de Blömkes,
De an de Seekante sind.

Un plückt se auk men[9] de wilden
Un lätt de tammen[10] stohn,   30
So segget doch alle de Lüde:
Dat het dat Künigskind dohn!

„O Moder", sede se, „Moder!
Mine Augen daht mi der so we;
Mag ik der nich gohn spatzeren   35
An de Kant von de ruskende See?"

„O Dochter", sede se, „Dochter!
Allene sast[11] du der nich gohn,
Weck up dinen jüngsten Broder,
Un de sall met di gohn." —   40

„Min allerjüngsten Broder
Is noch so'n unnüsel Kind,
He schütt[12] wull alle de Vügel,
De up de Seekante sind.

Un schütt he auk men de wilden   45
Un lätt de tammen gohn,
So segget doch alle de Lüde:
Dat het dat Künigskind dohn.

---

[2]=Leute [3]=die Augen saßen ihr zu (vom Weinen) [4]=sagte sie [5]=tun mir so weh (der is an expletive used to enliven an utterance) [6]=am Ufer des rauschenden Sees [7]=so ein [8]=unverständig [9]=nur [10]=zahmen [11]=sollst [12]=schießt

„O Moder", sede se, „Moder!
Min Herte doht mi der so we,
Laet[13] andere gohn tor Kerken![14]   50
Ick bed'[15] an de ruskende See."

Da sat[16] de Künigesdochter
Up't Hoefd[17] ere goldene Kron,
Se stack up eren Finger   55
En Rink von Demanten so schon.[18]

De Moder genk to de Kerken,
De Dochter genk en de Seekant,
Se genk der so lange spatzeren,
Bes se enen Fisker fand.   60

„O Fisker, leeveste Fisker!
Ji[19] könnt verdeenen grot Lohn:
Settet jue[20] Netkes to Water,
Fisket mi den Künigessohn!"

He sette sin Netkes to Water,   65
De Lotkes[21] sünken to Grund,
He fiskde un fiskde so lange,
De Künigssohn wurde sin Fund.

Do nam de Künigesdochter
Von Hoefd ere goldene Kron: 70
„Sü do, woledele[22] Fisker!
Dat is ju verdeende Lohn."[23]

Se trock[24] von eren Finger
Den Rink von Demanten so schon:
„Sü do, woledele Fisker!   75
Dat is ju verdeende Lon."

Se namm in ere blanke Arme
Den Künigssohn, o we!
Se sprank met em in de Wellen:
„O Vader un Moder, ade!"   80

---

[13]=laß [14]=Kirche [15]=bete [16]setzte [17]=Haupt [18]=schön [19]=Ihr (you) [20]=euere
[21]'sinkers' [22]'noble' [23]=euer verdienter Lohn [24]from trecken 'ziehen'

„Ich hört ein Sichelein rauschen"

Ich hört ein Sichelein rauschen,
Wohl rauschen durch das Korn,
Ich hört ein feine Magd klagen,
Sie hätt ihr Lieb verlorn.

„Laß rauschen, Lieb, laß rauschen,   5
Ich acht nit, wie es geh;
Ich hab mir ein Buhlen erworben
In Veiel[1] und grünem Klee."

„Hast du einen Buhlen erworben
In Veiel und grünem Klee,   10
So steh ich hier alleine,
Tut meinem Herzen weh."

„Es geht eine dunkle Wolk herein"

Es geht eine dunkle Wolk herein,
Mich deucht,[1] es wird ein Regen sein,
Ein Regen aus der Wolke
Wohl in das grüne Gras.

Und kommst du, liebe Sonn, nit bald,   5
So weset[2] all's im grünen Wald,
Und all die müden Blumen,
Die haben müden Tod.

Es geht eine dunkle Wolk herein,
Es soll und muß geschieden sein;   10
Ade, Feinslieb, dein Scheiden
Macht mir das Herze schwer.

---

[1]'violets'

[1]'methinks' [2]= *vergeht*

Wassernot

Zu Koblenz auf der Brücken[1]
Da lag ein tiefer Schnee,
Der Schnee, der ist verschmolzen,
Das Wasser fließt in See.

Es fließt in Liebchens Garten,   5
Da wohnet niemand drein,
Ich kann da lange warten,
Es wehn zwei Bäumelein.

Die sehen mit den Kronen
Noch aus dem Wasser grün,   10
Mein Liebchen muß drin wohnen,
Ich kann nicht zu ihr hin.

Wenn Gott mich freundlich grüßet
Aus blauer Luft und Tal,
Aus diesem Flusse grüßet   15
Mein Liebchen mich zumal.

Sie geht nicht auf der Brücken,
Da gehn viel schöne Fraun,
Sie tun mich viel anblicken,
Ich mag sie nicht anschaun.   20

Tamburgesell[1]

Ich armer Tamburgesell,
Man führt mich aus dem Gewölb,[2]
Ja aus dem Gewölb,
Wär ich ein Tambur blieben,
Dürft[3] ich nicht gefangen liegen,   5
Nicht gefangen liegen.

O Galgen, du hohes Haus,
Du siehst so furchtbar aus,
So furchtbar aus,
Ich schau dich nicht mehr an,   10
Weil i weiß, i gehör dran,
Daß i gehör dran.

---

[1]dative singular

[1]'drummer boy' [2]'vault' (used as prison) [3]=*brauchte*

Wenn Soldaten vorbeimarschieren,
Bei mir nit einquartieren,
Nit einquartieren,   15
Wann sie fragen, wer i gewesen bin:
Tambur von der Leibkompanie,[4]
Von der Leibkompanie.

Gute Nacht, ihr Marmelstein,[5]
Ihr Berg und Hügelein,   20
Und Hügelein,
Gute Nacht, ihr Offizier,
Korporal und Musketier,
Und Musketier.

Gute Nacht, ihr Offizier,   25
Korporal und Grenadier,
Und Grenadier.
Ich schrei mit heller Stimm,
Von euch ich Urlaub nimm,
Ich Urlaub nimm.   30

„Wenn ich ein Vöglein wär"

Wenn ich ein Vöglein wär
Und auch zwei Flüglein hätt,
Flög ich zu dir;
Weil's aber nicht kann sein,
Bleib ich allhier.   5

Bin ich gleich[1] weit von dir,
Bin ich doch im Schlaf bei dir
Und red mit dir;
Wenn ich erwachen tu,
Bin ich allein.   10

Es vergeht kein Stund in der Nacht,
Da mein Herze nicht erwacht
Und an dich gedenkt,
Daß du mir viel tausendmal
Dein Herz geschenkt.   15

---

[4]'bodyguard' [5]=*Marmorstein*

[1]=*obgleich ich ...*

Martin Opitz (1597–1639)

Martin Opitz, to whom we have already had occasion to refer, is a minor poet who occupies a major place in German literary history.

The rise of national literatures took place quite early in some countries, such as England and Italy, but very late in Germany. True, during the Middle Ages feudal society had produced a highly sophisticated literature — the *Minnesang* and the courtly epic — but with the rise of the burgher class in the 15th and 16th centuries this literature disappeared. It was replaced by the ludicrously inferior productions of the *Meistersinger*, of whom Wagner's Beckmesser is not an unfair caricature and Hans Sachs the most famous representative. The Renaissance humanists preferred to write in Latin, which naturally did not further the development of German as a literary idiom. The Reformation and the splitting of Germany into two camps brought with it a division of tongues: that of Luther's Bible and of the court chancelleries of Middle and Eastern Germany on the one hand, and the various local dialects of the Catholic lands of the South on the other. The former, which has become standard modern German, Jacob Grimm called "the Protestant dialect."

Meanwhile, neighboring countries, especially Holland and France, were producing poetry in their national languages, and Germany was becoming envious. Many German Protestants went to Holland, at that time the center of Protestant learning, for their university education and there came into contact with the new national literature of the Dutch. The return of these young men, fired with an enthusiasm to raise the level of German literature, could not fail to have an effect.

Ironically, the poet who was to have perhaps the greatest influence on the course of German literature did not go there to study. Martin Opitz, a Silesian like so many men of letters of his day, went to Holland to escape the Thirty Years' War. Inspired by the example of the Dutch, Opitz determined to do something about the state of poetry in Germany. With the methodicality typical of him he began by publishing (in 1624) a handbook of poetics, his *Buch von der deutschen Poeterey*, a completely unoriginal work except in one respect: it showed by means of actual examples that "correct" verse was possible even in German. About the same time, his *Teutsche Poemata* (German Poems) were published and the new era had begun. The Protestant poets threw themselves at his feet and hailed him as the "duke of German [lyre] strings" — *Herzog deutscher Saiten* — and the "Virgil of our day." The new poetry used "the Protestant dialect" and abjured local locutions and *das Fremdwort*. It introduced new meters and was especially careful to see that the metrical accent coincided with natural stress, for as self-evident as the necessity for this seems to us, it had not always been the case heretofore. The new poetry also took over lock, stock and barrel the Renaissance conventions of "decorum" — tragedy must always treat of persons of high estate, comedy of the lower classes, and so on.

The secular verse produced by Opitz and in his wake strikes the modern reader for the most part as cold and impersonal. It is impersonal. This age, the Baroque, had a concept of poetry rather different from ours. Above all, Baroque poetry is not confessional; it does not pretend to be a direct revelation of the poet's heart, but is rather a social expression, sometimes no more than a social grace, a representative gesture of the society from which it springs. By the 17th century this society had become almost wholly that of the courts, for Germany was a congeries of absolute principalities, and though the poets themselves usually belonged to the *Gelehrtenstand* — the scholar class — their poetry was oriented toward the nobility, the *Adel*. Baroque poetry is *ungemütlich*, unromantic, distant, rational. To a surprising degree it is a poetry of stereotypes. In certain situations it is necessary to say certain things — this is also part of the doctrine of "decorum" — much as at a formal reception. The ideal of the age was not originality but adroitness — it was the age of the virtuoso. The German Baroque possesses no Milton and no Donne, no Racine and no Lope; it has no literary figure of the stature of its great composers, no Johann Sebastian Bach.

„Jetzund kömmt die Nacht herbei"

Jetzund[1] kömmt die Nacht herbei,
Vieh und Menschen werden frei,
Die gewünschte Ruh geht an,[2]
Meine Sorge kömmt heran.

Schöne glänzt der Mondenschein   5
Und die güldnen Sternelein;
Froh ist alles weit und breit,
Ich nur bin in Traurigkeit.

Zweene mangeln überall[3]
An der schönen Sternen Zahl;   10
Diese Sternen, die ich mein',
Sind der Liebsten Äugelein.

Nach dem Monden[4] frag ich nicht,
Dunkel ist der Sternen Licht,

---

[1]=*jetzt* [2]=*beginnt* [3]'two things are lacking above all' [4]dative singular

Weil sich von mir weggewendt,   15
Asteris,[5] mein Firmament.

Wann sich aber neigt zu mir
Dieser meiner Sonnen[6] Zier,
Acht ich es das Beste sein,
Daß kein Stern noch Monde[7] schein'.   20

"Jetzund kömmt die Nacht herbei" is a gallant compliment in the form of a song. It is meant to delight by the form of its utterance; the question of its "sincerity" does not arise. The first two stanzas contrast the peace and happiness of all the world with the speaker's sadness and unrest. We naturally wonder what can be the matter with him. It turns out that two "stars" are missing, his loved one's eyes, and this of course makes the whole world dark, despite moon and stars. Then comes the final, not ungraceful erotic *pointe*: When "Asteris" (from Greek for 'star') bends to him, he thinks it better that there be neither moon nor stars. The poem is essentially a pun based on the double meaning in German of *Stern* and *Augensterne*, or pupils.

Friedrich von Logau (1604–1655)

Vom Opitio

Im Latein sind viel Poeten, immer aber ein Virgil;
Deutsche haben einen Opitz, Tichter[1] aber sonsten viel.

Die deutsche Sprache

Deutsche mühen sich jetzt hoch, deutsch zu reden fein und rein;[1]
Wer von Herzen redet deutsch, wird der beste Deutsche sein.

---

[5]proper name [6]genitive singular [7]singular

[1]=*Dichter*

[1]Reference to the *Sprachgesellschaften* of the day, societies for the purification of the German language

Frankreich

Frankreich hat es weit gebracht; Frankreich kann es schaffen,
Daß so manches Land und Volk wird zu seinem Affen.

Glauben

Lutherisch, Päbstisch und Calvinisch, diese Glauben alle drei
Sind vorhanden; doch ist Zweifel, wo das Christentum denn sei.

Gott dient allen; wer dient ihm?

Gott schafft, erzeugt, trägt, speist, tränkt, labt, stärkt, nährt, erquickt,
Erhält, schenkt, sorgt, beschert, vermehrt, gewähret, schickt,
Liebt, schützt, bewahrt, erlöst, beschattet, benedeit,
Schirmt, sichert, führt, regiert, errettet, hilft, befreit,
Erleuchtet, unterweist, erfreut, sterbt[1] und erweckt,   5
So daß sich fort und fort sein Heil auf uns erstreckt.
Mit allem dienstu, Gott, uns allen! ist auch wol,
Der dir dient, einer nur und dient dir, wie er sol?

Des Herren Abendmahl

Wie man Christi Leib kann essen, wie man Christi Blut kann trinken,
Läßt sich jener dies vernehmen, läßt sich dieser das bedünken.[1]
Der den Leib gab selbst zur Speise, der das Blut gab selbst zu trinken,
Der wird leisten, was versprochen; ich will glauben, du magst dünken.

Abgedankte Soldaten[1]

Würmer im Gewissen,
Kleider wol zerrissen,
Wolbenarbte Leiber,
Wolgebrauchte Weiber,
Ungewisse Kinder,   5
Weder Pferd noch Rinder,

---

[1] *sterbt* 'causes death'

[1] Logau addresses here the theological dispute between Catholics and Protestants over the nature of the Eucharist. *bedünken* 'be of the opinion,' 'opine'

[1] mustered-out soldiers (Thirty Years' War)

Nimmer Brot im Sacke,
Nimmer Geld im Packe[2]
Haben mit genummen
Die vom Kriege kummen.   10
Wer dann hat die Beute?
Eitel[3] fremde Leute.

Paul Fleming (1609–1640)

Auf die italienische Weise:[1] O fronte serena

O liebliche Wangen,
Ihr macht mir Verlangen,
Dies Rote dies Weiße
Zu schauen mit Fleiße!
Und dies nur alleine   5
Ists nicht, was ich meine:
Zu schauen, zu grüßen —
Zu rühren, zu küssen
Ihr macht mir Verlangen,
O liebliche Wangen!   10

O Sonne der Wonne
O Wonne der Sonne!
O Augen, so[2] saugen
Das Licht meiner Augen!
O englische Sinnen,   15
O himmlisch Beginnen![3]
O Himmel auf Erden,
Magst du mir nicht werden?[4]
O Wonne der Sonne,
O Sonne der Wonne!   20

O Schönste der Schönen,
Benimm mir dies Sehnen![5]
Komm, eile, komm, komme,

---

[2]All the things enumerated in lines 1-8 are objects of verbs in line 9: 'They have brought from the war maggoty consciences [cf. *Gewissenswürmer*] ... no money in their pack' [3]=*lauter* 'nothing but'

[1]'air,' 'melody' [2]=*die* [3]'doings' [4]'can't you be mine?' [5]'appease my longing'

Du Süße, du Fromme,[6]
Ach, Schwester, ich sterbe,   25
Ich sterb, ich verderbe.
Komm, komme, komm, eile,
Komm, tröste, komm, heile!
Benimm mir dies Sehnen,
O Schönste der Schönen!   30

Paul Fleming was one of the more important poets to follow in the footsteps of
Opitz. His best verse is as fresh and vital today as when it was written.
"O liebliche Wangen" is written in dactyls ($-\smile\smile$), a measure that enjoyed
great popularity among the poets of the seventeenth century:

O liebliche Wangen, / Ihr macht mir Verlangen
$\smile - \smile\smile - \smile \quad \smile - \smile\smile - \smile$

Dactyls usually, as here, give the impression of speed, since the fewer stresses
any given measure contains the faster it seems. Here the speed symbolizes the
breathless eagerness of the cavalier for the favors of his adored one. At the
same time, the dactyls lend a lightness, a scherzo-like quality. This contrasts
wittily with the avowed seriousness of the utterance, producing a tension
between *what* is said and the *way* it is said: *Ach, Schwester, ich sterbe, / Ich
sterb, ich verderbe.* Another way of putting the same thing would be to say
that the form exercises a restraining influence: it keeps the content within the
bounds of courtly decorum.

The meter is not the only means of restraint employed. The outpouring of
longing, which forms the overt content of the poem and which is intensified
from stanza to stanza — cheeks–eyes–complete surrender — is kept hovering,
as it were, by the reversed correspondence of the first and last two lines of
each stanza, so that the poem continually returns upon itself, its object
unattained. This, too, is symbolic, since the subject of the poem is longing
(*Sehnen*) and the condition of this state is non-fulfillment.

Towards Interpretation
1. Besides the intensification of longing from stanza to stanza, each contains within itself an intensification. See if you can point this out.
   (Hint: Consider the first four lines of each stanza and compare them
   with the last four.)

---

[6]'gentle one'

An sich

Sei dennoch unverzagt, gib dennoch unverloren,[1]
Weich keinem Glücke[2] nicht, steh höher als der Neid,
Vergnüge dich an dir[3] und acht es für kein Leid,
Hat sich gleich[4] wider dich Glück,[2] Ort und Zeit verschworen.

Was dich betrübt und labt, halt alles für erkoren,[5]   5
Nimm dein Verhängnis an, laß alles unbereut.[6]
Tu, was getan muß sein und eh man dirs gebeut.[7]
Was du noch hoffen kannst, das wird noch stets geboren.[8]

Was[9] klagt, was lobt man doch? Sein Unglück und sein Glücke
Ist sich ein jeder selbst. Schau alle Sachen an —   10
Dies alles ist in dir. Laß deinen eitlen Wahn,

Und eh du förder gehst, so geh in dich zurücke.
Wer sein selbst[10] Meister ist und sich beherrschen kann,
Dem ist die weite Welt und alles untertan.

Towards Interpretation
1. To whom are these lines addressed?
2. Look up the terms hedonistic, epicurean, stoic, and quietistic. Decide
   which best applies to the attitude expressed here.
3. What is "der eitle Wahn" we are urged to abandon?
4. Look up the article "Sonnet" in the *Encyclopedia Britannica*, then reread this poem.

Paul Fleming

Andreas Gryphius

---

[1]'be ever undaunted, never give up' [2]'fortune' [3]'be content with your lot' [4]'even
though [5]'fated' [6]'complain of nothing' [7]=*gebietet* [8]i.e., is continually coming into
being [9]=*warum* [10]'of himself'

Andreas Gryphius (1616–1664)

Though his theme is an ancient one — the transitoriness of all things earthly, the vanity of human wishes — Andreas Gryphius, of all the poets of the Baroque age, probably has the greatest appeal for the modern reader. Gryphius' manner of handling his theme is typical of his time: antithetical, passionately rational, yet deeply religious. His tones are somber but never without final hope, for as a Christian he keeps faith with the divine promise and looks forward to the day of its fulfillment. The basic antithesis of his work is that of earthly misery (even in grandeur) and heavenly glory (even for the miserable).

Abend

Der schnelle Tag ist hin, die Nacht schwingt ihre Fahn
Und führt die Sternen auf. Der Menschen müde Scharen
Verlassen Feld und Werk; wo Tier' und Menschen waren,
Traurt itzt die Einsamkeit. Wie ist die Zeit vertan![1]

Der Port naht mehr und mehr sich zu der Glieder Kahn.[2]   5
Gleich wie dies Licht verfiel, so wird in wenig Jahren
Ich, du, und was man hat, und was man sieht, hinfahren.
Dies Leben kommt mir vor wie eine Rennebahn.

Laß, höchster Gott, mich doch nicht auf dem Laufplatz gleiten,
Laß mich nicht Ach, nicht Pracht, nicht Lust, nicht Angst   10
Dein ewig heller Glanz sei vor und neben mir!   [verleiten.[3]

Laß, wenn der müde Leib entschläft, die Seele wachen,
Und wenn der letzte Tag wird mit mir Abend machen,
So reiß mich aus dem Tal der Finsternis zu dir!

It is apparent that this poem, despite its title, is not simply a description of evening, for after the first four lines there is not a single phrase we can apply to evening as such. What then is meant here by *Abend*? Line 13 tells us that evening stands for death: *Und wenn der letzte Tag wird mit mir Abend machen. . . .* Death is life's evening or sunset. Is this then a poem about death? Yes, but about life too, or rather about life's undeviating course toward death. The realm within which this ceaseless process takes place is the realm of time, and "Abend" is a poem about time.

---

[1]'spent to no end' [2]*der Glieder Kahn* 'the vessel of the limbs,' i.e., the body [3]'do not let ... lead me astray'

The first aspect of time stressed in our poem is its swiftness, its way of slipping past before we can accomplish anything: *Der s c h n e l l e Tag ist h i n ; Wie ist die Zeit v e r t a n !* In the second quatrain (i.e., second group of four lines), time is seen under the aspect of space: We, or our bodies, are a boat that is constantly drawing nearer the harbor, which is of course death (5); life is a racetrack upon which we must run (8).* Gryphius sees life as a confined, predetermined hastening toward an inevitable goal. Reason for hope is not to be found in the realm of time. Man can only submit to a hopeless situation. But beyond time there is hope — hence the prayer contained in the last six lines. The first tercet (i.e., group of three verses) continues the image of life as a racetrack; the second, which explicitly foresees day's last evening, implies the attainment of the harbor and the end of the race, since these are both one.

In the images of life as a race and as a sailing toward the harbor of death in the "vessel of the limbs," time is seen under the aspect of *horizontality*, as distance stretching out before us. Likewise in lines 2-3, *Der Menschen müde Scharen / Verlassen Feld und Werk* without looking up to see the stars led out by night: *Wo Tier' und Menschen waren, / Traurt itzt die Einsamkeit.* But now, in the magnificently forceful last line, *eternity* is suddenly seen under the aspect of *verticality*, of swift upward movement: *So reiß mich aus dem Tal der Finsternis zu dir!* Time as space on the horizontal plane is interrupted or displaced by timelessness as verticality. (The view of the divine implied by these images is that of a God who stands outside His creation rather than being immanent in it.)

The poem also operates with the contrast between darkness and light, bringing this contrast into relation with time. The first sentence juxtaposes day and night, but night itself brings light with it; in fact, to bring light seems to be night's main office: *. . . die Nacht schwingt ihre Fahn / Und f ü h r t d i e S t e r n e n a u f.* Stars, as we know, are a common symbol of hope, promise, fulfillment. The second quatrain speaks of the passing of the light of day. But that it is called "*d i e s Licht*" instead of simply "*das Licht*" suggests another light, one that will not pass away. It is this other light that the poet prays may guide him on life's *Laufplatz: Dein e w i g h e l l e r G l a n z sei vor und neben mir!* Thus the light of eternity is contrasted with the light of our day, and the latter, which fails so swiftly, seems only an aspect of darkness. In the last tercet the contrast is used once more: again the poet speaks of the coming of evening, or more precisely, of death *as* the coming of evening, then combining the space and light imagery, prays that he may, when his evening comes, be rapt out of the darkness of this failing light to the divine, unfailing light of eternity. He prays that the promise of the stars may be fulfilled.

"Abend," then, is built on the antithesis of time and eternity. This antithesis appears as horizontality and verticality and as darkness and light.

---

*The image is Biblical: cf. Hebrews 12:1 and I Corinthians 9:24ff.

None of these abstractions, however, is presented *per se*, but in the form of images and metaphors: as day and night, as light that fades and light that shines eternally, as a racecourse and as an instantaneous ascent. The "what" of the poem is contained in the "how."

Towards Interpretation

1. As what is night personified in lines 1-2?
2. What evaluation of existence is implied in calling the body *der Glieder Kahn*?
3. What do you understand by the line *laß mich nicht Ach . . . verleiten*?
4. The second edition of *The Oxford Book of German Verse* (1927) gave line 5 as *dem Port naht mehr und mehr der wildbewegte Kahn*. What do you think of the "improvement"? Give reasons for your approval or disapproval on the basis of the context, not in a vacuum!
5. The same anthology gave line 10: *Laß mich nicht S c h m e r z, nicht Pracht, nicht Lust, nicht Angst verleiten!* What is lost by this change? (Hint: Read both the original and the *Oxford Book* variant aloud.)

Tränen des Vaterlandes, Anno 1636

Wir sind doch nunmehr ganz, ja mehr denn ganz verheeret![1]
Der frechen Völker[2] Schar, die rasende Posaun',
Das vom Blut fette Schwert, die donnernde Kartaun'[3]
Hat aller[4] Schweiß und Fleiß und Vorrat aufgezehret.

Die Türme stehn in Glut, die Kirch ist umgekehret.   5
Das Rathaus liegt im Graus;[5] die Starken sind zerhaun,
Die Jungfern[6] sind geschändt;[7] und wo wir hin nur schaun
Ist Feuer, Pest und Tod, der Herz und Geist durchfähret.

Hier durch die Schanz[8] und Stadt rinnt allzeit frisches Blut.
Dreimal sind schon sechs Jahr, als[9] unsrer Ströme Flut,   10
Von Leichen fast verstopft, sich langsam fortgedrungen.[10]

Doch schweig ich noch von dem, was ärger[11] als der Tod,
Was grimmer denn die Pest und Glut und Hungersnot:
Daß auch der Seelen-Schatz[12] so vielen abgezwungen.[13]

---

[1] = *durch Heere zerstört* [2] = *Kriegsvölker (Soldaten)* [3] a kind of heavy cannon [4] genitive plural [5] = *Schutt* [6] 'young women' [7] 'violated' [8] 'ramparts' [9] = *Es sind schon 3x6 Jahre, daß* [10] *sich fortgedrungen* 'has been pressing onward' [11] = *schlimmer* [12] 'treasure of the soul' (also in sense of 'religion') [13] = *abgezwungen worden ist*

Towards Interpretation
1. What was going on in Germany in 1636? For how long had it been going on?
2. Count the nouns in this poem. Count the verbs. (Note that such constructions as *ist umgekehret, sind zerhaun* are merely copula plus participle, not auxiliary plus participle.) How many of the verbs show action, how many merely the result of action? How does the ratio of nouns to verbs reflect the message of the poem?
3. What seems to you to be the effect of the irregular metrical situation in line 3: *Das vom Blút fétte Schwért?* Compare the normal situation: *Der fréchen Vólker Schár.*

Tränen in schwerer Krankheit (Anno 1640)

Mir ist, ich weiß nicht wie, ich seufze für und für.[1]
Ich weine Tag und Nacht; ich sitz in tausend Schmerzen;
Und tausend fürcht ich noch; die Kraft in meinem Herzen
Verschwindt, der Geist verschmacht', die Hände sinken mir.

Die Wangen werden bleich, der muntern Augen Zier   5
Vergeht gleich als der Schein der schon verbrannten Kerzen.
Die Seele wird bestürmt gleich wie die See im Märzen.[2]
Was ist dies Leben doch, was sind wir, ich und ihr?

Was bilden wir uns ein, was wünschen wir zu haben?
Itzt sind wir hoch und groß, und morgen schon vergraben;   10
Itzt Blumen, morgen Kot. Wir sind ein Wind, ein Schaum,

Ein Nebel und ein Bach, ein Reif,[3] ein Tau, ein Schatten;
Itzt was und morgen nichts. Und was sind unsre Taten
Als ein mit herber Angst durchaus vermischter Traum.

Towards Interpretation
1. What is the nature of the sickness spoken of in this poem?
2. Into what error would we fall if we attempted to interpret Gryphius' view of life from this one poem? What is lacking here that is so important in "Abend"?
3. In what *verse* form are this and the two foregoing sonnets written? (Cf. Angelus Silesius.)

---

[1]'for ever and ever' [2]=*März* [3]'frost'

Über Nicolai Copernici Bild

Du dreimal weiser Geist! Du mehr denn großer Mann
Dem nicht die Nacht der Zeit, die alles pochen[1] kann,
Dem nicht der herbe Neid die Sinnen hat gebunden,
Die Sinnen, die den Lauf der schnellen Erden[2] funden;
Der du der Alten[3] Träum und Dünkel[4] wiederlegt   5
Und recht uns dargetan,[5] was lebt und was sich regt:
Schau! Itzund blüht dein Ruhm, den als[6] auf einem Wagen
Der Kreis, auf dem wir sind, muß um die Sonnen[2] tragen!
Wann dies, was irdisch ist, wird mit der Zeit vergehn,
Soll dein Lob unbewegt mit seiner Sonnen[2] stehn.   10

Towards Interpretation
   1. Who was Nicolas Copernicus and what is his claim to fame?

Johann Klaj (1616–1656)

From: *Der Engel- und Drachen-Streit*

Der Ober Feldherr Lucifer [spricht].[1]

Wollen wir heute die Beute recht kosten /
Lasset verwegen die Degen nicht rosten![2]
Setzet / versetzet gebrennete Pfosten[3] /
Wachet / verwachet die eussersten Posten!
Lasset nicht / fasset den Fürstlichen Muth /   5
zaget nicht / waget das Purpurne Blut!
giesset / vergiesset vor Englische[4] Krafft /
schrecklich und kecklich den Lebenden Safft!

Des Lucifers Soldaten [sprechen].

Lucifer wann deine Waffen rasseln
in dem blanckgeharnschten[5] Heer /
wann die heisern Kälberfelle[6] prasseln /   10

---

[1]'ravage' [2]singular [3]'ancients' [4]'false notions' [5]'shown' [6]=*wie*

[1]From a longer poem on the revolt of the angels called *Der Engel- und Drachen-Streit*.
Contemporary spelling and punctuation have been retained. [2]=*seid verwegen* (bold)
und laßt euere Degen nicht rosten! [3]The "burnt posts" are stakes used to make pa-
lisades. [4]'angelic' [5]'brightly armored' [6]The "hoarse calf hides" are drumheads.

dann erstaunet Land und Meer /
wenn die lautbar-hellen[7] Feldtrommeten
uns verjagen Todesnöthen.

Wann der helle Küriß[8] und die Schilde
halten inner[9] dampf bestaubt /   15
wann die milden Reiter werden wilde /
wenn das Pferd stoltz-dramplend schnaubt /
wenn ein Wald voll Piquen / voller Lantzen /
dich und uns nun wird ümschantzen,

Wollen wir als dapfre Männer stehen /   20
und verschiessen Loth und Kraut[10] /
üm ein Haar nicht auß den Gliedern gehen[11] /
den / der fürchtet seiner Haut[12] /
wollen wir bestrickt mit Lunten[13] stricken
unsern Feinden überschicken.   25

Himmelhertze / Schild des heitern Himmels[14] /
warüm schwärtzest du dein Haubt?[15]
Es wird wegen dieses Lustgetümmels
unser Haubt mit Laub ümlaubt /
Wann sich unser Pantzer nur erschüttert[16] /   30
Roß und Mann und alles zittert.

Christian Hofmann von Hofmannswaldau
(1616–1679)

Vergänglichkeit der Schönheit

Es wird der bleiche Tod mit seiner kalten Hand
Dir, Lesbie,[1] mit der Zeit um deine Brüste streichen,
Der liebliche[2] Korall der Lippen wird verbleichen;
Der Schultern warmer Schnee wird werden kalter Sand.

---

[7]=*laut und hell* [8]=*Küraß* [9]'press forward'(?) [10]=*Blei und Pulver* [11]'not move from
our ranks by a hair' [12]'whoever fears for his skin' [13]'fuses' [14]'The heart of heaven'
and 'shield of heaven serene' is Lucifer (in the eyes of his soldiers) [15]i.e., why do
your looks grow dark? [16]'shakes, rattles'

[1]Reference to the Greek poet Sappho of Lesbos, here a code name for the poet's supposed beloved. [2]=*liebreizend* 'fascinating'

Der Augen süßer Blitz, die Kräfte deiner Hand,   5
Für welchen solches fällt,[3] die werden zeitlich weichen,[4]
Das Haar, das itzund kann des Goldes Glanz erreichen,[5]
Tilgt endlich Tag und Jahr als ein gemeines Band.[6]

Der wohlgesetzte Fuß, die lieblichen Gebärden,
Die werden teils zu Staub, teils nichts und nichtig
                                    werden,[7] 10
Dann opfert keiner mehr der Gottheit[8] deiner Pracht.

Dies und noch mehr als dies[9] muß endlich untergehen,
Dein Herze kann allein zu aller Zeit bestehen,
Dieweil[10] es die Natur aus Diamant gemacht.

Towards Interpretation

1. Is the poet complimenting his Lesbia in saying that her heart is "made of diamond"?
2. Why is he reminding her of the *Vergänglichkeit der Schönheit*?

Gedanken über die Eitelkeit

Was ist die Welt und ihr berühmtes Glänzen?
Was ist die Welt und ihre ganze Pracht?
Ein schnöder Schein in kurzgefaßten Grenzen,
Ein schneller Blitz bei schwarzgewölkter Nacht,
Ein buntes Feld, da Kummerdisteln grünen,   5
Ein schön Spital, so voller Krankheit steckt,
Ein Sklavenhaus, da alle Menschen dienen,
Ein faules Grab, so Alabaster deckt.
Das ist der Grund, darauf wir Menschen bauen
Und was das Fleisch für einen Abgott hält.   10
Komm, Seele, komm und lerne weiter schauen,
Als sich erstreckt der Zirkel dieser Welt!
Streich ab von dir derselben[1] kurzes Prangen,
Halt ihre Lust für eine schwere Last:
So wirst du leicht in diesen Port gelangen,   15
Da Ewigkeit und Schönheit sich umfaßt.

---

[3] = *vor welchen so vieles besiegt niederfällt.* A typical Baroque compliment: nothing can withstand Lesbia's attractions. [4] = *besiegt abziehen* [5] 'compete with' [6] = *allgemeines Schicksal* [7] *teils ... teils:* The body will become dust; Lesbia's graces will return to nothingness and be forgotten. [8] = *Göttlichkeit* [9] Rhetorical turn for what has not been enumerated [10] = *weil*

[1] i.e., of this world

Wo sind die Stunden

Wo sind die Stunden
Der süßen Zeit,
Da ich zuerst empfunden,
Wie deine Lieblichkeit
Mich dir verbunden?   5
Sie sind verrauscht. Es bleibet doch dabei,
Daß alle Lust vergänglich sei.

Das reine Scherzen,
So mich ergetzt
Und in dem tiefen Herzen   10
Sein Merkmal eingesetzt,
Läßt mich in Schmerzen.
Du hast mir mehr als deutlich kund getan,
Daß Freundlichkeit nicht ankern kann.

Das Angedenken   15
Der Zuckerlust
Will mich in Angst versenken.
Es will verdammte Kost
Uns zeitlich¹ kränken.
Was man geschmeckt und nicht mehr schmecken   20
Ist freudenleer und jammervoll.   [soll,

Empfangne Küsse,
Ambrierter² Saft,
Verbleibt nicht lange süße
Und kommt von aller Kraft;   25
Verrauschte Flüsse
Erquicken nicht. Was unsern Geist erfreut,
Entspringt aus Gegenwärtigkeit.

Ich schwamm in Freude,
Der Liebe Hand   30
Spann mir ein Kleid von Seide;
Das Blatt hat sich gewandt,
Ich geh im Leide,
Ich wein itzund, daß Lieb' und Sonnenschein
Stets voller Angst und Wolken sein.   35

---

¹'in time'   ²'ambrosial'

Catharina von Greiffenberg (1633–1694)

Greiffenberg was beyond doubt one of the greatest lyric poets of the 17th century, and her work represents the very best of the meditative poetry of the German Baroque. Her poetry is filled with a sense of the wonder of God's mercy, for which she believed we owe Him our utmost faith and trust. As a Protestant poet in Catholic Austria during the Counter-Reformation, it is not surprising that a major theme of her poetry is Christian constancy in the face of hardship and suffering. Even in suffering, however, she sees a reason to praise God, since that suffering comes, as do all  things, from Him; through suffering we experience another aspect of His love, and our love for Him is tested. Because for her there is a oneness between the supernatural and natural phenomena, i.e., everything is *super*natural, she does not seek a "mystical" experience of divinity; rather, she views her poetry as a way of expressing her very personal experience of the infinite goodness of God that we see all around us. Greiffenberg employs to some extent a very mannered poetic language; that is, like her contemporary poets she expresses herself in a style which seems somewhat artificial and contains an abundance of those rhetorical flourishes that characterize the High Baroque style. Nevertheless, she often creates astonishingly fresh and daring images by coining compound words and conjoining unlike elements in order to translate into words her profound experience of faith. Her poetry was not intended to please or be understandable to the public: it was written for and to God.

„O Wort!"

O Wort![1] dem alle Wort zu wenig,[2] es zu preisen!
O Wort! durch welches ward, das man mit Worten nennt.
Durch dich, o Wesen-Wort! man dessen Selbstheit kennt,
Der seinen Allheit-Glanz, dich zeugend, wollte weisen.

O Wort! das auf das Wort des Engels wollte reisen   5
In keuschen Tugend-Thron! das bleibet ungetrennt

---

[1]Cf. John 1:1ff., "In the beginning was the Word ..." [2]'insufficient'

Von seinem Ausspruch-Mund, doch alle Welt durchrennt.
Wort! das mit Worten kann, die voll der Werke, speisen.

Wort! das eh als sein Mund und Zunge war geboren!
Ja, Wort! das seinen Mund und Zunge selbst erschuf!   10
Wort! das zu reden ihm[3] durch Schweigen hat erkoren!

Wort! des[4] Unmündigkeit[5] die ganze Welt ausruft,
O Wort! das Gott beredt zum Schaffen und Erlösen,
Wollst Worte dir zu Lob in mir jetzt auserlesen.

Über das unaussprechliche heilige Geistes-Eingeben!

Du ungesehner Blitz, du dunkel-helles Licht,
Du Herzerfüllte Kraft, doch unbegreiflichs Wesen!
Es ist was Göttliches in meinem Geist gewesen,
Das mich bewegt und regt: Ich spür ein seltnes Licht.

Die Seel ist von sich selbst nicht also löblich licht.   5
Es ist ein Wunder-Wind, ein Geist, ein webend Wesen,
Die ewig' Atem-Kraft, das Erz-Sein[1] selbst gewesen,
Das ihm[2] in mir entzünd dies Himmel-flammend Licht.

Du Farben-Spiegel-Blick, du wunderbuntes Glänzen!
Du schimmerst hin und her, bist unbegreiflich klar;   10
Die Geistes Taubenflüg'[3] in Wahrheits-Sonne glänzen.

Der Gott-bewegte Teich[4] ist auch getrübet klar!
Es will erst gegen ihr[2] die Geistes-Sonn beglänzen
Den Mond,[5] dann dreht er sich, wird Erden-ab[6] auch klar.

The Holy Spirit is that aspect of the Trinity which makes faith possible. The identical rimes of the octet reinforce formally the theme that the essence (*Wesen*) of the Holy Spirit is Light (*Licht*), which is perfect unto itself. That essential light, like the sun shining on the moon, has shone upon the speaker and imparted to her soul some of its own divine luminosity in the form of ineffable ("unaussprechlich") grace.

---

[3]=*sich* [4]=*dessen* [5]'immaturity,' 'mouthlessness'; i.e., creation is the expression of the unspoken word

[1]*Wunder-Wind ... Erz-Sein*, epithets for the Holy Spirit [2]*sich* [3]In Christian iconography, the dove symbolizes the Holy Spirit, cf. Matthew 3:16. [4]Cf. John 5:7, where the waters of the Pool of Bethesda are troubled by the "angel"; here the soul is the pool. [5]The moon receiving its light from the sun is one of Greiffenberg's favorite images for the relationship of the soul to God. [6]i.e., from the point of view of the earth

Towards Interpretation

1. What images does Greiffenberg use in this poem to represent the soul?
2. Can you visualize the astronomy of lines 12-13?
3. What is the relationship of the soul (*Mond*) to the divine (*Geistes-Sonne*)?

„Ich will ein Bienlein sein"

Ich will ein Bienlein sein, dem Jesus-Klee zufliegen.
Auror' und Tithon[1] ich lass' ruhig schlafen liegen;
Das selbste Feder-Volk noch schlummert auf dem Ast,
Da ich zu schiffen schon durch Lüfte bin gefaßt
Nach meinem Blumen-Port. Die Purpur-Perlen[2] scheinen   5
Den Sternen selber vor mit ihren Himmels-Feinen.
Sie machen seel-gesund, doch tödlich lieb-erkrankt.
Sie löschen Höllen-Glut, entzünden, daß es fankt,[3]
Das Feur der Dankbarkeit. Ich setze ganz mit Zittern
Die Zunge gierig an, besorge, anzubittern[4]   10
Den schon erz-großen Schmerz; saug also fein gemach
Das Mark des Himmels ein. O angenehme Sach!
Ich saug der Gottheit Saft. Ich trink den Bronn[5] der Sonnen.
Der Geist der selbsten Stärk' kommt her in mich geronnen.
Der Drei- und Einheit-Klee gibt hier sein Honig her.   15
Wenn man die Allheit hat, was will und wünscht man mehr?

What is perhaps most startling in this poem is not the figure of the bee sipping at the wounds of Christ, which can be found in other religious verse of the period, but the intense identification of the of poetic "I" with the bee. The poet becomes a bee, who "knows" that in sucking the nectar of the "Jesus-clover" it sucks "the source of the sun," since Christ is its creator and, at the same time, the creator of our own sun, the Sun of Life. The image of the bee is both wholly physical and wholly spiritual.

---

[1]Tithonus was the husband (lover) of Aurora, the dawn. [2]i.e., the wounds of the Savior [3]=*funkt* [4]'to make bitter' [5]=*Brunnen*

Kaspar Stieler (1632–1707)

Nacht-Glücke

Willkommen, Fürstin aller Nächte!
Prinz der Silberknechte,
Willkommen, Mon[1] aus düstrer Bahn
Vom Ozean!
Dies ist die Nacht, die tausend Tagen   5
Trotz kann sagen:[2]
Weil mein Schatz
Hier in Priapus' Platz[3]
Erscheinen wird, zu stillen meine Pein.[4]
Wer wird, wie ich, wohl so beglücket sein?   10

Beneidet, himmlische Laternen,
Weißgeflammte Sternen,
Mit einem scheelen Angesicht
Ach! mich nur nicht.
Kein Mensch, als ihr nur, möge wissen,   15
Wie wir küssen:
Alle Welt
Hat seine Ruh bestellt,
Wir beide nur, ich und mein Kind[5] sind wach,
Und, Flammen, ihr an Bronteus'[6] Wolkendach.   20

Es säuselt Zephir aus dem Weste,
Durch Pomonen-Äste,[7]
Es seufzet sein[8] verliebter Wind
Nach meinem Kind.
Ich seh es gerne, da er spielet   25
Und sie kühlet,
Weil[9] sie mir
Folgt durch die Gartentür,
Und doppelt den geschwinden Liebestritt.
Bring, West, sie bald und tausend Küsse mit!   30

---

[1] =*Mond*, which is also the *Fürstin aller Nächte* (Luna, Diana) and the *Prinz der Silberknechte* (the stars). [2]'can outdo' [3]As a god of fertility, Priapus' statue is often placed in gardens. [4]=*Liebespein* [5]'beloved' [6]=Brontēs 'thunderer,' one of the cyclopes who forge Zeus' thunderbolts. The flames are flashes of lightning. [7]'Pomona's branches'; Pomona is a fertility goddess. [8]Zephir's [9]'while'

Was werd ich, wenn sie kommt gegangen,
An- doch erstlich fangen,
Küß ich die Hand, die Brust, den Mund
Zur selben Stund?[10]
Ich werd (ich weiß) kein Wort nicht machen,   35
Soviel Sachen,
Die an Zier
Den Göttern gehen für[11]
Und auf dies Schönchen sein gewendet an,[12]
Erstaunen mich, daß ich nicht reden kann.   40

Komm, Flora,[13] streue dein Vermügen[14]
Dahin, wo wir liegen.
Es soll ein bunter Rosenhauf
Uns nehmen auf,
Und, Venus, du sollst in den Myrten[15]   45
Uns bewirten,
Bis das Blut
Der Röt' herfür sich tut.[16]
Was Schein ist das? Die Schatten werden klar.
Still, Lautenklang![17] Mein Liebchen ist schon dar.   50

Barthold Hinrich Brockes (1680–1747)

Mondschein

Der Abend kam, sobald der güldne Glanz
Des Sonnenlichts nicht mehr zu sehen war,
Mit seiner sanften Schatten Schar
Gemach, gemach heran:
Doch war der Schein nicht ganz   5
Vergangen und dahin, der Schatten auch noch nicht
Ganz ausgedehnt und schwarz, vielmehr schien Nacht und Licht
In einem sanften Grad vereint. Hieraus entsprung
Ein allgemeine rein und helle Dämmerung,
Voll Kühlung, Still' und Lust; als ich, von ungefähr,   10
An eines Grabens klarer Flut,

---

[10]=*zu gleicher Zeit* [11]'surpass the gods' [12]i.e., form part of her attractions [13]goddess of vegetation [14]=*Vermögen* 'riches' [15]The myrtle was sacred to Venus. [16]i.e., until dawn; *Röt'* =*Morgenröte* [17]*Laute* 'lute'

Auf welcher teils des Himmels heitrer Schein
Und teils ein Widerschein von hohen Bäumen ruht,
Mit sanften Schritten hin und her
Vergnügt spazieren ging. Ich konnte mich nicht satt   15
An diesem Erd- und Himmelsspiegel sehn,
Unglaublich eben, still und glatt
War die kristallengliche Fläche,
Der Abendröte Rest schien fast in größrer Schwäche
Am Himmel als auf ihr:[1] unglaublich rein und schön   20
War westenwärts die lichte Heiterkeit
Am Firmament, im Wasser auch zu sehn.
Zur Seiten kam ein Widerschein
Von einem lieblichen Gebüsch, von Binsen und von Rohr
Mir in natürlichster Vollkommenheit,   25
Als wär es alles doppelt, vor.
Absonderlich[2] nahm ein fast wahrer Schein
Von dicken Wipfeln hoher Linden,
Die an dem fetten[3] Strand sich da gepflanzet finden,
Mit einem dunklen Schmuck das klare Wasser ein.[4]   30
Ich hatte meine Lust, die Gleichheit dieser Schatten,
Die sie, im Widerschein, mit ihrem Urbild hatten,
Bewundernd anzusehn. Allein,
Wie stutzt' ich, als mein Blick, bei meinem sanften Schritte,
Auf dieser glatten Bahn gemächlich vor sich glitte,[5]   35
Und ich, ohn überwärts zu sehn,
Den hellen Mond in vollem Licht
An einem grünen Himmel fand.
Noch mehr, mir fiel zugleich noch einer ins Gesicht,[6]
Und zwar der wahre Mond, der eben übers Haupt   40
Der Bäume, die so dicht belaubt,
Hervortrat und am blauen Himmel stand.
Unglaublich ist, wie sehr mich dieser Anblick rührte.
Und unbeschreiblich ist die Lust,
Die ich darob[7] in meiner Brust   45
Und meinem ganzen Wesen spürte.
Der reine Glanz so schöner Lichter drang
Bei der so süßen Abendstille
Und kühlen Heiterkeit, mit einer rechten Fülle
Von Anmut mir ins Herz, daß ich, halb außer mir,   50

---

[1] i.e., the reflection of the sunset in the water was almost clearer than its reality in the sky [2] 'strangely,' 'particularly' [3] 'fertile' [4] *nahm ... ein* 'reflected' [5] =*glitt* [6] 'vision'
[7] =*darüber*

Ob[8] aller Kreaturen Zier
Dem Schöpfer dies zu Ehren sang:
Ach! laß die durch Dein Werk erfüllte Seele
Dir Herr so angenehm, als wie die durch den Schein
Des Monds erfüllte Flut mir angenehm ist, sein!   55
Laß mich oft ihren[9] Schmuck am grünen Himmel schauen,
Bis ich dereinsten[10] dort im Blauen
Dem wahren Licht so nah wie hier dem flücht'gen Schein,
Auch Deine Wunderwerk' zu sehn mag fähig sein!
Ach, laß zu diesem Zweck mir oft die Flut der Erden   60
So, wie es jetzt geschieht, zum Himmelsspiegel werden!

Gegenüber der schematisierenden Naturdarstellung der Barockpoesie tut
solch ein Gedicht wie Brockes' „Mondschein" den entscheidenden Schritt
hinaus in die leibhaftig-anwesende Sinnenwirklichkeit: die Natur — wenn
schon sie etwas gartenhaft Gehegtes und Umfriedetes behält — ist nicht
mehr bloße Kulisse oder bloßes Zeichengerüst [allegorical sign language],
sondern eigenwertiges Dasein und Inbegriff realistisch gesehener Erscheinungen. Sehend, hörend, fühlend, riechend, schmeckend ist das lyrische
Ich den Eindrücken offen, entzückt und angerührt von der Fülle und Viel-
falt der Wirklichkeit als solcher, die es mit zartester Treue einzufangen
versucht; und die sprachliche Vergegenwärtigung [realization] ist von einer
Dichte und Intensität, daß man nicht umhin kann, von Magie zu sprechen.
. . . Anderseits bringt das reflektierende Durchgehen der Erscheinungen
und die begriffliche Sorgfalt, ja Ängstlichkeit der malenden Ausschöpfung
eine steife und gestelzte Würde mit sich, die der Hingabe an den stim-
mungsbedeutsamen Gesamteindruck entgegenwirkt. So kommt es immer
wieder zum Bruch zwischen sinnlicher Erfassung und verstandesmäßiger
Zergliederung, zwischen unmittelbarer Einfühlung und gedanklich vermit-
telter Betrachtung, zwischen mitschwingender Teilhabe und distanziertem
Gegenüber. Die dichterische Anschauung neigt hier dazu, in lauter kleine
Einzelbeobachtungen auseinanderzufallen, die am Faden der Reflexion
aneinandergereiht werden. Die Mannigfaltigkeit der Sinneseindrücke wird
weniger von einem beseelenden Mittelpunkt her zur bildhaften Einheit
gerundet als vielmehr durch den klärenden Begriff in eine rationale
Ordnung gebracht. — Auf solche Weise ergibt sich ein ebenso befremdli-
ches wie reizvolles Ineinander und Gegeneinander von Logik und Magie.*

Towards Interpretation

1. Read the poem aloud. How does Brockes use sounds to create the
   proper mood (*Klangmalerei*) for his setting? Give examples.
2. What is the significance of the contrast between the green and blue

---

[8]=*über*   [9]refers to *Wunderwerke*, line 59   [10]=*einmal*

*Johannes Pfeiffer, *Wege zur Dichtung* (Hamburg: F. Wittig, [7]1969), 64f.

heavens? What is he saying about the relationship between God and Nature?

3. After reading the poem, do we need to rethink the meaning of the title, "Mondschein"?

Christiana Mariana von Ziegler (1695–1760)

Die Zieglerin was a fixture in the literary and cultural life of Leipzig during the first half of the eighteenth century. Having been twice widowed before the age of thirty, Ziegler was able to exercise a certain freedom from the social restrictions usually placed upon women, especially unmarried women and wives. In fact, her literary production is essentially limited to the twenty years of her widowhood; after she married for a third time, at the age of forty-six (1741), she published no more poetry. Ziegler is an important figure in German literary history because of the *public* nature of her accomplishments as a woman poet: obviously there were woman poets before her — and better poets, at that (one need only think of Greiffenberg!) — but the public recognition she received made it clear that there was a place in literary life for woman poets. She was the first woman to be offered membership in J. C. Gottsched's *Deutsche Gesellschaft*, the most important literary society of the day, and she twice received the *Gesellschaft*'s poetry prize. In 1733 she was crowned Imperial Poet Laureate of the University at Wittenberg, the first woman ever to receive such an honor in Germany.

Brief an ein Frauenzimmer

Apollens werte Braut nennt mich dein Dichterkiel![1]
Galante — — du denkst und schreibst zu viel;
Ach es erfordert mehr zum rechten Zweck zu kommen,
Und das was ich getan, heißt noch nichts unternommen.
Ein Reim zählt uns nicht gleich zu den Poeten mit,   5
Wenn man auch noch so schnell zum Musenhügel[2] tritt.
Der Hippokrenen Fluß dient auch zu Stümpereien;
Drum wirst du, Freundin, mir vor diesesmal verzeihen,
Ich schreibe deutsch heraus, so wie das Herze denkt;

---

[1] 'poet's quill'   [2] Mt. Helicon was sacred to Apollo and the Muses, hence *Musenhügel*; the Hippocrene, a fountain that is the source of poetic inspiration, flowed from Mt. Helicon.

Und da dein Schreiben mir so viele Neigung schenkt,   10
So offenbar ich dir, wie mir es sonst gegangen,
Mit was vergeb'ner Müh' ich manches angefangen.
Ein Dichter soll und muß dazu geboren sein,
Das lag mir in dem Kopf, ich schrieb in Tag hinein;[3]
Bis treuer Freunde Rat mich auf den Einfall brachte,   15
Daß ich bloß die Vernunft zu meiner Richtschnur machte.[4]
Die führte mich sogleich ganz einen andern Weg;
Gefällt dir mein Gesang, betritt auch diesen Steg,
Du wirst denselbigen sodann mit Ruhm beschreiten
Daferne[5] du dich läßt in diesen Schranken leiten.   20
Geduld, Vernunft und Zeit, die können uns belehren.
Anstatt daß Männer stets gelehrte Redner hören,
So nehmen wir ein Buch von einer klugen Hand,
Und machen uns daraus das was uns nützt, bekannt.[6]
Die Regeln muß man auch aus ihrem Grunde wissen,   25
Es muß uns keine Müh' bei dieser Kunst verdrießen;
Wenn man die Sätze nicht recht einzuteilen weiß,
So wird dem Leser kalt, bald übel und bald heiß.
Dem Unfall in der Zeit[7] mit Vorsicht vor zu kommen,
So hab ich manchen Rat mit Danken angenommen.   30
Es kömmt manch schönes Werk zu unsrer Zeit heraus,
Ich suche mir noch jetzt dergleichen Bücher aus,
Und lese stets mit Lust was andrer[8] Witz geschrieben,
Denn wer das Dichten liebt, der muß auch diese lieben.
So fahr ich täglich fort, und lerne was dabei;   35
Dadurch verlieret sich das wilde Waldgeschrei.
Die Vorschrift kann ich dir aus gutem Herzen geben;
Doch steht dir ferner frei derselben nach zu leben.[9]
Inliegendes[10] Gedicht stellt sich auch bei dir ein;
Es soll von meiner Gunst zum Schluß der Zeuge sein;   40
Nebst der Versicherung, du wirst mich stets so kennen,
Daß du mich in der Tat kannst deine Freundin nennen.

---

[3] =*in den Tag hineinschreiben* 'to dash off' [4] *Daß ... machte* 'that I should simply make Reason my guideline' [5] =*insofern* [6] *Anstatt ... bekannt*, i.e., since we cannot as women have access to learned lectures as men do, let us take a clever book and learn out of it what we need [7] *in der Zeit* 'early enough' [8] genitive plural [9] *derselben ... leben* 'to follow this [advice]' [10] 'the enclosed'

Johann Christian Günther (1695–1723)

Schreiben an seine Leonore[1]
Von Breslau A[nno] 1719. den 22. Dezembr.

Ach Kind, ach liebstes Kind, was war das vor Vergnügen!
Der Himmel geb' uns doch dergleichen Nächte viel
Und laß uns so vertraut bis an das letzte Ziel[2]
Mit Brust und Geist vermählt in Eintrachtsbanden[3] liegen;
Denn außer jener Welt und ohne diese Lust[4]   5
Ist doch wohl der Natur kein größrer Schatz bewußt.

Wir spielen unverstört mit Redlichkeit und Küssen,
Wir haben gleichen Sinn, wir wünschen einerlei,
Sind Sklaven süßer Macht, und niemand lebt so frei;
Wir schwatzen, daß uns auch die Worte mangeln müssen,   10
Wir schenken uns an uns und nähmen, könnt es sein,
Als Seelen wahrer Treu, nur einen Körper ein.

Uns darf kein Modebrief kein Ehverlöbnis stiften,[5]
Kein Kuppler und kein Geld verbindet unsre Glut,
Dein Mahlschatz[6] ist mein Herz, dein Herz mein Heiratsgut[7]   15
Und unser beider Ruhm die Dichtkunst meiner Schriften,
In welchen Lieb und Scherz so lange Lob gewinnt,
Als Kunst und Wissenschaft in Deutschland fruchtbar sind.

Wir haben unsern Bund die Zeit bewähren[8] lassen;
Vor dich ist auf der Welt kein beßrer Mann als ich,   20
Ich find auch auf der Welt kein treuer Weib als dich,
Wir müßten sonder[9] uns das beste Leben hassen;
Da, wo ich dich nicht seh, da ist mir alles leer,
Und wenn es auch der Schwarm des größten Hofes wär.

Versuchte[10] mich Eugen[11] und böte mir der Kaiser   25
Vor dich, du frommes[12] Kind, Gold, Thron und Purpur an,
So spräch ich, wie ich dir mit Wahrheit schwören kann:
Ich ehre, großer Held, die vielen Siegesreiser,[13]

---

[1]Leonore Jachmann was Günther's great love and poetic inspiration [2]i.e., until death [3]'bonds of harmony' [4]'for except for that world (of ours) and but for this joy' [5]'We need no fashionable announcement to confirm our engagement' [6]'pledge of marriage' [7]'dowry' [8]'confirm' [9]=*ohne* [10]'tempt' [11]Prince Eugene of Savoy, famous Austrian fieldmarshal [12]'gentle' [13]'wreathes of victory'

Ich weiß auch, großer Karl,[14] was Macht und Kronen sind —
Behaltet, was ihr habt, und laßt mir nur mein Kind!   30

Gesegnet sei der Tag, gesegnet sei die Kammer,
Der unsern Bund gesehn, die unsern Kuß gehört!
Wer jenen durch Verdruß und die mit Fluch entehrt,
Dem mach'[15] ein böses Weib den Ehstand[16] voller Jammer.
Gesegnet sei auch gar der Kummer und der Neid,   35
Der wegen deiner Gunst mir manchen Stoß verleiht!

O könnt ich doch, mein Kind, in allen Sprachen dichten
(So wünsch ich dann und wann wie einst Petrarchens[17] Mund),
So tät ich deinen Wert den meisten Ländern kund,
So ließ' ich jedes Volk von unsrer Liebe richten;[18]   40
Die Klügsten würden sehn, wie zärtlich meine Treu,
Wie redlich meine Brust, wie rein dein Herze sei.

Ich tu, so viel ich kann, dein Denkmal[19] auszubreiten,
Um bei der späten Welt[20] durch deinen Ruhm zu blühn;
Wie mancher wird noch Trost aus meinen Liedern ziehn,   45
Wie mancher wird mein Vers zur süßen Regung[21] leiten!
So merk ich, wenn mein Mund der Alten[22] Arbeit list,[23]
Daß unsre Liebe schon vordem[24] gewesen ist.

Was hat wohl unser Wunsch mehr auf der Welt zu suchen,
Und welches Glück ist noch wohl unsers Neides wert?   50
Wenn nur des Himmels Huld[25] dich vollends[26] ganz gewährt,
So wüte[27] Feind und Groll, so mag der Spötter fluchen;
Drei Dinge sind mein Trost: Gott, Wissenschaft[28] und du;
Bei diesen seh ich stets den Stürmen ruhig zu.

Johann Christian Günther, *der letzte Schlesier*, stands at the end of a line of
notable Silesians — among them Opitz, Heermann, Scheffler, and Gryphius —
who gave the German Baroque some of its most characteristic literature. Günther is Janus-faced: he looks back on the Baroque (which, to be sure, in arts
other than literature had not yet run its full course: Bach was at the height of
his powers, the magnificent Bavarian pilgrimage churches and the *Karlskirche*
in Vienna were just being or yet to be built), and he looks forward to the latter
part of the 18th century with its insistence on individual feeling and the artist's
right to create out of personal experience. It is the strong personal note, the
passionate stress on his own feeling and experience, that strikes us as "mod-

---

[14]the emperor, Charles VI [15]hortatory subjunctive [16]'married life' [17]Italian love poet,
of great influence on the 15th-17th centuries [18]'judge' [19]'fame' [20]'posterity' [21]'emotion' [22]'ancients' [23]=*liest* [24]=*vorher* [25]'grace' [26]'finally' [27]hortatory subjunctive
[28]'learning'

ern" in Günther. The form and conventions to which he adheres are, however, largely those of his time. He likes the alexandrine, not infrequently resorts to stereotyped emblemism, and has a strong tendency toward rationalistic reflection. This dissonance — or at least what seems to be so from our point of view — between form and content gives his work its peculiar stamp, which is often the stamp of torment, and becomes in itself symbolic of his situation between two epochs. We have already noted a parallel phenomenon in the work of Brockes.

Towards Interpretation

1. What does *Kind* mean in this poem?
2. Is the poet married to his Leonore?
3. Point out at least three passages indicating a conflict between the individual and society.
4. What parallel between himself and other poets does Günther draw in the next to the last stanza?
5. Point out passages especially indicative of Günther's *Selbstgefühl*.
6. Translate lines 31-34, making all references perfectly clear to the English reader.
7. What is this poem meant to convey to posterity? How does it relate to the work of *die Alten*?

„Was war das vor ein göttlich Paar?"

Was war das vor ein göttlich Paar?
Wo hat die Welt dergleichen Lüste?
So lacht' ihr Mund, so flog das Haar,
So hüpften die gefüllten Brüste.
Die Sehnsucht schilt den leeren Raum,   5
Ich weiß nicht, was ich selbst begehre.
Der Menschen Leben heißt ein Traum,
O wenn doch meins ein solcher wäre!

Towards Interpretation

1. Tell the story implied in this poem, deducing all your material from the poem itself.

Weihnachtsode

Die Nacht ist hin, nun wird es Licht,
Da Jakobs Stern[1] die Wolken bricht.
Ihr Völker, hebt die Häupter auf
Und merkt der goldnen Zeiten Lauf!

Du süßer Zweig aus Jesse Stamm,[2]   5
Mein Heil, mein Fürst, mein Schatz, mein Lamm,
Ach schau doch hier mit Freuden her,
Wie wenn mein Herz die Wiege wär!

Ach komm doch, liebster Seelenschatz!
Der Glaube macht dir reinen Platz,   10
Die Liebe steckt das Feuer an,
Das auch den Stall erleuchten kann.

Ihr Töchter Salems,[3] küßt den Sohn!
Des Höchsten Liebe brennet schon.
Kommt, küßt das Kind! Es stillt den Zorn.   15
Ach, nun erhebt der Herr mein Horn![4]

Towards Interpretation

1. Stanza 1: How can the night be past when the stars are still shining?
2. Stanzas 2-3: Where is the Christ Child's cradle? Explain the development of the metaphor in lines 8-12. What does the poet imply about himself in the word *Stall*?

Johann Günther

---

[1]Numbers 24:17 [2]Isaiah 11:1 and Romans 15:12 [3]*Salem* (Hebrew) 'peace'; perhaps here for Jeru*salem* 'city of peace.' [4]Psalms 92:10

Gerhard Tersteegen (1697–1769)

Andacht bei nächtlichem Wachen

Nun schläfet man,
Und wer nicht schlafen kann,
Der bete mit mir an[1]
Den großen Namen,
Dem Tag und Nacht   5
Wird von der Himmelswacht[2]
Preis, Lob und Ehr gebracht:
O Jesu, Amen.

Weg Phantasie!
Mein Herr und Gott ist hie.[3]   10
Du schläfst, mein Wächter, nie.
Dir will ich wachen.
Ich liebe dich,
Ich geb zum Opfer mich
Und lasse ewiglich   15
Dich mit mir machen.

Es leuchte[4] dir,
Der Himmelslichter Zier;
Ich sei[4] ein Sternlein hier
Und dort zu funkeln.   20
Nun kehr ich ein.[5]
Herr, rede du allein
Beim tiefen Stillesein
Zu mir im Dunkeln.

Toward the end of the 17th century there arose in Germany an anti-formalistic religious movement known as Pietism, which is characterized perhaps above all by a striving for a relationship of fervent inwardness between man and his creator, thus emphasizing and even glorifying individual feeling. This movement had a deep effect upon the development of German literature. It not only opened the way for the expression of personal feeling but was also instrumental in creating a new vocabulary in which this feeling could be enunciated. Goethe himself was strongly influenced by Pietism, as indeed were most German poets from Klopstock to Novalis. The new tone that this religious movement helped introduce into poetry is heard in Tersteegen's "Andacht bei nächt-

---

[1]'let him worship with me' [2]'heavenly host' [3]=*hier* [4]hortatory [5]'turn in' (go to bed)

lichem Wachen." *Andacht* comes from *denken an*; *Andacht* is an intensive thinking about the divine. In the midst of silent meditation stands the poem,* like silence made audible that we may be included in it: *Und wer nicht schlafen kann, / Der bete mit mir an / Den großen Namen. . . .*

Our immediate impression on reading this poem is that of a gentle murmur, as though someone were praying half aloud. This murmur varies in clarity and intensity. We are aware first of low sounds, then of high ones. The first stanza is dominated by the *a*-sound, especially in combination with the liquid consonants *n* and *m*, so that the final *amen* seems to sum up all that has gone before. The second stanza is dominated by *ie* and *i*. Here the poem reaches its greatest intensity and clarity. The central line, which contains the dominant vowels, is "*Ich liebe dich.*" At the same time the rimes *wachen-machen* assonate with the *Nacht-wacht-bracht* rimes of the first stanza and thus establish a firm connection between them. The last stanza is again bound to the middle one by assonance: *dir-Zier-hier* assonate with *sie-hie-nie*. In the final stanza the high (front) vowels and diphthongs (*ie, ei, eu*) are subdued by the low (back) vowels and liquids of *funkeln, Dunkeln* and the poem sinks off into darkness and sleep.

A Note on Vowel Symbolism

It would be nonsense to maintain that any phoneme (unit of sound) has a specific meaning *per se* — it can have a meaning only in connection with a meaningful word. Anyone can convince himself of this by considering the words for the same idea in various languages: *life / vie / Leben — death / mort / Tod*. However, once the significance of a certain sound has been established in a given context semantically, i.e., in accordance with meaning, then it can take on symbolic significance within that context. Thus if we say the poem "sinks off into darkness and sleep" in the *funkeln-Dunkeln* rime, it is not solely because of the low (back) vowels and liquids in these words but also because the context speaks of going to bed, of deep silence and of darkness. In the same way, when we say that the poem attains its greatest clarity and intensity in the middle stanza — the greatest wakefulness, as it were — it is not because of the high (front) vowels this stanza contains but because of the meaning of the text in which they occur in emphatic position; only then do they (especially in contrast with the *an*- and *am*-sounds in the preceding stanza) attain the (symbolic) significance of clarity. We know from *what* is said that the worshipper is awake, *how* it is said comes to symbolize wakefulness. Having recognized the system, we accept — within this context — the equations: high (front) vowels and diphthongs = clarity, awareness, intensity;

---

*The Pietists were known as *die Stillen im Lande*. In one of his letters Tersteegen writes: "Der Herr bringe all das Unsere zu einem tiefen Schweigen!"

low (back) vowels (plus nasals and/or liquids) = a lower degree of clarity, awareness, intensity.

Towards Interpretation

1. Examine lines 19-20 in "Andacht bei nächtlichem Wachen." How does the enjambement (run-over line) and the separation of *hier* from *dort* reflect the meaning expressed here?

„*Gleich wie ein leichtes Blatt*"

Gleich wie ein leichtes Blatt, also gleichgiltig schwebet
    In Gottes Luft mein willenloser Sinn;
Kein Wollen sonst in mir als Gottes Wollen lebet,
    Sein mindster Wink[1] bläst meinen Willen hin.
Zu lassen und zu tun, zu leiden oder nicht,
Es ist mir alles eins, Herr, wenn dein Will geschicht.[2]

Sidonia Hedwig Zäunemann (1714-1740)

Ode auf die . . . sämtliche Herren Hussaren[1]
Im Herbstmonat 1735

Ihr Dichter! wie so träg und kalt,
Den Helden jetzt ein Lied zu singen?
Kann denn ihr Adel und Gewalt
Den Kiel zu keinen Reimen bringen?
Soll Trau-Ring, Wiege, Leichenstein[2]   5
Nur bloß der Lieder würdig sein?
Fürwahr des Grossen **KARLS Hussaren,**
Mit ihrer tapfern Tapferkeit,
Verstatten nicht bei dieser Zeit
Mein Dichten länger zu versparen.   10

Kann wohl der Themis[3] Richter-Schwert
Den Purpur nur allein beschützen?

---

[1]'slightest sign' [2]=*geschieht*

[1]The full title is: *Ode auf die zum Dienst Sr. Römischen Kaiserlichen Majestät Karls des VI. am Rhein stehende sämtliche Herren Hussaren.* [2]i.e., themes deemed appropriate for *Gelegenheitsgedichte.* [3]Themis, the personification of justice, is represented as blindfolded and holding a sword and scales.

Muß nicht Bellonens[4] Opfer-Herd
Zugleich den Scepter unterstützen?
Man fällt nicht allzeit Schlüssen bei;[5]   15
Stahl, Eisen, Pulver, Schwert und Blei,
Karthaunen,[6] Mörser und Soldaten,
Die würken, daß die Majestät,
Auf ihrem Throne feste steht,
Und kämpfen vor[7] den Flor der Staaten. [. . .]   20

Zwar manchmal macht der Feind sich groß,
Und stark genug; allein weswegen?
Nur, daß **Ihr** auf der Erden Schoß
Noch mehr der Sinnen könnt erregen.[8]
Gewiß, **Ihr** bringt den Feind so weit,   85
Daß er vor Sieg um Gnade schreit,
Und sich vor euren Hieben schmieget.
G'nug, eure Säbel sind beglückt,
Mit Haar und Scheitel[9] ausgeschmückt,
Wenn Roß und Mann zu Boden liegen.   90

Gefangne, Beute, Wunden, Blut,
Bespritzte Säbel, Roß und Leichen,
Die sind von eurem Helden-Mut,
Und Eures Eifers echte Zeugen.
Des Gegners Angst und Todes-Schweiß,   95
Ist Euer größter Ruhm und Preis;
Das Glücke sucht Euch liebzukosen;
Denn wenn Ihr zieht, fällt's Euch nicht schwer,
Daß Ihr die Beute bringt, was mehr?
Auch blut'ge Köpfe der Franzosen.   100

Wie öfters würde nicht die Treu
Der tapfern Deutschen unterliegen,
Wofern Ihr nicht durch Stahl und Blei,
Und Eure Klugheit könntet siegen.
Ihr treibt die Marodeurs[10] zurück,   105
Ihr sorget vor[11] des Landmanns Glück,
Und rettet ihn aus Not und Eisen.
So mancher Mund, so mancher Mann,
Den Ihr befreit, sinnt, wie er kann,
Sich herzlich dankbar zu erweisen.   110

---

[4]Roman goddess of war [5]'one is not always bound by decisions' [6]type of canon;
Mörser 'mortars' [7]=*für* [8]i.e., can arouse wonder in us [9]'skull' [10]'marauders,'
'looters' [11]=*für*

Halt frecher Kiel! halt blöder Sinn!
Was willst du doch von Helden dichten?
Die Kraft gebricht, wo denkst du hin?
Ein solches Denkmal aufzurichten.
Wohlan! so soll hier zum Beschluß,   115
Weil ich Euch schweigend ehren muß,
Die Nachwelt meinen Wunsch erfahren.
Ein jeder Mund von Deutscher Treu,
Der sage ohne Heuchelei:
Es leben Kaiser KARLS Hussaren!   120
(Abridged)

Very few readers would suspect that this blood-thirsty celebration of warfare
was the work of a twenty-one-year-old woman who had seen almost nothing of
the world and who still lived with her parents. But Zäunemann was anything
but conventional, both in poetry and in life. For example, her habit of going
horseback riding unchaperoned, and doing so in men's clothing, was somewhat
troubling to the Erfurt bourgeoisie, and the local clergy was concerned that her
interest in poetry, men's work, was unwomanly and, as such, heretical. Her
lengthy poem "Das Ilmenauische Bergwerk" (1737), perhaps her most famous,
records her descent into a mine (dressed as a miner!) and incorporates elements
of miners' language in a description of the dangers of a miner's life. Her poem
celebrating the opening of the Georg-Augustus Universität, Göttingen, earned
her the title of Imperial Poet Laureate (1738). Zäunemann drowned at the age
of twenty-six, while attempting to cross the flooded Gera River on horseback.

Anna Louisa Karsch (1722–1791)

Few would nowadays agree with Karsch's mentor, Johann Wilhelm Gleim,
that she was "die deutsche Sappho"; in fact, contemporary literary figures like
Herder, Moses Mendelssohn, and Nicolai were pungently critical of her published poetry. Nevertheless, if not a great poet — or often not even a good one
— die Karschin was a literary phenomenon and, on occasion, not incapable of
poignant, poetic expression. Karsch was taken to represent an ideal: an
untutored Naturgenie, an "außerordentliche Tochter der Natur" (Wieland) who
had an almost incredible ability to produce rime and meter at the slightest
provocation. She moved in the literary circles of Berlin and engaged in a
literary correspondence with many of the important figures of contemporary
German letters, including even some communication with Goethe. She is the
first woman in German literature who was able to earn a livelihood, albeit a
poor one, exclusively from her poetry.

It is remarkable that *die Karschin* was able to make and sustain a poetic career on her natural talent; and it is somewhat ironic that her reputation actually suffered with the publication of her collected works (1763). As a genre, the *Gelegenheitsgedicht* (occasional poem) offers the poet a mixed blessing: the impact of the poetic moment lends the poem a certain importance, even *gravitas*, that often passes with the moment itself. It may also be true that Karsch, who enthusiastically cultivated her image as *Naturgenie*, was eventually trapped by it: as long as she produced her primitive folkish poetry, she represented a sentimental, literary ideal. But when she began to strive for a kind of profundity, she disappointed those, like Herder, who had praised her as an authentic voice of the *Volk*, but could no longer take her seriously once she exchanged the village for the metropolis.

Auf den Tod

des Prinzen Heinrich von Braunschweig[1]
zu Berlin den 12tn des Herbstmonats 1761

„Wo ist Er, daß ich Ihn mit Tränen salbe,
Mein Sohn? — Wo ist Er? bringt Ihn mir!"
So klagt die Fürstin! also ächzt das halbe
    Zerrißne Herz in Ihr!

Ach! in der Schlacht, voll von des Helden Ruhme   5
Dacht[2] Er Gefahr und Jugend nicht;
Er sank! — So sinkt am Abend eine Blume
    Die sonst ihr Angesicht

Vom Stengel nach der Sonnen Antlitz wandte,
Und nun gebogen niederhängt,   10
Er, dessen Brust zu grossen Taten brannte,
    Dem Bruder[3] nachgedrängt,

Stritt wie ein Held, der unterm Waffenrocke
Schon dreißigmal das Feld bezog;

---

[1]Heinrich (b. 1742), son of Charlotte (sister to Frederick the Great) and Duke Karl I of Braunschweig, fell in battle against the French at Hamm, Westphalia, during the Seven Years' War. [2]=*dachte ... an* [3]Karl, his oldest brother, also served in this campaign.

Staub trug er auf der jugendlichen Locke,   15
   Die um den Nacken flog.

Die Feinde flohn. Er, jung und schon ein Sieger,
Empfand den Sieg und eilte froh
Sie auzsuspähn. Den wundgeword'nen Tiger
   Verfolgt ein Löwe so!   20

Mit einer Kugel auf der Flucht verschossen,
Traf hinterlistig ihn der Tod.
Du, Stelle! wo sein Heldenblut geflossen,
   Bleib ewig purpurrot!

Klagt ihn, ihr Hügel! und ihr grünen Auen,   25
Ihr Wälder, klaget ihn bei Hamm!
Er fiel; so fällt, vom Künstler umgehauen,
   Der jungen Ceder Stamm;

Nach ihrem Umfall ein geschnitzter Götze,
Wird Weihrauch vor ihr aufgestreut.   30
So stirbt ein Held, daß Ihn der Nachruhm setze
   Hin zur Unsterblichkeit.[4]

Mit diesem grossen Mut, der im Gefechte
Ganz seinem Geiste beigewohnt,
Sah Er den Tod, der keinerlei Geschlechte[5]   35
   Und keine Tugend schont!

Den Helden-Lorbeer um sein Haupt gewunden,
Starb er den Tod fürs Vaterland!
Welch Dichter Moschus[6] Leier hat gefunden,
   Der nehme sie zur Hand,   40

Und singe dieses Helden Tod, und klage
Laut in der Landes-Töchter Ton:
„Hier fiel im Frühling Gott gelebter Tage,[7]
   Ein kriegrischer Adon!"[8]

Towards Interpretation
1. In an otherwise critical review of Karsch's poetry, Herder called this poem "eine der schönsten Threnodien unsrer Sprache." Herder also likens the poem to a *Volkslied*. What formal and lexical elements of the poem might justify this view?

---

[4]i.e., as the artist sacrifices the cedar to create a god, so fame sacrifices a boy to make him an immortal hero [5]'race,' 'family' [6]Greek poet of the 2nd century B.C., to whom a famous threnody for the poet Bion was attributed; Bion's chief extant poem is a "Lament for Adonis." [7]i.e., in the springtime (youth) of the days God granted to him [8]=Adonis, youth beloved of Venus, gored to death by a wild boar

Friedrich Gottlieb Klopstock (1724–1803)

Like Opitz, Klopstock is a great innovator, but unlike Opitz, he is also a major poet, not merely a purifier of language and literary law-giver.

Klopstock felt himself to be a man of destiny and that this destiny was to reveal the glory and mercy of God to mankind through poetry. His religious fervor is of pietistic origin, inward, deep, and emotional, though not without rationalistic overtones.

FRIEDR. GOTTL. KLOPSTOCK

The ancient concept of the poet as seer (*vates*) had been largely lost sight of by the 18th century; its reaffirmation in the person of a man who took his office of poet with great seriousness and whose work carried tremendous conviction came as a revelation to Klopstock's contemporaries. Through his example it became immediately apparent by what yardstick serious poetry was to be measured. When Klopstock first came upon the literary scene the ideal was polished fluency, the transference of not-too-profound thoughts into smooth-flowing meter and rime. Didactic and Anacreontic verse (the poetry of wine, women and song) were the order of the day. Such products began to seem rather shallow when one had felt the movement and heard the message of Klopstock's umrimed hexameters in the *Messias* (a verse epic dealing with man's salvation), the Alcaic and Asclepiadean measures of his odes, or the "free rhythms"* of his hymns. Klopstock's influence, not only on his contemporaries but also on later German poetry — down to and including Rilke — is inestimable. It is no exaggeration to say that without him the literature of Germany as we have it today is as unthinkable as the music of Germany without Beethoven.

---

*Klopstock invented the concept of *freie Rhythmen* in his poem "Dem Allgegenwärtigen" (1758). The form is characterized by rimeless lines of variable length and without consistent meter; however, they do possess a strong rythmic component based on the natural rhythm of the language.

Dem Unendlichen

Wie erhebt sich das Herz, wenn es dich,
Unendlicher, denkt!¹ wie sinkt es,
Wenn's auf sich herunterschaut!
Elend schaut's wehklagend dann, und Nacht und Tod!

Allein du rufst mich aus meiner Nacht, der² im Elend, der
im Tode hilft!   5
Dann denk ich es ganz, daß du ewig³ mich schufst,
Herrlicher!⁴ den kein Preis, unten am Grab, ob am Thron,
Herr, Herr, Gott! den dankend entflammt⁵ keinen Jubel genug
besingt.

Weht, Bäume des Lebens,⁶ ins Harfengetön!
Rausche mit ihnen ins Harfengetön, kristallner Strom!⁷   10
Ihr lispelt, und rauscht, und, Harfen, ihr tönt
Nie es⁷ ganz! Gott ist es, den ihr preist!

Donnert, Welten,⁸ in feierlichem Gang, in der Posaunen
Du Orion, Waage,⁹ du auch!   [Chor!
Tönt all' ihr Sonnen auf der Straße voll Glanz,¹⁰   15
In der Posaunen Chor!

Ihr Welten, donnert¹¹
Und du, der Posaunen Chor, hallest¹¹
Nie es ganz, Gott; nie es ganz, Gott,
Gott, Gott ist es, den ihr preist!   20

"To the Eternal" is a hymn, a song of praise to the deity, in *freie Rhythmen*. The length of the lines and the grouping of the stresses are determined not by a metrical scheme but by the surge and flow of the emotion conveyed. "To write successfully without metre," the English poet and critic Laurence Binyon once said, "needs stronger inspiration, more mastery of rhythm, and a severer sense of form, not less discipline but greater discipline than to write in metre." The poet who chooses to write in free verse must have the emotion he wishes to convey so perfectly under control that he is able to embody it in his poetry in a way that makes it impossible for us to misinterpret it, even though there is no metrical norm to serve as a guide. The movement of the emotion must constitute the rhythm and the rhythm must convey the emotion. Furthermore, if such verse is to be successful, we must feel that we are reading poetry, not merely agitated prose broken up into lines of unequal length.

---

¹transitive verb ²'you who' ³adjective ⁴vocative ⁵*dankend entflammt* goes with *Jubel*
⁶Revelation 22:1-2 ⁷*Es* is the object of the three preceding verbs. ⁸'planets' ⁹constellations Orion and Libra ¹⁰the Milky Way ¹¹transitive verb

The main stresses in the first stanza of "Dem Unendlichen" fall as follows:

> Wie erhébt sich das Hérz, wenn es dích,
> Unéndlicher, dènkt! Wie sínkt es,
> Wenn's auf sích herúnterschaut!
> Élend schaut's wéhklàgend dann, und Nácht und Tód!

Does this determination of the stresses elucidate the content of the lines? Yes; for the content is the up-and-down, the rising and sinking of feeling in connection with two activities: "thinking" the divine and contemplating self, and only those words that correspond to or symbolize the rise and fall of feeling connected with these activities (but not the activities themselves) receive primary stress.

Towards Interpretation

1. How is the *Elend, Nacht und Tod* felt by the heart in the first stanza overcome in the second?
2. A striking feature of Klopstock's language is the transitive use of intransitive verbs. Point out examples. What effect is achieved by this activation of intransitives?
3. Explain the meaning of *unten am Grab, oben am Thron* (line 7).
4. Does the inability of all creation to praise God enough make this poem a failure? Explain.

Die frühen Gräber

> Willkommen, o silberner Mond,[1]
> Schöner, stiller Gefährt[2] der Nacht!
> Du entfliehst? Eile nicht, bleib, Gedankenfreund!
> Sehet, er bleibt, das Gewölk wallte nur hin.[3]
>
> Des Maies Erwachen ist nur   5
> Schöner noch, wie die Sommernacht,
> Wenn ihm Tau, hell wie Licht, aus der Locke träuft,
> Und zu dem Hügel herauf rötlich er kömmt.
>
> Ihr Edleren, ach es bewächst
> Eure Male[4] schon ernstes Moos!   10

---

[1]The strophic form, one of Klopstock's own devising and one of his favorites, is a mixture of meters and contains a significant number of amphibrachs ($\smile - \smile$) and choriambs ($- \smile \smile -$): *Willkommen, o silberner Mond* ($\smile - \smile | \smile - \smile | \smile -$). Note that the rhythm makes it impossible to read verses as dactyls ($- \smile \smile$), though the meter might seem to allow it.   [2]'companion'   [3]'drifted past'   [4]=*Grabmale* (tombs)

O wie war glücklich ich, als ich noch mit euch
Sahe⁵ sich röten den Tag, schimmern die Nacht.

Towards Interpretation

1. One editor of Klopstock's works (K. A. Schleiden) says of "Die
   frühen Gräber": "Ode von echter unmittelbarer lyrischer Kraft. Verbindung von Naturbetrachtung und Besinnung auf den Menschen.
   Klopstock erweist sich hier als Meister der Gestaltung abendlicher
   Stimmungen und stiller Naturfreude."* Explain exactly how *Naturbe-*
   trachtung and *Besinnung auf den Menschen* are here combined.
2. How is the moon's apparent movement explained? Do you find such
   rationality to be disturbing? Do you find a parallel image (or images)
   in the poem that might account for the poet's calling our attention to
   das Bleibende?
3. How is May (or May's awakening) personified?
4. Who are the *Edleren* in line 9?
5. Substitute *dem Haare* for *der Locke* in line 7. Do you feel a loss?
   Why?
6. Give two reasons why Klopstock says (line 11) *O wie war glücklich*
   ich rather than *O wie war ich glücklich*.

Die Sommernacht

Wenn der Schimmer von dem Monde nun herab
In die Wälder sich ergießt, und Gerüche
Mit den Düften von der Linde
In den Kühlungen wehn;

So umschatten mich Gedanken an das Grab   5
Der Geliebten,¹ und ich seh in dem Walde
Nur es dämmern, und es weht mir
Von der Blüte nicht her.

Ich genoß einst, o ihr Todten, es mit euch!
Wie umwehten uns der Duft und die Kühlung,   10
Wie verschönt warst von dem Monde,
Du o schöne Natur!

---

⁵=*sah*

*F. G. Klopstock, *Ausgewählte Werke*, ed. Karl August Schleiden (München: Hanser, 1962), 1240.

¹plural, 'loved ones,' meaning here 'friends'

Towards Interpretation

1. In this ode, Klopstock creates another strophic form using the anapest
   (˘ ˘ _) and an a foot of his own invention (˘ ˘ _ ˘). Scan the poem
   and give your opinion as to whether the metrical form reinforces the
   natural rhythm of the language.

Die Frühlingsfeier

Nicht in den Ozean der Welten alle[1]
Will ich mich stürzen! schweben nicht,
Wo die ersten Erschaffenen, die Jubelchöre der Söhne des
Anbeten, tief anbeten! und in Entzückung vergehn!   [Lichts,[2]

Nur um den Tropfen am Eimer,[3]   5
Um die Erde nur, will ich schweben, und anbeten!
Halleluja! Halleluja! Der Tropfen am Eimer
Rann aus der Hand des Allmächtigen auch!

Da der Hand des Allmächtigen
Die größeren Erden entquollen[4]   10
Die Ströme des Lichts rauschten, und Siebengestirne[5] wurden,
Da entrannest du, Tropfen, der Hand des Allmächtigen!

Da ein Strom des Lichts rauscht', und unsere Sonne wurde,
Ein Wogensturz sich stürzte wie vom Felsen
Der Wolk[6] herab und den Orion gürtete,   15
Da entrannest du, Tropfen, der Hand des Allmächtigen!

Wer sind die tausendmal tausend, wer die Myriaden alle,
Welche den Tropfen bewohnen, und bewohnten? und wer
                                                          bin ich?
Halleluja dem Schaffenden! mehr wie die Erden, die quollen!
Mehr wie die Siebengestirne, die aus Strahlen zusammen-
                                                    strömten! —   20

Aber du, Frühlingswürmchen,
Das grünlichgolden neben mir spielt,
Du lebst; und bist vielleicht
Ach nicht unsterblich!

Ich bin heraus gegangen anzubeten,   25
Und ich weine? Vergib, vergib

---

[1]'ocean of all the worlds' = the creation   [2]The 'choirs of the sons of light' are the
angels and archangels. [3]Isaiah 40:15 [4]'ran forth from' [5]the Pleiades [6]dative

Auch diese Träne dem Endlichen,[7]
O du, der sein wird![8]

Du wirst die Zweifel alle mir enthüllen,
O du, der mich durch das dunkle Tal   30
Des Todes führen wird![9] Ich lerne dann,
Ob eine Seele das goldene Würmchen hatte.

Bist du nur gebildeter Staub,[10]
Sohn des Mais,[11] so werde denn
Wieder verfliegender Staub,   35
Oder was sonst der Ewige will!

Ergeuß[12] von neuem du, mein Auge,
Freudentränen!
Du, meine Harfe,
Preise dem Herrn!   40

Umwunden[13] wieder, mit Palmen[14]
Ist meine Harf' umwunden! ich singe dem Herrn!
Hier steh ich. Rund um mich
Ist alles Allmacht! Und Wunder alles!

Mit tiefer Ehrfurcht schau ich die Schöpfung an,   45
Denn du!
Namenloser, du!
Schufest sie!

Lüfte, die um mich wehn, und sanfte Kühlung
Auf mein glühendes Angesicht hauchen,   50
Euch, wunderbare Lüfte,
Sandte der Herr! der Unendliche!

Aber jetzt werden sie still, kaum atmen sie.
Die Morgensonne wird schwül!
Wolken strömen herauf!   55
Sichtbar ist, der kommt, der Ewige![15]

Nun schweben sie, rauschen sie, wirbeln die Winde!
Wie beugt sich der Wald! Wie hebt sich der Strom!
Sichtbar, wie du es Sterblichen[16] sein kannst,
Ja, das bist du, sichtbar, Unendlicher![17]   60

---

[7]'for that which is mortal' (the worm) [8]Exodus 3:14 [9]Psalms 23:4 [10]'formed dust'
[11]'son of May' (the worm) [12]=Ergieß [13]'enwreathed' [14]'sign of victory' [15]Exodus
13:21 and 16:10 [16]'mortals' [17]For the whole storm passage see Psalms 18:7-15 and
Nahum 1:3.

Der Wald neigt sich, der Strom fliehet, und ich
Falle nicht auf mein Angesicht?
Herr! Herr! Gott! barmherzig und gnädig!
Du Naher! erbarme dich meiner!

Zürnest du? Herr, 65
Weil[18] Nacht dein Gewand ist?
Diese Nacht ist Segen der Erde.[19]
Vater, du zürnest nicht!

Sie[20] kommt, Erfrischung auszuschütten
Über den stärkenden Halm![21] 70
Über die herzerfreuende Traube!
Vater, du zürnest nicht!

Alles ist still vor dir, du Naher!
Rings umher ist alles still!
Auch das Würmchen, mit Golde bedeckt, merkt auf! 75
Ist es vielleicht nicht seelenlos? ist es unsterblich?

Ach, vermöcht' ich dich, Herr, wie ich dürste, zu preisen!
Immer herrlicher offenbarest du dich!
Immer dunkler wird die Nacht um dich,
Und voller von Segen! 80

Seht ihr den Zeugen des Nahen, den zückenden Strahl?
Hört ihr Jehovas Donner?
Hört ihr ihn? hört ihr ihn,
Den erschütternden Donner des Herrn?

Herr! Herr! Gott! 85
Barmherzig, und gnädig!
Angebetet, gepriesen
Sei dein herrlicher Name!

Und die Gewitterwinde? sie tragen den Donner.
Wie sie rauschen! wie sie mit lauter Woge den Wald durch- 90
Und nun schweigen sie. Langsam wandelt   [strömen!
Die schwarze Wolke.

Seht ihr den neuen Zeugen des Nahen, den fliegenden Strahl!
Höret ihr hoch in der Wolke den Donner des Herrn?
Er ruft: Jehova! Jehova! 95
Und der geschmetterte Wald dampft![22]

---

[18]=da [19]dative [20]*diese Nacht*, i.e., the storm [21]'nourishing blades (of grain)' [22]'the riven forest steams'

Aber nicht unsre Hütte!
Unser Vater gebot
Seinem Verderber
Vor unsrer Hütte vorüberzugehn![23]   100

Ach, schon rauscht, schon rauscht
Himmel, und Erde vom gnädigen Regen!
Nun ist, wie dürstete sie! die Erd' erquickt,
Und der Himmel der Segensfüll' entlastet!

Siehe, nun kommt Jehova nicht mehr im Wetter[24]   105
In stillem, sanftem Säuseln
Kommt Jehova,[25]
Und unter ihm neigt sich der Bogen des Friedens![26]

Klopstock's "Frühlingsfeier" (first version, 1759) occupies a key position in the development of German lyric poetry. It opens two main paths future poets were to take, the one to poetry of mood (*Stimmungslyrik*) the other to the hymnic poetry of the sublime. The first finds its fulfillment in Goethe, the second in Hölderlin.

Like "Dem Unendlichen," "Die Frühlingsfeier" is a hymn (*Hymne*) in *freie Rhythmen*. The rhythms mirror the poet's mood and strive to recreate through their movement this mood in the listener. These "rites of spring" are a celebration of the divine through the celebration of nature:

> Mit tiefer Ehrfurcht schau ich die Schöpfung an,
> Denn du,
> Namenloser, du
> Schufest sie.

"The heavens declare the glory of God; and the firmament sheweth his handiwork." Like the singers of the Psalms, Klopstock is a *heiliger Dichter*, but with a difference. Klopstock knows and accepts the scientific discoveries of the 17th and 18th centuries; he is aware of the significance of Copernicus, Kepler, and Galileo, of Newton and Leibniz, of Harvey and Leeuwenhoek. The universe had expanded since Old Testament times and with the universe God. But man had become smaller and apparently less significant. Did man, in fact, still have any real significance at all? Was a "heiliger Dichter" still possible?

The enormity of the universe against the almost microscopic nature of our world and man's place in it is the theme of the first five stanzas. But since all creation is divine, all must partake of the one spirit, and man, despite his eccentric position in creation, is *mehr wie die Erden, die quollen*, because he has a soul, and is aware that he has one. The praise of creation as a whole,

---

[23]Exodus 12:23 [24]= *Gewitter* [25]I Kings 19:11-12 [26]Genesis 9:13

however, of the glory of God in its entirety, the poet leaves to the angels, whose proper office it is; he turns to our own sphere, the earth.

If all is divine, must not all that lives also live forever? Mustn't the *Frühlingswürmchen* which stands in relation to man as man to the world, have a soul? Klopstock leaves the question open, but his reverence even for this lowly form of life is apparent. He ensouls a living creature that is not aware of its divine origin — his relation to the worm is analogous to that of the angels to him. Man is the being in between: between the not yet aware (worm) and the perfectly aware (angels).

After a bridge passage (lines 37-48) in which the theme is again stated within its now defined limits (*die Schöpfung* here means specifically the earth), God manifests Himself in the storm. It is Klopstock's object to make us experience the soft breeze (49-56), the rising wind (57-64), the gathering darkness (65-72), the renewed hush (73-76), the lightning and thunder (81-88) as vividly as possible, never forgetting that these are aspects of the divine. By means of carefully controlled rhythmic language he arouses an inward response to phenomena that stand for a noumenon, i.e., *das Ding an sich*, for the non-empirical, for God. Klopstock's aim is always to make us feel the divine. His way of doing this is through movement, by leaping from contrast to contrast: universe – earth – man – worm; angel – man – worm; soft breeze – hush – violent wind; thunder and lightning – gentle rain; black cloud – rainbow. He is a motoric poet *par excellence*. *Wohllaut gefällt, Bewegung noch mehr*, we read in one of his poems, and Herder, speaking of Klopstock's odes, says in his declamatory way: "Wohlklang! er wird, was er war. Kein aufgezähltes Harmonienstück! Bewegung! Melodie des Herzens! Tanz! In Fehlern und Eigenheiten, wie ist ein Genie noch überall lehrend!"

The beginning of the poem speaks of the creation (stanzas 1-4), the end of the storm and the spring rain followed by the rainbow of peace (or promise). The Deluge is commonly interpreted (not only in the sacred writings of the Hebrews) as the second creation. It is a judgment but also a rebirth. The rainbow is the sign of God's covenant with his creation and especially of course with man. Christian doctrine has this covenant pointing to a final judgment and resurrection, the last rebirth and the Coming at the end of time. This symbolism was perfectly familiar to Klopstock's readers, though it is certainly less so to us. Only by keeping the symbolic references in mind can we fully understand what the poet is saying in "Die Frühlingsfeier" and fully empathize with his deeply emotional tone.

Towards Interpretation

1. Can you explain the title? (Remember that spring is the season of renewal.)
2. Typical of the hymnic poet and especially of Klopstock is the "long breath" or what one might call the "stretched period." In line 103, for

example, *wie dürstete sie!* is inserted between *ist* and *erquickt*, so that we are made to wait for the end of the period, or syntactic unit, as the earth for the rain. Examine stanzas 3 and 4 from this standpoint and see if you can determine why the poet makes us wait so long for the end of the period.

3. Is Klopstock a musical poet? A musical poet is not necessarily one who writes melodious verse. In fact, it is rather the *un*musical poet who writes in this way. A musical poet is one who achieves his effects the way music does, and in this sense, Klopstock is perhaps Germany's most musical poet. In discussing Klopstock in his famous essay "Über naive und sentimentalische Dichtung" (1796), Schiller says:

> Je nachdem . . . die Poesie entweder einen bestimmten *Gegenstand* nachahmt, wie die bildenden Künste [plastic arts] tun, oder je nachdem sie, wie die Tonkunst, bloß einen bestimmten *Zustand des Gemüts* hervorbringt, ohne dazu eines bestimmten Gegenstands nötig zu haben, kann sie bildend (*plastisch*) oder musikalisch genannt werden. Der letztere Ausdruck bezieht sich also nicht bloß auf dasjenige, was in der Poesie, wirklich und der Materie nach, Musik ist, sondern überhaupt auf alle diejenigen Effekte derselben, die sie hervorzubringen vermag, ohne die Einbildungskraft durch ein bestimmtes Objekt zu beherrschen; und in diesem Sinne nenne ich Klopstock vorzugsweise einen musikalischen Dichter.

Der Frohsinn[1]

Voller Gefühl des Jünglings, weil' ich Tage
Auf dem Roß, und dem Stahl,[2] ich seh des Lenzes
Grüne Bäume froh dann, und froh des Winters
    Dürre beblütet.

Und der geflohnen Sonnen, die ich sahe,   5
Sind so wenig doch nicht, und auf dem Scheitel
Blühet mir es winterlich schon, auch ist es
    Hier und da öde.

Wenn ich dies frische Leben regsam atme;
Hör ich dich denn auch wohl, mit Geistes Ohre,   10
Dich dein Tröpfchen leises Geräusches[3] träufeln,
    Weinende Weide.[4]

Nicht die Zypresse, denn nur traurig ist sie;
Du bist traurig und schön, du ihre Schwester,

---

[1]This poem is variation on the Sapphic ode form. [2]'ice skates' [3]genitive of manner
[4]= *Trauerweide*

O es pflanze dich an das Grab der Freund mir,   15
   Weide der Tränen!

Jünglinge schlummern hin, und Greise bleiben
Wach. Es schleichet der Tod nun hier, nun dort hin,
Hebt die Sichel, eilt, daß er schneide, wartet
   Oft nicht der Ähre.[5]   20

Weiß auch der Mensch, wenn ihm des Todes Ruf schallt?
Seine Antwort darauf? Wer dann mich klagen
Hört, verzeih dem Toren sein Ach; denn glücklich
   War ich durch Frohsinn!

Towards Interpretation

1. The poem states that the poet is *Voller Gefühl des Jünglings*. Is he a
   Jüngling?
2. What would you say is the true theme of this ode?

Das Rosenband

Im Frühlingsschatten fand ich sie;
Da band ich sie mit Rosenbändern:
Sie fühlt' es nicht und schlummerte.

Ich sah sie an; mein Leben hing
Mit diesem Blick an ihrem Leben;   5
Ich fühlt' es wohl und wußt' es nicht.

Doch lispelt' ich ihr sprachlos zu
Und rauschte mit den Rosenbändern:
Da wachte sie vom Schlummer auf.

Sie sah mich an; ihr Leben hing   10
Mit diesem Blick an meinem Leben,
Und um uns ward's Elysium.

Towards Interpretation

1. Is this poem atypical of Klopstock, insofar as it is unmusical (i.e.,
   plastic) in Schiller's sense? Is our imagination centered on a definite
   object or a state of feeling reflected in movement?
2. Explain the significance of the run-over lines in the second and fourth
   stanzas.

---

[5]'often doesn't wait for the ear (of grain),' i.e., maturity

Das Wiedersehn

Der Weltraum fernt[1] mich weit von dir,
So fernt mich nicht die Zeit.
Wer überlebt das siebzigste
Schon hat, ist nah bei dir.

Lang sah ich, Meta,[2] schon dein Grab,   5
Und seine Linde wehn;
Die Linde wehet einst auch mir,
Streut ihr Blum' auch mir,

Nicht mir! Das ist mein Schatten nur,
Worauf die Blüte sinkt;   10
So wie es nur dein Schatten war,
Worauf sie oft schon sank.

Dann kenn' ich auch die höh're Welt,
In der du lange warst;
Dann sehn wir froh die Linde wehn,   15
Die unsre Gräber kühlt.

Dann . . . Aber ach ich weiß ja nicht,
Was du schon lange weißt;
Nur daß es, hell von Ahndungen,
Mir um die Seele schwebt!   20

Mit wonnevollen Hoffnungen
Die Abendröte kommt:
Mit frohem, tiefen Vorgefühl,
Die Sonnen auferstehn!

---

[1]transitive verb [2]Klopstock's wife (1728–1758)

Ludwig Christoph Hölty (1748–1776)

Hölty was a charter member of the *Göttinger Hain*, a group of enthusiastic young Klopstockians who banded together in the spring of 1772 at the university in Göttingen. The members of the *Hain* ('sacred grove') passionately repudiated anything that seemed to them to "degrade Germany" (and this included a good deal of contemporary literature) and strove to produce works worthy both of mankind and their native land. Certainly the best, and perhaps the only true, poet among them was Hölty himself, whose verse has sweetness and purity and a harp-like tone peculiarly its own. What the theorists of the *Hain* might vow to do, he did because it was his nature.

Dein, o Hölty gedenk ich! Dein ist der liebliche Knabe,
der in Goethes Gesang reifte zum herrlichen Mann.
(Friedrich Rückert)

Elegie auf eine Nachtigall

Sie ist dahin, die Maienlieder tönte,
    Die Sängerin,
Die durch ihr Lied den ganzen Hain verschönte,
    Sie ist dahin.
Sie, deren Lied mir in die Seele hallte,   5
    Wenn ich am Bach,
Der durchs Gebüsch, im Abendgolde, wallte,
    Auf Blumen lag.

Sie schmelzete die Wipfel in Entzücken.
    Der Wiederklang   10
Entfuhr dem Schlaf, auf blauer Berge Rücken,
    Wenn ihr Gesang
Im Wipfel floß. Die ländlichen Schalmeien[1]
    Erklangen drein,

---

[1]'shawms'

Es tanzeten die Elfen ihre Reihen[2]   15
  Darnach im Hain.

Dann lauschten oft die jugendlichen Bräute,[3]
  Auf einer Bank
Von Rasen, an des trauten Lieblings Seite,
  Dem Zauberklang.   20
Sie drückten sich, bei jeder deiner Fugen,[4]
  Die Hand einmal,
Und hörten nicht, wenn deine Schwestern schlugen,[5]
  O Nachtigall.

Sie lauschten, bis der Hall der Abendglocke   25
  Im Dorfe schwieg,
Und Hesperus,[6] mit silberfarbner Locke,
  Dem Meer entstieg.
Und gingen dann, im Wehn der Abendkühle,
  Dem Dörfchen zu,   30
Mit einer Brust voll zärtlicher Gefühle,
  Voll süßer Ruh.

Towards Interpretation
1. See if you can, by a careful reading of this poem, determine the symbolism of the alternating long and short lines.

Die Schale der Vergessenheit

Eine Schale des Stroms, welcher Vergessenheit
  Durch Elysiums Blumen rollt,
Eine Schale des Stroms spende mir, Genius![1]
  Dort wo Phaons die Sängerin,[2]
Dort wo Orpheus vergaß seiner Eurydice,[3]   5
  Schöpf[4] die goldene Urne voll!
Dann versenk ich dein Bild, spröde[5] Gebieterin,
  In den silbernen Schlummerquell!
Den allsiegenden Blick, der mir im Marke zuckt,[6]

---

[2]'figure dances' (ring-around-a-rosy)   [3]=*Brautleute*   [4]'fugues'   [5]'sang'   [6]the evening star (Venus)

[1]'spirit,' probably Hermes, the conductor of the dead to Lethe, the River of Forgetfulness, which borders Hades   [2]*Sängerin* =Sappho, the Greek poet, who was vainly in love with Phaon; *vergessen* has two subjects and two genitive objects.   [3]Orpheus, legendary father of song, who descended to Hades to fetch his wife Eurydice.   [4]'dip'   [5]'unyielding'   [6]'that quivers in my marrow'

Und das Beben der weißen Brust,   10
Und die süße Musik, welche der Lipp' entfloß,
Tauch ich tief in den Schlummerquell!

Towards Interpretation
1. Why does the poet want to forget his *Gebieterin*?
2. Why is it especially fitting that Sappho and Orpheus are cited as examples of those who have found forgetfulness in Lethe? Many others have also found oblivion there.
3. What trope (figure of speech) is implied in line 9? (Note: The arrows of Cupid are symbols of the looks of love; cf. "Das Rosenband.")
4. Hölty was tubercular and died the year this poem was written. When we know this, we may find the poem more touching, since we will be aware that the poet's prayer to be allowed to forget this look, that body, that voice is almost a renunciation of life. But do we really need to know anything about Hölty's life to understand the poem and be moved by it?

Die Schiffende

Sie wankt dahin! Die Abendwinde spielen
    Ihr Apfelblüten zu,[1]
Die Vögellein, so[2] ihre Gottheit fühlen,
    Erwachen aus der Ruh.

Wie ihr Gewand, im Mondenglanze, flittert,   5
    Und ihres Busens Flor![3]
Sie wankt dahin! Der helle Vollmond zittert
    Aus jeder Well' hervor.

Da rauscht der Kahn durch hangende Gesträuche,
    Birgt mir das Engelbild,   10
Schwankt itzt hervor, tanzt wieder auf dem Teiche,
    Den ihre Gottheit[4] füllt.

Verdeckt mir nicht, ihr[5] hangenden Gesträuche,
    Ihr lächelndes Gesicht,
Sie tanzt so schön auf ihrem Silberteiche,   15
    Ihr[5] Erlen, bergt sie nicht!

Weht, Winde, weht, o flügelt sie, ihr[5] Winde,
    An diese Laub'[6] heran,

---

[1]*spielen ... zu* 'blow gently towards' (*zuwehen*) [2]=*die* [3]'thin scarf' [4]here, as in line 3, approximates *Göttlichkeit* [5]vocative [6]'arbor'

> Daß ich mich ihr, im Schauer[7] dieser Linde,
> Zu Füßen werfen kann!   20

Towards Interpretation

1. The poet says that the girl in this boat is "divine." How does he show that this is true?
2. What is the precise physical situation described here? Does the formal structure of the poem reflect it?

Die Mainacht

> Wenn der silberne Mond durch die Gesträuche blickt,
> Und sein schlummerndes Licht über den Rasen geußt,[1]
> Und die Nachtigall flötet,
> Wandl' ich traurig von Busch zu Busch.
>
> Selig preis' ich dich dann, flötende Nachtigall,   5
> Weil dein Weibchen mit dir wohnet in einem Nest,
> Ihrem singenden Gatten
> Tausend trauliche Küsse gibt.
>
> Überschattet von Laub, girret ein Taubenpaar
> Sein Entzücken mir vor; aber ich wende mich,   10
> Suche dunkle Gesträuche,
> Und die einsame Träne rinnt.
>
> Wann, o lächelndes Bild, welches wie Morgenrot
> Durch die Seele mir strahlt, find' ich auf Erden dich?
> Und die einsame Träne   15
> Bebt mir heißer die Wang' herab!

This elegaic ode (1774), written almost ten years after Klopstock's "Die frühen Gräber," reveals the great literary debt the younger Hölty owed Klopstock, whom he greatly admired. It is primarily from Klopstock that he derives his sense of rhythm and meter, as well as his poetic vocabulary and imagery.

Towards Interpretation

1. Reread "Die Mainacht," and Klopstock's "Die frühen Gräber" and "Sommernacht." Note the imagery these poems have in common.

---

[7] = *ehrfürchtige Scheu* (the feeling of the speaker is applied to the place; we might say 'reverent hush')

[1] = *gießt*

How does the natural world (e.g., the moon) affect the speakers of the poems? Where does the speaker's contemplation of nature lead him in each case?

2. Which of the two, Hölty or Klopstock, seems to you to control more strictly emotion through form? Defend your position.

Auftrag[1]

Ihr Freunde hänget, wann ich gestorben bin,
Die kleine Harfe hinter dem Altar auf,
    Wo an der Wand die Totenkränze[2]
        Manches verstorbenen Mädchens schimmern.

Der Küster[3] zeigt dann freundlich dem Reisenden   5
Die kleine Harfe, rauscht mit dem roten Band,
    Das, an der Harfe festgeschlungen,
        Unter den goldenen Saiten flattert.

This poem, written on the back of a lending slip from the Göttingen Library, was composed in the late summer of 1775, just a year before Hölty's early death. For the first collected edition of his poems (1783), edited by Christian and Friedrich Leopold zu Stolberg and J. H. Voß, Voß composed a third strophe for this ode, gave it the title by which we know it today, "Auftrag," and placed the expanded poem at the end of the collection. That is the form in which it is generally known today. While Voß's third strophe, meant no doubt as a tribute to their friendship, adds new images and thus changes the meaning of the entire poem — essentially creates a *new* poem — the degree to which Voß is able to recreate the sweet, sad lyricality of Hölty's poetic language is remarkable, even if he finally errs on the side of pathos:

Oft, sagt er staunend, tönen im Abendrot
Von selbst die Saiten, leise wie Bienenton;
    Die Kinder, hergelockt vom Kirchhof,   10
        Hörtens, und sahn, wie die Kränze bebten.

Towards Interpretation
1. Why is the harp to be hung with the *Mädchenkränze*?
2. What effect does the addition of the children in Voß's strophe have on the meaning of the "new" poem? Hölty spoke only of *die Reisenden*, wayfarers.

---

[1]The imitation of Greek meters came into German poetry with Klopstock. Here Hölty imitates the alcaic stanza (see Appendix). [2]'funeral wreaths' [3]'sexton'

Leopold von Göckingk (1748–1828)

Als der erste Schnee fiel

Gleich einem König, der in seine Staaten
Zurück als Sieger kehrt, empfängt ein Jubel dich!
Der Knabe balgt um deine Flocken sich,
Wie bei der Krönung um Dukaten.[1]

Selbst mir, obschon ein Mädchen und der Rute[2]   5
Lang nicht mehr untertan, bist du ein lieber Gast;
Denn siehst du nicht, seit du die Erde hast
So weich belegt, wie ich mich spute[3]

Zu fahren, ohne Segel, ohne Räder,
Auf einer Muschel,[4] hin durch den weißen Flor,   10
So sanft, und doch so leicht, so schnell, wie vor
Dem Westwind eine Flaumenfeder?

Aus allen Fenstern und aus allen Türen
Sieht mich der bleiche Neid aus hohlen Augen nach;
Selbst die Matrone wird ein leises Ach!   15
Und einen Wunsch um mich verlieren.

Denn der, um den wir Mädchen oft uns stritten,
Wird hinter mir, so schlank wie eine Tanne, stehn
Und sonst auf nichts mit seinen Augen sehn,
Als auf das Mädchen in dem Schlitten.   20

Towards Interpretation
1. Why is it easy in this poem to distinguish between the author and the "poetic I"?

---

[1]Coins were strewn among the crowd at coronations. [2]'rod' [3]=*eile* [4]i.e., sleigh in the form of a shell

80

Matthias Claudius (1740–1815)

Der Frühling
Am ersten Maimorgen

Heute will ich fröhlich, fröhlich sein,
Keine Weis und keine Sitte hören,[1]
Will mich wälzen und für Freude schrein,
Und der König[2] soll mir das nicht wehren.[3]

Denn er kömmt mit seiner Freuden Schar   5
Heute aus der Morgenröte Hallen,
Einen Blumenkranz um Brust und Haar
Und auf seiner Schulter Nachtigallen;

Und sein Antlitz ist ihm rot und weiß,
Und er träuft von Tau und Duft und Segen —   10
Ha! mein Thyrsus sei ein Knospenreis,[4]
Und so tauml' ich meinem Freund entgegen.

Towards Interpretation

1. Look up *Dionysos* in a classical dictionary and show how this information is essential to the understanding of the poem.
2. Would this poem be fully intelligible without the title? Explain.

Motett

Der Mensch lebt und bestehet
Nur eine kleine Zeit;
Und all die Welt vergehet
Mit ihrer Herrlichkeit.
Es ist nur Einer ewig und an allen Enden,[1]   5
Und wir in seinen Händen.

Towards Interpretation

1. An interpreter of Claudius has written of this poem: "Da haben wir noch einmal das Beispiel einer Gestaltungskraft [ability to endow with

---

[1]'heed no instructions and no moral advice' [2]'the king himself' [3]'prevent' [4]'let my thyrsus be a budding branch' The thyrsus, associated with Dionysus, is a staff topped with a pine cone or vines.

[1]'everywhere'

form], die Wort um Wort zu Glanz und Zauber weckt und die doch
wie verborgen wirkt, weil sie sich deckt [coincides] mit dem Gesetz
der Sache [subject]. Der Gegensatz zwischen der Unendlichkeit Gottes
und der Endlichkeit des Menschen . . . ist eingegangen in den
rhythmischen Wechsel. . . ."* Read the poem aloud several times,
then explain precisely what the critic means.

2. A motet is a *mehrstimmiger Gesang über einen Bibeltext.* What Biblical text might the poet have in mind?

Der Tod

Ach, es ist so dunkel in des Todes Kammer,
Tönt so traurig, wenn er sich bewegt
Und nun aufhebt seinen schweren Hammer
Und die Stunde schlägt.

Towards Interpretation

1. Explain how here also the form coincides with the *Gesetz der Sache.* Note especially the last verse.
2. Suppose we placed a semicolon after *bewegt* and changed *aufhebt* to *hebt er* — would you feel a loss? Can you say why?

Ein Wiegenlied bei Mondenschein zu singen

So schlafe nun, du Kleine!
Was[1] weinest du?
Sanft ist im Mondenscheine
Und süß die Ruh.

Auch kommt der Schlaf geschwinder   5
Und sonder[2] Müh,
Der Mond freut sich der Kinder
Und liebet sie.

Er liebt zwar auch die Knaben,
Doch Mädchen mehr,   10
Gießt freundlich schöne Gaben
Von oben her

---

*Johannes Pfeiffer, *Matthias Claudius, der Wandsbecker Bote* (Bremen: Storm, 1949), 25.

[1]=*warum*   [2]=*ohne*

Auf sie aus, wenn sie saugen,
Recht wunderbar;
Schenkt ihnen blaue Augen   15
Und blondes Haar.

Alt ist er wie ein Rabe,
Sieht manches Land;
Mein Vater hat als Knabe
Ihn schon gekannt.   20

Und bald nach ihren Wochen[3]
Hat Mutter mal[4]
Mit ihm von mir gesprochen:
Sie saß im Tal

In einer Abendstunde,   25
Den Busen bloß,[5]
Ich lag mit offnem Munde
In ihrem Schoß.

Sie sah mich an, für Freude
Ein Tränchen lief,   30
Der Mond beschien uns beide,
Ich lag und schlief;

Da sprach sie: „Mond, o scheine,
ich hab sie lieb,
Schein Glück für meine Kleine!"   35
Ihr Auge blieb

Noch lang am Monde kleben
Und flehte[6] mehr.
Der Mond fing an zu beben,
Als hörte er.   40

Und denkt nun immer wieder
An diesen Blick,
Und scheint von hoch hernieder
Mir lauter[7] Glück.

Er schien mir unterm Kranze[8]   45
Ins Brautgesicht
Und bei dem Ehrentanze;[9]
Du warst noch nicht.

---

[3]'childbed' [4]=*einmal* [5]'bare' [6]'besought' [7]'pure' [8]'bridal wreath' [9]'dance in bride's honor

Towards Interpretation

1. It is obvious that the enjambement (run-over line) connecting stanzas 3 and 4 symbolizes the pouring out of the moon's gifts. The way from sky to earth is open. Observe the enjambement between stanzas 6 and 7 and between 9 and 10 — what is the situation here? (Do lines 22ff. and 39ff. confirm your analysis?)
2. Trace the successive time references from stanza 5 on. Is there likelihood that the baby will sing this song to *her* baby?
3. What is the symbolism of the longer line followed by a shorter line?

Johann Georg Jacobi (1740–1814)

Abends

Komm, Liebchen! es neigen
Die Wälder sich dir;
Und alles mit Schweigen
Erwartet dich hier.

Der Himmel, ich bitte,   5
Von Wölkchen wie leer!
Der Mond in der Mitte,
Die Sternlein umher!

Der Himmel im glatten
Umdämmerten Quell!   10
Dies Plätzchen im Schatten,
Dies andre so hell!

Im Schatten, der Liebe
Dich lockendes Glück;
Dir flüsternd: es bliebe   15
Noch vieles zurück, —

Es blieben der süßen
Geheimnisse viel:
So festes Umschließen!
So wonniges Spiel! —   20

Da rauscht es! da wanken
Auf jeglichem Baum

Die Äste; da schwanken
Die Vögel im Traum.

Dies Wanken, dies Zittern   25
Der Blätter im Teich —
O Liebe! dein Wittern![1]
O Liebe! dein Reich!

Towards Interpretation

1. What gesture must one imagine in verse 5? Does gesture play a further role in this poem? What effect is thus produced?

2. How does the lover use nature to plead his case? Compare this poem with Stieler's "Nacht-Glücke" and Hofmannswaldau's "Vergänglichkeit der Schönheit" and try to characterize the tone of each.

Gottfried August Bürger (1747–1794)

Lenore[1]

Lenore fuhr ums Morgenrot
Empor aus schweren Träumen:
„Bist untreu, Wilhelm, oder tot?
Wie lange willst du säumen?" —
Er war mit König Friedrichs Macht   5
Gezogen in die Prager Schlacht[2]
Und hatte nicht geschrieben,
Ob er gesund geblieben.

Der König und die Kaiserin,
Des langen Haders müde,   10
Erweichten ihren harten Sinn
Und machten endlich Friede;
Und jedes Heer, mit Sing und Sang,

---

[1]*Wittern*, approximately, 'the weather you make,' 'your weather, atmosphere.' The entire poem is an evocation of love's *Wittern*.

[1]This ballad belongs to a well-established genre, that of the ghostly lover. "Sweet William's Ghost," an authentic folk-ballad passed down in oral tradition, is the best known representation of the theme in English. [2]At the Battle of Prague (Seven Years War) the Prussians under Frederick the Great defeated the Austrians on May 6, 1757. The *Kaiserin* (line 9) is Austrian Empress Maria Theresia.

Mit Paukenschlag und Kling und Klang,
Geschmückt mit grünen Reisern,   15
Zog heim zu seinen Häusern.

Und überall, allüberall,
Auf Wegen und auf Stegen,
Zog alt und jung dem Jubelschall
Der Kommenden entgegen.   20
„Gottlob!" rief Kind und Gattin laut,
„Willkommen!" manche frohe Braut.
Ach! aber für Lenoren
War Gruß und Kuß verloren.

Sie frug den Zug wohl auf und ab   25
Und frug³ nach allen Namen;
Doch keiner war, der Kundschaft gab,
Von allen, so da kamen.
Als nun das Heer vorüber war,
Zerraufte sie ihr Rabenhaar   30
Und warf sich hin zur Erde
Mit wütiger Gebärde.

Die Mutter lief wohl hin zu ihr:
„Ach, daß sich Gott erbarme!
Du trautes Kind, was ist mit dir?"   35
Und schloß sie in die Arme. —
„O Mutter, Mutter! hin ist hin!
Nun fahre Welt und alles hin!
Bei Gott ist kein Erbarmen.
O weh, o weh mir Armen!" —   40

„Hilf, Gott, hilf! Sieh uns gnädig an!
Kind, bet ein Vaterunser!
Was Gott tut, das ist wohlgetan;
Gott, Gott erbarmt sich unser!" —
„O Mutter, Mutter! eitler Wahn!   45
Gott hat an mir nicht wohlgetan!
Was half, was half mein Beten?
Nun ist's nicht mehr vonnöten." —

„Hilf, Gott, hilf! Wer den Vater kennt,
Der weiß, er hilft den Kindern.   50
Das hochgelobte Sakrament
Wird deinen Jammer lindern." —

---

³=*fragte* (archaic)

„O Mutter, Mutter, was mich brennt,
Das lindert mir kein Sakrament!
Kein Sakrament mag Leben   55
Den Toten wiedergeben." —

„Hör, Kind! Wie, wenn der falsche Mann
Im fernen Ungarlande
Sich seines Glaubens abgetan
Zum neuen Ehebande?   60
Laß fahren, Kind, sein Herz dahin!
Er hat es nimmermehr Gewinn!
Wenn Seel und Leib sich trennen,
Wird ihn sein Meineid brennen." —

„O Mutter! Mutter! hin ist hin!   65
Verloren ist verloren!
Der Tod, der Tod ist mein Gewinn!
O wär ich nie geboren!
Lisch aus, mein Licht, auf ewig aus!
Stirb hin, stirb hin in Nacht und Graus!   70
Bei Gott ist kein Erbarmen;
O weh, o weh mir Armen!"

„Hilf, Gott, hilf! Geh nicht ins Gericht
Mit deinem armen Kinde!
Sie weiß nicht, was die Zunge spricht;   75
Behalt ihr nicht die Sünde!⁴
Ach, Kind, vergiß dein irdisch Leid
Und denk an Gott und Seligkeit,
So wird doch deiner Seelen
Der Bräutigam nicht fehlen." —   80

„O Mutter! was ist Seligkeit?
O Mutter! was ist Hölle?
Bei ihm, bei ihm ist Seligkeit
Und ohne Wilhelm Hölle! —
Lisch aus, mein Licht, auf ewig aus!   85
Stirb hin, stirb hin in Nacht und Graus!
Ohn ihn mag ich auf Erden,
Mag dort nicht selig werden." —

So wütete Verzweifelung
Ihr in Gehirn und Adern.   90
Sie fuhr mit Gottes Vorsehung

---

⁴'Don't hold the sin against her!'

Vermessen fort zu hadern,
Zerschlug den Busen und zerrang
Die Hand⁵ bis Sonnenuntergang,
Bis auf am Himmelsbogen   95
Die goldnen Sterne zogen.

Und außen, horch! ging's trapp trapp trapp,
Als wie von Rosseshufen,
Und klirrend stieg ein Reiter ab
An des Geländers Stufen.   100
Und horch! und horch den Pfortenring,
Ganz lose, leise, klinglingling!
Dann kamen durch die Pforte
Vernehmlich diese Worte:

„Holla, holla! Tu auf, mein Kind!   105
Schläfst, Liebchen, oder wachst du?
Wie bist noch gegen mich gesinnt?
Und weinest oder lachst du?" —
„Ach, Wilhelm, du? . . . So spät bei Nacht? . . .
Geweinet hab ich und gewacht;   110
Ach, großes Leid erlitten!
Wo kommst du hergeritten?" —

„Wir satteln nur um Mitternacht.
Weit ritt ich her von Böhmen.
Ich habe spät mich aufgemacht   115
Und will dich mit mir nehmen." —
„Ach, Wilhelm, erst herein geschwind!
Den Hagedorn durchsaust der Wind,
Herein, in meinen Armen,
Herzliebster, zu erwarmen!"   120

„Laß sausen durch den Hagedorn,
Laß sausen, Kind, laß sausen!
Der Rappe⁶ scharrt; es klirrt der Sporn.
Ich darf allhier nicht hausen.
Komm, schürze, spring und schwinge dich   125
Auf meinen Rappen hinter mich!
Muß heut noch hundert Meilen
Mit dir ins Brautbett eilen." —

„Ach, wolltest hundert Meilen noch
Mich heut ins Brautbett tragen?   130
Und horch, es brummt die Glocke noch,

⁵plural ⁶'black horse'

Die elf schon angeschlagen." —
„Sieh hin, sieh her, der Mond scheint hell.
Wir und die Toten reiten schnell.
Ich bringe dich, zur Wette,   135
Noch heut ins Hochzeitbette." —

„Sag an, wo ist dein Kämmerlein?
Wo? wie dein Hochzeitbettchen?" —
„Weit, weit von hier! . . . Still, kühl und klein! . . .
Sechs Bretter und zwei Brettchen!" —   140
„Hat's Raum für mich?" — „Für dich und mich!
Komm, schürze, spring und schwinge dich!
Die Hochzeitgäste hoffen!
Die Kammer steht uns offen." —

Schön Liebchen schürzte, sprang und schwang   145
Sich auf das Roß behende;
Wohl um den trauten Reiter schlang
Sie ihre Lilienhände;
Und hurre hurre, hopp hopp hopp!
Ging's fort in sausendem Galopp,   150
Daß Roß und Reiter schnoben
Und Kies und Funken stoben.

Zur rechten und zur linken Hand,
Vorbei vor ihren Blicken,
Wie flogen Anger, Heid und Land!   155
Wie donnerten die Brücken! —
„Graut Liebchen auch? . . . Der Mond scheint hell!
Hurra! Die Toten reiten schnell!
Graut Liebchen auch vor Toten?" —
„Ach nein! . . . Doch laß die Toten!" —   160

Was klang dort für Gesang und Klang?
Was⁷ flatterten die Raben? . . .
Horch, Glockenklang! Horch, Totensang:⁸
„Laßt uns den Leib begraben!"
Und näher zog ein Leichenzug,   165
Der Sarg und Totenbahre trug.
Das Lied war zu vergleichen
Dem Unkenruf in Teichen.

---

⁷=*warum* ⁸'burial dirge'

„Nach Mitternacht begrabt den Leib
Mit Klang und Sang und Klage!   170
Jetzt führ ich heim mein junges Weib.
Mit, mit zum Brautgelage!
Komm, Küster, hier! komm mit dem Chor
Und gurgle mir das Brautlied vor!
Komm, Pfaff, und sprich den Segen,   175
Eh wir zu Bett uns legen!" —

Still, Klang und Sang . . . Die Bahre schwand . . .
Gehorsam seinem Rufen,
Kam's, hurre hurre! nachgerannt
Hart hinter's Rappen Hufen.   180
Und immer weiter, hopp hopp hopp!
Ging's fort in sausendem Galopp,
Daß Roß und Reiter schnoben
Und Kies und Funken stoben.

Wie flogen rechts, wie flogen links   185
Gebirge, Bäum' und Hecken!
Wie flogen links und rechts und links
Die Dörfer, Städt und Flecken! —
„Graut Liebchen auch? . . . Der Mond scheint hell!
Hurra! Die Toten reiten schnell!   190
Graut Liebchen auch vor Toten?" —
„Ach! Laß sie ruhn, die Toten!" —

Sieh da! sieh da! Am Hochgericht⁹
Tanzt um des Rades¹⁰ Spindel,
Halb sichtbarlich bei Mondenlicht,   195
Ein luftiges Gesindel. —
„Sasa! Gesindel, hier! komm hier!
Gesindel komm und folge mir!
Tanz uns den Hochzeitreigen,¹¹
Wenn wir zu Bette steigen!" —   200

Und das Gesindel, husch husch husch!
Kam hinten nachgeprasselt,
Wie Wirbelwind am Haselbusch
Durch dürre Blätter rasselt.
Und weiter, weiter, hopp hopp hopp!   205
Ging's fort in sausendem Galopp,

⁹'place of execution'   ¹⁰Criminals were bound on a wheel and their limbs broken.
¹¹'wedding dance'

Daß Roß und Reiter schnoben
Und Kies und Funken stoben.

Wie flog, was rund der Mond beschien,
Wie flog es in die Ferne!   210
Wie flogen oben überhin
Der Himmel und die Sterne! —
„Graut Liebchen auch? . . . Der Mond scheint hell!
Hurra! Die Toten reiten schnell!
Graut Liebchen auch vor Toten?" —   215
„O weh! Laß ruhn die Toten!" —

„Rapp'! Rapp'!¹² mich dünkt, der Hahn schon ruft . . .
Bald wird der Sand verrinnen . . .
Rapp'! Rapp'! ich wittre Morgenluft . . .
Rapp'! tummle dich von hinnen!   220
Vollbracht, vollbracht ist unser Lauf!
Das Hochzeitbette tut sich auf!
Die Toten reiten schnelle!
Wir sind, wir sind zur Stelle." —

Rasch auf ein eisern Gittertor   225
Ging's mit verhängtem Zügel.¹³
Mit schwanker Gert ein Schlag¹⁴ davor
Zersprengte Schloß und Riegel.
Die Flügel flogen klirrend auf,
Und über Gräber ging der Lauf.   230
Es blinkten Leichensteine
Rundum im Mondenscheine.

Ha sieh! Ha sieh! Im Augenblick,
Huhu! ein gräßlich Wunder!
Des Reiters Koller,¹⁵ Stück für Stück,   235
Fiel ab wie mürber Zunder.
Zum Schädel ohne Zopf und Schopf,
Zum nackten Schädel ward sein Kopf,
Sein Körper zum Gerippe
Mit Stundenglas und Hippe.¹⁶   240

Hoch bäumte sich, wild schnob der Rapp'
Und sprühte Feuerfunken;
Und hui! war's unter ihr hinab
Verschwunden und versunken.

---

¹²addressed to horse   ¹³'with loose rein'   ¹⁴'with a lax blow of his riding whip'
¹⁵'jerkin'   ¹⁶'scythe'

Geheul! Geheul aus hoher Luft,   245
Gewinsel kam aus tiefer Gruft.
Lenorens Herz mit Beben
Rang zwischen Tod und Leben.

Nun tanzten wohl bei Mondenglanz
Rundum herum im Kreise   250
Die Geister einen Kettentanz[17]
Und heulten diese Weise:
„Geduld! Geduld! Wenn's Herz auch bricht!
Mit Gott im Himmel hadre nicht!
Des Leibes bist du ledig;   255
Gott sei der Seele gnädig!"

Towards Interpretation

1. What is Lenore's sin?
2. Describe the stages of Lenore's ride. How are the stages marked linguistically?
3. Who does Wilhlem turn out to be? Whose agent is he?

Gottfried Bürger

J. W. von Goethe

---

[17]a circle dance (holding hands)

Johann Wolfgang von Goethe (1749–1832)

One can say without too great an oversimplification that the making of German poetry throughout the Baroque and a good deal of the 18th century (which was still under Baroque influence) was basically a kind of formal competition with rather well-understood rules. The doctrine of "decorum," based on Aristotle's immanent universal, that is "the general character in situations of a given kind, the 'sort of thing that might happen'" (C. S. Lewis) was the guiding principle behind poetic production. This doctrine, skillfully vulgarized and reduced to a system of fixed types and arbitrary rules by Horace in his *Ars poetica*, was introduced into Germany by Opitz, who thus made "correct" poetry possible. According to this doctrine, the work of art imposes its laws on the author. The author's aim is to find the most fitting, most "decorous," expression for the particular occasion, that is, the one expression which brings out its general character most vividly. Obviously, the individual and his own experience could play almost no part in such a system which led rather to the "set piece" and the cult of virtuosity. But it would be a gross error to think that this proce-dure was always harmful. On the contrary, it had a definitely liberating effect upon the literature of Germany, and even at its worst led to nothing more serious than bombast. But by the 18th century this normative poetics had hard-ened into superficial formalism, and the doctrine that had once liberated the poet now held him in bonds.

Both Goethe and Klopstock broke with this literary tradition in Germany, but each man, according to his genius, broke with it in a different way.

When Goethe came upon the literary scene, Klopstock had already reaf-firmed the seriousness of the poet's calling. By revivifying the ancient concept of the poet as seer, and by genially exploiting the resources given into his hands by Luther's Bible and Pietism, Klopstock had raised the whole level of poetry in Germany. As a natural consequence of his lofty concept of poetry, he had broken with current Anacreontic conventions and the shallow didacticism of the day. Led by his genius and his theory of verse as a means of outward realization of an inward state, he had introduced "freie Rhythmen," thus con-sciously and emphatically writing poetry "from the inside," letting the motif impose the form rather than imposing the form on the motif. As a student of the Greeks, he had introduced into German literature the imitation of ancient meters; he thought he recognized in these forms — as Goethe was later to recognize in the hexameter and the elegiac distich — an original coincidence of certain types of content and expression, in theory, at least, again working from within.

Klopstock fathered a tradition in German poetry, and there can be no doubt that Goethe profited from it. Yet it cannot be said that he followed it, and it is not without justice that one of the most perceptive German critics, Max Kommerell, has said: "Vor Goethe war Lyrik etwas anderes."*

For almost as long as a normative esthetic had existed, there had also existed, though less widely recognized, a counter-esthetic of "inward form." This held that a work of art comes into being, or should come into being, from within, according to its own laws, organically, as a particular kind of plant must develop from a particular kind of seed. The stress here was on the particular, not the general. Carried to its logical conclusion, this doctrine implied that each and every work of art is *sui generis*, incomparable and unique. The father of this esthetic was the neo-Platonist Plotinus (203-269 A.D.), whose ideas were kept alive by Giordano Bruno (1548-1600) and the Third Earl of Shaftesbury (1671-1713). From Shaftesbury they were taken over by Herder and Goethe.†

With Goethe the doctrine of inward or organic form received profound and influential poetic realization in works of a more personal and more subtly modern kind than those of Klopstock. Goethe's work represents the most brilliant exemplification of poetry "from within" in a period critical for the development of our concepts of the nature of poetry itself. After Goethe, it was no longer possible to judge a poem simply by its adherence to "rules," not because poetry had become lawless, but because each poem followed laws of its own. It was as though the doctrine of decorum had been transferred within: within the poet and within the poem. That the triumph of the principle of inward form was not without its perils is undeniable: it offered dangerous temptations to the *inwardly* lawless, of whom there were more than enough in a country like Germany, where the literary tradition was comparatively unstable and discontinuous. Not a few products of the *Sturm und Drang*, the late 18th century revolt against the reigning conventions, are ample witness of this. But for better or for worse, the new esthetic did triumph. It was taken over by the Romantics, the most influential of whom, it must be remembered, were younger contemporaries of Goethe himself, and thus a new epoch in literature and the history of the human spirit began.

Goethe's poetry is poetry of self. But, to quote Kommerell again, though it is indeed poetry of self, the self is seen as object — "Goethes Lyrik ist unmittelbare Dichtung des Ich . . . aber des Ich als Gegenstand gesehen!" The

---

*All quotations from Max Kommerell are taken from the chapter "Goethes Gedicht" in his *Dichterische Welterfahrung: Essays*, ed. H. G. Gadamer (Frankfurt a. M.: Klostermann, 1952), 23-52.

†During the same period, Kant's critical philosophy — the *Critique of Pure Reason* (1781) and the *Critique of Judgement* (1790) — furnished a solid theoretical basis for an esthetic of inward form by showing that the whole phenomenal world in its formal aspect is due to the time–space pattern *we* impose upon it: "Die Welt ist meine Vorstellung" (Schopenhauer). This meant that everything was subjective and norm an illusion. The door had been opened for "modern" art.

poet stands outside himself and observes himself "with sublime curiosity."
Kommerell regards this ability of Goethe's to see himself objectively as "das
Geheimnis seines Dichtens bis ins hohe Alter."

To Goethe's way of thinking, the subject is formed by the object. "Das
Auge ist das letzte, höchste Resultat des Lichts auf dem organischen Körper,"
is one of his most striking statements of this view. His lyrical poetry records
those moments when the external world, the child of light and ultimately light
itself, opens new eyes in him. It is this process that he beholds "with sublime
curiosity" and characteristic objectivity. Yet never coldly. On the contrary, he
recreates the moment of wonder, the *Augenblick* (how much more expressive is
the German word), with all the emotion of direct participation, for his aim is
also to open new eyes in *us*. On hundreds of occasions he records the unfold-
ing of new perceptual organs within himself. Hence his bewildering range. But
he records these events in direct, colloquial language, with the artlessness of
great art. Hence his accessibility.

The moment of revelation Goethe referred to as the *Gelegenheit*, and his
poetry he characterized as *Gelegenheitsdichtung*. With equal justice, he also
called his whole work *Bruchstücke einer großen Konfession*. We no longer
take these words in a narrow, purely autobiographical sense, but as meaning
fragments of a confession of grace granted, and beauty revealed.

Mit einem gemalten Band[1] (1771)

Kleine Blumen, kleine Blätter
Streuen mir mit leichter Hand
Gute, junge Frühlingsgötter
Tändlend auf ein luftig Band.

Zephir,[2] nimm's auf deine Flügel,   5
Schling's um meiner Liebsten Kleid!
Und dann tritt sie für[3] den Spiegel
Mit zufriedner Munterkeit.

Sieht mit Rosen sich umgeben,
Sie, wie eine Rose jung.   10
Einen Kuß, geliebtes Leben!
Und ich bin belohnt genung.

Schicksal, segne diese Triebe,[4]

---

[1]The title means that the poem accompanied a present of a painted ribbon, a fashionable way of showing a girl attention in the 1770's. (The Goethe poems are dated to
help give a picture of the poet's development.) [2]The West Wind, beneath whose
breath the snow melts and blossoms open. [3]= *vor* [4]Goethe later omitted this strophe.

Laß mich ihr und laß sie mein,
Laß das Leben unsrer Liebe   15
Doch kein Rosen-Leben sein!

Mädchen, das wie ich empfindet,
Reich mir deine liebe Hand!
Und das Band, das uns verbindet,
Sei kein schwaches Rosen-Band!   20

Even Goethe did not spring fully armed from the head of Jove. He began by
following the conventions in which he was brought up. "Mit einem gemalten
Band" is one of the so-called *Sesenheimer Lieder*, a group of poems addressed
to Friederike Brion, the daughter of a country parson. Goethe fell in love with
her while he was a student at the university in Strassburg. In this poem we can
observe, almost paradigmatically, the process of Goethe's disengagement from
the Anacreontic-Rococo conventions of his time; we can sense the birth of the
attitude that was to lead immediately afterward to the new tone in his poetry.*
The first half of "Mit einem gemalten Band" (through line 10) moves in the
world of the Rococo and neo-classical restraint, while the second half already
has much of the impetuosity of the *Sturm und Drang*. To be sure, the overall
tone remains that of the Rococo; nor are meter and rhythm in any way novel or
revolutionary, though handled with delightful freedom.

   The motif of the painted ribbon is itself typical of the delicate, half-
allegorical playfulness of the Rococo, when allusiveness was all and forth-
rightness merely bad taste. In the spirit of the Rococo, the emphasis is on
smallness and lightness: *K l e i n e Blumen, k l e i n e Blätter . . . mit l e i c h-
t e r Hand*; the airy deities at the service of lovers (cf. *The Rape of the Lock*);
above all the word *tändlend* (cf. 'dandle') with its denial of seriousness, and
the dainty, ballet-like gesture of strewing. The phrase *mit zufriedener Munterkeit* is Anacreontic-Rococo. *Zufrieden* is one of the most characteristic words
of the mid-18th century, when contentment with one's lot was considered a
prime virtue, while *Munterkeit* calls up the mood of mercurial, hedonistic joie
de vivre we think of in connection with the Anacreontics. We might translate:
"with seemly gaiety." The loved one is compared to a rose, the favorite flower
of the Rococo, and the symbolism of the *Rosenband* is also typical of the age
(cf. Klopstock's "Rosenband").

   Yet it is the comparison with the rose that forms the transition to the new
tone: *Sieht mit Rosen sich umgeben, / Sie, wie eine Rose jung*. The beloved,
who has just stepped before the mirror in a characteristic social gesture,
becomes a part of nature. The latter half of the poem seems to stand under different laws from the first: there a stylized playing with nature, here nature

---

*Our analysis follows in large part that of Kurt May, *Form und Bedeutung* (Stuttgart:
Klett, ²1963), 50ff.

itself. Hence the rejection, or at least the re-interpretation, of the Rosenband: *Doch kein Rosen-Leben . . . kein schwaches Rosen-Band.* . . . The *Tändeln* of the first half of the poem becomes a serious declaration of love, demanding complete union of I and Thou; above all, the merely imagined scene of the first half yields to the immediacy of the face-to-face encounter. The vocabulary is the antithesis of Anacreontic: in *geliebtes Leben, Leben unsrer Liebe,* and in the word *Schicksal* a much higher power than the *gute, junge Frühlingsgötter* is called upon with all earnestness.

Willkommen und Abschied[1] (1771)

Es schlug mein Herz. Geschwind, zu Pferde!
Und fort, wild wie ein Held zur Schlacht.
Der Abend wiegte[2] schon die Erde,
Und an den Bergen hing die Nacht.
Schon stund im Nebelkleid die Eiche   5
Wie ein getürmter[3] Riese da,
Wo Finsternis aus dem Gesträuche
Mit hundert schwarzen Augen sah.

Der Mond von einem Wolkenhügel
Sah schläfrig aus dem Duft[4] hervor;   10
Die Winde schwangen leise Flügel,
Umsausten schauerlich[5] mein Ohr.
Die Nacht schuf tausend Ungeheuer,
Doch tausendfacher war mein Mut,
Mein Geist war ein verzehrend Feuer,   15
Mein ganzes Herz zerfloß in Glut.

Ich sah dich, und die milde[6] Freude
Floß aus dem süßen Blick auf mich.
Ganz war mein Herz an deiner Seite,
Und jeder Atemzug für dich.   20
Ein rosenfarbes Frühlingswetter
Lag auf dem lieblichen Gesicht,
Und Zärtlichkeit für mich, ihr Götter!
Ich hofft' es, ich verdient' es nicht.

[1]The title was added much later to a revised version. *Willkommen* is used here in the old sense as a greeting given either by the guest or host, like *Guten Tag.* We should therefore render the title as "Hail and Farewell." [2]'cradled' (lit. 'rocked in a cradle') [3]'towering' (lit. 'towered') [4]=*leichter Nebel* [5]'in a way to make one shudder' [6]*Milde* is used here in the older sense of *gütig spendend* (generous out of kindness)

Der Abschied, wie bedrängt, wie trübe!   25
Aus deinen Blicken sprach dein Herz.
In deinen Küssen welche Liebe,
O welche Wonne, welcher Schmerz!
Du gingst, ich stund und sah zur Erden,
Und sah dir nach mit nassem Blick;   30
Und doch, welch Glück, geliebt zu werden,
Und lieben, Götter, welch ein Glück!

Best known and best loved of the Sesenheim lyrics is "Willkommen und Ab-schied." Here Goethe finds his own, unmistakable tone; here the Anacreontic conventions are definitely cast off as incommensurate with the new feeling; here — and through poems of a comparable kind — the German nation was to form its notions of the true nature of lyric poetry.

In such a "new" poem, one that breaks so radically with current poetical usage, we might also expect to find a break with traditional metrics. But this is not the case. The meter is the familiar four-stress iambic: *Es schlúg mein Hérz. Geschwínd, zu Pférde!* Yet, though there is never any doubt what the basic metrical pattern is, it is followed in the breach as much as the observance. Thus, already in the second line, we must read: *Und fórt, wíld wie ein Héld zur Schlácht* (and not: *Und fórt, wild wíe*, etc.), as though the heart in its excitement had skipped a beat. In some lines we have only two main stresses: *Und an den Bérgen hìng die Nácht*, or: *Wie ein getúrmter Ríese da*, where the isolated heavy stresses emphasize the idea of giganticness. Line 8 has three main stresses: *Mit húndert schwárzen Aúgen sàh.* Particularly expressive is the variation at the beginning of the third stanza, where we must read:

Ich sáh dích, und die mílde Fréude
Flóß aus dem süßen Blíck auf mích

and not: *Ich sáh dich, únd . . . Floß aús dem süßen. . . .* In short, the basic pattern is handled with great freedom, being varied to conform to the emo-tional structure rather than rigidly following a strict, formalistic scheme. Nonetheless, it is our awareness of such a scheme that gives the poem much of its charm. A tension is set up between law, as represented by the metrical pat-tern, and freedom, as expressed by the variations which the rhythm, the exponent of emotion, imposes on this pattern. The handling of the meter shows that freedom under the law is not only possible but also esthetically highly effective.

Since a work of art is a whole, it should be possible to arrive at a fairly satisfactory interpretation from whatever angle we approach it, provided the angle is given by the work itself. We have begun with a formal aspect of the poem and have summarized our findings rather abstractly as "freedom under the law." Will an analysis of other aspects bear this out? Let us turn to the content and the imagery through which it is expressed.

"Willkommen und Abschied" is a lyrical ballad or balladesque lyric. It tells the story of a heart: *Es schlug mein Herz.* The heart of the first two stanzas is untamed, arbitrary, willful. It is symbolized, as elsewhere in Goethe's work, by the galloping horse. Or it is a raging fire: *Mein Geist war ein verzehrend Feuer, / Mein ganzes Herz zerfloß in Glut.* As the imagery indicates, this heart is at odds with nature: calm evening cradles the earth, while man rides wildly forth, in time to his own heartbeat, not nature's. The wild heart conjures up threatening images: the great oak in its veil of mist is a towering giant, darkness peers out of the undergrowth with a hundred eyes, the winds beat eerie wings around the rider's ears. The *tausend Ungeheur* are not created by night so much as by the protagonist's heated imagination, as a foil to his rampant will. To put it bluntly, he is dramatizing himself. The overtones of this part of the poem are mildly ironic. This becomes plain with the change of key at the beginning of the second part (lines 17ff.).

The basic situation of this poem is one to which the youthful Goethe often gave form. In the first half of the poem nature stands over against man, the wild rider. But nature and the beloved are one: *Ein rosenfarbes Frühlings-wetter / Lag auf dem lieblichen Gesicht. . . .* What a contrast with the demonic imaginings of the first sixteen lines. As to which vision of nature is truer, the tone of the poem leaves no doubt. With this nature the heart seeks to identify itself (proving after all that it does "deserve it"): *Ganz war mein Herz an deiner Seite, / Und jeder Atemzug für dich.*

In his capacity as poet, Goethe cannot be wholly identified either with the wild rider or the recipient of the gentle glances. As a poet, he is giving form to a motif, which in abstract terms we can call the polarity of the masculine and feminine. He presents this motif through nature images interwoven in, or, more precisely, telling the story of a lover's ride to his sweetheart. In actuality, the process may have been the reverse, i.e., he came to see in his personal experience the underlying motif. Be that as it may, we must try to find that layer of meaning which most satisfactorily accounts for the basic configuration of a work. The configurations that rule the mind of an artist often to the point of obsession are his "themes," are he. Even very great artists do not have many themes; their greatness consists partly in "seeing them into" many situations. The theme of polarity or complementary opposites receives hundreds of exemplifications in Goethe's work. Yet it attains true importance only when the complementary poles find each other. Then something happens that causes them to become more than either was as a mere opposite. What happens then Goethe later termed *Steigerung. Polarität und Steigerung* is the truly fundamental configuration in his work.

The polarity in "Willkommen und Abschied" is too obvious to require further comment. That a *Steigerung* also takes place is apparent as soon as we think of looking for it. The union of the poles comes in the third stanza, the separation in the last. Wherein lies the *Steigerung*? In answer, we need only ask ourselves if we can conceive of the lover riding back through the night as he came, his heart full of strange, wild imaginings, outside of nature rather than in it. Certainly this is no longer the heart that created a "thousand monsters"; this spirit is no longer a "raging fire" — the masculine pole has been transformed, *gesteigert*, by the "eternal feminine." It has not *become* feminine — to think this would be a misinterpretation of the nature of *Steigerung* — it has become more truly itself: still passionate, but no longer wild and unclarified, not *dumpf*, but rejoicing and liberated. What the experience of love is, has perhaps never been expressed more infectiously than in the last two lines:

> Und doch, welch Glück, geliebt zu werden,
> Und lieben, Götter, welch ein Glück!

"A passive, an active, both *Glück*, and in the midst of this happiness gratitude to the gods, to whom every great love is deeply indebted" (Erich Trunz).

The extent of the transformation is the difference between the first and last two lines, our sense of the deep change between the beginning and the end. Or, to return to our point of departure: the heart whose story this poem tells has accepted the law of love over its untamed will, and finds in this bondage a higher freedom — freedom under the law. The message implied by the formal aspect of the poem and its content is the same.

Mailied (1771)

> Wie herrlich leuchtet
> Mir die Natur!
> Wie glänzt die Sonne!
> Wie lacht die Flur![1]
>
> Es dringen Blüten   5
> Aus jedem Zweig
> Und tausend Stimmen
> Aus dem Gesträuch
>
> Und Freud und Wonne
> Aus jeder Brust.   10
> O Erd', o Sonne!
> O Glück, o Lust!
>
> O Lieb', o Liebe!
> So golden schön,
> Wie Morgenwolken   15
> Auf jenen Höhn![2]
>
> Du[3] segnest herrlich
> Das frische Feld,

---

[1]'meadow' [2]'yonder heights' [3]i.e., *die Liebe*

Im Blütendampfe[4]
Die volle Welt.   20

O Mädchen, Mädchen,
Wie lieb' ich dich!
Wie blinkt[5] dein Auge!
Wie liebst du mich!

So liebt die Lerche   25
Gesang und Luft,
Und Morgenblumen
Den Himmelsduft,[6]

Wie ich dich liebe
Mit warmen[7] Blut,   30
Die du[8] mir Jugend
Und Freud' und Mut

Zu neuen Liedern
Und Tänzen gibst.
Sei ewig glücklich,   35
Wie du mich liebst!

"Die Lieder seiner [Goethes] Jugend," the Austrian poet Hugo von Hofmannsthal wrote, "sind nichts als ein Hauch. Jedes ist der entbundene Geist eines Augenblickes, der sich aufgeschwungen hat in den Zenith und dort strahlend hängt und alle Seligkeit des Augenblickes rein in sich saugt und verhauchend sich löst in den klaren Äther."* Here the world is seen as a metaphor of divine love expressed in nature and in man, and the sense of the world's oneness, of the immanence of the divine, has been given compelling expression.

Towards Interpretation
1. In lines 5-10, how many different spheres are made the subject of *Es dringen*? What two spheres are combined in the exclamations in verses 11-12?
2. "Es ist der versteckte Grundsatz dieser Vers- und Reimkunst," Max Kommerell writes, "die Worte genau so zu setzen, wie die ungesuchteste [most natural] Prosa sie setzen würde." Can you find any passage in the poem that might disprove this?
3. Despite its seemingly unpremeditated immediacy, "Mailied" is an eminently artful poem. The secret of its charm lies of course primarily in

---

[4]'blossom vapor'   [5]=*glänzt*   [6]*Duft* 'dünner Nebel'   [7]=*warmem*   [8]'you who'

*Hugo von Hofmannsthal, "Das Gespräch über Gedichte," in *Ausgewählte Werke in zwei Bänden* (Frankfurt a.M.: S. Fischer, 1957), 2:377.

its form, which is based on the principle of polar complementaries. Read the poem again aloud and see if you can detect the *formal* exemplification of this polarity. (Hint: What keeps "answering" what?)

Sehnsucht (1775)

Dies wird die letzte Trän' nicht sein
Die glühend Herz-auf[1] quillet,
Das[2] mit unsäglich neuer Pein
Sich schmerzvermehrend stillet.

O laß doch immer hier und dort   5
Mich ewig Liebe fühlen,
Und möcht' der Schmerz auch[3] also fort
Durch Nerv und Adern wühlen.

Könnt' ich doch ausgefüllt einmal
Von dir, o Ew'ger, werden!   10
Ach, diese lange tiefe Qual,
Wie dauert sie auf Erden!

Herbstgefühl (1775)

Fetter grüne, du Laub,
Das Rebengeländer[1]
Hier mein Fenster herauf![2]
Gedrängter[3] quillet,
Zwillingsbeeren, und reifet   5
Schneller und glänzend voller!
Euch brütet der Mutter Sonne
Scheideblick, euch umsäuselt
Des holden Himmels
Fruchtende[4] Fülle.   10
Euch kühlet des Monds
Freundlicher Zauberhauch,
Und euch betauen,[5] ach!

---

[1] =*nach dem Herzen herauf* [2]*Das* is not an "oversight" for *die*, but refers to *das Herz* in the Goethean coinage *Herz-auf*. Such constructions are common in Goethe. [3]*möcht ... auch* 'even though ... should'

[1]'grapevine trellis' [2]*heraufgrünen* is a transitive verb in Klopstock's manner. [3]'more concentratedly' [4]'fructifying' [5]'bedew'

Aus diesen Augen
Der ewig belebenden Liebe   15
Vollschwellende⁶ Tränen.

The first step in understanding this poem is to grasp the syntax. Verses 1-6 contain three parallel imperatives (*grüne - quillet - reifet*); verses 7-16 contain four parallel statements (*Euch brütet - umsäuselt - kühlet - betauen*).

Unlike "Mailied," "Herbstgefühl" is no outburst of joy in life, but an insight into the relationship between fullness of life and death. Hence the elegiac tone. The emphasis, however, is altogether on fullness, vitality, completion, not death, which is only the *implied* polar complement, perceptible above all in the tone. The three apostrophic imperatives with their heavy load of adverbs — three of them in the comparative, thus adding to their "weight" — evoke the sense of swelling and ripening. (Note also the progressive series: *grünen - quellen - reifen*.) Then the poem opens out — from microcosmos to macrocosmos, from the poet's window to the world (*Sonne - Himmel - Mond*). Lines 7-12 show nature's part in the process of maturation, lines 13-16 return again to man, whose "full-swelling" tears both contribute to, and interpret the meaning of, ripening. In mankind "eternally animating love," for Goethe the prime mover in all nature, becomes conscious. Thus the tears both ripen the grape and prove that man ripens with it, that he understands the meaning of ripening.

Mahomets Gesang (1772-73)

Seht den Felsenquell,¹
Freudehell,
Wie ein Sternenblick!²
Über Wolken
Nährten³ seine Jugend   5
Gute Geister
Zwischen Klippen im Gebüsch.

Jünglingfrisch
Tanzt er aus der Wolke
Auf die Marmorfelsen nieder,   10
Jauchzet wieder
Nach dem Himmel.⁴

---

⁶*Vollschwellend* means here both 'full-swelling' and 'causing to swell fully.'

¹'spring gushing from rocks' ²*Blick* 'flash' ³'nourished' ⁴*Jauchzet ... Himmel* 'bounds rejoicing back toward heaven'

Durch die Gipfelgänge[5]
Jagt er bunten Kieseln nach,
Und mit frühem Führertritt   15
Reißt er seine Bruderquellen
Mit sich fort.

Drunten werden in dem Tal
Unter seinem Fußtritt Blumen,
Und die Wiese   20
Lebt von seinem Hauch.

Doch ihn hält kein Schattental,
Keine Blumen,
Die ihm seine Knie' umschlingen,
Ihm mit Liebes-Augen schmeicheln;   25
Nach der Ebne[6] dringt sein Lauf
Schlangewandelnd.[7]

Bäche schmiegen
Sich gesellig an.
Nun tritt er   30
In die Ebne silberprangend,
Und die Ebne prangt mit ihm,
Und die Flüsse von der Ebne
Und die Bäche von Gebürgen
Jauchzen ihm und rufen: „Bruder,   35
Bruder, nimm die Brüder mit,
Mit zu deinem alten Vater,
Zu dem ew'gen Ozean,
Der mit weitverbreit'ten Armen
Unsrer wartet,[8]   40
Die[9] sich, ach! vergebens öffnen,
Seine Sehnenden[10] zu fassen;
Denn uns frißt in öder Wüste
Gier'ger Sand,
Die Sonne droben   45
Saugt an unserm Blut
Ein Hügel
Hemmet uns zum Teiche.[11]
Bruder,
Nimm die Brüder von der Ebne,   50

---

[5]'passages among the peaks' [6]'plain' [7]= *wandelnd wie eine Schlange* [8]'waits for us' (*unsrer* is genitive) [9]refers to *Armen* [10]'those longing for him' [11]'dams us to a pond'

Nimm die Brüder von Gebürgen
Mit, zu deinem Vater mit!"

„Kommt ihr alle!" —
Und nun schwillt er
Herrlicher; ein ganz Geschlechte[12]   55
Trägt den Fürsten hoch empor,
Und im rollenden Triumphe
Gibt er Ländern Namen, Städte
Werden unter seinem Fuß.

Unaufhaltsam rauscht er über,[13]   60
Läßt der Türne Flammengipfel,[14]
Marmorhäuser, eine Schöpfung
Seiner Fülle, hinter sich.

Zedernhäuser[15] trägt der Atlas
Auf den Riesenschultern, sausend   65
Wehen[16] über seinem Haupte
Tausend Segel auf zum Himmel
Seine Macht und Herrlichkeit.

Und so trägt er seine Brüder,
Seine Schätze, seine Kinder   70
Dem erwartenden Erzeuger[17]
Freudebrausend[18] an das Herz.

This is a song *to* Mohammed, not *by* him. It was originally intended to be sung by the prophet's first converts in a drama about the great religious leader. With the image of the river the poem depicts the nature of the prophet as such (not only Mohammed). It says nothing about his teaching. Since the poem speaks only of the river, tracing its course from the mountains to the sea, one might take it as "simply a nature lyric," as at least one critic has maintained. That is, one might think so, were it not for the title. The title is essential: it adds another dimension to the poem.

Towards Interpretation

1. What is implied about the subject's ability to shape his own ends in the equation river = prophet? (Note especially the first stanza.)
2. Where does the river become aware of its obligations to its "brothers"? Is there a religious note here? Would we expect this if the poem were simply a nature lyric?

---

[12]'race' [13]=*vorüber* [14]'spires flaming in the sun' [15]'cedar houses' (ships) [16]transitive verb [17]'begetter' [18]goes with *trägt*

3. Think the poem to the end in meteorological terms. If we take the meteorology symbolically and make religious-philosophical equivalencies, what do we get? Does this view include a "heaven"?

4. The poem contains many compounds, some of them Goethe's own creations: *freudehell, Sternenblick, jünglingfrisch, Gipfelgänge, Führertritt, Liebes-Augen, silberprangend, Flammengipfel, Riesenschultern, freudebrausend.* Translate these compounds into conventional German. What is gained by the use of words such as these?

5. Make a careful translation of lines 65-68. Explain the words *Brüder, Schätze, Kinder.* Is there possible (perhaps intentional) ambiguity in the possessive adjectives in line 66?

6. Scansion of lines 60-64:

    _ ◡ _ ◡ _ ◡ _ ◡
    _ ◡ _ ◡ _ ◡ _ ◡
    _ ◡ _ ◡ _ ◡ _ ◡
    _ ◡ _ ◡ _ ◡ _

Scansion of lines 8-12:

    _ ◡ _
    _ ◡ _ ◡ _ ◡
    _ ◡ _ ◡ _ ◡ _ ◡
    _ ◡ _ ◡
    _ ◡ _ ◡

Erich Trunz, the editor of the *Hamburger Ausgabe* of Goethe's works, has written: "Die Abschnitte des Gedichts entsprechen genau den Abschnitten im Leben des Stroms" (1:470). Comment on the difference between these two stanzas from this standpoint.

An Schwager Kronos[1]
in der Postchaise d[en] 10 Oktbr 1774

Spude dich,[2] Kronos!
Fort den rasselnden Trott!
Bergab gleitet der Weg;
Ekles Schwindeln zögert[3]
Mir vor die Stirne dein Haudern.[3]   5
Frisch den holpernden
Stock Wurzeln Steine den Trott
Rasch in's Leben hinein![4]

---

[1]'To Coachman Time' Goethe confuses here Kronos, the father of Zeus, with Chronos, Time. We give this poem in its earliest known form. [2]=*spute dich* 'hurry up' [3]*zögert,* transitive, 'brings through delay' The subject is *Haudern,* Rhineland dialect for 'ride in a hack,' 'poke along.' [4]Lines 6-8 later became: *Frisch, holpert es gleich* (= *obgleich es holpert*), / *Über Stock und Steine den Trott / Rasch ins Leben hinein!* But here, in the full vigor of the *Sturm und Drang,* the words *Frisch den holpernden Trott* are torn

Nun, schon wieder?
Den eratmenden[5] Schritt   10
Mühsam Berg hinauf.
Auf denn, nicht träge denn!
Strebend und hoffend an.

Weit hoch herrlich der Blick
Rings in's Leben hinein   15
Vom Gebürg zum Gebürg
Über[6] der ewige Geist
Ewigen Lebens ahndevoll.[7]

Seitwärts des Überdachs[8] Schatten
Zieht dich an   20
Und der Frischung verheißende Blick
Auf der Schwelle des Mädchens da. —[9]
Labe dich! — Mir auch, Mädchen,
Diesen schäumenden Trunck
Und den freundlichen Gesundheitsblick!   25

Ab dann, frischer hinab!
Sieh, die Sonne sinkt!
Eh' sie sinkt, eh' mich faßt
Greisen im Moore Nebelduft,
Entzahnte Kiefer schnattern   30
Und das schlockernde Gebein,

Trunknen vom letzten Strahl
Reiß mich, ein Feuermeer
Mir im schäumenden Aug',
Mich geblendeten, Taumelnden,   35
In der Hölle nächtliches Tor![10]

Töne, Schwager, dein Horn,
Raßle den schallenden Trab,

---

apart and the nouns *Stock, Wurzeln, Steine* inserted. Grammatically they are nonsense, psychologically they are very effective. First the *Holpern* is perceived, then its cause, the sticks, roots and stones, which, inserted between *holpernden* and *Trott*, make a *holpernden Trott*. James Joyce was to do a great deal of this sort of thing over a century later. [5]'panting' [6]The later version has *Schwebet*. [7]=*ahnungsvoll* [8]'projecting roof' [9]=*Und der Blick des Mädchens auf der Schwelle da, der (Er-)Frischung verheißt* (promises) [10]Prose paraphrase of lines 28-36: ... *ehe mich Greisen* (old man) *Nebelduft im Moore faßt, ehe entzahnte Kiefer* (toothless jaws) *schnattern und mein Gebein schlockert* (my frame totters, or: my bones rattle), [*ehe das geschieht,*] *möge ich, vom letzten Strahl trunken, ein Feuermeer in meinem schäumenden Auge, geblendet, taumelnd, ins nächtliche Tor der Hölle gerissen werden!*

Daß der Orkus[11] vernehme, ein Fürst kommt,
Drunten von ihren Sitzen   40
Sich die Gewaltigen lüften.[12]

There is no more characteristic expression of the *Lebensgefühl* of the *Sturm und Drang* than Goethe's "An Schwager Kronos"; yet this poem, perhaps more than any other by the youthful Goethe, reveals the influence of his great predecessor Klopstock. It can hardly be an accident that the poem was written directly after Goethe had been in personal touch with Klopstock, at that time still the undisputed leader of German letters, for a period of two weeks, and had then accompanied him from Frankfurt a good distance on his way to Karlsruhe. Returning home alone *in der Postchaise*, the young author of *Götz* and *Werther*, then on the threshold of world fame, an inexhaustible well of song in his breast, passes his life in symbolic review in rhythm to the *rasselnden Trott* and *eratmenden Schritt* of the horses of Coachman Time.

But it is not the feeling and tone of this poem that is Klopstockian, and it is certainly not its sentiment. It is the technique and the poetics behind the technique. *Wohllaut gefällt, Bewegung noch mehr* was Klopstock's creed, and his striving for *Darstellung der (inneren) Bewegung* by means of syntax and rhythm. In this, Goethe follows the acknowledged master.

The most striking example is the magnificent "stretched period" in lines 28-36, where syntax and rhythm reflect in positively physical fashion the force of the *Hinab-Reißen* which is its content. This is brought about by the preponement of the subordinate clauses (*Eh' sie sinkt, eh'* . . .), by the insertion of appositives to the three *mich*'s ([*mich*] Greisen, Trunknen [*mich*], [*mich*] geblendeten, taumelnden), and by the insertion of an absolute construction (*ein Feuermeer / Mir im schäumenden Aug'*). The word *Trunknen*, boldly isolated from its appositive (*mich*, l. 33), appears at the crest of this syntactical wave as the dominant mood word. Then the wave begins to break, that is, the main clause begins and the melodic line starts to fall. Drunk with life — and therefore a *Fürst* — the poet triumphantly enters the realm of death. The idea underlying this poem and "Herbstgefühl" is the same; here the motif is realized hymnically, there elegiacally.

Ganymed (1774?)

Wie im Morgenrot
Du rings mich anglühst,
Frühling, Geliebter!
Mit tausendfacher Liebeswonne
Sich an mein Herz drängt   5

---

[11]i.e., the Underworld   [12]=*erheben*

Deiner ewigen Wärme
Heilig Gefühl,
Unendliche Schöne![1]
Daß ich dich fassen möcht'[2]
In diesen Arm!   10

Ach, an deinem Busen
Lieg' ich, schmachte,
Und deine Blumen, dein Gras
Drängen sich an mein Herz.
Du kühlst den brennenden   15
Durst meines Busens,
Lieblicher Morgenwind,
Ruft drein die Nachtigall
Liebend nach mir aus dem Nebeltal.

Ich komme! ich komme!   20
Wohin? Ach, wohin?

Hinauf, hinauf strebt's,[3]
Es schweben die Wolken
Abwärts, die Wolken
Neigen sich der sehnenden Liebe,   25
Mir, mir!

In eurem[4] Schoße
Aufwärts,
Umfangend umfangen!
Aufwärts   30
an deinem Busen,
Alliebender Vater!

Towards Interpretation

1. In Greek myth Ganymede was a beautiful youth whom Zeus's eagle
   lifted to Olympus. How does this Ganymede attain levitation?
2. Point out the ways in which the spring calls to Ganymede and the
   ways in which he answers. What senses are appealed to?
3. The answer to Ganymede's longing for union is expressed in the
   words umfangend umfangen. How would you translate this? Can one
   say that the river in "Mahomets Gesang" is tragend getragen? (Cf.
   lines 51f. and 65ff.) Wherein lies the difference between the river and

---

[1]Lines 6-8 are the subject of drängt, l. 5. They may be construed: a) [das] heilig(e)
Gefühl [und] unendliche Schöne (=Schönheit) deiner ewigen Wärme; b) [das] heilig(e)
Gefühl deiner ewigen Wärme, [o] unendliche Schöne! [2]=könnt(e) [3]Approximately: 'I
feel an upward striving' [4]i.e., the clouds'

Ganymede? What are the social and religious implications of this difference?

4. Compare the religious feeling here with that in "Die Frühlingsfeier." For which poet, Klopstock or Goethe, is the divine more *in* the world?

Harzreise im Winter (1777)

Dem Geier[1] gleich,
Der auf schweren Morgenwolken
Mit sanftem Fittig[2] ruhend
Nach Beute schaut
Schwebe[3] mein Lied.   5

Denn ein Gott hat
Jedem seine Bahn
Vorgezeichnet,
Die der Glückliche
Rasch zum freudigen   10
Ziele rennt;
Wem aber Unglück
Das Herz zusammenzog,
Er sträubt vergebens
Sich gegen die Schranken[4]   15
Des ehernen[5] Fadens,
Den die doch bittre Schere[6]
Nur einmal löst.

In Dickichts-Schauer[7]
Drängt sich das rauhe Wild.[8]   20
Und mit den Sperlingen
Haben längst die Reichen
In ihre Sümpfe sich gesenkt.[9]

Leicht ist's, folgen dem Wagen,
Den Fortuna führt,   25
Wie der gemächliche Troß[10]
Auf gebesserten Wegen
Hinter des Fürsten Einzug.[11]

---

[1]any bird of prey, not necessarily 'vulture' [2]'pinion' [3]'hortatory: let ... hover' [4]'limits' [5]'brazen,' 'pitiless' [6]'shears' (of the Fate who cuts the thread of life) [7]'uncanniness of the thicket' [8]'game' [9]According to German folklore, certains birds hibernated under water. [10]'comfortable (easy-going) retinue' [11]'entry' (into a town)

Aber abseits, wer ist's?
Ins Gebüsch verliert sich sein Pfad,   30
Hinter ihm schlagen
Die Sträuche zusammen,
Das Gras steht wieder auf,
Die Öde[12] verschlingt ihn.

Ach, wer heilet die Schmerzen   35
Des,[13] dem Balsam zu Gift ward?
Der sich Menschenhaß
Aus der Fülle der Liebe trank!
Erst verachtet, nun ein Verächter,
Zehrt er heimlich auf   40
Seinen eigenen Wert
In ungenügender[14] Selbstsucht.

Ist auf deinem Psalter,[15]
Vater der Liebe, ein Ton
Seinem Ohre vernehmlich,   45
So erquicke sein Herz!
Öffne den[16] umwölkten Blick
Über[17] die tausend Quellen
Neben dem Durstenden
In der Wüste!   50

Der du der Freuden[18] viel schaffst,
Jedem ein überfließend Maß,[19]
Segne die Brüder der Jagd
Auf der Fährte[20] des Wilds
Mit jugendlichem Übermut[21]   55
Fröhlicher Mordsucht,[22]
Späte Rächer des Unbills
Dem schon Jahre vergeblich
Wehrt mit Knütteln der Bauer.[23]

Aber den Einsamen hüll   60
In deine Goldwolken!
Umgib[24] mit Wintergrün,
Bis die Rose wieder heranreift,[25]

---

[12]'wilderness' [13]=*dessen* 'of him' [14]'dissatisfied' [15]=*Harfe* [16]=*seinen* [17]'to' [18]genitive with *viel* [19]'measure' [20]'trail' [21]'enthusiasm' [22]'yearning to kill' [23]Lines 57-59: Peasants were not allowed to kill game, though it often ruined their crops; hence the hunters are 'late revengers of an injustice the peasant has been vainly trying to ward off for years with clubs.' [24]'enclose' [25]'begins to mature'

Die feuchten Haare,
O Liebe, deines Dichters!   65

Mit der dämmernden Fackel[26]
Leuchtest du ihm[27]
Durch die Furten[28] bei Nacht,
Über grundlose[29] Wege
Auf öden Gefilden;[30]   70
Mit dem tausendfarbigen Morgen
Lachst du ins Herz ihm;
Mit dem beizenden[31] Sturm
Trägst du ihn hoch empor.
Winterströme stürzen vom Felsen   75
In seine Psalmen,
Und Altar des lieblichsten Danks
Wird ihm des gefürchteten Gipfels
Schneebehangner Scheitel,
Den mit Geisterreihen[32]   80
Kränzten ahnende[33] Völker.[34]

Du stehst mit unerforschtem Busen
Geheimnisvoll-offenbar
Über der erstaunten Welt
Und schaust aus Wolken   85
Auf ihre Reiche und Herrlichkeit,
Die du aus den Adern deiner Brüder
Neben dir wässerst.

More than forty years after its conception, Goethe himself wrote a commentary on this fascinating but difficult poem.* Even more illuminating than the commentary, however, are his letters to Frau von Stein and his diary of the same

---

[26]the moon [27]i.e., Love lights the way for the poet (*ihm*) [28]'fords' [29]'deep' (with mud) [30]'fields' [31]Two meanings of *beizen* are probably active here: *Mit dem Falken beizen* 'hunt with a hawk' and *beizen* 'bite' (as with an acid), 'tan.' The storm is a hawk sent up by love and as it rises, it carries the poet with it (at the end of the stanza he is on top of the mountain); at the same time it is a "biting" wind. (Goethe speaks elsewhere of a *beizender Tabak*.) [32]'spirit dances' (revels) [33]'foreknowing' [34]Lines 78-80: The "feared peak" is the Brocken, highest point in the Harz, in Goethe's day seldom, if ever, climbed in winter until climbed by the poet himself on this very occasion. The *Geisterreihen* are the witches' orgies held on the Brocken on Walpurgis Eve (see *Faust* Part I).

*Available in the *Jubiläums-Ausgabe* of Goethe's works, *Sämtliche Werke*, ed. E. v. d. Hellen *et al.*, 40 vols. (Stuttgart and Berlin: Cotta, 1902-1912), 2:283ff. Details of the commentary do not always agree with the diary Goethe kept of his journey.

period (December, 1777). From these sources we learn that Goethe left Weimar on a stormy November 29th for the Harz mountains. He had two ostensible purposes for his journey: to inspect the mining industry of the Harz and to visit a man named Plessing, an *äußerst hypochondrischen Selbstquäler*, who had turned to the poet for help. His chief reason for undertaking this arduous journey he seems, however, to have kept secret. He wrote to Frau von Stein on December 10th: "Ich will Ihnen entdecken (sagen Sie's niemand) daß meine Reise auf den Harz war, daß ich wünschte den Brocken zu besteigen. . . ." He had good reason for keeping this quiet — in those days people would have considered him crazy. All these, plus a hunting party of Goethe's duke, the Duke of Weimar, which Goethe knew was out to check the ravages of wild boar in another vicinity, provide motifs for the poem.

The following notes make no claim to solving all the difficulties in the poem or to exhausting its meaning:

Lines 1-5: Barker Fairley* suggests that the image of the bird of prey — for him, specifically a vulture — "makes better sense if we read 'mein Lied' as meaning not the completed song, but the uncompleted, i.e., the creative impulse looking for prey." In the lines that follow the prey is found.

Lines 6-18: The song proper begins with an announcement of the main theme: the contrast between the man destined to happiness and the man destined to sorrow. The former attains his goal almost without effort; the only goal attained by the latter is a death unwelcome even to him: *die doch bittre Schere.*

Lines 19-23: Free association seems to be at work here. Goethe's own comment: "Wer seine Bequemlichkeit aufopfert, verachtet gern diejenigen, die sich darin behagen. . . . Unser Reisende hat alle Bequemlichkeiten zurückgelassen und verachtet die Städter [apparently *die Reichen*, line 22], deren Zustand er gleichnisweise [figuratively] schmählich herabsetzt." In any event, "the rich" have retired, like the sparrows, to their swamps (see footnote 9), to their safe retreats, figuratively also "swamps." For the rich the traveler has only contempt, and his sense of superiority continues in

---

*Barker Fairley, ed., *Goethe: Selected Poems* (London/Toronto: Heinemann, 1954), 209. For other interpretations of metaphors in this poem, see Heinrich Henel, "Der Wanderer in der Not: Goethes 'Wanderers Sturmlied' und 'Harzreise im Winter,'" in *Goethe Zeit: ausgewählte Aufsätze* (Frankfurt a.M.: Insel, 1980), 76-101; Bernd Leistner, "Goethes Gedicht 'Harzreise im Winter': Versuch einer Interpretation," in *Impulse: Aufsätze, Quellen, Berichte zur deutschen Klassik und Romantik 4*, ed. Walter Dietze and Peter Goldammer (Berlin: Aufbau, 1982), 70-117; Albrecht Schöne, *Götterzeichen, Liebeszauber, Satanskult: Neue Einblicke in alte Goethetexte* (Munich: Beck, 1982), 15-52; Jochen Schmidt, "Goethes Bestimmung der dichterischen Existenz im Übergang zur Klassik: 'Harzreise im Winter,'" *Deutsche Vierteljahrsschrift* 57 (1983): 613-635; David E. Wellbery and Klaus Weimar, *Johann Wolfgang v. Goethe, "Harzreise im Winter": Eine Deutungskontroverse*, Modellanalysen: Literatur 14 (Paderborn: Schoningh, 1984); Wolf von Engelhardt, "Goethes Harzreise im Winter 1777," *Goethe Jahrbuch* 104 (1987): 192-211.

Lines 24-28, for he feels himself above the "easy-going retinue" that follows "Fortune's car" along "improved ways." More than anything else, lines 21-28 serve to dissociate the traveler from a certain *kind* of fortunate person.

Lines 29-34 take up the second part of the theme announced in the second strophe, after the examples of the (despised) fortunate ones: "he whose heart is constricted by misfortune." Like the hunted game (lines 19ff.), he disappears in the underbrush without a trace.

Lines 35-42: Sympathy for the one *abseits*, though it is by no means implied that the *Abseitiger* is in the right. Introduction of the image of drinking and giving drink, which is continued in the next two strophes (47ff. and 51ff.) and which occurs again at the end of the poem. As usual in Goethe, this image is associated with the principle of love.

Lines 43-50 contain a prayer to the "father of love" for the unhappy one. This stanza is the pivot of the poem — here it turns from the negative to the positive.

Lines 51-59: Another contrast: from the hunted to the hunters, from the denier to the affirmers, who are also included in the traveler's prayer (perhaps with a slightly ironic overtone). Note that the "brothers of the chase" are no more in the same category with the "rich" and the "easy-going retinue" (lines 22 and 26) than is

Lines 60-65: "the lonely one" in the same category with the man *abseits*. For though the traveler-poet is lonely and thus related to the *Abseitiger*, he is also an affirmer and a *Glücklicher* and hence related to the *Brüder der Jagd*. Is not *his* image that of the bird of prey? The universality of Goethe's art begins to become apparent here. It also becomes apparent that "Harzreise im Winter" is fundamentally a poem dealing with the nature of art and the artist. In these lines, the most intense in the whole hymn, the poet prays for himself, prays that, whatever may come, he may endure and be fruitful through love, that the rosebud may be enclosed in frost-resistant leaves until the time comes for it to unfold.

Lines 66-81: As he thinks of what love has done for him — the imagery contrasts and compares the poet's way both with that of the Abseitiger and the comfortable retinue behind the prince's coach — it is as though his prayer were answered, and standing now on top of the windswept Brocken — carried there by Love's *beizender Sturm* — he consecrates it as an altar of thanksgiving, thus fulfilling in the way of love the presentiment of *ahnende Völker*. The *Geisterreihen* that encircle this peak shall no longer be those of witches, but angels.

Lines 82-88: Though Goethe himself cannily speaks of geology in his comments on these lines, it is surely not geology alone that the poem has in mind. The mountain, with its unfathomed (and unfathomable?) bosom, *geheimnisvoll-offenbar*, i.e., mysterious and yet perfectly evident (Goethe's formula for the divine), looking out over the "realms and their splendor," which it "waters" from the "veins" (of ore) of its brother mountains, is an image of blessing. That the mountain is more than a mountain, or that for Goethe a mountain is more than it is for us, every reader must feel. The *Du* in line 82 is disturbingly ambiguous; it is only after some thought that we decide the mountain must be meant. The *du*'s of the preceding strophe, which refer to love, are still in our ear, and it may also occur to us that Goethe could be addressing himself as a poet — after Klopstock such a grand conception of the poet would not seem overdrawn. Almost certainly we are *meant* to be aware of this plurality of references. The mountain is first of all itself, but it is also a symbol of blessing and love (connected throughout the poem with images of giving as the mountain is here) *and* of the poet, who has identified himself with love through prayer and through sympathy with the *Abseitiger* and with the mountain by climbing it and consecrating it as an altar of thanksgiving.*

Like so many of Goethe's poems, "Harzreise im Winter" leads us back to its starting point — compare the first five verses with the last seven and note the motif of viewing from a height in both. The measure of the heart's progress, however, is contained in the contrast between the hunting image at the beginning and the image of blessing at the end.

Auf dem See (1775/89)[1]

Und frische Nahrung, neues Blut
Saug' ich aus freier Welt;
Wie ist Natur so hold und gut,
Die mich am Busen hält!
Die Welle wieget unsern Kahn   5
Im Rudertakt hinauf,
Und Berge, wolkig himmelan,[2]
Begegnen unserm Lauf.[3]

Aug', mein Aug', was sinkst du nieder?
Goldne Träume, kommt ihr wieder?   10
Weg, du Traum! so gold du bist;
Hier auch Lieb' und Leben ist.

---

*A passage in a letter to Frau von Stein (11 December 1777) helps confirm our interpretation of the poet's identification of himself with the mountain: "... ich trat ans Fenster und er [der Brocken] lag vor mir klar *wie mein Gesicht im Spiegel*, da ging mir das Herz auf und ich rief [to the forester with whom he was staying]: Und ich sollte nicht hinaufkommen!" (Emphasis added.)

[1]The first version of this poem was entered in Goethe's diary as *15. Junius 1775, aufm Zürichersee*; this text is the revised version of 1789.   [2]=*nach dem Himmel zu*
[3]'course'

Auf der Welle blinken
Tausend schwebende Sterne,
Weiche Nebel trinken   15
Rings die türmende Ferne;
Morgenwind umflügelt[4]
Die beschattete Bucht,
Und im See bespiegelt
Sich die reifende Frucht.   20

The metrical situation in this poem, along with certain other considerations, has led some commentators to believe that "Auf dem See" is really jottings for three different poems. It must be admitted that the metrical situation is striking, even strange. In the first stanza, a four-beat iambic line alternating with one of three beats and a rising confident rhythm; in the second, a trochaic measure and falling rhythm; in the third, trochees again, but combined with dactyls: $\_ \; \smile \_ \; \smile \_ \; \smile \; / \; \_ \; \smile \_ \; \smile \smile \_ \; \smile$, and a peaceful, meditative rhythm. Is there a connection between these stanzas or are the skeptics right?

Stanza 1 shows a mother-child relationship between *Ich* and *Welt*. Nature holds man to her bosom and suckles him. He takes the breast with evident relish.* The boat rocking on the waves is like a cradle or like being cradled in a mother's arms and rocked to and fro. The mountains could easily be interpreted as a breast image. The rhythm is usually said to reflect the rowing, but it also, and much more significantly, symbolizes Mother Nature's rocking of her child.

In stanza 2, the *Ich* turns away from the scene about it and gazes within itself. A memory has suddenly come to the surface, the memory of some other harmony — "a golden dream" that in some unexplained way nullifies the present harmony. With an effort of the will — *Weg, du Traum!* — the dream is dismissed and the *Ich* returns to the Here and Now.

But now — stanza 3 — how different is the Here! Nature is no longer an indulgent mother rocking and nursing her infant. In fact, and this is the most striking thing about the last stanza, the *Ich* has entirely disappeared. Not only has it disappeared, but the form seems to exclude any attempt at entrance into this new world. Each pair of these magically evocative verses is a self-contained unit describing some part of nature and nothing but nature. Entrance of any human element is symbolically forbidden by the run-over lines:

Auf der Welle blinken
Tausend schwebende Sterne. . . .

---

[4]'wings about'

*In the first version of this poem, one could doubt whether the child had even been born: *Ich saug' an meiner N a b e l s c h n u r / Nun Nahrung aus der Welt.* . . .

Each aspect of nature is related to another: the stars gleam in the water, the soft mists "drink" the peaks, the breeze wings about the bay, the ripening fruit is mirrored in the lake. In the first stanza, by contrast, each aspect of nature was related to man. Here all is "blessed unto itself" and man is nowhere. No, not nowhere. Man is the beholder of this harmony. Through him it attains meaning, without him there would be no harmony. But as long as he was merely nature's child, he could not give it this meaning. Basically, indeed, it was then meaningless, for it meant only *him*, like the phantasmagoric shapes in the first half of "Willkommen und Abschied." It was necessary for him to lose paradise and turn his back on the "golden dream" in order to discover what paradise is. The poem exemplifies the *process* of maturation. It closes with a symbol of itself:

> Und im See bespiegelt
> Sich *die reifende Frucht.*

„*Warum gabst du uns die tiefen Blicke*" (1776)

> Warum gabst du uns die tiefen Blicke,
> Unsre Zukunft ahndungsvoll zu schaun,
> Unsrer Liebe, unserm Erdenglücke
> Wähnend selig nimmer hinzutraun?[1]
> Warum gabst uns, Schicksal, die Gefühle,   5
> Uns einander in das Herz zu sehn,
> Um durch all' die seltenen Gewühle[2]
> Unser wahr Verhältnis auszuspähn?
>
> Ach, so viele tausend Menschen kennen,
> Dumpf sich treibend,[3] kaum ihr eigen Herz,   10
> Schweben zwecklos hin und her und rennen
> Hoffnungslos in unversehnem Schmerz;[4]
> Jauchzen wieder, wenn der schnellen Freuden
> Unerwart'te Morgenröte tagt.
> Nur uns armen liebevollen beiden   15
> Ist das wechselseit'ge Glück versagt,[5]
> Uns zu lieben, ohn' uns zu verstehen,

---

[1]Lines 1-4: *du* (line 1) refers to *Schicksal* (l. 5), *uns* to Goethe and Frau von Stein, to whom this poem was sent as a letter, 14 April 1776. *Wähnend selig* '(foolishly) imagining ourselves blissful' [cf. *Wahn* 'illusion']. To paraphrase: 'Why (o Fate) did you endow us with the power of divining the future, so that we can never abandon ourselves in imaginary bliss to our love, our earthly happiness?' [2]'strange confusions' [3]'drifting purposelessly, unawares' [4]The dative shows that they run about *in* 'unforeseen pain' (not *into* it). [5]'the mutual happiness denied'

In dem andern sehn, was er nie war,
Immer frisch auf Traumglück auszugehen[6]
Und zu schwanken auch in Traumgefahr.   20

Glücklich, den[7] ein leerer Traum beschäftigt!
Glücklich, dem[8] die Ahndung[9] eitel wär'!
Jede Gegenwart[10] und jeder Blick bekräftigt
Traum und Ahndung leider uns noch mehr.
Sag', was will das Schicksal uns bereiten?   25
Sag', wie band es uns so rein genau?
Ach, du warst in abgelebten Zeiten[11]
Meine Schwester oder meine Frau.

Kanntest jeden Zug[12] in meinem Wesen,
Spähtest, wie die reinste Nerve[13] klingt,   30
Konntest mich mit *einem* Blicke lesen,
Den[14] so schwer ein sterblich[15] Aug' durchdringt.
Tropftest Mäßigung dem heißen Blute,
Richtetest[16] den wilden irren Lauf,
Und in deinen Engelsarmen ruhte   35
Die zerstörte Brust sich wieder auf.

Hieltest zauberleicht ihn[17] angebunden
Und vergaukeltest[18] ihm[17] manchen Tag.
Welche Seligkeit glich jenen Wonnestunden,
Da er[17] dankbar dir zu Füßen lag,   40
Fühlt' sein Herz an deinem Herzen schwellen,
Fühlte sich in deinem Auge gut,
Alle seine Sinnen sich erhellen[19]
Und beruhigen[19] sein brausend Blut.

Und von allem dem schwebt ein Erinnern   45
Nur noch um das ungewisse Herz,
Fühlt[20] die alte Wahrheit ewig gleich im Innern,
Und der neue Zustand wird ihm Schmerz.
Und wir scheinen uns nur halb beseelet,
Dämmernd ist um uns der hellste Tag.   50
Glücklich, daß das Schicksal, das uns quälet,
Uns doch nicht verändern mag.[21]

---

[6]*auf etwas ausgehen* 'go looking for something' [7]'he whom' [8]'he to whom' [9]=*Ahnung* [10]i.e., every time we are together [11]'in times gone by' (*not* in this life!) [12]'trait' [13]'nerve,' 'string' (music) [14]'me whom' [15]'mortal' [16]'made straight' [17]These pronouns have no grammatical referent, but the meaning is obvious: the poet refers to his former incarnation in the third person. [18]'caused to pass as by magic' [19]dependent on *fühlte* [20]Supply *er* as subject of *fühlt*. [21]=*kann*

Hier ist Goethes Art zu sein und zu dichten leicht anschaulich zu machen: Er hat von Anfang an alle seine Erlebnisse *begriffen*. Im Erleben das Erlebte begreifend, aber nicht in gewollter Besinnung [deliberation], sondern in einer ungewollten Anwandlung von Sinn [involuntary insight into the meaning], so schreibt er dies hin, und diese wissendsten Worte sind intim wie ein Brief oder wie etwas halblaut in die Dämmerung Geredetes, wo man das Gegenüber nicht deutlich sieht, aber seine Hand spürt und einmal einen bedeutenden Blick von ihm auffängt. Die Worte sind so unscheinbar [plain] als die gesagten Dinge groß und heilig — auch als Gedicht scheint alles nur für *einen* Menschen gesagt, so allgemein es ist. . . . Anfang und Ende wenden sich an das Schicksal, das von Goethe mit der Einfalt eines Menschen des Altertums geglaubt wird. . . . Und worüber klagt er denn, klagt wie über etwas Schweres, das man doch nicht anders haben will? Darüber, daß ihm und ihr allein versagt ist, was allen andern Liebenden gegönnt ist: Täuschung! . . .

Das Erkennen, dieser selbstlose, sachliche, reine Bezug [relation] von Ich und Gegenstand, das Erkennen ist hier auch der Inbegriff [essence] der Liebe. . . .

Kein einziges leidenschaftliches Wort, sondern der Friede der tiefsten Verständigung. Schmerz, weil dem letzten Wissen umeinander, als das hier die Liebe erscheint, das Leben mit keiner Form genügt. . . . Man hört es den Worten nicht an, daß sie ein Mysterium eröffnen werden. Und plötzlich ist es da. „Ach, du warst in abgelebten Zeiten. . . ." Das wunderbare Bekanntsein miteinander, das Leben ineinander wie in einem Zimmer, wo man jedes Ding seit der Kindheit kennt: Das wird erklärt, aus Vergangenem hergeleitet. Denn die ganzen Imperfekta, die jenem „Ach, du warst" folgen, sind aufs Deutlichste unterschieden von den Präsentia des gegenwärtigen Zustandes, malen eine frühere Verkörperung der Liebenden aus. [Is this reference to metempsychosis due to the influence of Indian philosophy, the author asks, but dismisses such speculation as beside the point. The poet's relation to such mysteries is not that of belief or unbelief; he uses them as he sees fit, symbolically.] Ein Mysterium der Liebe, sonst nichts, spielt sich vor ihm [dem Dichter] — der Liebe, die täuschungsloses Wissen umeinander ist, und er und die Freundin werden Paradigma für Urbildliches [prototypical forms]. . . .

Indem Goethe schlicht sagt, was ist, entsteht ein Gedicht von seltenster Originalität. So ist nie gedichtet, fast möchte man sagen, nie geliebt worden. . . .   (Max Kommerell)

An den Mond (1776-78)[1]

Füllest[2] wieder Busch und Tal
Still mit Nebelglanz
Lösest[3] endlich auch einmal
Meine Seele ganz;

Breitest über mein Gefild[4]   5
Lindernd deinen Blick,
Wie des Freundes Auge mild[5]
Über mein Geschick.

Jeden Nachklang fühlt mein Herz
Froh- und trüber Zeit   10
Wandle[6] zwischen Freud' und Schmerz
In der Einsamkeit.

Fließe, fließe, lieber Fluß!
Nimmer[7] werd' ich froh,
So verrauschte[8] Scherz und Kuß,   15
Und die Treue so.

Ich besaß es doch einmal,
Was so köstlich ist!
Daß man doch zu seiner Qual
Nimmer es vergißt!   20

Rausche, Fluß, das Tal entlang,
Ohne Rast und Ruh,
Rausche, flüstre meinem Sang
Melodien zu,

Wenn du in der Winternacht   25
Wütend überschwillst,
Oder um die Frühlingspracht
Junger Knospen quillst.

Selig, wer sich vor der Welt
Ohne Haß verschließt,[9]   30
Einen Freund am Busen hält
Und mit dem genießt,[10]

---

[1]The original version of the poem is undated, but was contained in a letter to Frau v. Stein; this text follows the revision of 1789. [2]The unspoken *du* refers to the moon. [3]'dissolve,' 'release,' 'restore' [4]"all within my view" [5]'kindly' [6]The subject is *ich*, understood [7]=*nie mehr* [8]'passed away' (like rushing water) [9]Cf. "Harzreise im Winter" [10]Not so much 'enjoy' as 'experience together'; cf. "Genosse"

Was, von Menschen nicht gewußt
Oder nicht bedacht,
Durch das Labyrinth der Brust   35
Wandelt in der Nacht.

"An den Mond" is one of Goethe's greatest but also most enigmatic lyrics; not to be moved by it is proof enough that one has no ear for poetry, at least German poetry; to pretend to be able to interpret it fully is proof of purblind arrogance. The following remarks merely try to point out some relationships between theme and structure; the enigma remains.

It is the moon that makes this experience possible. Its vague light that fills bush and valley as water fills a bowl also fills the restless soul and brings it peace. We should notice the *wieder* in the first verse and the *auch einmal* in the third. The moon has shone on this valley many times without bringing the soul release; this time it finally does. The poem records an act of grace. It seems to be dedicated to the moon out of gratitude, a kind of *ex voto*.

In the second stanza, the moon is said to "spread" its glance* over all within view: *Wie des Freundes Auge mild / Über mein Geschick*. At the end of the poem, the friend has taken the place of the moon; this better moon wanders with the speaker through the dark "labyrinth of the breast" as does the moon itself across the nocturnal sky. Moon and friend both bring release and restore the soul. Beginning and end are thus joined. In this way we can more or less "account for" stanzas 1-2 and 8-9 in structural terms.

"An den Mond" is not, however, only a poem of friendship, but of friendship and *time*. The time motif, implicit even in the first two stanzas (*endlich auch einmal* implies long, perhaps even desperate waiting; *Geschick* is that which is "sent" as one's temporal lot), becomes explicit in the third. But not in the mode of temporality, not as successiveness, but as simultaneity, the negation of time:

Jeden Nachklang fühlt mein Herz
Froh- und trüber Zeit,
Wandle zwischen Freud' und Schmerz
In der Einsamkeit.

This is the effect of the moon. We see how exact Goethe's language was when he said, *Lösest meine Seele ganz* — the soul is literally "dissolved," it is everywhere at once, like salt suspended in a cup of water. It hears every echo of both sad and happy times, it wanders between joy and pain, but it does not identify itself with any of these things. At most, it feels kinship with the wandering moon.

---

*A bold metaphor, but like most Goethean metaphors so consonant with nature that we hardly notice it.

The next four stanzas form a kind of poem within a poem — they are devoted to the stream, an ancient symbol of time. It is striking, when one comes
to think of it, that the stream, to which the poem is *not* addressed, should be
apostrophized, while the moon, to which it *is* addressed, is not. The poet talks
with the moon, but *to* the stream. It is as though he were on an island in the
stream of time, surrounded by it, but not of it. It was the moon's light that
created this island. The word *lösest* in line 3 begins to take on the further
meaning of *los-lösen*.

The stream stanzas show a 2+2 structure (*Fließe* + *Rausche*). In contrast
to the releasing and restoring effect of the moon (=timelessness), that of the
stream (=time) is deeply saddening, even tormenting (*Qual*), for it recalls that
which is irretrievably lost, *das verrauschte Einmal*. Yet the stream is a *lieber
Fluß*, and it is expressly bidden to follow its nature, to express the mode of
successiveness, to flow and rush. The polarity we find everywhere in Goethe's
work is clearly present here also: time and timelessness. In these middle
stanzas the poles are brought together: man, granted the grace of release from
time, affirms that from which he has been released. The second pair of stream
stanzas (6-7) overcomes the melancholy of the first pair and brings the *Steigerung.** Yet in a way that at first seems suspiciously particular: *Rausche, flüstre
m e i n e m Sang / Melodien zu. . . .* Does this mean that Goethe, like so many
poets of our own day, would narrow the application to the poet alone and let
the rest of us go hang? We can rest assured that this is not the case; or rather:
we can rest assured that this is not the whole story. Certainly, "my song" does
mean my art, my poetry, and it naturally has a special application to Goethe
the poet, but it also means all of life's activities, the "song" we all sing to the
melody time "whispers." The poet is only paradigmatic. Stanza 7 says yes to
all that time may bring, *Winternacht* or *Frühlingspracht*. Only after this affirmation does the poem return to its beginning, but now on a higher plane: the
friend supplants the moon.

Towards Interpretation

1. Study the last two stanzas carefully and show wherein lies the supe-
    riority of the friend as opposed to the moon.

---

*Stanzas 4-7 form a little elegy within the framework of the poem: they discover the
positive meaning in sorrow.

Wanderers Nachtlied[1] (1776)

Der du[2] von dem Himmel bist,
Alles Leid und Schmerzen stillest,
Den, der doppelt elend ist,
Doppelt mit Erquickung füllest,
Ach, ich bin des Treibens[3] müde!   5
Was soll all der Schmerz und Lust?[4]
Süßer Friede,
Komm, ach komm in meine Brust!

Ein gleiches[1] (1780)

Über allen Gipfeln
Ist Ruh,
In allen Wipfeln
Spürest du
Kaum einen Hauch;   5
Die Vögelein schweigen im Walde.
Warte nur, balde
Ruhest du auch.

These two poems, the most famous of all German lyrics, stand to each other in the relation of prayer and fulfillment, or at least the promise of fulfillment.

> "Wandrers Nachtlied." In this prayer for peace, the unbearable tension of the soul is neither described, nor yet evoked by image or analogy. It is transmuted directly into the syntactical structure of the verse. . . . By piling up subordinate clauses, three of them, one on another, by placing inside the last of them yet another subordinate clause, which is itself dependent upon the object of the first,
>
> > Den, der doppelt elend ist,
> > Doppelt mit Erquickung füllest,
>
> thus making the construction even more tortuous than ever, Goethe has

---

[1]This text follows the first printed edition of 1780. *Nacht*, here 'after sunset,' 'evening' [2]'You who' [3]'pointless doings,' but also with the sense of driving and being driven [4]"*Schmerz* and *Lust* are nouns of different gender and would normally require an article each. But here they are bound together by the single article *der*. The effect is to reveal pain and pleasure for what they are, opposite poles of one and the same thing, the ambivalent manifestation of that restless *Treiben*, from which the poet implores release" (Elizabeth M. Wilkinson, "Goethe's Poetry," *German Life and Letters* n. s. 2 [1948/49]: 325).

[1]i.e., also a "Wanderers Nachtlied"

rendered an utter knottedness of feeling *directly*, through the 'turnings intricate of verse.' The piling up of initial dentals increases the effect of clenched frustration. Language so pent and strained can only find an outlet in sheer exclamation:

> Ach, ich bin des Treibens müde!
> Was soll all der Schmerz und Lust?

And only then is the being, so long invoked, finally called by name, and the brief main clause pronounced:

> Süßer Friede,
> Komm, ach komm in meine Brust!*

In discussing "Ein gleiches," the critic just quoted points out that, as surely and powerfully as these eight lines evoke a mood — not by describing the stillness of evening, but by *becoming* evening stillness itself — we have hardly begun to understand the poem if we simply stop there.

Towards Interpretation

1. The poet speaks first of hilltops, then tree-tops, then birds, then man. What might be the significance of this sequence? (Hint: Is a hierarchy of inanimate–animate nature implied?)
2. People often misquote the poem, placing *Gipfeln* before *Wipfel*. How does this destroy the sense of the poem?

Der Fischer (1778/89)[1]

> Das Wasser rauscht', das Wasser schwoll,
> Ein Fischer saß daran,
> Sah nach dem Angel ruhevoll,
> Kühl bis ans Herz hinan.
> Und wie er sitzt, und wie er lauscht,   5
> Teilt sich die Flut empor;[2]
> Aus dem bewegten Wasser rauscht
> Ein feuchtes Weib hervor.
>
> Sie sang zu ihm, sie sprach zu ihm:
> „Was lockst du meine Brut   10
> Mit Menschenwitz und Menschenlist
> Hinauf in Todesglut?[3]
> Ach, wüßtest du, wie's Fischlein[4] ist
> So wohlig auf dem Grund,[5]

---

*Wilkinson, "Goethe's Poetry," 323f.

[1]Composed in 1778; we follow the revised version of 1789. [2]'divides upwards [3]'deadly heat' [4]dative plural [5]'so snug here on the bottom'

Du stiegst[6] herunter, wie du bist,   15
Und würdest erst[7] gesund.

Labt sich die liebe Sonne nicht,
Der Mond sich nicht im Meer?
Kehrt wellenatmend[8] ihr Gesicht
Nicht doppelt schöner her?   20
Lockt dich der tiefe Himmel nicht,
Das feuchtverklärte[9] Blau?
Lockt dich dein eigen Angesicht
Nicht her in ew'gen Tau?"

Das Wasser rauscht', das Wasser schwoll,   25
Netzt'[10] ihm den nackten Fuß;
Sein Herz wuchs ihm so sehnsuchtsvoll,
Wie bei der Liebsten Gruß.[11]
Sie sprach zu ihm, sie sang zu ihm;
Da war's um ihn geschehn: 30
Halb zog sie ihn, halb sank er hin,
Und ward nicht mehr gesehn.

Towards Interpretation

1. Wolfgang Kayser* classifies "Der Fischer" and "Erlkönig" (which follows below) as "naturmagische Balladen." According to Kayser, the characteristics of such ballads are:
   a) Das Geschehen ist überzeitlich (timeless).
   b) Die menschlichen Gestalten sind überindividuell, „ein Fischer", „ein Vater mit seinem Kind", so unbestimmt wie nur möglich.
   c) Das Geschehen geht nicht von den Menschen aus, sondern diese werden von anderen Mächten, von Naturmächten erfaßt. Diese Mächte haben sich in den Balladen zu Gestalten verdichtet.
   Following Kayser's lead, what natural force (*Naturmacht*) does the woman in "Der Fischer" represent?
2. How much of the ballad is devoted to actual description of the narrative situation and where do we find the narrative details?
3. Do you feel that the poet has succeeded in thinking himself into the role of the *Wasserweib*? What details seem to you especially convincing? Point out false notes, if you find any.
4. Are the arguments in the speech of the *Wasserweib* (stanza 3) logical?

---

[6]subjunctive [7]'only then' [8]'wave-breathing' [9]'transfigured by the wet' [10]'wets' [11]'as at his darling's greeting'

*Wolfgang Kayser, *Geschichte der deutschen Ballade* (Berlin: Junker und Dünnhaupt, 1936), 161ff.

Erlkönig[1] (1782)

Wer reitet so spät durch Nacht und Wind?
Es ist der Vater mit seinem Kind;
Er hat den Knaben wohl in dem Arm,
Er faßt ihn sicher, er hält ihn warm. —

Mein Sohn, was birgst du so bang dein Gesicht? — 5
Siehst, Vater, du den Erlkönig nicht?
Den Erlenkönig mit Kron' und Schweif?[2] —
Mein Sohn, es ist ein Nebelstreif.[3] —

„Du liebes Kind, komm, geh mit mir!
Gar schöne Spiele spiel' ich mit dir; 10
Manch' bunte Blumen sind an dem Strand;
Meine Mutter hat manch' gülden Gewand."

Mein Vater, mein Vater, und hörest du nicht,
Was Erlenkönig mir leise verspricht? —
Sei ruhig, bleibe ruhig, mein Kind! 15
In dürren Blättern säuselt der Wind. —

„Willst, feiner Knabe, du mit mir gehn?
Meine Töchter sollen dich warten[4] schön;
Meine Töchter führen den nächtlichen Reihn[5]
Und wiegen und tanzen und singen dich ein."[6] 20

Mein Vater, mein Vater, und siehst du nicht dort
Erlkönigs Töchter am düstern Ort? —
Mein Sohn, mein Sohn, ich seh' es genau;
Es scheinen die alten Weiden[7] so grau. —

„Ich liebe dich, mich reizt[8] deine schöne Gestalt; 25
Und bist du nicht willig; so brauch' ich Gewalt." —
Mein Vater, mein Vater, jetzt faßt er mich an!
Erlkönig hat mir ein Leids[9] getan! —

Dem Vater grauset's,[10] er reitet geschwind,
Er hält in Armen das ächzende Kind, 30
Erreicht den Hof mit Mühe und Not;
In seinen Armen das Kind war tot.

In "Der Erlkönig" the narration is divided among three "voices": the human,
as represented by father and son; the supernatural, as represented by the *Erl-*

---

[1]Corruption of *Elbkönig* 'king of the elves' [2]'train' (of a garment) [3]*Streif* 'streak'
[4]'wait upon' [5]a round dance [6]*ein* separable prefix that goes with all three preceding
verbs, meaning 'to sleep' [7]'willows' [8]'tempts,' 'charms' [9]'injury' [10]'is horrified'

könig; and that of the impartial poet-narrator. These voices are divided among the strophes as follows:

1. Narrative strophe (the poet speaks)
2. Dialog (father - son - father)
3. The *Erlkönig* speaks
4. Dialog (son - father)
5. The *Erlkönig* speaks
6. Dialog (son - father)
7. The *Erlkönig* speaks - the son cries out to father
8. Narrative strophe

As the poem progresses, the voice of the father is increasingly supplanted by that of the *Erlkönig*. In *stanza 2* the father is the master of the situation: he speaks first and last, his voice surrounds that of his son with the same security as does his protecting arm. In *stanzas 4 and 6*, the words of the father no longer surround the son. The *Erlkönig* has entered into the sequence of speeches, and the son is surrounded on one hand by the *Erlkönig* and on the other by the father, both of whom compete for him. In *stanza 7* the father's voice disappears completely from the poem: the last human voice is the cry of the son, *Erlkönig hat mir ein Leids getan!*

Towards Interpretation

1. Each time the *Erlkönig* speaks with the son, the son perceives him through a different sensory organ. How does the *Erlkönig* communicate with him?
2. The *Erlkönig* also uses a different appeal to "charm" the son every time he speaks. How does he try to convince the son to go with him?
3. The poem rimes *Kind-Wind*/(*gesch w i n d*) three times, twice in the speeches of the narrator, the objective voice, once in those of the father. Does this rime contribute to the sense of the poem?
4. What is the *Erlkönig*? What does he represent in the poem?
5. What is being described in "Der Erlkönig"? What is the theme of the poem?

Das Göttliche (1783)

Edel sei[1] der Mensch,
Hilfreich und gut!
Denn das allein
Unterscheidet ihn
Von allen Wesen,   5
Die wir kennen.

Heil den unbekannten
Höhern Wesen,
Die wir ahnen![2]
Ihnen gleiche[3] der Mensch!   10
Sein Beispiel lehr'[4] uns
Jene glauben.[5]

Denn unfühlend
Ist die Natur:
Es leuchtet die Sonne   15
Über Bös' und Gute,
Und dem Verbrecher
Glänzen wie dem Besten
Der Mond und die Sterne.

Wind und Ströme,   20
Donner und Hagel
Rauschen ihren Weg
Und ergreifen
Vorüber eilend
Einen um den andern.[6]   25

Auch so das Glück[7]
Tappt[8] unter die Menge,
Faßt bald des Knaben
Lockige Unschuld
Bald auch den kahlen   30
Schuldigen Scheitel.

Nach ewigen, ehrnen,[9]
Großen Gesetzen
Müssen wir alle
Unseres Daseins   35
Kreise vollenden.

---

[1]hortatory: 'let ... be' [2]'have a premonition of' [3]'let ... resemble' [4]'let ... teach' [5]'to believe in' [6]i.e., now the good, now the bad [7]'fortune' [8]'gropes' [9]'immutable'

Nur allein der Mensch
Vermag das Unmögliche:
Er unterscheidet,
Wählet und richtet;   40
Er kann dem Augenblick
Dauer[10] verleihen.

Er allein darf
Den Guten lohnen,
Den Bösen strafen,   45
Heilen und retten,
Alles Irrende, Schweifende[11]
Nützlich verbinden.

Und wir verehren
Die Unsterblichen[12]   50
Als wären sie Menschen,
Täten im großen[13]
Was der Beste im kleinen
Tut oder möchte.

Der edle Mensch   55
Sei hilfreich und gut!
Unermüdet schaff'[14] er
Das Nützliche, Rechte,
Sei uns ein Vorbild[15]
Jener geahneten Wesen!

Towards Interpretation

1. Note carefully the things here designated as peculiar to man. What is peculiar to the divine, as expressed in this poem? Might the poem also be called "Das Menschliche"? Why isn't it?
2. The Romantics would later suggest that nature and human beings were two faces of the same thing. Would you call the view of nature expressed in this poem "romantic"?
3. If you have read Goethe's *Iphigenie*, compare the heroine's view of the gods with the attitude expressed here.

---

[10]'permanence' [11]'unstable,' 'aimlessly roaming' [12]'immortals,' 'gods' [13]'on a grand scale' [14]hortatory subjunctive [15]'model,' 'prototype'

Mignons Lied[1] (1783/95)

Kennst du das Land? wo die Zitronen blühn,
Im dunkeln Laub die Gold–Orangen glühn,
Ein sanfter Wind vom blauen Himmel weht,
Die Myrte still und hoch der Lorbeer steht,
Kennst du es wohl?
     Dahin! Dahin   5
Möcht' ich mit dir, o mein Geliebter, ziehn!

Kennst du das Haus? auf Säulen ruht sein Dach,
Es glänzt der Saal, es schimmert das Gemach,
Und Marmorbilder stehn und sehn mich an:
Was hat man dir, du armes Kind, getan?   10
Kennst du es wohl?
     Dahin! Dahin
Möcht' ich mit dir, o mein Beschützer, ziehn!

Kennst du den Berg und seinen Wolkensteg?
Das Maultier sucht im Nebel seinen Weg,
In Höhlen wohnt der Drachen alte Brut,   15
Es stürzt der Fels und über ihn die Flut:
Kennst du ihn wohl?
     Dahin! Dahin
Geht unser Weg; o Vater, laß uns ziehn!

„*Cupido, loser, eigensinniger Knabe!*" (1787/88)

Cupido, loser,[1] eigensinniger Knabe!
Du batst mich um Quartier auf einige Stunden.
Wie viele Tag' und Nächte bist du geblieben!
Und bist nun herrisch[2] und Meister im Hause geworden!

Von meinem breiten Lager bin ich vertrieben;   5
Nun sitz' ich an der Erde, Nächte[3] gequälet;
Dein Mutwill'[4] schüret Flamm' auf Flamme des Herdes,
Verbrennet den Vorrat des Winters und senget mich Armen.

Du hast mir mein Geräte verstellt und verschoben;[5]
Ich such' und bin wie blind und irre geworden.   10

---

[1]Mignon is a child of indeterminate background from Goethe's novel, *Wilhelm Meister*.

[1]'impudent' [2]'bossy' [3]=*nachts, nächtelang* [4]'arbitrariness' [5]'you've misplaced all my things'

Du lärmst so ungeschickt, ich fürchte, das Seelchen
Entflieht, um dir zu entfliehn, und räumet die Hütte.

„Noch etwas Eigenes", sagte ich, „hat das Gedicht. Es ist mir immer, als
wäre es gereimt, und doch ist es nicht so. Woher kommt das?" „Es liegt im
Rhythmus", sagte Goethe. „Die Verse beginnen mit einem Vorschlag [un-
accented syllable], gehen trochäisch fort, wo denn der Daktylus gegen das
Ende eintritt, welcher eigenartig wirkt und wodurch es einen düster kla-
genden Charakter bekommt." Goethe nahm eine Bleifeder und teilte so ab:

Von / meinem / breiten / Lager / bin ich ver / trieben.

Wir sprachen über Rhythmus im allgemeinen und kamen darin überein,
daß sich über solche Dinge nicht denken lasse. „Der Takt", sagte Goethe,
„kommt aus der poetischen Stimmung, wie unbewußt. Wollte man darüber
denken, wenn man ein Gedicht macht, man würde verrückt und brächte
nichts Gescheites zustande."*

Towards Interpretation

1. Does Goethe in the passage above answer Eckermann's question?
2. How does Cupido (= Love) show his power in this poem?
3. What 'story' is implied in these lines?

J. H. W. Tischbein, "Goethe in der römischen Campagna"
Städelsches Kunstinstitut, Frankfurt

---

* J. P. Eckermann, *Gespräche mit Goethe*, ed. Conrad Höfer (Leipzig: Hesse und
Becker, 1913), 318f. (6. April 1829).

Römische Elegien[1] (1788-90)

I

Saget, Steine, mir an, o sprecht, ihr hohen Paläste!
  Straßen, redet ein Wort! Genius,[2] regst du dich nicht?
Ja, es ist alles beseelt in deinen heiligen Mauern,
  Ewige Roma; nur mir schweiget noch alles so still.
O wer flüstert mir zu, an welchem Fenster erblick' ich   5
  Einst[3] das holde Geschöpf, das mich versengend erquickt?[4]
Ahn' ich die Wege noch nicht, durch die ich immer und immer,
  Zu ihr und von ihr zu gehn, opfre die köstliche Zeit?
Noch betracht' ich Kirch' und Palast, Ruinen und Säulen,
  Wie ein bedächtiger Mann schicklich die Reise benutzt.   10
Doch bald ist es vorbei; dann wird ein einziger Tempel,
  Amors Tempel, nur sein, der den Geweihten empfängt.
Eine Welt zwar bist du, o Rom; doch ohne die Liebe
  Wäre die Welt nicht die Welt, wäre denn Rom auch nicht Rom.

V

Froh empfind' ich mich nun auf klassischem Boden begeistert;
  Vor- und Mitwelt[5] spricht lauter und reizender mir.
Hier befolg' ich den Rat, durchblättre die Werke der Alten[6]
  Mit geschäftiger Hand, täglich mit neuem Genuß.
Aber die Nächte hindurch hält Amor mich anders beschäftigt;   5
  Werd' ich auch halb nur gelehrt,[7] bin ich doch doppelt beglückt.
Und belehr' ich mich nicht, indem ich des lieblichen Busens

I: [1]Goethe here uses the word "elegy" in its ancient technical sense of "a poem written in distichs." The employment of this form in poems of mourning led to the modern usage of the word. The first two lines of the first elegy scan as follows:

$$- \smile \quad - \smile \quad \smile \quad - \quad \| \quad \smile \quad - \quad \smile \quad - \smile \quad - \smile$$
Saget, Steine, mir an, $\quad\|\quad$ o sprecht, ihr hohen Paläste!

$$- \smile \quad - \smile \quad \smile \quad - \quad \| \quad - \smile \smile \quad - \quad \smile \quad \smile \quad -$$
Straßen, redet ein Wort! $\quad\|\quad$ Genius, regst du dich nicht?

The first line is a hexameter, the second a classical pentameter. Together they make up a distich. Each distich usually forms a self-contained unit. The tone of the *"Römische Elegien"* — there are twenty-four in all — is one of celebration. They thankfully celebrate a Northerner's discovery of the possibility of harmony between mind and body, *Natur und Geist*. They are Goethe's most "pagan" poetry. The *Hamburger Ausgabe* of Goethe's works, I:489-96, contains an excellent discussion of these poems by Erich Trunz. [2]i.e., *genius loci* (spirit of the place) [3]'someday' [4]=*das mich erquickt, indem es mich versengt* (burns, i.e., with the fires of love)

V: [5]'past and present' [6]'the ancients' [7]'even if I only become half learned/taught'

Formen spähe,[8] die Hand leite die Hüften hinab?
Dann versteh' ich den Marmor[9] erst recht; ich denk' und vergleiche,
    Sehe mit fühlendem Aug', fühle mit sehender Hand.   10
Raubt die Liebste denn gleich mir einige Stunden des Tages,[10]
    Gibt sie Stunden der Nacht mir zur Entschädigung[11] hin.
Wird doch nicht immer geküßt, es wird vernünftig gesprochen;
    Überfällt sie der Schlaf, lieg' ich und denke mir viel.
Oftmals hab' ich auch schon in ihren Armen gedichtet   15
    Und des Hexameters Maß leise mit fingernder Hand
Ihr auf den Rücken gezählt. Sie atmet in lieblichem Schlummer,
    Und es durchglühet ihr Hauch mir bis ins Tiefste die Brust.
Amor schüret[12] die Lamp' indes und denket der Zeiten,
    Da er den nämlichen Dienst seinen Triumvirn[13] getan.   20

VII

O wie fühl' ich in Rom mich so froh! gedenk' ich der Zeiten
    Da mich ein graulicher[14] Tag hinten im Norden[15] umfing,
Trübe der Himmel und schwer auf meine Scheitel sich senkte,
    Farb- und gestaltlos die Welt um den Ermatteten lag,
Und ich über mein Ich, des unbefriedigten Geistes   5
    Düstre Wege zu spähn, still in Betrachtung versank.
Nun umleuchtet der Glanz des helleren Äthers die Stirne;
    Phöbus[16] rufet, der Gott, Formen und Farben hervor.
Sternhell glänzet die Nacht, sie klingt von weichen Gesängen,
    Und mir leuchtet der Mond heller als nordischer Tag.   10
Welche Seligkeit ward mir Sterblichem![17] Träum' ich? Empfänget
    Dein ambrosisches[18] Haus, Jupiter Vater, den Gast?
Ach! hier' lieg ich und strecke nach deinen Knieen die Hände
    Flehend aus.[19] O vernimm, Jupiter Xenius,[20] mich!
Wie ich hereingekommen, ich kann's nicht sagen: es faßte   15
    Hebe[21] den Wandrer und zog mich in die Hallen heran.
Hast du ihr einen Heroen herauf zu führen geboten?
    Irrte die Schöne? Vergib! Laß mir des Irrtums Gewinn!

---

[8]'explore'   [9]i.e., the marble statues   [10]*obgleich die Liebste mir ... raubt*   [11]'repayment'
[12]'trims'   [13]Amor's triumvirate: the Latin poets Ovid, Tibullus, and Propertius, all of
whom wrote elegiac verse on erotic themes.

VII: [14]'grayish'   [15]i.e., in Germany   [16]Phoebus Apollo, the sun god   [17]'what bliss fell
to the lot of a mortal like me'   [18]'ambrosial' Ambrosia was the food and drink of the
gods and made immortal those who partook of it.   [19]Embracing the knees was the ritual
gesture of pleading in antiquity. Cf. "Ganymed."   [20]*Xenius = der Gastfreundliche*; cf.
line 21.   [21]goddess of youth and cup-bearer to the gods (before Ganymede)

Deine Tochter Fortuna, sie auch! die herrlichen Gaben
    Teilt als ein Mädchen sie aus, wie es die Laune gebeut.[22]   20
Bist du der wirtliche Gott? O dann so verstoße den Gastfreund
    Nicht von deinem Olymp wieder zur Erde hinab!
„Dichter! wohin versteigest du dich?"[23] — Vergib mir: der hohe
    Kapitolinische Berg ist dir ein zweiter Olymp.[24]
Dulde mich, Jupiter, hier, und Hermes[25] führe mich später   25
    Cestius' Mal vorbei, leise zum Orkus hinab.[26]

„In goldnen Frühlingssonnenstunden"

In goldnen Frühlingssonnenstunden
Lag ich gebunden
An dies Gesicht.[1]
In holder Dunkelheit der Sinnen
Konnt' ich wohl diesen Traum beginnen,   5
Vollenden nicht.

The following nine poems come from the cycle, *West-östlicher Divan* (1819). *Divan* is a Persian word meaning 'gathering,' especially 'collection of poems.' Goethe's *Divan* is a cycle, in which the poems illuminate and refer to one another. It stands under the spiritual aegis of the great fourteenth-century Persian poet Hafis ('Knower of the Koran'), with whose work Goethe became acquainted in translation. The *West-östlicher Divan* is an astounding example of vitality in old age, of rebirth. The tone is sovereign, almost nonchalant, often ironical, the method highly symbolical. In no work is Goethe more wholly present and at the same time more elusive.

---

[22]=*gebietet* [23]'where do you think you're climbing to?' [24]*der hohe ... Olymp*: Jupiter has called the poet to order, he is not to think Olympus is for him. The poet explains that the Mons Capitolinus (a hill in Rome with the temple of Jupiter) is the god's "*second* Olympus"; the poet only meant to ask leave to stay *here* (l. 25). [25]*Hermes psychagogos* (soul-leader) [26]The pyramid of Cestius (*Mal* 'monument') is just outside the walls of Rome near the Protestant cemetery; the poet asks to be buried here. Through an irony of fate, not Goethe, but his son, was laid to rest in this cemetery, where Keats is also buried.

[1]The "vision" is usually presumed to be *Faust*. These lines (from around 1800) were hastily scribbled on a sheet of paper containing notes for that work.

Erschaffen und Beleben

Hans Adam war ein Erdenkloß,[1]
Den Gott zum Menschen machte;
Doch bracht' er aus der Mutter Schoß[2]
Noch vieles Ungeschlachte.[3]

Die Elohim[4] zur Nas' hinein   5
Den besten Geist ihm bliesen;
Nun schien er schon was mehr zu sein,
Denn er fing an zu niesen.

Doch mit Gebein und Glied und Kopf
Blieb er ein halber Klumpen,   10
Bis endlich Noah für den Tropf[5]
Das Wahre fand — den Humpen.[6]

Der Klumpe fühlt sogleich den Schwung,
So bald er sich benetzet,[7]
So wie der Teig durch Säuerung[8]   15
Sich in Bewegung setzet.

So, Hafis,[9] mag dein holder Sang,
Dein heiliges Exempel
Uns führen, bei der Gläser Klang,
Zu unsres Schöpfers Tempel.   20

Towards Interpretation
1. The tone of this poem — a drinking song — is what the Germans call
   burschikos (from *Bursche* 'university student'), that is, disrespectful
   and slangy. See if you can put your finger on some of the turns that
   help produce this effect. What role is played by foreign words? Does
   the poem say anything serious beyond its playfulness?
2. What does the title mean?

Es ist gut

Bei Mondenschein im Paradeis
Fand Jehovah im Schlafe tief
Adam versunken, legte leis
Zur Seit' ein Evchen, das auch entschlief.

---

[1]'lump of clay' [2]'womb' [3]'uncouthness' [4]'deity' (Hebrew, plu.) [5]'poor devil' [6]'tankard' (cf. Genesis 9:20) [7]'wets' (his throat) [8]'fermentation' [9]i.e., the Persian poet whose *Divan* in part inspired Goethe's cycle.

Da lagen nun, in Erdesschranken,[1]   5
Gottes zwei lieblichste Gedanken. —
„Gut!!!" rief er sich zum Meisterlohn,
Er ging sogar nicht gern davon.

Kein Wunder, daß es uns berückt,[2]
Wenn Auge frisch in Auge blickt,   10
Als hätten wir's so weit gebracht
Bei dem zu sein, der uns gedacht.[3]
Und ruft er uns: wohlan, es sei![4]
Nur, das beding' ich,[5] alle zwei.
Dich halten dieser Arme Schranken,[6]   15
Liebster von allen Gottes-Gedanken.[7]

Towards Interpretation
1. What does the title refer to?
2. Observe the rime scheme. What is symbolized by the change to couplets?
3. In the first stanza, God's thoughts are put in bonds of earth by the creation of Adam and Eve: the abolute expresses itself in the particular. What does the particular do, or strive to do, in the second stanza?

Selige Sehnsucht

Sagt es niemand, nur den Weisen,
Weil die Menge gleich verhöhnet,[1]
Das Lebend'ge will ich preisen,
Das nach Flammentod sich sehnet.

In der Liebesnächte Kühlung,   5
Die dich zeugte, wo du zeugtest,[2]
Überfällt dich fremde Fühlung,
Wenn die stille Kerze leuchtet.

Nicht mehr bleibest du umfangen
In der Finsternis Beschattung,   10

---

[1]'bonds of earth' [2]'enchants' [3]Lines 11-12: 'as though we had managed to catch up with Him who conceived of us' [4]'let there be!' [5]'I (the poet, not God) make only this condition' [6]'the bonds of these arms' [7]line 16 refers to *dich* (line 15)

[1]Cf. Matthew 7:6: "Give not that which is holy unto the dogs, neither cast ye your pearls before swine, lest they trample them under their feet, and turn and rend you." [2]'that begot you (and) where you begot.' The personal pronouns in this and the next two stanzas refer to *Schmetterling*, line 16.

Und dich reißet neu Verlangen
Auf zu höherer Begattung.[3]

Keine Ferne macht dich schwierig,[4]
Kommst geflogen und gebannt,[5]
Und zuletzt, des Lichts begierig[6]
Bist du Schmetterling verbrannt.[7]

Und so lang du das nicht hast,
Dieses: Stirb und werde![8]
Bist du nur ein trüber Gast
Auf der dunklen Erde.

15

20

Lesebuch

Wunderlichstes Buch der Bücher
Ist das Buch der Liebe;
Aufmerksam hab' ich's gelesen:
Wenig Blätter Freuden,
Ganze Hefte Leiden;
Einen Abschnitt macht die Trennung.
Wiedersehn — ein klein Kapitel,
Fragmentarisch! Bände Kummers,
Mit Erklärungen verlängert,
Endlos, ohne Maß.
O Nisami![1] — doch am Ende
Hast den rechten Weg gefunden;
Unauflösliches, wer löst es?
Liebende sich wieder findend.

5

10

---

[3]'procreation,' 'pairing' [4]'is too far for you' [5]'enthralled' [6]'greedy (for)' [7]The moth and the flame is an ancient symbol a) of love's impelling magnetism, b) of the longing of the soul for death in order to attain release from the body, c) of the union of the soul with the divine. The flame is death and also the way to higher existence. It is also a symbol of the divine (as is all light in Goethe). The applicability of the image is heightened by the fact that the ancients often represented the soul as a butterfly (or moth). [8]Cf. John 12:24: "Except a corn of wheat fall into the ground and die, it abideth alone: but if it die, it bringeth forth much fruit."

[1]Here Goethe confuses the Turkish poet Nisami with the Persian poet Nischani, whose poetry he was imitating.

„Ist's möglich, daß ich, Liebchen, dich kose"

Ist's möglich, daß ich, Liebchen, dich kose,
Vernehme[1] der göttlichen Stimme Schall!
Unmöglich scheint immer die Rose,
Unbegreiflich die Nachtigall.

„Volk und Knecht"

Suleika[1] [spricht]
Volk und Knecht und Überwinder,[2]
Sie gestehn, zu jeder Zeit,
Höchstes Glück der Erdenkinder
Sei nur die Persönlichkeit.

Jedes Leben sei zu führen,   5
Wenn man sich nicht selbst vermißt;
Alles könne man verlieren,
Wenn man bliebe, was man ist.

Hatem [antwortet]
Kann wohl sein! so wird gemeinet;
Doch ich bin auf andrer Spur: 10
Alles Erdenglück vereinet
Find' ich in Suleika nur.

Wie sie sich an mich verschwendet,
Bin ich mir ein wertes Ich;
Hätte sie sich weggewendet,   15
Augenblicks verlör' ich mich.

Nun, mit Hatem wär's zu Ende;
Doch schon hab' ich umgelost:[3]
Ich verkörpre mich behende
In den Holden, den sie kost.   20

Wollte, wo nicht gar ein Rabbi,
Das will mir so recht nicht ein,

---

[1]subject *ich* understood

[1]Hatem is Goethe's name for himself within the frame of the *Divan*; Suleika is Hatem's beloved, i.e., the female pole in the *Divan*. [2]i.e., everyone: common people, *Volk und Knecht*, and the mighty, *Überwinder*. [3]'changed my lot (*Los*)'

Doch Ferdusi, Motanabbi,[4]
Allenfalls der Kaiser sein.

Towards Interpretation

1. Hatem's answer takes up themes and concepts introduced in Suleika's poem, *Glück* (v. 3), *sich vermissen* (v. 6), *bleiben* (v.8). What is the implied synthesis of these elements?

„*Locken, haltet mich gefangen*"

Hatem [spricht]

Locken, haltet mich gefangen
In dem Kreise des Gesichts![1]
Euch geliebten braunen Schlangen
Zu erwidern hab' ich nichts.[2]

Nur dies Herz, es ist von Dauer,   5
Schwillt in jugendlichstem Flor;[3]
Unter Schnee und Nebelschauer
Rast ein Ätna dir[4] hervor.

Du[5] beschämst wie Morgenröte
Jener Gipfel ernste Wand,[6]   10
Und noch einmal fühlet Hatem
Frühlingshauch und Sommerbrand.

Schenke her![7] Noch eine Flasche!
Diesen Becher bring' ich ihr![8]
Findet sie ein Häufchen Asche,   15
Sagt sie: „Der verbrannte mir."[9]

Suleika [antwortet]

Nimmer will ich dich verlieren!
Liebe gibt der Liebe Kraft.
Magst du meine Jugend zieren
Mit gewalt'ger Leidenschaft.

---

[4]Abul Kasim Mansur, called Firdausi (ca. 940-1021), Persian epic poet; Motanabbi (ca. 915-965), Arabic poet.

[1]'Locks, keep me prisoner within the circle of the face (that you surround)' [2]i.e., my locks are no longer brown [3]'bloom' [4]ethical dative [5]The heart is addressed. [6]Elliptical: As the dawn 'shames' the mountains' forbidding sides, so the heart the poet's aging exterior. [7]'Cupbearer, come here!' [8]'This cup I pledge to her' [9]*mir* 'on my account'

Ach! wie schmeichelt's meinem Triebe,   5
Wenn man meinen Dichter preist:
Denn das Leben ist die Liebe,
Und des Lebens Leben Geist.

Towards Interpretation
Hatem:
1. What is the "snow and fog" of line 7? the "Etna" of line 8?
2. Translate carefully verses 9-12. How is the imagery of the second stanza varied in the third?
3. What name must one read for "Hatem" in verse 11 to make the rime?
4. Point out the thematic kinship between this poem and "Selige Sehnsucht."
Suleika:
5. What does Suleika see as Hatem's special contribution to their union?
6. Does Suleika mean to imply that *Geist* is all that is needed?

Wiederfinden

Ist es möglich! Stern der Sterne,
Drück' ich wieder dich ans Herz!
Ach, was ist die Nacht der Ferne
Für ein Abgrund, für ein Schmerz!
Ja, du bist es! meiner Freuden   5
Süßer, lieber Widerpart;[1]
Eingedenk[2] vergangner Leiden,
Schaudr' ich vor[3] der Gegenwart.

Als die Welt im tiefsten Grunde
Lag an Gottes ew'ger Brust,   10
Ordnet' er die erste Stunde
Mit erhabner Schöpfungslust,
Und er sprach das Wort: „Es werde!"
Da erklang ein schmerzlich Ach!
Als das All mit Machtgebärde   15
In die Wirklichkeiten brach.[4]

Auf tat sich[5] das Licht! So trennte
Scheu sich Finsternis von ihm,
Und sogleich die Elemente
Scheidend auseinander fliehn.   20

---

[1]'companion' [2]'mindful of' [3]=*bin ich erschüttert von* [4]i.e., became reality [5]*sich auftun* 'open'

Rasch, in wilden, wüsten Träumen
Jedes[6] nach der Weite rang,[7]
Starr, in ungemess'nen Räumen,
Ohne Sehnsucht, ohne Klang.

Stumm war alles, still und öde,   25
Einsam Gott zum erstenmal!
Da erschuf er Morgenröte,
Die erbarmte sich der Qual;
Sie entwickelte dem Trüben
Ein erklingend Farbenspiel,[8]   30
Und nun konnte wieder lieben
Was erst auseinander fiel.

Und mit eiligem Bestreben
Sucht sich, was sich angehört;
Und zu ungemess'nem Leben   35
Ist Gefühl und Blick gekehrt.
Sei's Ergreifen, sei es Raffen,[9]
Wenn es nur sich faßt und hält!
Allah braucht nicht mehr zu schaffen,
Wir erschaffen seine Welt.   40

So, mit morgenroten Flügeln,
Riß es mich[10] an deinen Mund,
Und die Nacht mit tausend Siegeln[11]
Kräftigt[12] sternehell den Bund.
Beide sind wir auf der Erde   45
Musterhaft[13] in Freud' und Qual,
Und sein zweites Wort: Es werde!
Trennt uns nicht zum zweitenmal.

Gott, All-Einheit, schuf Welt als seinen Gegen-Stand. Welt ist bedingt, begrenzt, ist daher Zweiheit, Polarität, ist Licht und Finsternis, rechts und
links, männlich und weiblich; und darum auch Leid (vgl. V. 14). Die Welt
war zunächst völlige Trennung von Gott, Chaos, jedes Ding vereinzelt
(24). Darum schuf er eine Kraft, die wieder alles zu allem in Beziehung
brachte (31-32). Ihr Sinnbild [symbol] sind die Farben. Das Licht (so lehrt
Goethes *Farbenlehre*) wird zur Farbe durch ein trübendes Medium. Gott ist

---

[6]i.e., *jedes Element* [7]'strove' [8]'It [the dawn] developed out of the darkness a ringing
play of colors.' Goethe did not accept Newton's theory that the colors of the spectrum
are caused by the refraction of white light, but maintained that white light was original
and an entity in itself, and that the prismatic colors were a modification of light through
das Trübe, darkness or unlighted matter. [9]'snatching' [10]'I was irresistibly drawn'
[11]'seals' (the stars) [12]'confirms' [13]'typical,' 'serving as models'

das Licht; die Materie ist Finsternis. Aber die Materie steigert sich ins Leichte, Geistige empor; das Licht fällt in sie hinein; so entsteht das Spektrum der Farben, in seiner Mitte das Rot (27). Auch die welt der Töne ist Verbindung, kosmische Ordnung, Harmonie (24, 30). Gott und Welt sind nun verbunden und ebenso alle Dinge untereinander: das polar Getrennte zieht sich gegenseitig an [is mutually attracted], und im Einander-Finden erlebt es sein höchstes Glück; denn Einheit ist Gottes Wesen, und jede Vereinigung sein Gleichnis, ein Hinstreben zu ihm. Das All erfuhr erst das *schmerzlich Ach* der Vereinzelung und dann das *ungemess'ne Leben* seliger Vereinigung; so auch das Ich und das Du; darum sind sie beispielhaft, *musterhaft* in Qual und Freude. . . .*

Towards Interpretation

1. The last stanza returns to the lover's embrace of stanza 1. In what context does the poet now understand his love?
2. How do lovers reverse the process of Creation?

„In tausend Formen"

In tausend Formen magst du dich verstecken,
Doch, Allerliebste, gleich erkenn' ich dich;
Du magst mit Zauberschleiern dich bedecken,
Allgegenwärtige, gleich erkenn' ich dich.

An der Zypresse reinstem, jungem Streben,   5
Allschöngewachsne, gleich erkenn' ich dich;
In des Kanales reinem Wellenleben,
Allschmeichelhafte, wohl erkenn' ich dich.

Wenn steigend sich der Wasserstrahl entfaltet,
Allspielende, wie froh erkenn' ich dich;   10
Wenn Wolke sich gestaltend umgestaltet,
Allmannigfaltige, dort erkenn' ich dich.

An des geblümten Schleiers Wiesenteppich,
Allbuntbesternte, schön erkenn' ich dich;
Und greift umher ein tausendarm'ger Eppich,[1]   15
O Allumklammernde, da kenn' ich dich.

Wenn am Gebirg der Morgen sich entzündet,
Gleich, Allerheiternde, begrüß' ich dich,

Goethes Werke, Hamburger Ausgabe, ed. Erich Trunz *et al.*, 14 vols. (Hamburg: Wegner, ¹1952), 2:571.

[1]Generic word for vines, especially 'ivy'

Dann über mir der Himmel rein sich ründet,
Allherzerweiternde, dann atm' ich dich.   20

Was ich mit äußerm Sinn, mit innerm kenne,
Du Allbelehrende, kenn' ich durch dich;
Und wenn ich Allahs Namenhundert nenne,
Mit jedem klingt ein Name nach für dich.

[End of selections from *West-östlicher Divan*]

„*Dämmrung senkte sich von oben*" (1827)

Dämmrung senkte sich von oben,
Schon ist alle Nähe fern;
Doch zuerst emporgehoben
Holden Lichts der Abendstern![1]
Alles schwankt ins Ungewisse,   5
Nebel schleichen in die Höh';
Schwarzvertiefte Finsternisse
Widerspiegelnd ruht der See.

Nun am östlichen Bereiche
Ahn' ich Mondenglanz und -glut,   10
Schlanker Weiden Haargezweige
Scherzen auf der nächsten Flut.
Durch bewegter Schatten Spiele
Zittert Lunas Zauberschein,
Und durchs Auge schleicht die Kühle   15
Sänftigend ins Herz hinein.

Towards Interpretation
1. A critic has maintained that the order in this poem is "eternally and objectively true." Is the language of the poem similarly objective? (Hint: *hold, schleichen, scherzen,* etc.)
2. Can you surmise by whom or what the Evening Star is *emporgehoben*?
3. What do you think the poet means to imply by *Kühle*: a) meteorologically, b) emotionally?
4. Translate lines 5-8 and 9-12.
5. Would you say this is a pure "nature" poem? Defend your standpoint.

---

[1] = *doch zuerst wird der Abendstern mit seinem holden Licht emporgehoben*

St. Nepomuks Vorabend[1]
Karlsbad, den. 15. Mai 1820

Lichtlein schwimmen auf dem Strome,
Kinder singen auf der Brücken,[2]
Glocke, Glöckchen fügt vom Dome
Sich der Andacht, dem Entzücken.

Lichtlein schwinden, Sterne schwinden;   5
Also löste sich die Seele
Unsres Heil'gen, nicht verkünden
Durft' er anvertraute Fehle.[3]

Lichtlein, schwimmet! Spielt, ihr Kinder!
Kinder-Chor, o singe, singe!   10
Und verkündiget nicht minder,
Was den Stern zu Sternen bringe.[4]

Proœmion[1] (1816)

Im Namen dessen, der Sich selbst erschuf!
Von Ewigkeit in schaffendem Beruf;
In Seinem Namen, der den Glauben schafft,
Vertrauen, Liebe, Tätigkeit und Kraft;
In Jenes Namen, der, so oft genannt,   5
Dem Wesen nach[2] blieb immer unbekannt:

So weit das Ohr, so weit das Auge reicht,
Du findest nur Bekanntes, das Ihm gleicht,
Und deines Geistes höchster Feuerflug
Hat schon am Gleichnis, hat am Bild genug;   10
Es zieht dich an, es reißt dich heiter fort,[3]
Und wo[4] du wandelst, schmückt sich[5] Weg und Ort;
Du zählst nicht mehr, berechnest keine Zeit,
Und jeder Schritt ist Unermeßlichkeit.

---

[1]St. Nepomuk of Bohemia was thrown into the Moldau because he would not betray to King Wenceslas IV the secret of the confessional of Queen Johanna (6f.). As his body was carried downstream it was accompanied by strange lights or stars, which showed that his soul had already been received into heaven (11f.). In honor of their saint, the Bohemians hold lighted processions on the water on St. Nepomuk's Eve. [2]feminine singular [3]'misdeed' [4]'what brings the star (the saint) to the stars'

[1]'Foreword,' 'Preface' (Greek) This and the next two poems appear at the beginning of the collection "Gott und Welt" [2]'in his essence' [3]*reißt ... fort* 'carries along,' 'compels' [4]'wherever' [5]Cf. Greek *kosmēó* (from *kosmós*) 'order,' 'adorn'

Towards Interpretation

1. Make a careful translation of verses 7-10, paying special attention to the words *gleicht* and *Gleichnis*.
2. The last two verses of this poem describe a mystical experience — time is no more and "every step is infinity"; the individual is united with the One. Yet the individual remains in the world of natural phenomena, which is the world of individuation, and God remains in his essence unknowable. Through what then is the mystical experience possible?
3. Compare the mystical experience here to that a) in "Ganymed", b) in Klopstock's "Die Frühlingsfeier," c) in Knorr von Rosenroth's "Morgenlied," d) in Brockes' "Mondschein."

„Was wär ein Gott, der nur von außen stieße"

Was wär ein Gott, der nur von außen stieße,
Im Kreis das All am Finger laufen ließe![1]
Ihm ziemt's,[2] die Welt im Innern zu bewegen,
Natur in Sich, Sich in Natur zu hegen,[3]
So daß, was in Ihm lebt und webt und ist,   5
Nie Seine Kraft, nie Seinen Geist vermißt.[4]

„Im Innern ist ein Universum auch"

Im Innern ist ein Universum auch;
Daher der Völker löblicher Gebrauch,[1]
Daß jeglicher das Beste, was er kennt,
Er Gott, ja seinen Gott benennt,
Ihm Himmel und Erden übergibt,[2]   5
Ihn fürchtet und womöglich[3] liebt.

Towards Interpretation

1. First poem: Is God seen here as *imminent* or *immanent*?
2. Second poem: Compare with „Das Göttliche."
3. Both poems: The divine is here seen under two aspects. Which is the moral aspect?

---

[1]The figure is that of spinning a ball on one's finger.   [2]'it befits Him'   [3]'comprise'
[4]'lacks'

[1]'praisewothy custom'   [2]'surrenders'   [3]'perhaps even'

ΔΑΙΜΩΝ *Dämon*[1] (1817)

Wie an dem Tag, der dich der Welt verliehen,
Die Sonne stand zum Gruße der Planeten,[2]
Bist alsobald[3] und fort und fort gediehen
Nach dem Gesetz, wonach du angetreten.
So mußt du sein, dir kannst du nicht entfliehen,   5
So sagten schon Sibyllen, so Propheten;[4]
Und keine Zeit und keine Macht zerstückelt
Geprägte Form,[5] die lebend sich entwickelt.

Towards Interpretation

1. Point out the connection between the doctrine expressed here and a)
"Mahomets Gesang," b) "Harzreise im Winter."

Epirrhema[1] (1820)

Müsset[2] im Naturbetrachten
Immer eins wie alles achten;
Nichts ist drinnen, nichts ist draußen:
Denn was innen, das ist außen.
So ergreifet ohne Säumnis[3]   5
Heilig öffentlich Geheimnis.

Towards Interpretation

1. In his *Maximen und Reflexionen*, Goethe says: "Man suche nichts
hinter den Phänomenen, sie selbst sind die Lehre." Applying this dic-
tum to "Epirrhema," try to show how nature can be both *öffentlich*
and a *Geheimnis*. Why is it also *heilig*? (Cf. "Prooemion" and "Was
wär ein Gott. . . .")
2. What light does "Epirrhema" throw on the last stanza of "Harzreise
im Winter"?

---

[1]'individuality,' 'personality,' 'innate character'   [2]i.e., the constellation under which
one is born; purely emblematic — Goethe did not believe in astrology.   [3]'forthwith'
[4]*Sibylle*, pagan prophetess; *Prophet*, Biblical prophet   [5]'Stamped form,' i.e., form
predestined to evolve according to a certain pattern. W. N. Guthrie translates, "the
shape, seed hidden." This is of course the doctrine of inward or organic form applied
to the development of the personality.

[1]'one word more' (Greek)   [2]Supply *ihr*.   [3]'hesitation'

[*Lied des Türmers*][1]

Zum Sehen geboren,
Zum Schauen bestellt,
Dem Turme geschworen,[2]
Gefällt mir die Welt.

Ich blick' in die Ferne   5
Ich seh' in der Näh'
Den Mond und die Sterne,
Den Wald und das Reh.

So seh' ich in allen
Die ewige Zier,[3]   10
Und wie mir's gefallen,
Gefall' ich auch mir.

Ihr glücklichen Augen,
Was je ihr gesehn,
Es sei wie es wolle,   15
Es war doch so schön!

Towards Interpretation
1. Lines 5-6: Why *blick'* in line 5 and *seh'* in line 6?
2. Lines 11-12: What is the precise meaning of these lines?
3. Last stanza: What is symbolized by the interruption of the rime scheme (*Augen – wolle*)?
4. Lynceus ('lynx-eyed') is a man who can see through everything; in addition his post is on a tower: What does Goethe imply by putting these words in the mouth of such a figure?

Marianne von Willemer (1784-1860)

Until the last decade of her life, only one other person knew for certain that Willemer had written great poetry, and that person was Goethe. She met Goethe for the first time in 1814, shortly before her marriage to Johann von

---

[1]Goethe's last lyrical poem (1831). These lines actually have no title; they are sung by the watchman Lynceus in *Faust II* at the beginning of the scene "Tiefe Nacht" (lines 11,288-303), where they contrast with Faust's inner darkness. [2]'bound by oath to the duties of tower watchman' [3]*die ewige Zier*, i.e., the cosmic order; cf. "Proœmion": "Und wo du wandelst, *schmückt sich* Weg und Ort."

Willemer, a prosperous banker who had taken her into his household as his ward when she was sixteen. The following year, Goethe spent five weeks with the Willemers at their estate outside Frankfurt, after which they joined him in Heidelberg for three days. It was during this period that Goethe composed the "Buch Suleika" section of his *West-östlicher Divan*, and it was then that it took on its final form as a poetic "dialog" between the lovers, Hatem and Suleika. While it was known that Marianne von Willemer had inspired powerful feelings in the sixty-six-year-old Goethe and came to serve as the embodiment of Suleika for him, no one seems to have shared the real secret, which Willemer herself kept until 1851, long after Goethe's death: five of the Suleika-poems in the *Divan* were actually written by her. Although they corresponded for the rest of Goethe's life, they never saw each other again. Many women inspired Goethe to poetic expression, but Marianne von Willemer may have been the only one who was actually able to share in the creative act itself.

„*Was bedeutet die Bewegeung*"[1]

Suleika [spricht]

Was bedeutet die Bewegung?
Bringt der Ostwind frohe Kunde?
Seiner Schwingen frische Regung
Kühlt des Herzens tiefe Wunde.

Kosend spielt er mit dem Staube,   5
Jagt ihn auf in leichten Wölkchen,
Treibt zur sichern Rebenlaube
Der Insekten frohes Völkchen.

Lindert sanft der Sonne Glühen,
Kühlt auch mir die heißen Wangen,   10
Küßt die Reben noch im Fliehen,
Die auf Feld und Hügel prangen.

---

[1]This poem was written on a journey from Frankfurt to visit Goethe in Heidelberg, September 23, 1815. It appears in the *Divan* with some modifications as an answer to the poem "Deinem Blick mich zu bequemen. . . ."

Und mich soll sein leises Flüstern
Von dem Freunde lieblich grüßen;
Eh' noch diese Hügel düstern,   15
Sitz' ich still zu seinen Füßen.

Und du magst nun weiterziehen,
Diene Frohen und Betrübten;
Dort, wo hohe Mauern glühen,
Finde ich den Vielgeliebten.   20

Ach, die wahre Herzenskunde,
Liebeshauch, erfrischtes Leben
Wird mir nur aus seinem Munde,
Kann mir nur sein Atem geben.

„Ach, um deine feuchten Schwingen"[1]

Suleika [spricht]

Ach, um deine feuchten Schwingen,
West, wie sehr ich dich beneide:
Denn du kannst ihm Kunde bringen,
Was ich durch die Trennung leide.

Die Bewegung deiner Flügel   5
Weckt im Busen stilles Sehnen;
Blumen, Augen, Wald und Hügel
Stehn bei deinem Hauch in Tränen.

Doch dein mildes, sanftes Wehen
Kühlt die wunden Augenlider;   10
Ach, für Leid müßt' ich vergehen,
Hofft' ich nicht, wir sehn uns wieder.

Geh' denn hin zu meinem Lieben,
Spreche sanft zu seinem Herzen;
Doch vermeid', ihn zu betrüben   15
Und verschweig' ihm meine Schmerzen.

Sag' ihm nur, doch sag's bescheiden:
Seine Liebe sei mein Leben;
Freudiges Gefühl von beiden
Wird mir seine Nähe geben.   20

---

[1]This poem was written on the return from Heidelberg after her final meeting with
Goethe, September 26, 1815. It appears in the *Divan* with slight modifications as an
answer to the poem "Es klingt so prächtig. . . ."

Friedrich von Schiller (1759-1805)

Schiller's poetry revolves around three poles: the good, the true, the beautiful. Of the poems included here, "Die Götter Greichenlands" and "Nänie" are concerned with the nature of the beautiful — their center is esthetic; "Die Kraniche des Ibykus" concerns the triumph of good over evil — its center is moral; "Die Worte des Glaubens" and "Die Worte des Wahns" concern human freedom — they have to do with the nature of truth.

Schiller has a deep-seated longing to see the ideal embodied in the real, the noumenal in the phenomenal. To find the *Idee in der Erscheinung* fills him with passionate though unselfinterested enthusiasm and he knows how to inspire this enthusiasm in us, his readers. This is the beauty of Schiller's poetry, whether lyric or dramatic; it is also the beauty of his philosophical essays, which rank very high, perhaps highest, among all his writings.

In "Die Götter Greichenlands" Schiller mourns the passing of what was, as he conceives it, the world's most perfect exemplification of the ideal in the real, the mythical pantheism of early Greece. Not that he wants to reinstate the gods of Greece — no one is more aware of the impossibility of such a thing than Schiller — but he wants to bring to our consciousness a sense of loss, and thus make us see the nature of the age we live in, its barrenness (from a poetic standpoint) and its lack of beauty. Because a mechanical explanation of the universe, such as that of the Enlightenment in which Schiller lived, excludes the ideal, the noumenal, this means for Schiller that it excludes the possibility of beauty.

Die Götter Greichenlands

Da ihr noch die schöne Welt regieret[1]
An der Freude leichtem Gängelband,[2]
Selige Geschlechter noch geführet,[1]
Schöne Wesen aus dem Fabelland!
Ach, da euer Wonnedienst[3] noch glänzte,   5
Wie ganz anders, anders war es da!

---

[1]Supply *habt.* [2]'leading harness (for small children)' [3]'rapturous rites'

Da man deine Tempel noch bekränzte,
Venus Amathusia![4]

Da der Dichtung zauberische Hülle
Sich noch lieblich um die Wahrheit wand —   10
Durch die Schöpfung floß da Lebensfülle,
Und was nie empfinden wird, empfand.
An der Liebe Busen sie zu drücken,
Gab man höhern Adel der Natur,[5]
Alles wies den eingeweihten Blicken,[6]   15
Alles eines Gottes Spur.

Wo jetzt nur, wie unsre Weisen sagen,
Seelenlos ein Feuerball sich dreht,
Lenkte damals seinen Goldnen Wagen
Helios in stiller Majestät.   20
Diese Höhen füllten Oreaden,[7]
Eine Dryas[8] lebt' in jenem Baum,
Aus den Urnen lieblicher Najaden[9]
Sprang der Ströme Silberschaum.

Jener Lorbeer wand sich einst um Hilfe,[10]   25
Tantals Tochter schweigt in diesem Stein,[11]
Syrinx' Klage tönt aus jenem Schilfe,[12]
Philomelas Schmerz aus diesem Hain;[13]
Jener Bach empfing Demeters Zähre,
Die sie um Persephonen geweint,[14]   30
Und von diesem Hügel rief Cythere
Ach, umsonst! dem schönen Freund.[15]

Zu Deukalions Geschlechte[16] stiegen
Damals noch die Himmlischen herab;
Pyrrhas schöne Töchter zu besiegen,   35
Nahm der Leto Sohn[17] den Hirtenstab.
Zwischen Menschen, Göttern und Heroen[18]
Knüpfte Amor einen schönen Bund,

---

[4]Venus (=Aphrodite) of Amathus in Cyprus, where the goddess was specially honored. [5]dative [6]'to the initiated glance' [7]mountain nymphs [8]tree spirit [9]water nymphs [10]Daphne, protesting the attentions of Apollo, was turned into a laurel. [11]Niobe, daughter of Tantalus, did not cease lamenting her children until she turned to stone. [12]Syrinx, fleeing from Pan, was changed into a reed. [13]Philomela, endlessly lamenting the death of her son, became a nightingale. [14]Demeter's daughter Persephone was abducted by Hades, lord of the Underworld. [15]*Cythere* =Aphrodite, who lamented her 'handsome friend' Adonis, slain by a boar. [16]'Deukalion's race' is the human race; Pyrrha (l. 35) was his wife. [17]Apollo [18]Greek heroes were often demi-gods or at least supermen.

Sterbliche mit Göttern und Heroen
Huldigten[19] in Amathunt.[20]   40

Finstrer Ernst und trauriges Entsagen
War aus eurem heitern Dienst verbannt;
Glücklich sollten alle Herzen schlagen,
Denn euch war der Glückliche verwandt.[21]
Damals war nichts heilig als das Schöne,   45
Keiner Freude schämte sich der Gott,
Wo die keusch errötende Kamöne,[22]
Wo die Grazie gebot.

Eure Tempel lachten gleich Palästen,
Euch verherrlichte das Heldenspiel   50
An des Isthmus kronenreichen Festen,[23]
Und die Wagen donnerten zum Ziel.
Schön geschlung'ne, seelenvolle Tänze
Kreisten um den prangenden Altar,
Eure Schläfe schmückten Siegeskränze,   55
Kronen euer duftend Haar.

Das Evóe muntrer Thyrsusschwinger
Und der Panther prächtiges Gespann
Meldeten den großen Freudebringer,[24]
Faun und Satyr taumeln ihm voran;   60
Um ihn springen rasende Mänaden,
Ihre Tänze loben seinen Wein,
Und des Wirtes[25] braune Wangen laden
Lustig zu dem Becher ein.

Damals trat kein gräßliches Gerippe   65
Vor das Bett des Sterbenden. Ein Kuß
Nahm das letzte Leben von der Lippe,
Seine Fackel senkt' ein Genius.[26]
Selbst des Orkus strenge Richterwage[27]
Hielt der Enkel einer Sterblichen,   70

---

[19]'paid homage to' [20]=Amathus (see l. 8) [21]i.e., he who was happy was god-like. [22]a Roman Muse [23]Games held on the Isthmus of Corinth in honor of the gods; *kronenreich* because attended by many kings (or because many crowns of victory were awarded?) [24]Bacchantes (maenads) swinging the thyrsus and crying "*Evoe!*" accompanied Bacchus (Dionysos) as he rode in his car drawn by panthers. Cf. Claudius, "Der Frühling." [25]Bacchus himself [26]Sleep and Death (Hypnos and Thanatos) were represented as winged deities with torches turned upside down. [27]'scales of judgment'

Und des Thrakers seelenvolle Klage
Rührte die Erinnyen.²⁸

Seine Freuden traf der frohe Schatten
In Elysiens Hainen wieder an,
Treue Liebe fand den treuen Gatten   75
Und der Wagenlenker²⁹ seine Bahn;
Linus'³⁰ Spiel tönt die gewohnten Lieder,
In Alcestens Arme sinkt Admet,³¹
Seinen Freund erkennt Orestes wieder,³²
Seine Pfeile Philoktet.³³   80

Höh're Preise stärkten da den Ringer
Auf der Tugend arbeitvoller Bahn,
Großer Taten herrliche Vollbringer
Klimmten zu den Seligen hinan;
Vor dem Wiederforderer der Toten   85
Neigte sich der Götter stille Schar;
Durch die Fluten leuchtet dem Piloten
Vom Olymp das Zwillingspaar.³⁴

Schöne Welt, wo bist du? Kehre wieder,
Holdes Blütenalter der Natur!   90
Ach, nur in dem Feenland der Lieder
Lebt noch deine fabelhafte Spur.
Ausgestorben trauert das Gefilde,
Keine Gottheit zeigt sich meinem Blick,
Ach, von jenem lebenswarmen Bilde   95
Blieb der Schatten nur zurück.

Alle jene Blüten sind gefallen
Von des Nordes schauerlichem Wehn;
Einen zu bereichern unter allen,³⁵
Mußte diese Götterwelt vergehn.   100
Traurig such' ich an dem Sternenbogen,
Dich, Selene,³⁶ find' ich dort nicht mehr,
Durch die Wälder ruf' ich, durch die Wogen,
Ach, sie widerhallen leer!

---

²⁸The Thracian is Orpheus, who successfully pled for the release of his wife Eurydice from the Underworld. *Erinnyen,* 'Furies' ²⁹'charioteer' ³⁰legendary father of song ³¹Alceste, wife of Admetus, died in her husband's stead ³²Orestes' friend = Pylades; cf. Goethe's *Iphigenie,* Act III, sc. 3. ³³famous archer ³⁴Heroes, 'splendid accomplishers of great deeds,' were sometimes translated to the gods (*Seligen*). The examples given are Hercules (*Wiederforderer der Toten,* i.e., of the dead Alceste) and Castor and Pollux, *das Zwillingspaar.* ³⁵The One is the Christian God. ³⁶Greek for 'moon' and also the moon goddess (Latin *Luna*); Schiller finds the moon, but not "Selene."

Unbewußt der Freuden, die sie schenket,   105
Nie entzückt von ihrer Herrlichkeit,
Nie gewahr des Geistes, der sie lenket,
Sel'ger nie durch meine Seligkeit,
Fühllos selbst für ihres Künstlers Ehre,[37]
Gleich dem toten Schlag der Pendeluhr,   110
Dient sie knechtisch dem Gesetz der Schwere,[38]
Die entgötterte Natur.

Morgen wieder neu sich zu entbinden,
Wühlt sie heute sich ihr eignes Grab,
Und an ewig gleicher Spindel winden   115
Sich von selbst die Monde auf und ab.[39]
Müßig kehrten zu dem Dichterlande
Heim die Götter, unnütz einer Welt,
Die, entwachsen ihrem Gängelbande,
Sich durch eignes Schweben hält.   120

Ja, sie kehrten heim, und alles Schöne,
Alles Hohe nahmen sie mit fort,
Alle Farben, alle Lebenstöne,
Und uns blieb nur das entseelte Wort.
Aus der Zeitflut weggerissen, schweben   125
Sie gerettet auf des Pindus[40] Höhn:
Was unsterblich im Gesang soll leben,
Muß im Leben untergehn.[41]

Towards Interpretation

1. What adjectives does Schiller use to distinguish the Greek world from the modern world and vice versa?

Die Teilung der Erde

„Nehmt hin die Welt!" rief Zeus von seinen Höhen
Den Menschen zu. „Nehmt, sie soll euer sein;
Euch schenk' ich sie zum Erb' und ew'gen Lehen;[1]
Doch teilt euch brüderlich darein."

---

[37]'the honor her artist does her' [38]'law of gravity' [39]Allusion to Thessalian witches who pulled the moon down by a thread — their services are no longer needed. [40]range of mountains in northern Greece. [41]See "Nänie," p. 165f.

[1]'fief'

Da eilt, was Hände hat, sich einzurichten,   5
Es regte sich geschäftig jung und alt.
Der Ackermann griff nach des Feldes Früchten,
Der Junker birschte² durch den Wald.

Der Kaufmann nimmt, was seine Speicher³ fassen,
Der Abt wählt sich den edeln Firnewein,⁴   10
Der König sperrt die Brücken und die Straßen⁵
Und sprach: „Der Zehente⁶ ist mein."

Ganz spät, nachdem die Teilung längst geschehen,
Naht der Poet, er kam aus weiter Fern';
Ach, da war überall nichts mehr zu sehen,   15
Und alles hatte seinen Herrn.

„Weh' mir! so soll ich denn allein von allen
Vergessen sein, ich, dein getreuster Sohn?"
So ließ er laut der Klage Ruf erschallen
Und warf sich hin vor Jovis'⁷ Thron.   20

„Wenn du im Land der Träume dich verweilet",⁸
Versetzt der Gott, „so had're nicht mit mir.
Wo warst du denn, als man die Welt geteilet?"⁸
„Ich war", sprach der Poet, „bei dir.

Mein Auge hing an deinem Angesichte,   25
An deines Himmels Harmonie mein Ohr;
Verzeih' dem Geiste, der, von deinem Lichte
Berauscht, das Irdische verlor!" —

„Was tun?" spricht Zeus. „Die Welt ist weggegeben,
Der Herbst,⁹ die Jagd, der Markt ist nicht mehr mein.   30
Willst du in meinem Himmel mit mir leben:
So oft du kommst, er soll dir offen sein."

Towards Interpretation
1. What social classes do *Herbst*, *Jagd*, and *Markt* (line 30) represent?
2. Where does the poet belong in society?

---

²=*ging auf die Jagd* ³'warehouses' ⁴=*alter, daher kostbarer Wein* ⁵The king closes
off the roads so that he can collect tolls more easily. ⁶'tithe' ⁷'Jove's' ⁸Supply auxiliary. ⁹'harvest'

Die Kraniche des Ibykus

1

Zum Kampf der Wagen und Gesänge,[1]
Der auf Korinthus' Landesenge
Der Griechen Stämme froh vereint,
Zog Ibykus, der Götterfreund.
Ihm schenkte[2] des Gesanges Gabe,   5
Der Lieder süßen Mund Apoll;
So wandert' er, an leichtem Stabe,
Aus Rhegium,[3] des Gottes voll.[4]

2

Schon winkt auf hohem Bergesrücken
Akrokorinth des Wandrers Blicken,[5]   10
Und in Poseidons Fichtenhain
Tritt er mit frommem Schauder ein.
Nichts regt sich um ihn her, nur Schwärme
Von Kranichen begleiten ihn,
Die fernhin nach des Südens Wärme   15
In graulichtem[6] Geschwader ziehn.

3

„Seid mir gegrüßt, befreund'te Scharen,
Die mir zur See Begleiter waren!
Zum guten Zeichen nehm' ich euch,
Mein Los, es ist dem euren gleich: 20
Von fernher kommen wir gezogen
Und flehen um ein wirtlich[7] Dach.
Sei uns der Gastliche[8] gewogen,[9]
Der von dem Fremdling wehrt die Schmach!"

4

Und munter fördert er die Schritte   25
Und sieht sich in des Waldes Mitte;
Da sperren auf gedrangem[10] Steg
Zwei Mörder plötzlich seinen Weg.

---

[1]The Isthmian Games, held every four years near Corinth in honor of Poseidon (Neptune). *Wagen und Gesänge*, i.e., chariot races and choral (dramatic) contests [2]The subject is *Apoll*, line 6. [3]city in southern Italy [4]'full of the god,' i.e., inspired [5]'beckons to the wanderer's eyes'; *Akrokorinth*, fortified hill (acropolis) above Corinth [6]'grayish' [7]'hospitable' [8]Zeus, protector of strangers; cf. Goethe's 7th *Römische Elegie* [9]'well disposed' [10]=*engem*

Zum Kampfe muß er sich bereiten,
Doch bald ermattet sinkt die Hand,   30
Sie hat der Leier zarte Saiten,
Doch nie des Bogens Kraft gespannt.

5

Er ruft die Menschen an, die Götter,
Sein Flehen dringt zu keinem Retter;
Wie weit er auch die Stimme schickt,   35
Nichts Lebendes wird hier erblickt.
„So muß ich hier verlassen sterben,
Auf fremdem Boden, unbeweint,
Durch böser Buben[11] Hand verderben,
Wo auch kein Rächer mir erscheint!"   40

6

Und schwer getroffen sinkt er nieder,
Da rauscht der Kraniche Gefieder;
Er hört, schon kann er nicht mehr sehn,
Die nahen Stimmen furchtbar krähn.
„Von euch, ihr Kraniche dort oben,   45
Wenn keine andre Stimme spricht,
Sei meines Mordes Klag' erhoben!"
Er ruft es, und sein Auge bricht.

7

Der nackte Leichnam wird gefunden,
Und bald, obgleich entstellt[12] von Wunden,   50
Erkennt der Gastfreund in Korinth
Die Züge,[13] die ihm teuer sind.
„Und muß ich so dich wieder finden,
Und hoffte mit der Fichte Kranz
Des Sängers Schläfe zu umwinden,   55
Bestrahlt von seines Ruhmes Glanz!"

8

Und jammernd hören's alle Gäste,
Versammelt bei Poseidons Feste,
Ganz Greichenland ergreift der Schmerz,
Verloren hat ihn jedes Herz.   60

---

[11]'rogues' [12]'disfigured' (It is of course Ibykus, not his friend, who is *entstellt von Wunden*.) [13]'features'

Und stürmend drängt sich zum Prytanen[14]
Das Volk, es fordert seine Wut,[15]
Zu rächen des Erschlag'nen Manen,[16]
Zu sühnen[17] mit des Mörders Blut.

9

Doch wo[18] die Spur, die aus der Menge,   65
Der Völker flutendem Gedränge,[19]
Gelocket von der Spiele Pracht,
Den schwarzen Täter kenntlich macht?
Sind's Räuber, die ihn feig erschlagen?[20]
Tat's neidisch ein verborg'ner Feind?   70
Nur Helios vermag's zu sagen,
Der alles Irdische bescheint.

10

Er[21] geht vielleicht mit frechem Schritte
Jetzt eben durch der Griechen Mitte,
Und während ihn die Rache sucht,   75
Genießt er seines Frevels Frucht.
Auf ihres eignen Tempels Schwelle
Trotzt er vielleicht den Göttern, mengt
Sich dreist in jene Menschenwelle
Die dort sich zum Theater drängt.   80

11

Denn Bank an Bank gedränget sitzen,
Es brechen fast der Bühne[22] Stützen,
Herbeigeströmt von fern und nah,
Der Griechen Völker wartend da;
Dumpfbrausend[23] wie des Meeres Wogen,   85
Von Menschen wimmelnd, wächst der Bau
In weiter stets geschweiftem[24] Bogen
Hinauf bis in des Himmels Blau.[25]

12

Wer zählt die Völker, nennt die Namen,
Die gastlich[26] hier zusammenkamen?   90

---

[14]highest official [15]'its (the people's) rage demands' [16]*Manen* 'spirits of forebears'
[17]'atone' [18]Supply *findet man*. [19]Line 66 is in apposition to *Menge*. [20]Supply
auxiliary. [21]the murderer [22]here, the theater itself [23]'hollowly echoing' [24]'curved'
[25]The Greek theater was an open stadium. [26]'as guests'

Von Kekrops Stadt, von Aulis' Strand,
Von Phocis, vom Spartanerland,
Von Asiens entleg'ner[27] Küste,
Von allen Inseln kamen sie
Und horchen von dem Schaugerüste[28]   95
Des Chores grauser[29] Melodie,

13

Der streng und ernst, nach alter Sitte,
Mit langsam abgemess'nem Schritte
Hervortritt aus dem Hintergrund,
Umwandelnd des Theaters[30] Rund.   100
So schreiten keine ird'schen Weiber!
Die zeugete kein sterblich Haus![31]
Es steigt das Riesenmaß der Leiber
Hoch über Menschliches hinaus.[32]

14

Ein schwarzer Mantel schlägt die Lenden,[33]   105
Sie schwingen in entfleischten Händen
Der Fackel düsterrote Glut,
In ihren Wangen fließt kein Blut;
Und wo die Haare lieblich flattern,
Um Menschenstirnen freundlich wehn,   110
Da sieht man Schlangen hier und Nattern
Die giftgeschwoll'nen Bäuche blähn.

15

Und schauerlich, gedreht im Kreise,
Beginnen sie des Hymnus Weise,[34]
Der durch das Herz zerreißend dringt,   115
Die Bande um den Frevler[35] schlingt.
Besinnungraubend, herzbetörend[36]
Schallt der Erinnyen[37] Gesang;
Er schallt, des Hörers Mark[38] verzehrend,
Und duldet nicht der Leier Klang:[39]   120

---

[27]'distant' [28]'tiers of seats' [29]= *Grauen erregend* [30]here, the stage [31]'mortal race'
[32]The Greek tragic actor wore the cothurn, a boot with a very thick sole. [33]'flaps
against the loins' [34]*Weise* 'melody' [35]'evil-doer' [36]*betören* 'beguile' [37]the Furies
[38]'marrow' [39]The Furies' fierce chorus is incompatible with the sweet sound of the
lyre.

16

„Wohl dem, der frei von Schuld und Fehle
Bewahrt die kindlich reine Seele!
Ihm dürfen wir nicht rächend nahn.
Er wandelt frei des Lebens Bahn.
Doch wehe, wehe, wer verstohlen   125
Des Mordes schwere Tat vollbracht!
Wir heften uns an seine Sohlen,
Das furchtbare Geschlecht der Nacht.[40]

17

„Und glaubt er fliehend zu entspringen,
Geflügelt sind wir da, die Schlingen   130
Ihm werfend um den flücht'gen Fuß,
Daß er zu Boden fallen muß.
So jagen wir ihn, ohn' Ermatten,
Versöhnen kann uns keine Reu',
Ihn fort und fort bis zu den Schatten,   135
Und geben ihn auch dort nicht frei."

18

So singend, tanzen sie den Reigen,
Und Stille, wie des Todes Schweigen,
Liegt überm ganzen Hause schwer,
Als ob die Gottheit nahe wär'.   140
Und feierlich, nach alter Sitte,
Umwandelnd des Theaters Rund,
Mit langsam abgemess'nem Schritte
Verschwinden sie im Hintergrund.

19

Und zwischen Trug und Wahrheit schwebet   145
Noch zweifelnd jede Brust und bebet,
Und huldiget[41] der furchtbar'n Macht,
Die richtend im Verborg'nen wacht,
Die unerforschlich, unergründet
Des Schicksals dunkeln Knäuel[42] flicht,   150
Dem tiefen Herzen sich verkündet,
Doch fliehet vor dem Sonnenlicht.

[40]Line 128 is in apposition to *wir*, line 127. [41]'pay homage to' [42]'skein'

20

Da hört man auf den höchsten Stufen
Auf einmal eine Stimme rufen:
„Sieh da! Sieh da, Timotheus,   155
Die Kraniche des Ibykus!" —
Und finster plötzlich wird der Himmel,
Und über dem Theater hin
Sieht man in schwärzlichem Gewimmel,
Ein Kranichheer vorüberziehn.   160

21

„Des Ibykus!" — Der teure Name
Rührt jede Brust mit neuem Grame,[43]
Und wie im Meere Well' auf Well',
So läuft's von Mund zu Munde schnell:
„Des Ibykus? den wir beweinen?   165
Den eine Mörderhand erschlug?
Was ist's mit dem? Was kann er meinen?
Was ist's mit diesem Kranichzug?"

22

Und lauter immer wird die Frage,
Und ahnend fliegt's mit Blitzesschlage   170
Durch alle Herzen: „Gebet acht,
Das ist der Eumeniden[44] Macht!
Der fromme Dichter wird gerochen,[45]
Der Mörder bietet selbst sich dar.
Ergreift ihn, der das Wort gesprochen,   175
Und ihn, an den's gerichtet war!"

23

Doch dem[46] war kaum das Wort entfahren,
Möcht' er's im Busen gern bewahren —
Umsonst! der schreckenbleiche Mund
Macht schnell die Schuldbewußten kund.   180
Man reißt und schleppt sie vor den Richter,
Die Szene[47] wird zum Tribunal,
Und es gestehn die Bösewichter,
Getroffen von der Rache Strahl.

---

[43]'bitter sorrow' [44]'the good-tempered ones' (Greek), euphemism for the *Erinnyen*, the Furies [45]'is being avenged' [46]i.e., the guilty one [47]'Theater'; the word is used here with purposeful ambiguity.

Schiller's artistically most perfect ballad is a product of the so-called "Balladenjahr," the year 1797, in which he and Goethe worked together in friendly rivalry to produce some of the most famous art ballads in German literature. Goethe's interest in the "Kraniche" was especially marked, though the poem remains thoroughly Schillerian.

Stanzas 1-3 contain the exposition.* A connection is established between the poet-singer Ibykus, on his way to the feast of Poseidon in Corinth, and the flocks of cranes that have been accompanying him by sea and land. Like him, they come from afar; like him, they seek a *wirtlich Dach*.

Stanzas 4-6 tell of the wanton murder in the sacred wood. Ibykus calls upon the cranes to avenge him, futile as such an act seems — only in the world of fairy-tale might cranes assume such a role. But the ballad, by a circuitous path, makes the impossible possible. This path leads to the Greek theater and the true center of the poem.

In *stanzas 7-8* the corpse is found. All Greece is incensed over the murder of its beloved singer.

Stanzas 9-10 introduce with great artistry the theatrical performance and the *theme of the hidden*; as the poem progresses the two threads are further interwoven. The murder belongs of course to the hidden; it is hidden by the very multitude of those who would revenge it. Schiller depicts with great plasticity the swarms of people streaming into the theater.

Stanzas 13-15 give an inaccurate, but unforgettable, picture of the Greek chorus. It is a *Chor von erhabener Scheußlichkeit* (von Wiese), which now in

Stanzas 16-17 begins a song that robs men of their judgment and leads the guilty to acts of self-destruction. The chorus tells of the sure retribution that must overtake any guilty person whom they, the Furies, pursue: nemesis.

Stanzas 18-19 bring the stage action to a close and describe the effect of the chorus upon the audience (and, by suggestion, upon the reader). What we have just witnessed was illusion, art theater. The Eumenides on the stage are not actual spirits of retribution, but only their artistic representation. Yet they, an illusion, reveal, and even in a sense become, reality. The audience is still as death *Als ob die Gottheit nahe wär'*; it hovers between *Trug und Wahrheit*, solemnly aware of the power *die richtend im Verborg'nen wacht*. Were they the Eumenides? At any rate appearance becomes reality to this extent: the mummers of the spirits of retribution become the retributive power that overtakes the murderers who watch them. For a moment, art exceeds the mere "appearance of truth" and becomes "truth itself." Schiller believed that art alone can transform the real into the ideal (which is truth), and so reestablish the moral order.

Stanza 20. Not that these hardened murderers suddenly break down in tearful confession. We know only indirectly that they have been struck, if not

---

*Our analysis follows in broad outline that of Benno von Wiese, "Friedrich von Schiller," in his *Die deutsche Lyrik* (Düsseldorf: Schwann-Bagel, ²1981), 1:351-63.

exactly moved perhaps, by what they have seen and heard. Then the cranes appear and they betray themselves.

Stanzas 21-23. The moral order is reestablished: the poet has been avenged through poetry.

Towards Interpretation

1. From at least line 81 to line 156 (more than nine stanzas) we hear nothing of Ibykus. Is this a defect or a virtue? Why?
2. In line 156, does the murderer mean he sees the *same* cranes that were present at the scene of the crime? Is it necessary that they be the same cranes?
3. Does Ibykus have a special relationship with the gods (e.g., Zeus, *der Gastfreundliche,* lines 21ff.) in the way the Poet does in "Die Teilung der Erde"?

Die Worte des Glaubens

Drei Worte nenn' ich euch, inhaltschwer,
Sie gehen von Munde zu Munde;
Doch stammen sie nicht von außen her,
Das Herz nur gibt davon Kunde.
Dem Menschen ist aller Wert geraubt,   5
Wenn er nicht mehr an die drei Worte glaubt.

Der Mensch ist frei geschaffen, ist frei,
Und würd' er in Ketten geboren.
Laßt euch nicht irren des Pöbels Geschrei,
Nicht Mißbrauch rasender Toren![1]   10
Vor dem Sklaven, wenn er die Kette bricht,
Vor dem freien Menschen erzittert nicht!

Und die Tugend, sie ist kein leerer Schall,
Der Mensch kann sie üben im Leben,
Und sollt' er auch[2] straucheln überall,   15
Er kann nach der göttlichen[3] streben,

---

[1]Probably a reference to the excesses of the French Revolution when the mob misused its self-given (physical) freedom and so became the slave of its own desires. To be free in Schiller's sense is to use our innate reason (*Vernunft*) to gain mastery over our physical chains even while being forced to submit to them. This is of course ideal, not physical, freedom. [2]'and even if he should' [3]Supply *Tugend.*

Und was kein Verstand der Verständigen sieht,
Das übet in Einfalt ein kindlich Gemüt.[4]

Und ein Gott ist, ein heiliger Wille lebt,
Wie auch[5] der menschliche wanke;   20
Hoch über der Zeit und dem Raume webt
Lebendig[6] der höchste Gedanke.
Und ob[7] alles in ewigem Wechsel kreist,
Es beharret[8] im Wechsel ein ruhiger Geist.

Die drei Worte bewahret[9] euch, inhaltschwer,   25
Sie pflanzet[9] von Munde zu Munde,
Und stammen sie gleich nicht von außen her,[10]
Euer Inn'res gibt davon Kunde.
Dem Menschen ist nimmer sein Wert geraubt,
Solang' er noch an die drei Worte glaubt.   30

Die Worte des Wahns

Drei Worte hört man, bedeutungschwer,
Im Munde der Guten und Besten;
Sie schallen vergeblich, ihr Klang ist leer,
Sie können nicht helfen und trösten.
Verscherzt[1] ist dem Menschen des Lebens Frucht,   5
Solang' er die Schatten zu haschen sucht.

Solang' er glaubt an die goldene Zeit,
Wo das Rechte, das Gute wird siegen;
Das Rechte, das Gute führt ewig Streit,
Nie wird der Feind ihm erliegen,[2]   10
Und erstickst du ihn nicht in den Lüften frei,
Stets wächst ihm die Kraft aus der Erde neu.[3]

Solang' er glaubt, daß das buhlende Glück[4]
Sich dem Edeln vereinigen werde;
Dem Schlechten folgt es mit Liebesblick,   15

---

[4]*Ein kindlich Gemüt* (mind, disposition) practices virtue without 'stumbling' because its
natural inclinations coincide with the strictest moral demands. This is Schiller's concept of the *schöne Seele*. [5]'however much' [6]*webt lebendig*, cf. *leben und weben* 'to
live and pursue one's natural ways' [7]=*obwohl* [8]'there persists' [9]imperative [10]'even if
they do not derive from without'

[1]'forfeited through folly' [2]'the enemy will never succumb to it' [3]Allusion to the giant
Anteus, who remained invincible as long as he could touch his mother, the earth. Hercules strangled him in mid-air. [4]'wanton fortune'

Nicht dem Guten gehöret die Erde.
Er[5] ist ein Fremdling, er wandert aus
Und suchet ein unvergänglich Haus.

Solang' er glaubt, daß dem ird'schen Verstand
Die Wahrheit je wird erscheinen;   20
Ihren Schleier hebt keine sterbliche Hand,
Wir können nur raten und meinen.
Du kerkerst den Geist in ein tönend Wort,
Doch der freie wandelt im Sturme fort.

Drum, edle Seele, entreiß' dich dem Wahn   25
Und den himmlischen Glauben bewahre!
Was kein Ohr vernahm, was die Augen nicht sahn,
Es ist[6] dennoch, das Schöne, das Wahre!
Es ist nicht draußen, da sucht es der Tor,
Es ist in dir, du bringst es ewig hervor.   30

Wahn is delusion, error; cf. *wähnen* 'ween,' 'be of the opinion.' The two poems, "Worte des Glaubens" and "Worte des Wahns," stand in clear relationship to each other. One editor of Schiller, Ludwig Bellermann, makes the following comment:

> *Glaube*, daß wir frei sind, also unabhängig von allem Bösen außer uns und in uns, aber *wähne* nicht, daß das Böse in der wirklichen Welt jemals völlig besiegt werden könne. *Glaube*, daß wir Tugend üben können, aber *wähne* nicht, daß dem Tugendhaften das (äußere) Glück folge. *Glaube*, daß es einen Gott gibt, aber *wähne* nicht, daß wir die Wahrheit (deren letzter Grund in Gott liegt) voll erkennen können. Wer sich solchem Wahn hingibt, sucht „Schatten zu haschen."*

Nänie[1]

Auch das Schöne muß sterben! Das[2] Menschen und Götter
                      bezwinget,
  Nicht die eherne Brust rührt es des stygischen Zeus.[3]

---

[5]i.e., *der Gute*   [6]*ist* is used here in a pregnant sense: 'it *does* exist'

*Ludwig Bellermann, ed., *Schillers Werke*, 14 vols. (Leipzig und Wien: Bibliographisches Institut, n.d. [1895?]), 1:258, note 1.

[1]*Totenlied, Klagegesang bei der Leiche'* (Lat. *naenia*)   [2]'that which'   [3]The 'Stygian (from *Styx*) Zeus' is Hades, lord of the Underworld.

Einmal nur erweichte die Liebe den Schattenbeherrscher,[4]
Und an der Schwelle noch, streng, rief er zurück sein
                                                      Geschenk.
Nicht stillt Aphrodite dem schönen Knaben die Wunde,   5
Die in den zierlichen Leib grausam der Eber geritzt.[5]
Nicht errettet den göttlichen Held die unsterbliche Mutter,
Wann er, am skäischen Tor[6] fallend, sein Schicksal erfüllt.
Aber sie steigt aus dem Meer mit allen Töchtern des Nereus,
Und die Klage hebt an[7] um den verherrlichten Sohn.[8]   10
Siehe, da weinen die Götter, es weinen die Göttinnen alle,
Daß das Schöne vergeht, daß das Vollkommene stirbt.
Auch ein Klaglied zu sein im Mund der Geliebten ist herrlich,
Denn das Gemeine geht klanglos zum Orkus hinab.

Unlike Goethe's "Römische Elegien," Schiller's "Nänie" is an elegy both in content and form. The elegiac distich, we know, consists of a hexameter plus a pentameter: in the hexameter the rhetorical line unfolds, in the pentameter it sinks to a close. Schiller himself has given the classic description of this form:

> Im Hexameter steigt des Springquells flüssige Säule,
> Im Pentameter drauf fällt sie melodisch herab.

In "Nänie" each distich forms a separate unit: seven distichs, seven sentences. The flowing quality of the hexameter is constantly limited by the pentameter and brought to a complete stop — there is no enjambement between distichs, neither is there any between hexameter and pentameter. In content, this means here: *Auch das Schöne muß sterben.*

In the middle of the pentameter two stressed syllables collide, making a heavy pause, the caesura, necessary. Schiller uses this to point up the "message": on one side of the caesura, beauty, life; on the other, death:

> An der Schwelle noch, stréng, ‖ ríef er zurück sein Geschenk.

(The *Schwelle* is the *Schwelle des Lebens*.)

> Die in den zierlichen Leíb ‖ gráusam der Eber geritzt.

It is very interesting to observe what happens in the fourth distich (lines 7-8), which occupies the center of the elegy. Here the caesura in the pentameter falls in such a way as to divide the syntactical unit unnaturally:

---

[4]*Schattenbeherrscher* =Hades; the 'one time' was when Orpheus pleaded for Eurydice. Hades granted his plea, but on condition that Orpheus not look back at her until he had reached the Upper World. Overcome by longing, Orpheus did look back just as he was about to reenter the Upper World ("an der Schwelle") and Eurydice was taken from him. [5]Cf. "Die Götter Griechenlands," ll. 30ff. [6]a gate of Troy [7]*anheben* =*anfangen* [8]For this whole passage see the 24th book of *The Odyssey.* The hero is Achilles, his mother Thetis, a sea divinity. The daughters of Nereus are her sisters.

Wann er, am skäischen Tór ‖ fállend, sein Schicksal erfüllt.

The syntax here disregards the break between life and death. In other words, the form gives symbolic indication that death is not the end of the beautiful and perfect, but the fulfillment of Achilles' fate by and through which he becomes *vollkommen*. The next distich then begins with an *Aber* (in contrast to the three foregoing *Nicht*'s), introducing that part of the poem that tells why *das Schöne* does not perish utterly.

Let us now see what happens *formally* in the last three distichs. In the first part of the poem it was the beautiful that flowered in the hexameter and "died" in the pentameter; in the last part it is the *lament* for the beautiful that rises with the hexameter and falls with the pentameter. The latter, we note, no longer contains antithetical contrasts (though there is balance: *Daß das Schöne vergeht, ‖ daß das Vollkommene stirbt*). The form here implies acceptance of death even the death of the beautiful; the contrast — which implied that such an event was a *Widersinn* — is gone. The last verse is not halved, the balance being cancelled by the hovering stress on *klánglòs*. The development of the elegy has now progressed beyond lament and death — it has reached a new plane, that of eternal life in the spirit. The sorrow lamented has been overcome by the lamentation. This is what the form implies and the content expresses. The earthly, no matter how beautiful, must die and its death must be accepted, but it may nonetheless live forever in the spirit, where it is truly *herrlich*: "*Was unsterblich im Gesang soll leben, / Muß im Leben untergehn.*"

Towards Interpretation

1. Look up "Achilles" in a classical dictionary and note what bargain he struck in order to achieve lasting fame.
2. Analyze this poem by stating its content in *general* terms, according to the following division: Lines 1-2; 3-4; 5-6; 7-10 + 11-12; 13-14. Do you notice a *Steigerung* in this progression?
3. According to line 13, what has Achilles become?

Columbus

Steure, mutiger Segler! Es mag der Witz dich verhöhnen,
Und der Schiffer am Steu'r senken[1] die lässige Hand.
Immer, immer nach West! Dort muß die Küste sich zeigen,
Liegt sie doch deutlich und liegt schimmernd vor deinem
                                                                Verstand.
Traue dem leitenden Gott und folge dem schweigenden
                                                                Weltmeer![2]   5
Wär' sie[3] noch nicht, sie stieg' jetzt aus den Fluten empor.
Mit dem Genius[4] steht die Natur in ewigem Bunde:
Was der eine verspricht, leistet die andre gewiß.

Johann von Salis-Seewis (1762-1834)

Lied, zu singen bei einer Wasserfahrt

Wir ruhen, vom Wasser gewiegt,
Im Kreise vertraulich und enge;
Durch Eintracht wie Blumengehänge
Verknüpft und in Reihen gefügt;
Uns sondert von lästiger Menge   5
Die Flut, die den Nachen umschmiegt.

So gleiten, im Raume vereint,
Wir auf der Vergänglichkeit Wellen,
Wo Freunde sich innig gesellen
Zum Freunde, der redlich es meint,   10
Getrost, weil die dunkelsten Stellen
Ein Glanz aus der Höhe bescheint.

Ach trüg' uns die fährliche[1] Flut
Des Lebens so friedlich und leise!
O drohte nie Trennung dem Kreise,   15
Der sorglos um Zukunft[2] hier ruht!
O nähm' uns am Ziele der Reise
Elysiums Busen in Hut![3]

---

[1]dependent on *mag*   [2]=Latin *oceanus*, Atlantic   [3]=*die Küste*   [4]used here in the English sense

[1]= *gefährliche*   [2]=*ohne Sorgen um die Zukunft*   [3]'care, keeping'

Verhallen mag unser Gesang
Wie Flötenhauch schwinden das Leben;   20
Mit Jubel und Seufzern verschweben
Des Daseins zerfließender Klang!
Der Geist wird verklärt sich erheben,
Wann Lethe sein[4] Fahrzeug verschlang.

Friedrich Hölderlin (1770-1843)

Hölderlin continues and carries to its highest point the vatic tradition encountered with full force in German literature for the first time in the poetry of Klopstock. Hölderlin is above all a seer, but a seer as poet, not as philosopher or moralist.

No one can read Hölderlin without being struck by the intense purity of emotion and sense of reverence that pervade his work. The clarity and simple grandeur of his language, with its broad, generic vocabulary, is a reflection of an inner state. There is no "wit" in Hölderlin, nor is there any pretense. He is, to characterize him by contrast with a poet known to most English-speaking readers, the diametrical opposite of Heine. Hölderlin and Heine might, indeed, be taken as the extreme limits of the German spirit.

If reverence is the keynote in Hölderlin, it is because he is by nature a worshipper. The central event in his work is the epiphany, the manifestation of the god. When the god appears, the historical night in which we live will give birth to day, disunity will be overcome, and man again become one with all creation. All his visions are visions of the advent of the god, all his hope is hope of this advent, his despair the despair of it, and all his indignation at his own nation is indignation at men of little faith in the Coming. In three things especially Hölderlin found a warranty of the divine and a promise of the millennium: in nature, in a woman ("Diotima"), and in (his conception of) the ancient Greeks. For this reason these form the constant theme of his work. Hölderlin was raised in a strict pietistic atmosphere and educated to become a Lutheran minister, a post he never filled. Among his fellow students at the theological seminary in Tübingen were the later philosophers Hegel and

---

[4]=*des Geistes*

Schelling. Although, except for the figure of Christ, Christian dogma plays no direct role in Hölderlin's mature poetry, his whole thinking about the divine and the new age to come can be called secularized eschatology* of a Pietistic kind, a pattern clearly evident beneath the surface of his work. Hölderlin's later "hymns," none of which is included here, are of extreme difficulty and have been the subject of much investigation and speculation.

Hölderlin is not a poet of private moods and feelings in the sense of the *Erlebnisdichter* (the younger Goethe, for example). The "I" in his work is meant to be in relation to something transcending any personal pain or bliss. He wanted it to be representative; he wanted it to represent his people, the *Germania* and *heilig Herz der Völker* of his longing, a people ready to receive the god. But it was not to be. Hölderlin was largely rejected or misunderstood in his own time and throughout the 19th century. During the last thirty-eight years of his life he was hopelessly insane. The first complete edition of his works did not appear until eighty years after his death. It remained for another poet and his followers (Stefan George and his circle) to rediscover Hölderlin.

„Da ich ein Knabe war . . ."

Da ich ein Knabe war,
Rettet' ein Gott mich oft
Vom Geschrei und der Rute[1] der Menschen,
Da spielt' ich sicher und gut
Mit den Blumen des Hains,   5
Und die Lüftchen des Himmels
Spielten mit mir.

Und wie du[2] das Herz
Der Pflanzen erfreust,
Wenn sie entgegen dir[2]   10
Die zarten Arme strecken,

So hast du[2] mein Herz erfreut,
Vater Helios! und, wie Endymion,
War ich dein Liebling,
Heilige Luna![3]   15

---

*scheme of salvation looking forward to a "millenium" of some nature, i.e., a "thousand year" rule under divine guidance

[1]'rod,' 'scourge' [2]refers to *Helios*, line 13 [3]The beautiful shepherd Endymion was given immortality, perpetual youth and perpetual sleep so as to make love with the moon-goddess, Luna, in his eternal dreams.

O all ihr treuen
Freundlichen Götter!
Daß ihr wüßtet,
Wie euch meine Seele geliebt!

Zwar damals rief ich noch nicht   20
Euch mit Namen, auch ihr
Nanntet mich nie, wie die Menschen sich nennen,
Als kennten sie sich.

Doch kannt' ich euch besser,
Als ich je die Menschen gekannt,   25
Ich verstand die Stille des Aethers,[4]
Der Menschen Worte verstand ich nie.

Mich erzog der Wohllaut
Des säuselnden Hains
Und lieben lernt' ich   30
Unter[5] den Blumen.

Im Arme der Götter wuchs ich groß.

Towards Interpretation
1. Is man here seen as the master of nature or vice versa?
2. A defection is implied — defection from what? Is the *Ich* of the poem also guilty of this defection? Wherein does this defection especially show itself?
3. Compare lines 1-7 with 24-27 and comment on the auditory imagery.

An die Parzen[1]

Nur Einen Sommer gönnt, ihr Gewaltigen!
    Und einen Herbst zu reifem Gesange mir,
        Daß williger mein Herz, vom süßen
            Spiele gesättiget, dann mir sterbe.

Die Seele, der im Leben ihr göttlich Recht   5
    Nicht ward,[2] sie ruht auch drunten im Orkus nicht;

---

[4]*Der Aether*, upper regions of space, the empyrean, in Hölderlin a more intense word for the sky, connoting a harmony undisturbed by the misunderstandings of men. Hölderlin makes the *Aether* his most personal diety.   [5]'among'

[1]The three "Fates" who spin, measure, and cut the thread of life.   [2]*der ... ward* 'which did not receive its ...'; *der* is dative feminine.

> Doch ist mir einst das Heil'ge, das am
> Herzen mir liegt, das Gedicht, gelungen,
>
> Willkommen dann, o Stille der Schattenwelt!
> Zufrieden bin ich wenn auch mein Saitenspiel[3]   10
> Mich nicht hinab geleitet; Einmal
> Lebt' ich, wie Götter, und mehr bedarf's nicht.[4]

Towards Interpretation

1. This poem is prayer. To whom? For that?
2. What comparison is the basis of the metaphor in lines 1-2?
3. Comment on the attitude toward poetry expressed here. In whose work have we found this attitude before?
4. "An die Parzen" is written in a stanzaic form we have seen before. Which one?
5. Read Keats' sonnet "When I Have Fears" and compare and contrast it to "An die Parzen."

Hyperions Schicksalslied

> Ihr wandelt droben im Licht
> Auf weichem Boden, selige Genien![1]
> Glänzende Götterlüfte
> Rühren euch leicht,
>   Wie die Finger der Künstlerin   5
> Heilige Saiten.
>
> Schicksallos, wie der schlafende
> Säugling, atmen die Himmlischen;[1]
> Keusch bewahrt
>   In bescheidener Knospe,   10
> Blühet ewig
> Ihnen der Geist,
>   Und die seligen Augen
> Blicken in stiller
>   Ewiger Klarheit.   15
>
> Doch uns ist gegeben,
> Auf keiner Stätte zu ruhn,
> Es schwinden, es fallen
> Die leidenden Menschen

---

[3]'lyre' [4]'and no more is needed'

[1]= *Umschreibung für die Götter*

Blindlings von einer   20
    Stunde zur andern,
        Wie Wasser von Klippe
        Zu Klippe geworfen,
            Jahr lang ins Ungewisse hinab.

Towards Interpretation
1. Explain why *Klarheit* (line 15) is in the dative rather than the accusative.
2. Comment on the imagery of temporality in the final strophe. How does Hölderlin convey a sense of timelessness in the first two strophes?
3. How does the form of the poem (especially in the last strophe) contribute to its meaning?

An unsere großen Dichter[1]

Des Ganges[2] Ufer hörten des Freudengotts
    Triumph, als allerobernd vom Indus[2] her
        Der junge Bacchus kam, mit heil'gem
        Weine vom Schlafe die Völker weckend.[3]

O weckt, ihr Dichter! weckt sie vom Schlummer auch,   5
    Die jetzt noch schlafen, gebt die Gesetze, gebt
        Uns Leben, siegt, Heroën! ihr nur
        Habt der Eroberung Recht, wie Bacchus.

Towards Interpretation
1. The first stanza of this ode tells a piece of mythical news: the triumphal procession of Bacchus through Asia, bringing the East the blessings of civilization and awakening the peoples with "sacred wine." The second stanza interprets the triumph of Bacchus metaphorically. Explain how.

---

[1]i.e., Goethe and Schiller [2]Rivers of India; the Indus is west of the Ganges. [3]Dionysos (Bacchus) brought the Asians the cultivation of the vine, symbolic here of civilization itself.

Die scheinheiligen Dichter

Ihr kalten Heuchler, sprecht von den Göttern nicht!
Ihr habt Verstand! ihr glaubt nicht an Helios,
    Noch an den Donnerer und Meergott;
        Tot ist die Erde, wer mag ihr danken?[1] —

Getrost,[2] ihr Götter! zieret ihr doch[3] das Lied,   5
    Wenn schon aus euren Namen die Seele schwand,
        Und ist ein großes Wort vonnöten,[4]
            Mutter Natur! so gedenkt man deiner.[5]

Towards Interpretation

1. What role do the gods play in the works of the *scheinheilige Dichter?*
   Why have the *Scheinheilige* no real need of the gods? Why do they
   use them?
2. In what poem have we met the idea of the *tote Erde* before?
3. How would you characterize the tone of this poem?

Sonnenuntergang

Wo bist du? trunken dämmert die Seele mir
Von aller deiner Wonne; denn eben ist's,
    Daß ich gelauscht, wie goldner Töne
        Voll, der entzückende Sonnenjüngling

Sein Abendlied auf himmlischer Leier spielt';[1]   5
    Es tönten rings die Wälder und Hügel nach.
        Doch fern ist er zu frommen Völkern,
            Die ihn noch ehren,[2] hinweggegangen.

Towards Interpretation

1. How does the setting sun reveal its divine nature?
2. Are the *goldne Töne* heard by anyone besides the poet? What do the
   last two lines imply about the poet's contemporaries?

---

[1]'who wants to thank her (the earth)?'   [2]'take heart'   [3]'after all you do adorn'
[4]=*notwendig* [5]'then they remember you'

---

[1]The sun-god Apollo is also the god of music. [2]The Hyperboreans, a mythical people
who were said to live at the end of the earth in a land of perpetual sunshine, are especially associated with the cult of Apollo.

„Geh unter, schöne Sonne . . ."

Geh unter, schöne Sonne, sie achteten
  Nur wenig dein,[1] sie kannten dich, Heil'ge, nicht,
    Denn mühelos und stille bist du
      Über den Mühsamen aufgegangen.

Mir gehst du freundlich unter und auf, o Licht!   5
  Und wohl erkennt mein Auge dich, Herrliches!
    Denn göttlich stille ehren lernt' ich,
      Da Diotima[2] den Sinn mir heilte.

O du des Himmels Botin! wie lauscht' ich dir!
  Dir, Diotima! Liebe! wie sah von dir   10
    Zum goldnen Tage dieses Auge
      Glänzend und dankend empor. Da rauschten

Lebendiger die Quellen, es atmeten
  Der dunkeln Erde Blüten mich liebend an,
    Und lächelnd über Silberwolken   15
      Neigte sich segnend herab der Aether.[3]

Towards Interpretation

1. Did the *Ich* of this ode ever belong to the *Mühsamen*? What makes the *Mühsamen mühsam*?
2. Indicate how Diotima, who reveals to the poet the meaning of the sun becomes identified with it in the course of the poem. How does German grammar help make this identification possible?
3. Comment on the significance of the enjambement, verses 12ff.
4. In the last part of the poem a marriage between heaven and earth, a frequent occurrence in Hölderlin's poetry, is consummated. Show how this is indicated.

---

[1]*dein* (gen. with *achten*) 'to (of) you' [2]*Diotima*: In Plato's *Symposium*, a wise woman who teaches Socrates about the nature of love; in Hölderin's life, the beautiful and intelligent wife of the Frankfurt banker, Gontard, in whose house the poet was employed as a tutor. Susette Gontard became for Hölderlin the living embodiment of his dreams of Greece and the first and last great happiness of his life. [3]Cf. "Da ich ein Knabe war. . . ."

Abbitte[1]

Heilig Wesen! gestört hab' ich die goldene
Götterruhe dir oft, und der geheimeren
Tieferen Schmerzen[2] des Lebens
Hast du manche gelernt von mir.

O vergiß es, vergib! gleich dem Gewölke dort   5
Vor dem friedlichen Mond, geh' ich dahin, und du
Ruhst und glänzest in deiner
Schöne wieder, du süßes Licht!

Menons Klagen um Diotima[1]

1

Täglich geh' ich heraus, und such' ein Anderes immer,
    Habe längst sie befragt, alle die Pfade des Lands;
Droben die kühlenden Höhn, die Schatten alle besuch' ich,
    Und die Quellen; hinauf irret der Geist und hinab,
Ruh' erbittend; so flieht das getroffene Wild[2] in die Wälder,   5
    Wo es um Mittag sonst sicher im Dunkel geruht;
Aber nimmer[3] erquickt sein grünes Lager das Herz ihm,
    Jammernd und schlummerlos treibt es der Stachel umher.
Nicht die Wärme des Lichts, und nicht die Kühle der Nacht
                                                           hilft,
    Und in Wogen des Stroms taucht es die Wunden umsonst.   10
Und wie ihm vergebens die Erd' ihr fröhliches Heilkraut[4]
    Reicht, und das gärende Blut keiner der Zéphyre stillt,
So, ihr Lieben![5] auch mir, so will es scheinen,[6] und niemand
    Kann von der Stirne mir nehmen den traurigen Traum?

2

Ja! es frommet[7] auch nicht, ihr Todesgötter! wenn einmal
    Ihr ihn haltet, und fest habt den bezwungenen Mann,
Wenn ihr Bösen[8] hinab in die schaurige Nacht ihn genommen,
    Dann zu suchen, zu flehn, oder zu zürnen mit euch,

---

[1]'prayer for forgiveness' [2]*der ... Schmerzen*, partitive genitive

1: [1]An elegy. Menon (Greek) means 'he who remains/abides/waits'; for Diotima, see "Geh unter, schöne Sonne. . . ." [2]'stricken deer' [3]=*nicht mehr* [4]'healing herb' [5]'my loved ones' [6]*auch ... scheinen* 'and thus also it is with me, it seems'

2: [7]*frommen* 'be of avail' [8]i.e., the *Todesgötter*

Oder geduldig auch wohl im furchtsamen Banne[9] zu wohnen,   5
  Und mit Lächeln von euch hören das nüchterne Lied.
Soll es sein, so vergiß dein Heil, und schlummere klanglos![10]
  Aber doch quillt ein Laut hoffend im Busen dir auf,
Immer kannst du noch nicht, o meine Seele! noch kannst du's
  Nicht gewohnen,[11] und träumst mitten im eisernen Schlaf!   10
Festzeit hab ich nicht, doch möcht' ich die Locke bekränzen;
  Bin ich allein denn nicht? aber ein Freundliches muß
Fernher nahe[12] mir sein, und lächeln muß ich und staunen,
  Wie so selig doch auch mitten im Leide mir ist.

3

Licht der Liebe! scheinest du denn auch Toten,[13] du goldnes!
  Bilder aus hellerer Zeit, leuchtet ihr mir in die Nacht?[14]
Liebliche Gärten seid,[15] ihr abendrötlichen Berge,
  Seid willkommen und ihr, schweigende Pfade des Hains,
Zeugen[16] himmlischen Glücks, und ihr, hochschauende Sterne,   5
  Die mir damals so oft segnende Blicke gegönnt!
Euch, ihr Liebenden[17] auch, ihr schönen Kinder des Maitags,
  Stille Rosen und euch, Lilien, nenn' ich noch oft!
Wohl gehen Frühlinge fort,[18] ein Jahr verdränget das andre,
  Wechselnd und streitend, so tost[19] droben vorüber die Zeit   10
Über sterblichem Haupt, doch nicht vor seligen Augen,[20]
  Und den Liebenden ist anderes Leben geschenkt.
Denn sie alle, die Tag' und Jahre der Sterne,[21] sie waren
  Diotima! um uns innig und ewig vereint;

4

Aber wir, zufrieden gesellt, wie die liebenden Schwäne,
  Wenn sie ruhen am See, oder, auf Wellen gewiegt,
Niedersehn in die Wasser, wo silberne Wolken sich spiegeln,

---

[9]'in fearful compliance to banishment' [10]Line 7 could be taken as the words to the "sober song of the gods of death" but more likely the poet is addressing himself. [11]'become used to, resigned to' [12]*fernher nahe*, an oxymoron, 'from a distance near.' The oxymoron is the typical rhetorical figure of this strophe and of strophe 5. More than that, however, it characterizes the whole elegy and, in a sense, *all* elegies, insofar as they overcome suffering through lamentation (*Klagen*). Cf. Schiller's "Nänie."

3: [13]dative plural [14]Note that *Nacht* is accusative [15]*seid* goes with *willkommen* (line 4). [16]'witnesses' [17]vocative, in apposition to *Kinder des Maitags* (the roses and lilies) [18]'It is true that springs must pass' [19]*tosen* 'rage,' 'storm' [20]Cf. "Hyperions Schicksalslied." [21]"The days and years of the stars" are not the same as the years of this earth; the next strophe tells what they were like for Menon and Diotima.

Und ätherisches Blau unter den Schiffenden[22] wallt,
So auf Erden wandelten wir. Und drohte der Nord auch,[23]   5
Er, der Liebenden Feind, klagenbereitend,[24] und fiel
Von den Ästen das Laub, und flog im Winde der Regen,
Ruhig lächelten wir, fühlten den eigenen Gott[25]
Unter trautem Gespräch;[26] in Einem Seelengesange,
Ganz in Frieden mit uns kindlich und freudig allein.   10
Aber das Haus[27] ist öde mir nun, und sie haben mein Auge[28]
Mir genommen, auch mich hab' ich verloren mit ihr.
Darum irr' ich umher, und wohl, wie die Schatten, so muß ich
Leben, und sinnlos dünkt lange das Übrige mir.[29]

5

Feiern[30] möcht' ich; aber wofür? und singen mit Andern,
Aber so einsam fehlt jegliches Göttliche mir.
Dies ist's, dies mein Gebrechen,[31] ich weiß, es lähmet ein
Fluch mir
Darum die Sehnen,[32] und wirft, wo ich beginne,[33] mich hin,
Daß ich fühllos sitze den Tag, und stumm wie die Kinder,   5
Nur vom Auge mir kalt öfters die Träne noch schleicht,
Und die Pflanze des Felds, und der Vögel Singen mich trüb
macht,
Weil[34] mit Freuden auch sie Boten des Himmlischen sind,
Aber mir in schaudender Brust die beseelende Sonne,
Kühl und fruchtlos mir dämmert, wie Strahlen der Nacht,[35]   10
Ach! und nichtig und leer, wie Gefängniswände, der Himmel
Eine beugende Last über dem Haupte mir hängt!

6

Sonst mir anders bekannt![36] o Jugend, und bringen Gebete
Dich nicht wieder, dich nie? führet kein Pfad mich zurück?
Soll es werden auch mir, wie den Götterlosen, die vormals

4: [22]i.e., the swans   [23]'though the north wind threatened'   [24]'presaging lamentations'
[25]In another poem ("Die Liebenden") we read: *Trennen wollten wir uns, wähnten es
gut und klug;/ Da wir's taten, warum schreckt' uns, wie Mord, die Tat? / Ach! wir
kennen uns wenig, / Denn e s w a l t e t e i n G o t t in uns.* [26]'as we spoke intimate-
ly together'   [27]=the poet himself   [28]=Diotima   [29]The poem has now returned to its
beginnning.

5: [30]*feiern* = *das Göttliche rühmen* (cf. next line)   [31]*Gebrechen* is both subjective and
objective: 'my lack, weakness,' and 'that which I lack'   [32]'sinews'   [33]i.e., *wo ich zu
feiern beginne*   [34]=*während*   [35]Note the oxymoron.

6: [36]Nature (verses 7-12, strophe 5) is that which once had such a different aspect.

Glänzenden Auges[37] doch auch saßen an seligem Tisch,[38]
Aber übersättiget[39] bald, die schwärmenden[40] Gäste,   5
    Nun verstummet, und nun, unter der Lüfte Gesang,
Unter blühender Erd' entschlafen sind, bis dereinst[41] sie
    Eines Wunders Gewalt, sie, die Versunkenen, zwingt,[42]
Wiederzukehren und neu auf grünendem Boden zu wandeln. —
    Heiliger Othem[43] durchströmt göttlich die lichte Gestalt,[44]   10
Wenn das Fest sich beseelt, und Fluten der Liebe sich regen,[45]
    Und vom Himmel getränkt,[46] rauscht der lebendige Strom,[47]
Wenn es drunten ertönt, und ihre Schätze die Nacht zollt,[48]
    Und aus Bächen herauf glänzt das begrabene Gold. —

7

Aber o du,[49] die schon am Scheidewege[50] mir damals,
    Da ich versank vor dir, tröstend ein Schöneres[51] wies,
Du, die Großes zu sehn, und froher die Götter zu singen,
    Schweigend, wie sie, mich einst stille begeisternd gelehrt;[52]
Götterkind! erscheinest du mir, und grüßest, wie einst, mich,   5
    Redest wieder, wie einst, höhere Dinge mir zu?
Siehe! weinen vor dir, und klagen muß ich, wenn schon noch,
    Denkend edlerer Zeit, dessen[53] die Seele sich schämt.
Denn so lange, so lang auf matten Pfaden der Erde
    Hab ich, deiner gewohnt,[54] dich in der Irre gesucht,[55]   10
Freudiger Schutzgeist! aber umsonst, und Jahre zerrannen,
    Seit wir ahnend[56] um uns glänzen die Abende sahn.

8

Dich nur, dich erhält dein Licht, o Heldin! im Lichte,[57]
    Und dein Dulden[58] erhält liebend, o Gütige, dich;

---

[37]genitive of manner   [38]Before the Greeks became godless through overweening they sat at the table of the gods.   [39]'surfeited'   [40]'rapturous'   [41]'one day'   [42]The subject of *zwingt* is *eines Wunders Gewalt*; *sie* is the object.   [43]=*Atem*   [44]Lines 10-14 are a vision of the reawakening of the *Versunkenen* in another aeon when mankind, nature and the gods are again one.   [45]'begin to stir'   [46]'watered'   [47]i.e., the *Fluten der Liebe*   [48]*zollen* 'pay toll'; Night must also contribute to the festival of Oneness: it causes its buried gold to gleam in the streams.

7: [49]Diotima   [50]'at the parting of the ways'   [51]i.e., something more beautiful that our earthly union   [52]Cf. "Geh unter, schöne Sonne," 2nd stanza.   [53]refers to *weinen* and *klagen*   [54]'used to you'   [55]Since he sought Diotima on an earthly plane, he sought her *in der Irre*.   [56]'giving promise' (take with *glänzen*)

8: [57]The "light" reference is multiple: a) to the last verse of the preceding strophe (in the case of Diotima the *Ahnung* has already proven true); b) to the contrast with those

Und nicht einmal bist du allein; Gespielen[59] genug sind,
  Wo du blühest und ruhst unter[60] den Rosen des Jahrs;[61]
Und der Vater, er selbst, durch sanftumatmende Musen   5
  Sendet die zärtlichen Wiegengesänge dir zu.
Ja! noch ist sie es ganz! noch schwebt vom Haupte zur Sohle,
  Stillherwandelnd,[62] wie sonst, mir die Athenerin vor.
Und wie, freundlicher Geist! von heitersinnender[63] Stirne
  Segnend und sicher dein Strahl unter die Sterblichen fällt,   10
So bezeugest du mir's, und sagst mir's, daß ich es andern
  Wiedersage, denn auch andere glauben es nicht,
Daß unsterblicher doch, denn[64] Sorg' und Zürnen, die Freude
  Und ein goldener Tag täglich[65] am Ende noch ist.

9

So will ich, ihr Himmlischen! denn auch danken, und endlich
  Atmet aus leichter Brust wieder des Sängers Gebet.[66]
Und wie, wenn ich mit ihr, auf sonniger Höhe mit ihr stand,
  Spricht belebend ein Gott innen vom Tempel[67] mich an.
Leben will ich denn auch! schon grünt's! wie von heiliger Leier   5
  Ruft es von silbernen Bergen Apollons[68] voran!
Komm! es war wie ein Traum! Die blutenden Fittige[69] sind ja
  Schon genesen, verjüngt leben die Hoffnungen all.
Großes zu finden, ist viel, ist viel noch übrig, und wer so
  Liebte, gehet, er muß, gehet zu Göttern die Bahn.   10
Und geleitet ihr[70] uns, ihr Weihestunden![71] ihr ernsten,
  Jugendlichen! o bleibt, heilige Ahnungen, ihr
Fromme Bitten! und ihr Begeisterungen und all ihr
  Guten Genien, die gerne bei Liebenden sind;
Bleibt so lange mit uns, bis wir auf gemeinsamem Boden[72]   15
  Dort, wo die Seligen all niederzukehren bereit,[73]

---

who "sleep *beneath* the flowering earth" (strophe 6, line 7) and Diotima who "rests *among* the roses of the [eternal] year"; c) to the contrast between Diotima and Menon himself as we saw him in strophe 2. [58]'patience' (with me) [59]'companions' [60]see note 57 [61]Cf. strophe 3, line 13. [62]'taking her quiet way' [63]'serenely thoughtful' [64]=*als* [65]*täglich* 'in the way of day,' i.e., as we mortals experience a "golden day" here in our time. This may give us a presentiment of a different, perfect time, such as the end of the next strophe evokes.

9: [66]i.e., *feiern, das Göttliche rühmen* (strophe 5, verse 1) [67]*Tempel,* cf. *Haus,* strophe 4, verse 11. [68]i.e., Parnassus, which is snow-capped (*silbern*) and double-peaked (hence plural) [69]'pinions' [70]*geleitet ihr* is imperative [71]'hours of consecration' [72]Supply *uns begegnen* at the end of this verse; *gemeinsamem Boden,* 'common ground,' i.e., where both Menon (a man) and Diotima (a spirit) will be at home. [73]The "Blessed" (i.e., the gods) are all ready to descend to earth when the time is ripe.

Dort, wo die Adler[74] sind, die Gestirne, die Boten des Vaters,
    Dort, wo die Musen, woher[75] Helden und Liebende sind,
Dort uns, oder auch hier, auf tauender Insel[76] begegnen,
    Wo die Unsrigen erst,[77] blühend in Gärten gesellt,   20
Wo die Gesänge wahr, und länger die Frühlinge schön sind,
    Und von neuem ein Jahr unserer Seele[78] beginnt.

"Menons Klagen um Diotima" is an elegy. The fundamental striving of all elegies (insofar as they are laments) is to overcome the lamented sorrow through the lamentation itself.* The elegy seeks a positive in a negative; it seeks to spiritualize suffering and so lend it meaning, for meaning is found only in the realm of the spirit. Therefore it is not surprising that, of all forms, the elegy should operate with polar opposites, opposing pairs that constitute a unity, since the elegy is by nature a union of (seeming) contradictories. It is in terms of such polarities that "Menons Klagen" is composed.

These polarities are darkness and light, separation and oneness. Darkness, night, is a metaphor for loneliness and separation, not only from the beloved but also from nature and the divine. Light, day, is a metaphor for love and oneness, not only with the loved one but also with nature and the divine. Since Hölderlin regarded his poetry primarily as praise of the "higher," to be godless is for him death:

Beruf ist mir's
Zu rühmen Höhers, darum gab die
Sprache der Gott und den Dank ins Herz mir.
        ("Der Prinzessin Auguste von Homburg")

This task set by the elegy is a double one: to find the way back through darkness and night, loneliness and separation, to light and day, love and oneness, *and* to show how true light and oneness are not possible without darkness and separation. Through his love for Diotima Menon learned the meaning of oneness; in losing her he learned the meaning of separation. The elegy traces the way back from separation to a new union, but the new union is not on the same plane as the original: it is purely spiritual and hence indestructible — *this* union was not possible without separation. Thus a positive is derived from a negative, light from darkness.

---

[74]messengers of Zeus   [75]The muses *are* there, heroes and lovers *from* there.   [76]A sudden switch from "there" to "here," but at any event beyond ordinary, strife-riven time, where there is no difference between "there" and "here." The dewy island now replaces the Islands of the Blest, the home of the blessed in the afterlife.   [77]*erst*, take with *wahr … sind* in next verse.   [78]Cf. *Jahr*, strophe 3, verse 13, and strophe 8, verse 4. Verses 15-22 are a vision of the millenium to come. For Hölderlin, the millenium meant the reunion of all things — *alles Getrennte findet sich wieder.*

*Cf. Schiller's "Nänie" and the analysis, pp. 165ff.

Darkness and light, separation and oneness, are in themselves only concepts, and useless as such for poetry, which operates with images. Up to now we have abstracted the concepts from the images; the next, and more important step, is to observe how the concepts appear as specific images.

Strophes 1-2. Separation and darkness — the stricken deer vainly seeking comfort from nature, with which it was once one; a mythical picture of Hades.

Strophes 3-4. Light and Oneness — *Bilder aus hellerer Zeit,* the landscape of love (Arcadia); the image of the swans with heaven above and beneath, completely one with the *All;** the strolling lovers, who feel the god within. At the end of strophe 4 (as conversely at the end of strophe 2) light becomes darkness: the Hadean imagery reappears.

Strophe 5. Separation from nature and the divine. For the poet, lamed by a "curse," the planets and birds are no longer heaven's messengers but reminders of separateness; the sun's rays are "rays of night," the dome of the sky a prison wall. All that formerly united now excludes; all is bottomless despair for the poet, who feels himself incapable of his only true office: *Feiern.*

Strophe 6 is the fulcrum of the elegy. Here we find 1) imagery of oneness: those who once sat at the table of the gods; 2) of separation: the fall of the wanton guests; 3) a vision of reunion: the reawakening of the *Versunkenen* (those who fell from the divine table). This last element — an epiphany, for the awakening is accompanied by a vision of the return of the gods — is new. This is the turning point.

Strophe 7. The vision of Diotima. Here that which was implied in the imagery of the preceding strophe is given discursive affirmation. The separation from the divine that befell those once privileged to sit at the table with the gods, this was also the fate of Menon, who has become what his name implies a "waiting one," like those *unter blühender Erd entschlafen.* He too is a *Versunkener.* But at the parting of the ways (*da ich v e r s a n k vor dir*), Diotima had comforted him with the promise of a *Schöneres.* This can only mean reunion on a higher plane, a reawakening paralleling that envisioned at the end of strophe 6. The meaning of the parting has now been found: separation meant higher union.

Strophe 8 is a flood of moving light, for Diotima *is* light and these lines express her spiritual essence. To what degree the language is here spiritualized becomes apparent when we try to say precisely what the basis of the imagery is. We are aware of a softly undulating light-filled vision, an eternal inward blooming like that of the *selige Genien* in "Hyperions Schicksallied." Hölderlin is here comparable only with himself. The verbs, rather than the nouns, bear the imagery: *blühest und ruhst, sanftumatmend, schwebst stillher-*

---

*But not with men — the realization that their love was not meant as a merely private revelation comes later: ... *und sagst mir's, daß ich es andern / Wiedersage ...* (strophe 8).

wandelnd. The dialectic advances still another step in the last four verses: the poet realizes that the message sent him by the gods through Diotima is expressly meant for him *as a poet*, not as a private individual. It is a task imposed from above, and the horrible separation he was forced to undergo was only the divine way of making mankind realize the spiritual nature of the task. (Beneath the poem's Hellenistic surface lie continual reminders of the Christian scheme of redemption.)

Strophe 9 shows the poet beginning the fulfillment of the divinely imposed task: *feiern, danken*. The first part of the strophe (through verse 10) contains images of expansion and light, the latter part images of concentration and union. The final vision, another epiphany, is symbolic not only of the spiritual reunion of the lovers but of all mankind with nature and the divine. The *Jahr der Seele* will be beyond strife and separation, the world raised to the realm of the spirit.

Towards Interpretation

1. Point out specific examples illustrating the statement made in the above analysis about the imagery of strophe 9.
2. In discussing the poem, nothing was said about some important threads of imagery, notably the *path* images. Trace this imagery throughout the poem. Note especially when and why the poem becomes "pathless."
3. Comment in some detail on the manner in which continuity is established from strophe to strophe.

Lebenslauf

Größers wolltest auch du, aber die Liebe zwingt
    All uns nieder, das Leid beuget gewaltiger,
        Doch es kehret umsonst nicht
           Unser Bogen,[1] woher er kommt.

Aufwärts oder hinab! Herrschet in heil'ger Nacht,   5
    Wo die stumme Natur werdende Tage sinnt,
        Herrscht im schiefesten Orkus
           Nicht ein Grades,[2] ein Recht noch auch?

Dies erfuhr ich. Denn nie, sterblichen Meistern gleich,
    Habt ihr Himmlischen, ihr Alleserhaltenden,   10
        Daß ich wüßte, mit Vorsicht
           Mich des ebenen Pfades geführt.

---

[1] i.e., the 'arch' of our life   [2] 'something straight'

Alles prüfe[3] der Mensch, sagen die Himmlischen,
    Daß er, kräftig genährt, danken für Alles lern',
        Und verstehe die Freiheit,   15
            Aufzubrechen, wohin er will.

Towards Interpretation

1. Show how "Menons Klagen" and "Lebenslauf" complement and
   explain each other.

Gesang des Deutschen

O heilig Herz der Völker,[1] o Vaterland!
    Allduldend, gleich der schweigenden Mutter Erd',
        Und allverkannt, wenn schon aus deiner
            Tiefe die Fremden ihr Bestes haben!

Sie ernten den Gedanken, den Geist von dir,   5
    Sie pflücken gern die Traube, doch höhnen sie
        Dich, ungestalte Rebe! daß du
            Schwankend den Boden und wild umirrest.[2]

Du Land des hohen ernsteren Genius!
    Du Land der Liebe! bin ich der deine schon,[3]   10
        Oft zürnt' ich weinend, daß du immer
            Blöde[4] die eigene Seele leugnest.

Doch magst[5] du manches Schöne nicht bergen mir;
    Oft stand ich überschauend das holde Grün,
        Den weiten Garten hoch in deinen   15
            Lüften auf hellem Gebirg' und sah dich.[6]

An deinen Strömen ging ich und dachte dich,
    Indes die Töne schüchtern die Nachtigall
        Auf schwanker[7] Weide sang, und still auf
            Dämmerndem Grunde die Welle weilte.   20

Und an den Ufern sah ich die Städte blühn,
    Die Edeln, wo der Fleiß in der Werkstatt schweigt,[8]

---

[3]hortatory subjunctive

[1]Germany is a *Herz der Völker* also in a geographical sense.   [2]=*daß du schwankend
und wild auf dem Boden umirrest*   [3]'though I am yours'   [4]'foolishly, weakly, fearfully'
[5]=*kannst*   [6]Verses 14-16: *Oft stand ich in deinen Lüften auf hellem Gebirg und sah
dich, indem ich das holde Grün, den weiten Garten, überschaute.*   [7]'swaying'   [8]i.e.,
does not boast

Die Wissenschaft, wo deine Sonne
   Milde dem Künstler zum Ernste leuchtet.[9]

Kennst du Minervas Kinder?[10] sie wählten sich   25
   Den Ölbaum[11] früh zum Lieblinge; kennst du sie?
     Noch lebt, noch waltet der Athener[12]
       Seele, die sinnende, still bei Menschen,

Wenn Platons frommer Garten[13] auch schon nicht mehr
   Am alten Strome grünt und der dürft'ge Mann   30
     Die Heldenasche pflügt, und scheu der
       Vogel der Nacht auf der Säule trauert.[14]

O heil'ger Wald! o Attika! traf Er[15] doch
   Mit seinem furchtbarn Strahle[16] dich auch, so bald,
     Und eilten sie, die dich belebt, die   35
       Flammen entbunden, zum Aether über?

Doch, wie der Frühling, wandelt der Genius
   Von Land zu Land. Und wir? ist denn Einer auch
     Von unsern Jünglingen, der nicht ein
       Ahnden,[17] ein Rätsel der Brust, verschwiege?   40

Den deutschen Frauen danket! sie haben uns
   Der Götterbilder freundlichen Geist bewahrt,
     Und täglich sühnt der holde klare
       Friede das böse Gewirre wieder.

Wo sind jetzt Dichter, denen der Gott es gab,   45
   Wie unsern Alten, freudig und fromm zu sein,
     Wo Weise, wie die unsern sind? die
       Kalten und Kühnen, die Unbestechbaren![18]

Nun! sei gegrüßt in deinem Adel, mein Vaterland,
   Mit neuem Namen, reifeste Frucht der Zeit!   50
     Du letzte und du erste aller
       Musen, Urania,[19] sei gegrüßt mir!

---

[9]'kindly lights the artist at his serious work' [10]'Minerva's children' =the Athenians; Minerva (Pallas Athene) was patroness of Athens and the teacher of all crafts. [11]'olive' [12]genitive plural [13]Grove of the Academy beside the River Cephissus, where Plato taught. [14]The owl was sacred to Minerva. [15]*Er* =*der Gott des Schicksals* (Beissner). [16]'lightning' [17]=*Ahnen* 'premonition' [18]The poets Hölderlin has in mind are probably Klopstock, Goethe, and Schiller. The philosophers (*Weise*), whose coolness, daring, and intellectual honesty he praises, may be Kant, Fichte (whose lectures Hölderlin attended), and his personal friends and fellow students Hegel and Schelling. [19]Muse of Astronomy, who gave order to Chaos.

Noch säumst und schweigst du, sinnest ein freudig Werk,
Das von dir zeuge,[20] sinnest ein neu Gebild,[21]
Das einzig, wie du selber, das aus   55
Liebe geboren und gut, wie du, sei —

Wo ist dein Delos,[22] wo dein Olympia,[23]
Daß wir uns alle[24] finden am höchsten Fest? —
Doch wie errät der Sohn, was du den
Deinen, Unsterbliche, längst bereitest?   60

"Gesang des Deutschen," one of Hölderlin's "vaterländische Oden," shows strict symmetry of form: 6 + 3 + 6, each group of six stanzas being again subdivided into 3 + 3. The first three stanzas speak of the *Verkennung* of the fatherland, the refusal of others to recognize Germany's worth, while exploiting Germany's genius. But the son knows the secret worth of his native land and sets his *doch* (verse 13) against the general estimate, yes, even against that of Germany itself, whose foolish modesty makes it deny its soul (11-12). Stanzas 4-6 discover the soul of the fatherland, as yet, however, principally as a setting, a landscape.

Stanzas 7-9 remember Athens, its political impotence, its spiritual greatness. "Minerva's children" chose the olive branch (not the sword), yet the Athenian spirit still holds quiet sway (*waltet still*) among men — at least among such men as Hölderlin — though Plato's grove is gone and the ploughshare turns the ashes of the heroes of Greece. Plato's was a "holy grove" and Attica a holy land because there the highest things that Western man has known were striven for. But Fate's lightning struck, and the physical *Gebild* that was Athens is no more; it has become pure spirit (stanza 9), but for that very reason freed for re-embodiment.

The last six stanzas express an ardent hope and a hesitant prophecy. The poem attempts to look into the "seeds" of time: Is Germany to be the chosen land of the Spirit, the New Athens? *Alles Getrennte findet sich wieder* — like the spring, so also does the Spirit move from land to land (from South to North). The signs that give reason for hope are named: the prescience of German youth (stanza 10), German womanhood as the preserver of sacred traditions and soother of strife (stanza 11), Germany's great poets and philosophers (12). This section of the poem is the counterpart of stanzas 4-6: there

---

[20]'shall bear witness' [21]'configuration' [22]In Hölderlin's novel *Hyperion*, we read of Delos: "Hier wohnte der Sonnengott einst, unter den himmlischen Festen, wo ihn, wie goldnes Gewölk, das versammelte Griechenland umglänzte." [23]where the Games were held [24]That is, all the peoples of Germany, like the Greeks at their festivals — again the ideal of Oneness.

the landscape of the fatherland, here its people. Together, they make up its "soul" (verse 12).*

The last division of the ode begins with an emphatic *Nun!* Having vindicated the honor of his homeland, the poet now hails it in its new nobility as the "ripest fruit of Time," that is as the land most fitted to re-embody in its own way the Greek ideal, or more accurately: Hölderlin's concept of the Greek ideal. Will Urania create *ein neu Gebild* that shall give worthy witness of her? Will *der Genius* come to Germany as the spring comes north?

The last stanza seems to be addressed to both Urania and Germania, to the mother of cosmic harmony and the mother of men. The poet is the "son" of both — a *Musensohn* and a child of Germany. He asks his "mother": *Wo ist dein Delos, wo dein Olympia. . . ?* Shall his homeland ever be privileged to welcome the gods back to earth? The final answer must be left to the future. But his hope is strong.

Heidelberg

Lange lieb' ich dich schon, möchte dich, mir zur Lust,
    Mutter nennen, und dir schenken ein kunstlos Lied,
        Du, der Vaterlandsstädte
        Ländlichschönste, so viel ich sah.

Wie der Vogel des Walds über die Gipfel fliegt,   5
    Schwingt sich über den Strom, wo er vorbei dir glänzt,[1]
        Leicht und kräftig die Brücke,
        Die von Wagen und Menschen tönt.

Wie von Göttern gesandt, fesselt' ein Zauber einst
    Auf die Brücke mich an, da ich vorüber ging,   10
        Und herein in die Berge
        Mir die reizende Ferne schien,

Und der Jüngling, der Strom, fort in die Ebne zog,[2]
    Traurigfroh, wie das Herz, wenn es, sich selbst zu schön,
        Liebend unterzugehen,[3]   15
        In die Fluten der Zeit sich wirft.

---

*The influence of Herder, from whom so many of our ideas of nationality stem, seems apparent here.

[1] =*wo er glänzend an dir vorbeifließt* [2] The Neckar leaves the hills of the Odenwald at Heidelberg and enters the plain of the Rhine, emptying into this river some miles west of the town. [3] i.e., *um "liebend unterzugehen"*; excess of beauty or happiness leads to the desire for self-destruction, a common feeling in youth and the root of many enthusiasms.

Quellen hattest du ihm,[4] hattest dem Flüchtigen
Kühle Schatten geschenkt, und die Gestade[5] sahn
All' ihm nach, und es bebte
Aus den Wellen ihr lieblich Bild.   20

Aber schwer in das Tal hing die gigantische,
Schicksalskundige Burg[6] nieder bis auf den Grund,
Von den Wettern zerrissen;
Doch die ewige Sonne goß

Ihr verjüngendes Licht über das alternde   25
Riesenbild, und umher grünte lebendiger
Efeu; freundliche Wälder
Rauschten über die Burg herab.

Sträuche blühten herab, bis wo im heitern Tal,
An den Hügel gelehnt, oder dem Ufer hold,[7]   30
Deine[8] frölichen Gassen
Unter duftenden Gärten ruhn.

Towards Interpretation

1. Note the use of tenses in this poem. Can you suggest a reason for this usage?

2. Castle and stream here seem over time to experience two fates. How does the poem develop this idea?

3. Note the various directions and movements involved in the poem: The bridge "swings itself" from one bank to the other; men and vehicles move back and forth on the bridge; the stream flows at right angles to the bridge; the shores "gaze after" the fleeting river; the ruined castle "hangs down into the valley"; the vegetation pours down over the castle and the sun pours down from above; the streets of the town run at right angles to the hill and along the shore — a directional system composed almost like a painting. What is the poet's relation to all this movement? Is he involved? How would you describe his state (or attitude)?

5. The meter of this poem is an imitation of the Asclepiadean ode:

$$- \smile - \smile \smile - \mid - \smile \smile - \smile -$$
$$- \smile - \smile \smile - \mid - \smile \smile - \smile -$$
$$- \smile - \smile \smile - \smile$$
$$- \smile - \smile \smile - \smile -$$

Note, however, what happens to the final stresssed syllable in verses 17, 21, 25, 26. The fact that these syllables occur in a system that

---

[4]*du ihm*: *du* is the Heidelberg landscape, *ihm* is the Neckar. [5]=*Ufer* [6]Heidelberg Castle, blown up by the French in 1689. The "storms" (*Wetter*) of the next verse are those of war rather than nature. [7]'true to (hugging) the shore' [8]i.e., Heidelberg's

would require their being stressed may make us stress them (*System-zwang*), but obviously they do not naturally take stress. Can you derive from the *content* of these lines a reason for this anomalous *formal* situation?

Hälfte des Lebens

Mit gelben Birnen hänget
Und voll mit wilden Rosen
Das Land in den See,
Ihr holden Schwäne,
Und trunken von Küssen   5
Tunkt ihr das Haupt
Ins heilignüchterne[1] Wässer.

Weh mir, wo nehm' ich, wenn
Es Winter ist, die Blumen, und wo
Den Sonnenschein,   10
Und Schatten der Erde?
Die Mauern stehn
Sprachlos und kalt, im Winde
Klirren die Fahnen.[2]

Towards Interpretation

1. What season is being described in each strophe? Horticulturally speaking, what is "wrong" with the description in strophe 1? What might be Hölderlin's purpose in altering the facts of nature?
2. The swan is a common symbol of the poet. Might the poet be "talking to himself," as it were, in this stanza as in the second?
3. What crisis is described in this poem? What do you think is meant by "taking" the flowers, sunshine, shadows?

---

[1]'sacredly sober' Since classical times, the phrase "sober drunkenness" (*nüchterne Trunkenheit*) has been used to describe the poet's state of mind.   [2]'weather vanes'

Friedrich Leopold Freiherr von Hardenberg, "Novalis" (1772-1801)

Novalis' "Hymnen an die Nacht" are a central document not only of German but of European Romanticism, which later found its highest fulfillment in Wagner's operas. They represent a consistent working out in poetry of its basic striving, the fusion of the real with the ideal. In the *Fragmente* of Novalis we find the Romantic method of procedure formulated in very precise terms:

> The world must be romanticized. In this way we will find again its primal meaning. Romanticizing is nothing but raising to a higher power in a qualitative sense. In this process the lower Self becomes identified with a better Self. . . . When I give a lofty meaning to the commonplace, a mysterious prestige to the usual, the dignity of the unknown to the known, an aura of infinity to the finite, then I am romanticizing. — For the higher, the unknown, the mystical, the infinite, the process is reversed — these are reduced to their logarithms by such a connection — they are expressed in familiar terms.*

This is exactly what happens in the "Hymnen an die Nacht." Students of English literature will recognize the parallel with what Wordsworth and Coleridge (uninfluenced by Novalis as he by them) were simultaneously trying to accomplish in the *Lyrical Ballads*: Wordsworth endeavored to poetize (i.e., romanticize) the common and familiar, Coleridge the uncommon and fantastic.

The metaphorical material of the "Hymnen" is based primarily upon the commonest and most obvious of antitheses, darkness and light. Through romanticizing, these are rendered strange and unfamiliar and their normal connotations reversed, so that darkness finally becomes light and light darkness. This happens twice, once on the autobiographical level and once on the level of the history of mankind. This parallelism is Novalis's way of saying in poetry that the individual is the analogue of the whole, the microcosm the logarithm of the macrocosm. And, as light comes to take on the significance of darkness and darkness of light, so does birth come to mean death and death birth. The evaluation thus arrived at

---

*Novalis, *Schriften*, ed. Paul Kluckhohn and Richard Samuel, 5 vols. (Stuttgart: Kohlhammer, ²1960-1988), 2:545, no. 105 (translated here by R. M. Browning).

is of course the Christian one, and the poem might be called a Christianization of existence with almost as good a right as a romanticization.

It is not as an apologist of Christianity, however, that Novalis primarily speaks. Rather he *uses* Christianity as the most suitable medium for romanticizing. For Christianity is the romantic religion *par excellence*. In its view nothing is what it seems at first blush. A prime example is the Christian view of death as the gate to true life. This doctrine becomes, when translated into Romantic terms, a doctrine of self-transcendence, and self-transcendence becomes self-dissolution, a cancellation of the individuality so that it may become part of a larger and higher whole (the "better Self"). If then a poet, as is true of Novalis, regards the "goal of all goals" of poetry as *die Erhebung des Menschen über sich selbst,* it is not surprising that he should have a high regard for Christianity. Romanticism (in this sense at least) and Christianity play into each others' hands.

Hymnen an die Nacht[1]

1

Welcher Lebendige, Sinnbegabte, liebt nicht vor allen Wundererscheinungen des verbreiteten Raums um ihn, das allerfreuliche Licht — mit seinen Farben, seinen Strahlen und Wogen; seiner milden Allgegenwart, als weckender Tag. Wie des Lebens innerste Seele atmet es der rastlosen Gestirne Riesenwelt,[2] und schwimmt [5] tanzend in seiner blauen Flut — atmet es der funkelnde, ewigruhende Stein, die sinnige, saugende Pflanze, und das wilde, brennende, vielgestaltete Tier — vor allen aber der herrliche Fremdling[3] mit den sinnvollen Augen, dem schwebenden Gange, und den zartgeschlossenen, tonreichen Lippen. Wie ein König der [10] irdischen Natur ruft es[4] jede Kraft zu zahllosen Verwandlugen, knüpft und löst unendliche Bündnisse, hängt sein himmlisches Bild jedem irdischen Wesen um. — Seine Gegenwart allein offenbart die Wunderherrlichkeit der Reiche der Welt.

Abwärts wend' ich mich zu der heiligen, unaussprechlichen, [15] geheimnisvollen Nacht. Fernab liegt die Welt — in eine tiefe Gruft versenkt — wüst und einsam ist ihre Stelle. In den Saiten der

---

[1]The version given here is that published in the *Athenäum* (1800), as reprinted in Novalis, *Schriften*, 1:131-153. For difficult passages, students may also wish to consult the translation in *German Poetry from 1750 to 1900*, ed. Robert M. Browning, The German Library 39 (New York: Continuum, 1984), 108-131. [2]'the gigantic world of the restless planets' (subject of *atmet*) [3]i.e., man, who, as becomes evident as the poem develops, does not properly belong to the world of light, therefore a 'stranger.' [4]=*das Licht* (subject)

Brust weht tiefe Wehmut. In Tautropfen will ich hinuntersinken
und mit der Asche mich vermischen. — Fernen der Erinnerung,
Wünsche der Jugend, der Kindheit Träume, des ganzen langen [20]
Lebens kurze Freuden und vergebliche Hoffnungen kommen in
grauen Kleidern, wie Abendnebel nach der Sonne Untergang. In
anderen Räumen schlug die lustigen Gezelte das Licht auf.[5] Sollte
es nie zu seinen Kindern wiederkommen, die mit der Unschuld
Glauben seiner harren?[6]   [25]
      Was quillt auf einmal so ahndungsvoll unterm Herzen, und
verschluckt der Wehmut weiche Luft? Hast auch du ein Gefallen
an uns, dunkle Nacht? Was hältst du unter deinem Mantel, das mir
unsichtbar kräftig in die Seele geht? Köstlicher Balsam träuft aus
deiner Hand, aus dem Bündel Mohn.[7] Die schweren Flügel des [30]
Gemüts hebst du empor. Dunkel und unaussprechlich fühlen wir
uns bewegt — ein ernstes Antlitz seh ich froh erschrocken,[8] das
sanft und andachtsvoll sich zu mir neigt, und unter unendlich ver-
schlungenen Locken der Mutter liebe Jugend zeigt.[9] Wie arm und
kindisch dünkt mir das Licht nun — wie erfreulich und gesegnet [35]
des Tages Abschied. — Also nur darum, weil die Nacht dir[10] ab-
wendig macht die Dienenden, säetest du in des Raumes Weiten die
leuchtenden Kugeln, zu verkünden deine Allmacht — deine Wiederkehr — in den Zeiten deiner Entfernung. Himmlischer, als jene
blitzenden Sterne, dünken uns die unendlichen Augen, die die [40]
Nacht in uns geöffnet. Weiter sehn sie als die blässesten jener
zahllosen Heere[11] — unbedürftig des Lichts durchschaun sie die
Tiefen eines liebenden Gemüts — was einen höhern Raum mit unsäglicher Wollust füllt.[12] Preis der Weltkönigin,[13] der hohen
Verkündigerin heiliger Welten, der Pflegerin seliger Liebe — sie [45]
sendet mir dich — zarte Geliebte — liebliche Sonne der Nacht, —
nun wach' ich — nun bin ich dein und mein — du hast die Nacht
mir zum Leben verkündet — mich zum Menschen gemacht[14] —
zehre mit Geisterglut meinen Leib, daß ich luftig mit dir inniger
mich mische und dann ewig die Brautnacht währt.[15]   [50]

---

[5]*aufschlagen* 'pitch (a tent)' [6]*seiner* (genitive) *harren* 'wait for it' [7]Night holds in her
hand a bundle of poppies out of which a precious balm (opium) drips. [8]*froh
erschrocken* modifies *ich*. [9]Beneath its locks the face of Night reveals 'a mother's dear
youthfulness.' [10]Light is addressed. [11]The palest stars are the most distant. [12]The
'depths of a loving heart and mind' (*Gemüt*) that the inner eye 'sees through' are those
of Night or the divine itself, which delights to be 'seen through' (comprehended) by
man. [13]'Praise to the Queen of Creation' (Night) [14]By making Night, his true home,
meaningful to him, the beloved makes a *Mensch* out of him who was a *Fremdling* in
the world of light. [15]The image is chemical: consumation by fire, i.e., transformation
into gas (*luftig*), so that a more intimate (*inniger*) union may be possible.

2

Muß immer der Morgen wiederkommen? Endet nie des Irdischen
Gewalt? Unselige Geschäftigkeit verzehrt den himmlischen An-
flug der Nacht. Wird nie der Liebe geheimes Opfer ewig brennen?
Zugemessen ward dem Lichte seine Zeit; aber zeitlos und raumlos
ist der Nacht Herrschaft. — Ewig ist die Dauer des Schlafs. Heili- [5]
ger Schlaf — beglücke zu selten nicht der Nacht Geweihte[16] in
diesem irdischen Tagewerk. Nur die Toren verkennen dich und
wissen von keinem Schlafe, als dem Schatten, den du in jener
Dämmerung der wahrhaften Nacht mitleidig auf uns wirfst.[17] Sie
fühlen dich nicht in der goldnen Flut der Trauben — in des [10]
Mandelbaums Wunderöl, und dem braunen Safte des Mohns.[18] Sie
wissen nicht, daß du es bist, der des zarten Mädchens Busen um-
schwebt und zum Himmel den Schoß macht — ahnden nicht, daß
aus alten Geschichten du himmelöffnend entgegentrittst und den
Schlüssel trägst zu den Wohnungen der Seligen, unendlicher Ge- [15]
heimnisse schweigender Bote.[19]

3

[20]Einst da ich bittre Tränen vergoß, da in Schmerz aufgelöst
meine Hoffnung zerrann, und ich einsam stand am dürren Hügel,[21]
der in engen dunkeln Raum die Gestalt meines Lebens barg[22] —
einsam, wie noch kein Einsamer war, von unsäglicher Angst getrieben — kraftlos, nur ein Gedanken des Elends noch. — Wie ich [5]
da nach Hülfe umherschaute, vorwärts nicht konnte und rückwärts
nicht, und am fliehenden, verlöschten Leben mit unendlicher
Sehnsucht hing: — da kam aus blauen Fernen — von den Höhen
meiner alten Seligkeit ein Dämmerungsschauer[23] — mit einem
Male riß das Band der Geburt — des Lichtes Fessel.[24] Hin floh die [10]
irdische Herrlichkeit und meine Trauer mit ihr — zusammenfloß
die Wehmut in eine neue, unergründliche Welt — du Nachtbegei-
sterung, Schlummer des Himmels kamst über mich — die Gegend

---

[16]'those dedicated to Night' [17]i.e., sleep as ordinarily understood [18]Alcohol, bitter oil
of almonds (benzaldehyde), and opium — narcotics (in ascending scale of strength) that
induce the "artificial paradise." [19]This happens, for example, in dreams, which bring
us promise of the end of the rule of Light and separateness. The theme of this whole
hymn is death (sleep) in life. [20]This hymn, as we know from the poet's diary, is based
on an actual experience which Novalis underwent at the grave of his betrothed, Sophie
von Kühn. Day's reign is here broken forever, so far as the "I" of the hymns is concerned. [21]=*Grabhügel* [22]*bergen* 'keep safe' *and* 'conceal' [23]Comparison with 5th
hymn, where a similar birth-death occurs, leads one to conclude that the "heights of
my former bliss" from which comes the "thrill of dusk" refer to the time when the "I"
was still part of the divine, still unindividuated, still in the womb of Night. [24]The
trauma of birth is overcome; the "I" is reborn into Night.

hob sich sacht empor;[25] über der Gegend schwebte mein entbund-
ner, neugeborner Geist. Zur Staubwolke wurde der Hügel — [15]
durch die Wolke sah ich die verklärten Züge der Geliebten. In
Ihren[26] Augen ruhte die Ewigkeit — ich faßte Ihre[26] Hände, und
die Tränen wurden ein funkelndes, unzerreißliches Band. Jahrtau-
sende zogen abwärts in die Ferne, wie Ungewitter.[27] An Ihrem[26]
Halse weint' ich dem neuen Leben entzückende Tränen. — Es [20]
war der erste, einzige Traum — und erst seitdem fühl' ich ewigen,
unwandelbaren Glauben an den Himmel der Nacht und sein Licht,
die Geliebte.

4

Nun[28] weiß ich, wenn der letzte Morgen sein wird — wenn
das Licht nicht mehr die Nacht und die Liebe scheucht — wenn
der Schlummer ewig und nur *ein* unerschöpflicher Traum sein
wird. Himmlische Müdigkeit fühl' ich in mir. — Weit und
ermüdend ward mir die Wallfahrt zum Heiligen Grabe, drückend [5]
das Kreuz.[29] Die kristallene Woge, die, gemeinen Sinnen
unvernehmlich, in des Hügels dunkeln Schoß quillt,[30] an dessen
Fuß die irdische Flut bricht, wer sie gekostet, wer oben stand auf
dem Grenzgebirge der Welt,[31] und hinübersah in das neue Land,
in der Nacht Wohnsitz — wahrlich der kehrt nicht in das Treiben [10]
der Welt zurück, in das Land, wo das Licht in ewiger Unruh
hauset.

---

[25]movement of giving birth   [26]'her' (capitalized for emphasis)   [27]The overcoming of
time is seen as the passing of a thunderstorm.   [28]i.e., after the experience described in
the foregoing hymn. The first sentence answers the questions posed at the beginning of
the 2nd hymn.   [29]The figure is that of a pilgrimage to the Holy Sepulchre. From now
on, Christ, though not mentioned by name, displaces *die Geliebte,* whose function was
to lead the *poet* to the belief to which Christ leads us *all.* Cf. Mark 8:34, where Jesus
says to the multitude: "If any man would come after me, let him deny himself and take
up his cross and follow me."   [30]The "crystal wave" that "wells up in the grave's dark
depths," i.e., in Christ, has several counterparts in the New Testament. For example,
John 4:13f., Jesus says to the Samaritan woman at Jacob's well: "Every one who
drinks of this water will thirst again, but whoever drinks of the water that I shall give
him will never thirst; [it] will become in him a spring of water welling up to eternal
life." And Rev. 22:1, the angel shows John "the river of the water of life, bright as
crystal, flowing from the throne of God and of the Lamb [Christ]."   [31]The image of the
"frontier-forming mountain" develops from the (*Grab-*)*hügel* that divides life from
death, day from night. As the juxtaposition of the words *Berg* and *Hütten* (next paragraph) shows, the image comes from Mark 9:2-5: "Und nach sechs Tagen nahm Jesus
zu sich Petrus, Jakobus und Johannes und führte sie auf einen hohen *Berg* und
verklärte sich [was transfigured] vor ihnen. [His clothing becomes white as snow.
Elijah and Moses appear and speak with Jesus.] Und Petrus ... sprach zu Jesu: Rabbi,
hier ist gut sein; *lasset uns drei Hütten machen,* dir eine, Mose eine und Elia eine."

Oben baut er sich Hütten, Hütten des Friedens, sehnt sich und liebt, schaut hinüber, bis die willkommenste aller Stunden hinunter ihn in den Brunnen der Quelle zieht,[32] — das Irdische [15] schwimmt obenauf, wird von Stürmen zurückgeführt, aber was heilig durch der Liebe Berührung ward, rinnt aufgelöst in verborgenen Gängen auf das jenseitige Gebiet, wo es, wie Düfte, sich mit entschlummerten Lieben mischt.[33]

Noch weckst du, muntres Licht, den Müden zur Arbeit — [20] flößest fröhliches Leben mir ein[34] — aber du lockst mich von der Erinnerung moosigem Denkmal[35] nicht. Gern will ich die fleißigen Hände rühren, überall umschaun, wo du mich brauchst — rühmen deines Glanzes volle Pracht — unverdrossen verfolgen deines künstlichen Werks schönen Zusammenhang — gern betrachten dei- [25] ner gewaltigen, leuchtenden Uhr sinnvollen Gang[36] — ergründen der Kräfte Ebenmaß und die Regeln des Wunderspiels unzähliger Räume und ihrer Zeiten.[37] Aber getreu der Nacht bleibt mein geheimes Herz, und der schaffenden Liebe, ihrer Tochter. Kannst du mir zeigen ein ewig treues Herz? Hat deine Sonne freundliche [30] Augen, die mich erkennen? Fassen deine Sterne meine verlangende Hand? Geben mir wieder den zärtlichen Druck und das kosende Wort? Hast du mit Farben und leichtem Umriß Sie[38] geziert — oder war Sie[38] es, die deinem Schmuck höhere, liebere Bedeutung gab? Welche Wollust, welchen Genuß bietet dein [35] Leben, die   aufwögen[39] des Todes Entzückungen? Trägt nicht alles, was uns begeistert, die Farbe der Nacht? Sie trägt dich mütterlich und ihr verdankst du all deine Herrlichkeit. Du verflögst in dir selbst — in endlosen Raum zergingst du, wenn sie dich nicht hielte, dich nicht bände, daß du warm würdest und [40] flammend die Welt zeugtest. Wahrlich ich war, eh' du warst — die Mutter schickte mit meinen Geschwistern mich, zu bewohnen deine Welt, sie zu heiligen mit Liebe, daß sie ein ewig angeschautes Denkmal[40] werde — zu bepflanzen sie mit unverwelklichen Blumen. Noch reiften sie nicht diese göttlichen Gedanken — [45] Noch sind der Spuren unserer Offenbarung wenig[41] — Einst zeigt deine Uhr das Ende der Zeit, wenn du wirst wie unser einer, und

---

[32]i.e., into Christ the Grave whence flows the water of life. [33]What is immortal combines "like aromas with the loved ones who have gone before." The imagery continues that at the end of the 1st hymn. [34]*einflößen* 'infuse (with)' [35]i.e., the grave, which becomes a symbol of memory and *Treue* [36]i.e., the course of the sun [37]The tasks here mentioned belong to the field of physics. [38]i.e., the Night (capitalized for emphasis) [39]'would equal' [40]Not a monument that is eternally viewed but a monument made eternal by viewing: man gives the world spiritual (eternal) meaning. [41]Cf. MS version: *Mit meinem Geschlecht / Schickte die Mutter mich / Zu bewohnen deine Welt / Und zu heiligen sie / Mit Liebe. / Und zu geben / Menschlichen Sinn / Deinen Schöpfungen. / Noch reiften sie nicht / Diese göttlichen Gedanken / Noch sind der Spuren / Unsrer*

voll Sehnsucht und Inbrunst auslöschest und stirbst. In mir fühl'
ich deiner Geschäftigkeit Ende[42] — himmlische Freiheit, selige
Rückkehr. In wilden Schmerzen erkenn' ich deine Entfernung von [50]
unsrer Heimat, deinen Widerstand gegen den alten herrlichen
Himmel. Deine Wut und dein Toben ist vergebens. Unverbrenn-
lich steht das Kreuz — eine Siegesfahne unsers Geschlechts.[43]

Hinüber wall'[44] ich,
Und jede Pein   55
Wird einst ein Stachel
Der Wollust sein.[45]

Noch wenig Zeiten,
So bin ich los,
Und liege trunken   60
Der Lieb' im Schoß.

Unendliches Leben
Wogt[46] mächtig in mir
Ich schaue von oben
Herunter nach dir.[47]   65

An jenem Hügel
Verlischt dein Glanz[48] —
Ein Schatten bringet
Den kühlenden Kranz.

Gegenwart / Wenig. The Mother is of course Night, the *Weltgemüt* and feminine aspect
of the divine. For the idea of man's task as the spiritualization of the material, cf.
Angelus Silesius. [42]Since man is making the world into an image of himself and since
he feels a longing to return to the primal source, he knows that one day the world of
Light must also feel this longing: *Zugemessen ward dem Licht seine Zeit...* [43]*in hoc
signo vinces* (under this sign shalt thou conquer), the heavenly message to Constantine,
the first Christian emperor. The cross is the symbol of the overcoming of life through
death to gain true life. [44]*wallen* 'undulate, flow' *and* 'go on a pilgrimage' (*Wallfahrt*);
both meanings are active: see first paragraph of this hymn. [45]When this world is overcome, Novalis says elsewhere, *wir werden mehr genießen als je, denn unser Geist hat
entbehrt*: i.e., every present pain will become a *Stachel der Wollust*. [46]'undulates' —
further development of water imagery: life eternal springs within. [47]i.e., the World of
Light — the poet is *auf dem Grenzgebirge der Welt*. [48]The "hill" is the grave, one's
own and the Holy Sepulchre (which is on a hill, Golgatha). *Glanz* is of course here a
negative concept.

O! sauge, Geliebter,   70
Gewaltig mich an,[49]
Daß ich entschlummern
Und lieben kann.

Ich fühle des Todes
Verjüngende Flut,   75
Zu Balsam und Äther[50]
Verwandelt mein Blut —

Ich lebe bei Tage
Voll Glauben und Mut
Und sterbe die Nächte   80
In heiliger Glut.[51]

5

[52]Über der Menschen weitverbreitete Stämme herrschte vor
Zeiten ein eisernes Schicksal mit stummer Gewalt. Eine dunkle,
schwere Binde lag um ihre bange Seele. — Unendlich war die
Erde — der Götter Aufenthalt, und ihre Heimat.[53] Seit Ewigkeiten
stand ihr geheimnisvoller Bau. Über des Morgens roten Bergen, in   [5]
des Meeres heiligem Schoß wohnte die Sonne, das allzündende,
lebendige Licht. Ein alter Riese[54] trug die selige Welt. Fest unter
Bergen lagen die Ursöhne der Mutter Erde,[55] ohnmächtig in ihrer
zerstörenden Wut gegen das neue herrliche Göttergeschlecht und
dessen Verwandten, die fröhlichen Menschen. Des Meers dunkle,   [10]
grüne Tiefe war einer Göttin Schoß.[56] In den kristallenen Grotten
schwelgte ein üppiges Volk. Flüsse, Bäume, Blumen und Tiere
hatten menschlichen Sinn.[57] Süßer schmeckte der Wein von sicht-
barer Jugendfülle geschenkt[58] — ein Gott in den Trauben — eine
liebende, mütterliche Göttin, emporwachsend in vollen goldenen   [15]
Garben,[59] — der Liebe heilger Rausch ein süßer Dienst der schönsten Götterfrau[60] — ein ewig buntes Fest der Himmelskinder und
der Erdbewohner rauschte das Leben, wie ein Frühling, durch die

---

[49]Christ (*Geliebter*) as Death; *saugen* resumes the imagery of the first part of the 2nd
paragraph of this hymn: *bis die willkommenste aller Stunden hinunter ihn in den Brunnen der Quelle zieht.* [50]Development of motif of aromas and miscible gases introduced
at end of 1st hymn and continued here. The *Äther* meant is the chemical. [51]The last
four verses depict *das Doppelleben auf dem Grenzgebirge.* [52]The process we have just
followed in hymns 1-4 on a personal plane now unfolds on the plane of the history of
mankind. [53]The gods did not merely sojourn on earth, they lived there; there was no
transcendence. [54]Atlas [55]the Titans [56]Tethys, wife of Oceanus [57]Cf. "Die Götter
Griechenlands," to which Novalis is making indirect reference throughout this part of
the hymn. [58]'poured' (by Hebe) [59]Demeter [60]Aphrodite

Jahrhunderte hin — Alle Geschlechter verehrten kindlich die zarte, tausendfältige Flamme,[61] als das Höchste der Welt. E i n Ge- [20] danke nur war es, e i n entsetzliches Traumbild,

> Das furchtbar zu den frohen Tischen trat
> Und das Gemüt in wilde Schrecken hüllte.[62]
> Hier wußten selbst die Götter keinen Rat,
> Der die beklommne Brust mit Trost erfüllte.   25
> Geheimnisvoll war dieses Unholds[63] Pfad,
> Des Wut kein Flehn und keine Gabe stillte;
> Es war der Tod, der dieses Lustgelag[64]
> Mit Angst und Schmerz und Tränen unterbrach.
>
> Auf ewig nun von allem abgeschieden,   30
> Was hier das Herz in süßer Wollust regt,
> Getrennt von den Geliebten, die hienieden[65]
> Vergebne Sehnsucht, langes Weh bewegt,
> Schien matter Traum dem Toten nur beschieden,
> Ohnmächt'ges Ringen nur ihm auferlegt.[66]   35
> Zerbrochen war die Woge des Genusses
> Am Felsen des unendlichen Verdrusses.
>
> Mit kühnem Geist und hoher Sinnenglut
> Verschönte sich der Mensch die grause Larve,[67]
> Ein sanfter Jüngling löscht das Licht und ruht[68] —   40
> Sanft wird das Ende, wie ein Wehn der Harfe.
> Erinnrung schmilzt in kühler Schattenflut,[69]
> So sang das Lied dem traurigen Bedarfe.
> Doch unenträtselt blieb die ew'ge Nacht,
> Das ernste Zeichen einer fernen Macht.   45

Zu Ende neigte die alte Welt sich. Des jungen Geschlechts Lust-garten verwelkte — hinauf in den freieren, wüsten Raum strebten die unkindlichen, wachsenden Menschen.[70] Die Götter verschwan-den mit ihrem Gefolge — Einsam und leblos stand die Natur. Mit eiserner Kette band sie[71] die dürre Zahl und das strenge Maß. Wie [50] in Staub und Lüfte zerfiel in dunkle Worte die unermeßliche Blüte

---

[61]i.e., life in its thousandfold individuation [62]The hymn now returns to the opening sentence: the joyful pantheism of the pagan world is literally enclosed and vitiated by the thought of death. [63]'monster' — one thinks of Grendel. [64]'merry revel' [65]'here below' [66]Cf. the quite different picture painted by Schiller, "Die Götter Griechen-lands," lines 73ff. Novalis is nearer to the Greek idea. [67]'horrible mask' (death) [68]Cf. "Die Götter Griechenlands," 66ff. and note. [69]Lethe [70]The period of science and philosophy succeeds that of myth and poetry; space is "freer" and "barren" because the gods have gone. [71]accusative

des Lebens. Entflohen war der beschwörende[72] Glauben, und die allverwandelnde, allverschwisternde Himmelsgenossin, die Phantasie. Unfreundlich blies ein kalter Nordwind über die erstarrte Flur, und die erstarrte Wunderheimat verflog in den Äther.[73] Des [55] Himmels Fernen füllten mit leuchtenden Welten sich.[74] Ins tiefre[75] Heiligtum, in des Gemüts höhern[75] Raum zog mit ihren Mächten die Seele der Welt — zu walten dort bis zum Anbruch der tagenden[76] Weltherrlichkeit. Nicht mehr war das Licht der Götter Aufenthalt und himmlisches Zeichen — den Schleier der Nacht [60] warfen sie über sich. Die Nacht ward der Offenbarung mächtiger Schoß — in ihn kehrten die Götter zurück— schlummerten ein, um in neuen herrlichen Gestalten auszugehn über die veränderte Welt.[77] Im Volk, das vor allen verachtet, zu früh reif und der seligen Unschuld der Jugend trotzig fremd geworden war, erschien [65] mit niegesehenem Angesicht die neue Welt — In der Armut dichterischer Hütte — Ein Sohn der ersten Jungfrau und Mutter — Geheimnisvoller Umarmung unendliche Frucht. Des Morgenlands ahndende, blütenreiche Weisheit erkannte zuerst der neuen Zeit Beginn[78] — Zu des Königs demütiger Wiege wies ihr[79] ein Stern [70] den Weg. In der weiten Zukunft Namen huldigten sie ihm mit Glanz und Duft,[80] den höchsten Wundern der Natur. Einsam entfaltete das himmlische Herz sich zu einem Blütenkelch[81] allmächtiger Liebe — des Vaters hohem Antlitz zugewandt und ruhend an dem ahndungssel'gen Busen der lieblich ernsten Mutter. [75] Mit vergötternder Inbrunst schaute das weissagende Auge des blühenden Kindes auf die Tage der Zukunft, nach seinen Geliebten, den Sprossen seines Götterstammes,[82] unbekümmert über seiner Tage irdisches Schicksal. Bald sammelten die kindlichsten Gemüter, von inniger Liebe wundersam ergriffen, sich um ihn her. [80] Wie Blumen keimte ein neues fremdes Leben in seiner Nähe. Unerschöpfliche Worte und der Botschaften fröhlichste[83] fielen wie

---

[72]'invoking'; belief invokes the gods [73]Cf. "Die Götter Griechenlands," 96ff. [74]i.e., new planets were discovered, or a new interpretation was given to those already known. [75]Note completely figurative use of *tief* and *hoch*. [76]'dawning' [77]*Ins tiefre Heiligtum ... veränderte Welt:* "The world's soul with its powers" =the gods, who no longer manifest themselves in nature but have returned to the *Weltgemüt*, of which Night is here the symbol, to await the dawn of a new epoch of religious consciousness. The gods, like man, must be born again — they return to the womb to undergo a new gestation and rebirth. This parallels what happened to the "I" in the first part of the poem. [78]The Magi were first to worship the Christ Child. [79]=*der Weisheit* [80]i.e., with gold (*Glanz*) and frankincense and myrrh (*Duft*) [81]'blossom cup'; in the word *Kelch* lies a reference to the Eucharist. [82]'the shoots of his divine family tree (trunk)' =those who will believe in him; cf. John 15:5. [83]=*die fröhlichste der Botschaften*

Funken eines göttlichen Geistes von seinen freundlichen Lippen.
Von ferner Küste, unter Hellas' heiterm Himmel geboren, kam ein
Sänger nach Palästina und ergab sein ganzes Herz dem Wunder-   [85]
kinde:

> „Der Jüngling bist du, der seit langer Zeit
> Auf unsen Gräbern steht in tiefem Sinnen;[84]
> Ein tröstlich Zeichen in der Dunkelheit —
> Der höhern Menschheit freudiges Beginnen.   [90]
> Was uns gesenkt in tiefe Traurigkeit,
> Zieht uns mit süßer Sehnsucht nun von hinnen.
> Im Tode ward das ew'ge Leben kund,
> Du bist der Tod und machst uns erst gesund."

Der Sänger zog voll Freudigkeit nach Indostan — das Herz von   [95]
süßer Liebe trunken; und schüttete in feurigen Gesängen es unter
jenem milden Himmel aus, daß tausend Herzen sich zu ihm neigten, und die fröhliche Botschaft tausendzweigig emporwuchs.[85]
Bald nach des Sängers Abschied ward das köstliche Leben ein
Opfer des menschlichen tiefen Verfalls — Er starb in jungen   [100]
Jahren, weggerissen von der geliebten Welt, von der weinenden
Mutter und seinen zagenden Freunden. Der unsäglichen Leiden
dunkeln Kelch leerte der liebliche Mund — In entsetzlicher
Angst nahte die Stunde der Geburt der neuen Welt. Hart rang er
mit des alten Todes Schrecken — Schwer lag der Druck der alten   [105]
Welt auf ihm. Noch einmal sah er freundlich nach der Mutter —

---

[84]Cf. "Die Götter Griechenlands," 65ff. [85]The *Sänger* has given rise to much speculation. John 12:20ff. affords a hint, though not an explanation. Here we read of some
Greeks who have come to worship at the feast of the Passover and ask to see Jesus.
When He hears of this, He at once begins to speak of His approaching death and its
meaning. The singer's route: Greece — Palestine — India — reminds one of that of
Alexander the Great, who Hellenized the East, and above all of that of Dionysus, the
great *Freudebringer* (cf. Hölderlin's "An unsere großen Dichter"). Both proceeded in
triumph to India, bringing a *fröhliche Botschaft* (evangel, gospel). The singer is a
Westerner (Greek) who receives light from the Near East and carries it to the more
distant East, this being in fact what the Greeks, strongly influenced by the religious
thought of Asia Minor, actually did. More important than any historical or mythical
parallel, however, is the function of the singer within the poem: his *eastward* progress
balances that of the Magi *westward*: the latter proceed westward at Christ's birth, the
singer eastward just before the Passion. Separating the two journeys are the verses
interpreting Christ as Death and the overcoming of Death. The wisdom of the East
(philosophy) has a *presentiment* of the meaning of the *birth* of the Saviour (*des
Morgenlands ahnende ... Weisheit*), the singer from Hellas (poetry) *knows* the meaning
of his *death*. A new (transcendentalizing) poetry succeeds the old (mythologizing)
philosophy.

da kam der ewigen Liebe lösende Hand — und er entschlief.[86]
Nur wenig Tage hing ein tiefer Schleier über das brausende
Meer, über das bebende Land[87] — unzählige Tränen weinten die
Geliebten — Entsiegelt ward das Geheimnis — himmlische Geis-   [110]
ter hoben den uralten Stein vom dunkeln Grabe.[88] Engel saßen
bei dem Schlummernden — aus seinen Träumen zartgebildet[89] —
Erwacht in neuer Götterherrlichkeit erstieg er die Höhe der
neugebornen Welt — begrub mit eigner Hand der Alten Leich-
nam[90] in die verlaßne Höhle und legte mit allmächtiger Hand den   [115]
Stein, den keine Macht erhebt, darauf.

Noch weinen deine Lieben Tränen der Freude, Tränen der
Rührung und des unendlichen Danks an deinem Grabe — sehn
dich noch immer, freudig erschreckt, auferstehn — und sich mit
dir;[91] sehn dich weinen mit süßer Inbrunst an der Mutter seligem   [120]
Busen,[92] ernst mit Freunden wandeln, Worte sagen, wie vom
Baum des Lebens[93] gebrochen; sehen dich eilen mit voller Sehnsucht in des Vaters Arm,[94] bringend die junge Menschheit, und
der goldnen Zukunft unversieglichen Becher.[95] Die Mutter eilte
bald dir nach — in himmlischem Triumph — Sie war die Erste   [125]
in der neuen Heimat bei dir.[96] Lange Zeiten entflossen seitdem,
und in immer höherm Glanze regte deine neue Schöpfung sich[97]
— und Tausende zogen aus Schmerzen und Qualen, voll Glauben
und Sehnsucht und Treue dir nach — walten mit dir und der
himmlischen Jungfrau im Reiche der Liebe — dienen im Tempel   [130]
des himmlischen Todes und sind in Ewigkeit dein.

> Gehoben ist der Stein —
> Die Menschheit ist erstanden —

---

[86]*In entsetzlicher Angst ... entschlief*: Christ's struggle with death to give birth to the
new life parallels the poet's experience at the grave of his beloved (3rd hymn) — in
both instances unbearable anguish (the "old world's" view of death), in both instances
help "from above," in both instances death which leads to life. [87]Matthew 27:51; Luke
22:44-45 [88]Mentioned in all the synoptic Gospels. The grave was new, but the stone
uralt, for up to then it had separated life from death. [89]Cf. MS: *Engel saßen bei dem
Schlummernden, / Lieblicher Träume / Zartes S i n n b i l d.* Implied in John 20:12.
[90]The MS version makes it clear that *der Alten Leichnam* is *die alte mit ihm gestorb'ne
Welt.* [91]John 20:14-16 and 19ff. Cf. 1st hymn (end): *ein ernstes Antlitz seh ich f r o h
e r s c h r o c k e n, das ... sich zu mir neigt,* and the experience at the grave of the beloved (3rd hymn). [92]Not mentioned in New Testament. [93]Luke 24:13ff. and Acts 1:3
[94]Acts 1:9 [95]'cup that never runs dry' [96]The Assumption of the Virgin is not mentioned in the Gospels, though it has become a Roman Catholic dogma. Though from a
strict pietistic family, Novalis has a strong tendency toward Mariolatry, not suprising,
considering his devotion to the feminine aspect of the divine. [97]The realm of death,
which is night, becomes brighter and brighter as the poem progresses and as, within
the poem, Christianity spreads.

Wir alle bleiben dein
Und fühlen keine Banden.
Der herbste Kummer fleucht[98]   135
Vor deiner goldnen Schale,[99]
Wenn Erd' und Leben weicht,
Im letzten Abendmahle.[100]

Zur Hochzeit ruft der Tod —   140
Die Lampen brennen helle —
Die Jungfraun sind zur Stelle —
Um Öl ist keine Not[101] —
Erklänge doch die Ferne
Von deinem Zuge schon,[102]   145
Und ruften uns die Sternest
Mit Menschenzung' und Ton.

Nach dir, Maria, heben
Schon tausend Herzen sich.
In diesem Schattenleben[103]   150
Verlangten sie nur dich.
Sie hoffen zu genesen
Mit ahndungsvoller Lust —
Drückst du sie, heil'ges Wesen,
An deine treue Brust.   155

So manche, die sich glühend
In bittrer Qual verzehrt
Und dieser Welt entfliehend
Nach dir sich hingekehrt;
Die[104] hülfreich uns erschienen   160
In mancher Not und Pein —
Wir kommen nun zu ihnen,
Um ewig da zu sein.[105]

Nun[106] weint an keinem Grabe,
Für Schmerz, wer liebend glaubt.   165
Der Liebe süße Habe

---

[98]=*flieht* [99]Christ is the "cup." [100]Lord's Supper, Eucharist. [101]Cf. Matth. 25:1-13.
[102]Verses 13-14: 'Oh, if we could only hear thy (Christ's) procession approaching from
a distance' — the metaphor of the wedding party is continued. [103]Life in the realm of
this light has now become a *Schattenleben*. [104]The construction is broken off after the
semicolon, line 28; *Die* 'those who.' [105]*Sein* used in pregnant sense: not merely 'to be
there eternally,' but 'to exist in the way of eternity.' [106]*Nun* — in contrast to the time
before Christ.

Wird keinem nicht geraubt[107] —
Die Sehnsucht ihm zu lindern,
Begeistert ihn die Nacht[108] —
Von treuen Himmelskindern   170
Wird ihm sein Herz bewacht.

Getrost, das Leben schreitet
Zum ew'gen Leben hin;
Von innrer Glut geweitet
Verklärt sich unser Sinn.   175
Die Sternwelt wird zerfließen[109]
Zum goldnen Lebenswein,
Wir werden sie genießen
Und lichte Sterne sein.

Die Lieb' ist frei gegeben,   180
Und keine Trennung mehr.
Es wogt das volle Leben
Wie ein unendlich Meer.[109]
Nur e i n e Nacht der Wonne —
E i n ewiges Gedicht[110] —   185
Und unser aller Sonne[111]
Ist Gottes Angesicht.[112]

Towards Interpretation

1. The "Hymnen an die Nacht" tend to present the known as the unknown and vice versa. Indicate how this principle is applied in the 5th hymn in the case of the Greek gods, the river Lethe, the Jewish people, the Three Kings, the disciples, the Passion. Find examples of the opposite procedure. What is the poet, according to his own definition, doing when he does this?

2. List the first 100 adjectives used in the "Hymnen" (note those used more than once). Do these adjectives tend to specify in the direction of concreteness and plasticity? What force would you say they have?

3. Comment at some length on the development of the *Schoß* image. First record each instance of its occurrence, noting context, then com-

[107]The double negative, as well as many other turns, imitates the style of old church hymns. [108]Cf. first four hymns — the experience of the "I" is universalized. [109]The imagery of liquidity is resumed; compare end of fourth hymn. [110]This metaphor throws much light not only on Novalis's conception of poetry but also on that of the Romantics in general: Poetry is the finding of analogies which lead to a sense of oneness. [111]The "sun of *us all*" is God, in contrast to the *zarte Geliebte — liebliche Sonne der Nacht* at the end of the first hymn, who was only the poet's personal "sun." See also end of third hymn. [112]The final hymn, "Sehnsucht nach dem Tode," is omitted here.

pare these passages. Remember that *Schoß* has a wide range of meaning: 'lap,' 'womb,' 'bosom' (in Abraham's bosom, in the bosom of the Father), 'depths.'

4. Find as many analogies as you can between the personal "conversion" of the poet to the worship of Night and the conversion of mankind to Christianity. Look especially for similar turns of phrase in these two divisions of the poem.

5. We have stressed the thematic unity of the "Hymnen." Is there a similar stylistic unity? What seems to guide the poet in his choice of form? Why is *Gehoben ist der Stein* (end of 5th hymn) composed in the manner of a *Kirchenlied*? Can you think why the poem at the end of the 4th hymn is not written in this style?

6. "Absolute Abstraktion, Annihilation des Jetzigen — Apotheose der Zukunft, dieser eigentlichen, bessern Welt: dies ist der Kern der Geheiße [commandments] des Christentums. . ." (Novalis, *Fragmente*). How does this accord with what you found out in Exercise 2 about the use of adjectives in the "Hymnen"?

7. In the "Hymnen an die Nacht" Novalis operates very largely with what we might call "metaphysical irony." This takes the form of showing that that to which absolute value is attributed is in fact limited and dependent. Trace this procedure in the first and fifth hymns.

8. In the second hymn the universal which displaced that which was first posited as universal is in its turn displaced, i.e., we have double irony. How does this happen? By what means does the "I" seek to overcome this second limitation? Is this a true solution? If not, where and how does the true solution come about?

9. Presumably not everyone can be granted the experience described in the third hymn. What experience is posited as possible for all?

Sophie Mereau (Brentano) (1770-1806)

An einen Baum am Spalier

Armer Baum! — an deiner kalten Mauer
fest gebunden, stehst du traurig da,
fühlest kaum den Zephyr, der mit süßem Schauer
in den Blättern freier Bäume weilt
und bei deinen leicht vorübereilt.   5

O! dein Anblick geht mir nah!
und die bilderreiche Phantasie
stellt mit ihrer flüchtigen Magie
eine menschliche Gestalt schnell vor mich hin,
die, auf ewig von dem freien Sinn   10
der Natur entfernt, ein fremder Drang
auch wie dich in steife Formen zwang.

"An einen Baum am Spalier" uses a nature metaphor to illustrate just how difficult emotional — and intellectual — freedom is to achieve. Notice how the poem is slowly paced by long, open vowel sounds on the accented syllables (*a*, *au*, *ü*, *ä*, *äu*, *ei*) in the first five verses, but then, as the tree becomes ever more representative of human experience, the open sounds give way to a more consonantal and constricted (*flüchtigen*, *menschliche*) sound environment, only to end on the one word that summarizes the theme of the poem: *zwang*.

Towards Interpretation

1. Accepting Mereau's conceit *Baum=Mensch*, suggest: 1) Why would a person be espaliered? Hint: why is a tree espaliered? 2) Who would be the gardener? 3) What would be the trellis?
2. Can you think of one reason why this conceit might be considered an inadequate representation of the human experience?

Sophie Mereau Brentano

Clemens Brentano

Clemens Brentano (1778-1842)

„Was reif in diesen Zeilen steht"

Was reif in diesen Zeilen steht,
Was lächelnd winkt und sinnend fleht,
Das soll kein Kind betrüben,
Die Einfalt hat es ausgesät,
Die Schwermut hat hindurchgeweht,   5
Die Sehnsucht hat's getrieben;[1]
Und ist das Feld einst abgemäht,
Die Armut durch die Stoppeln geht,
Sucht Ähren, die geblieben,
Sucht Lieb', die für sie untergeht,   10
Sucht Lieb', die mit ihr aufersteht,
Sucht Lieb', die sie kann lieben.
Und hat sie einsam und verschmäht
Die Nacht durch, dankend in Gebet,
Die Körner ausgerieben,[2]   15
Liest sie, als früh der Hahn gekräht,
Was Lieb' erhielt, was Leid verweht,[3]
Ans Feldkreuz[4] angeschrieben:
„O Stern und Blume, Geist und Kleid,
Lieb', Leid und Zeit und Ewigkeit!"   20

Towards Interpretation

1. What is the basic metaphor of this poem?
2. How are the abstractions (*Einfalt, Schwermut, Sehnsucht, Armut*) given life?
3. Work out the rime scheme and note the way in which the poem is built up. Do any of the rimes seem forced?
4. Does the poem make sense when we examine it closely? What *does* stand ripe? Why should the gleanings Poverty finds be the essence of the poet's work? Surely other ears also "stood ripe in these lines"? Or are the things enumerated in the last two lines all-inclusive, even "cosmically" inclusive?

---

[1] 'made grow' [2] 'rubbed the kernels out (of the husks)' [3] The line may mean: 'what has preserved love and dispersed sorrow' or 'what love has preserved and sorrow dispersed.' [4] A crucifix in the fields is a common sight in Catholic lands.

Wiegenlied

Singet leise, leise, leise,
Singt ein flüsternd Wiegenlied,
Von dem Monde lernt die Weise,[1]
Der so still am Himmel zieht.

Singt ein Lied so süß gelinde,   5
Wie die Quellen auf den Kieseln,
Wie die Bienen um die Linde
Summen, murmeln, flüstern, rieseln.

Towards Interpretation
1. If the book is available to you, read what Wolfgang Kayser has to say about this poem in his *Kleine deutsche Versschule.**
2. The poem *is* what it tells us to *do*. Explain. Is this possible in anything but poetry?
3. What kinds of sounds predominate in these lines? What is their effect?

Sprich aus der Ferne!

Sprich aus der Ferne
Heimliche Welt,
Die sich so gerne
Zu mir gesellt!

Wenn das Abendrot niedergesunken,   5
Keine freudige Farbe mehr spricht,
Und die Kränze stilleuchtender Funken
Die Nacht um die schattigte Stirne flicht:[1]

Wehet der Sterne
Heiliger Sinn   10
Leis durch die Ferne
Bis zu mir hin.

Wenn des Mondes still lindernde Tränen
Lösen der Nächte verborgenes Weh,
Dann wehet Friede. In goldenen Kähnen   15
Schiffen die Geister im himmlischen See.

[1]'melody'

*Wolfgang Kayser, *Kleine deutsche Versschule* (Bern: Francke, 21 1982), 103ff.

[1]'braids'

Glänzender Lieder
Klingender Lauf
Ringelt sich nieder,
Wallet hinauf.   20

Wenn der Mitternacht heiliges Grauen[2]
Bang durch die dunkeln Wälder hinschleicht,
Und die Büsche gar wundersam schauen,
Alles sich finster, tiefsinnig bezeugt:[3]

Wandelt im Dunkeln   25
Freundliches Spiel,
Still Lichter funkeln
Schimmerndes Ziel.

Alles ist freundlich wohlwollend verbunden,
Bietet sich tröstend und traurend die Hand,   30
Sind durch die Nächte die Lichter gewunden,[4]
Alles ist ewig im Innern verwandt.

Sprich aus der Ferne,
Heimliche Welt,
Die sich so gerne   35
Zu mir gesellt!

Towards Interpretation

1. Do we find the basic striving of Romanticism, the fusion of the real with the ideal (cf. p. 162), reflected in this poem? Explain.
2. Lines 17-20 constitute the mathematical axis of the poem. Do they also constitute its thematic axis? Explain.
3. What are the "wreaths of softly glowing sparks" that Night braids about her brow in lines 7-8?
4. How does the use of personification throughout the poem help make us assent to the statement in lines 29-30?
5. The syntax here is that of rational argumentation: When so and so happens, it shows so and so. Does rationalism play a decisive role in the poem?

---

[2]'dread'   [3]'shows itself to be'   [4]'twined'

Der Spinnerin Nachtlied

Es sang vor langen Jahren
Wohl auch die Nachtigall,
Das war wohl süßer Schall,
Da wir zusammen waren.

Ich sing' und kann nicht weinen   5
Und spinne so allein
Den Faden klar und rein,
Solang der Mond wird scheinen.

Als wir zusammen waren,
Da sang die Nachtigall;   10
Nun mahnet mich ihr Schall,
Daß du von mir gefahren.

So oft der Mond mag scheinen,
Denk' ich wohl dein[1] allein;
Mein Herz ist klar und rein,   15
Gott wolle uns vereinen!

Seit du von mir gefahren,
Singt stets die Nachtigall;
Ich denk' bei ihrem Schall,
Wie wir zusammen waren.   20

Gott wolle uns vereinen,
Hier spinn' ich so allein,
Der Mond scheint klar und rein,
Ich sing' und möchte weinen!

"Der Spinnerin Nachtlied"* charms first of all by its artful riming: only two vowels, *a* and *ei*, are employed and only one of the two is used in any one stanza; the first and last verses of each stanza have feminine endings, the middle verses masculine. *a*- and *ei*-stanzas alternate regularly throughout. And not only do we find the same riming *vowels* but also the same *words* — in addition to those in stanzas 1 and 2, only two others are added (in stanzas 3 and 4): *gefahren* and *vereinen* (these reflect the contrast between plaint and longing that runs through the whole poem). *Gefahren* enters in the *a*-stanza (the

---

[1]genitive, 'of you'

*This analysis follows closely that of Erich Hock in *Motivgleiche Gedichte: Lehrerband*, Am Born der Literatur A7L (Bamberg: Bayerische Verlagsanstalt, [7]1963), 34ff. The student's attention is also called to the excellent interpretation by Wilhelm Schneider, *Liebe zum deutschen Gedicht* (Freiburg: Herder, [5]1963), 247ff.

nightingale stanza), which speaks of the past, but opens into the present (verse 11); *vereinen* enters in the *ei*-stanza (moon), which speaks of the present and looks forward to the future (verse 16). In a constant back-and-forth between Then and Now, the whole poem revolves monotonously about the one thing that occupies the mind of the *Spinnerin*. One at first has the impression the song could be spun out forever.

Let us examine the way in which Brentano joins the threads. The final verse of each stanza appears (sometimes varied) as the first verse of the stanza after the next, so that all stanzas except the first and last are enclosed by like verses. But while the position of the enclosing verses constantly shifts, the interior verses repeat in the stanza after the next in the same order. In the *ei*-stanzas, however, the repetitive phrase *klar und rein* is always associated with a different word: *Faden – Herz – Mond*. These are the elements that build up the situation delineated in the song: the *thread* represents the activity of spinning; the lonely *heart* sings of its sorrow; the *moon* shines into the room. Only the nightingale is lacking, and to it the other three stanzas are given. When the words *klar und rein* have been applied to *Faden, Herz, Mond*, all three, the variation is at an end. To continue, another element would need to be introduced. Thus, though the impression of an endless plaint persists, we see that the song could not go on forever and that it does not just end by chance after six stanzas.

In motif, vocabulary and mood, "Der Spinnerin Nachtlied" is reminiscent of the folksong, though of folksong in highly artistic transformation. Together with his brother-in-law Achim von Arnim (whose idea it was), Brentano collected and edited a famous anthology of German folksongs called *Des Knaben Wunderhorn* (first volume, 1805), one of the most significant achievements of the German Romantic movement. The impulse to collect such pieces goes back to Johann Gottfried Herder (1744-1803), one of the fathers of Romanticism, and, ultimately, to England and Percy's *Reliques of Ancient English Poetry* (first edition, 1765). So great was Brentano's affinity for the *Volkslied* that he not only applied its techniques and turns of phrase in his own verse but also actually wrote some of the "folksongs" included in the *Wunderhorn*, passing them off without any difficulty as genuine. After the publication of the *Wunderhorn*, the *Volkslied* became one of the most pervasive influences in German poetry. We hear the *Volksliedton* throughout the nineteenth century, though not of course in all writers. The so-called *Volksliedstrophe* has the rime scheme *a b a b* (although not followed in "Der Spinnerin Nachtlied"), usually with alternating masculine and feminine endings. Each stanza forms a clear-cut unit, emphasized by the nearness of the rimes. "Große Aufgipfelungen und starke Erregtheit haben in ihr [der Volksliedstrophe] keinen Platz," writes Wolfgang Kayser, "der Ton ist vielmehr verhalten [restrained]."*

---

*Kayser, *Kleine deutsche Versschule*, 39.

In the following ballad composed in the folksong manner we see Brentano as myth-maker. The figure of the Lore Lay (also Lorelei and Lurelay) is wholly his own creation (though influenced by the Tannhäuser legend), but it first became a permanent part of German imaginative culture largely through Heine's later treatment of the theme.* For most people the story is what Heine called it: "ein Märchen aus alten Zeiten," and few realize that the "olden times" are no older than 1801, the probable date of Brentano's "Lore Lay."

Lore Lay

Zu Bacharach am Rheine
Wohnt' eine Zauberin,
Sie war so schön und feine
Und riß viel Herzen hin.

Und brachte viel zuschanden   5
Der Männer[1] ringsumher;
Aus ihren Liebesbanden
War keine Rettung mehr.

Der Bischof ließ sie laden
Vor geistliche Gewalt[2] —   10
Und mußte sie begnaden,
So schön war ihr' Gestalt.

Er sprach zu ihr gerühret:
„Du arme Lore Lay!
Wer hat dich denn verführet   15
Zu böser Zauberei?"

„Herr Bischof, laßt mich sterben,
Ich bin des Lebens müd,
Weil jeder muß verderben,
Der meine Augen sieht.   20

Die Augen sind zwei Flammen,
Mein Arm ein Zauberstab —

---

*Heine's poem does not go back directly to Brentano's but to another version of the Lorelei "legend" in a poem by Otto Heinrich von Loeben. Loeben is, however, dependent on Brentano, both on the latter's poem "Lore Lay" and his "Frau Lure Lay" in the *Rheinmärchen*. Eichendorff also wrote a poem on this theme (see p. 225).

[1]*viel ... der Männer* 'many men'   [2]'summoned her before ecclesiastical authority'

O legt mich in die Flammen!
O brechet mir den Stab!"[3]

„Ich kann dich nicht verdammen,   25
Bis du mir erst bekennt,
Warum in diesen Flammen
Mein eigen Herz schon brennt.

Den Stab kann ich nicht brechen,
Du schöne Lore Lay!   30
Ich müßte dann zerbrechen
mein eigen Herz entzwei!"

„Herr Bischof, mit mir Armen[4]
Treibt nicht so bösen Spott,
Und bittet um Erbarmen   35
Für mich den lieben Gott!

Ich darf nicht länger leben,
Ich liebe keinen mehr —
Den Tod sollt Ihr mir geben,
Drum kam ich zu Euch her. —   40

Mein Schatz hat mich betrogen,
Hat sich von mir gewandt,
Ist fort von hier gezogen,
Fort in ein fremdes Land.

Die Augen sanft und wilde,   45
Die Wangen rot und weiß,
Die Worte still und milde,
Das ist mein Zauberkreis.

Ich selbst muß drin verderben,
Das Herz tut mir so weh,   50
Vor Schmerzen möcht' ich sterben,
Wenn ich mein Bildnis seh'.

Drum laßt mein Recht mich finden,
Mich sterben, wie ein Christ,
Denn alles muß verschwinden,   55
Weil er nicht bei mir ist."

Drei Ritter läßt er holen:
„Bringt sie ins Kloster hin!

---

[3]A staff was broken over a condemned person as a symbol of the death decree. [4]'with me poor woman'

Geh, Lore! — Gott befohlen[5]
Sei dein berückter[6] Sinn!   60

Du sollst ein Nönnchen werden,
Ein Nönnchen schwarz und weiß,
Bereite dich auf Erden
Zu deines Todes Reis'."

Zum Kloster sie nun ritten,   65
Die Ritter alle drei,
Und traurig in der Mitten
Die schöne Lore Lay.

„O Ritter, laßt mich gehen
Auf diesen Felsen groß!   70
Ich will noch einmal sehen
Nach meines Lieben Schloß.

Ich will noch einmal sehen
Wohl in den tiefen Rhein
Und dann ins Kloster gehen   75
Und Gottes Jungfrau sein."

Der Felsen ist so jähe,[7]
So steil ist seine Wand,
Doch klimmt sie in die Höhe,
Bis daß sie oben stand.   80

Es binden die drei Ritter
Die Rosse unten an
Und klettern immer weiter
Zum Felsen auch hinan.

Die Jungfrau sprach: „Da gehet   85
Ein Schifflein auf dem Rhein;
Der in dem Schifflein stehet,
Der soll[8] mein Liebster sein.

Mein Herz wird mir so munter,
Er muß mein Liebster sein! — "   90
Da lehnt sie sich hinunter
Und stürzet in den Rhein.

Die Ritter mußten sterben,
Sie konnten nicht hinab;

---

[5]'commended unto' [6]'enchanted,' 'strayed' [7]'steep' [8]Note that the Lore Lay does not
say he *is* her lover.

Sie mußten all verderben,   95
Ohn' Priester und ohn' Grab.

Wer hat dies Lied gesungen?
Ein Schiffer auf dem Rhein,
Und immer hat's geklungen
Von dem Dreiritterstein:⁹   100

Lore Lay!
Lore Lay!
Lore Lay!
Als wären es meiner drei.¹⁰

Frühlingsschrei eines Knechtes aus der Tiefe

Meister, ohne dein Erbarmen
Muß im Abgrund ich verzagen,
Willst du nicht mit starken Armen
Wieder mich zum Lichte tragen.

Jährlich greifet deine Güte   5
In die Erde, in die Herzen,
Jährlich weckest du die Blüte,
Weckst in mir die alten Schmerzen.

Einmal nur zum Licht geboren,
Aber tausendmal gestorben,   10
Bin ich ohne dich verloren,
Ohne dich in mir verdorben.

Wenn sich so die Erde reget,
Wenn die Luft so sonnig wehet,
Dann wird auch die Flut beweget,   15
Die in Todesbanden stehet.

Und in meinem Herzen schauert
Ein betrübter, bittrer Bronnen,
Wenn der Frühling draußen lauert,
Kommt die Angstflut angeronnen.   20

---

⁹"Bei Bacharach steht dieser Felsen, Lore Lay genannt, alle vorbeifahrende Schiffer rufen ihn an und freuen sich des vielfachen Echos" (Brentano's note). Actually, the *Loreleifelsen* (or *Lurlei*) is a good way down the Rhine from Bacharach. The name means *Elfenstein*, its echo having been interpreted as the calling of an elf from the bluff. Brentano was no doubt attracted to the name (as also to Bacharach) by its melodiousness. ¹⁰'as though there were three of me'

Weh! durch gift'ge Erdenlagen,
Wie die Zeit sie angeschwemmet,[1]
Habe ich den Schacht geschlagen,
Und er ist nur schwach verdämmet.[2]

Wenn nun rings die Quellen schwellen,   25
Wenn der Grund gebärend ringet,
Brechen her die bittern Wellen,
Die kein Witz,[3] kein Fluch mir zwinget.[4]

Andern ruf' ich: „Schwimme, schwimme!"
Mir kann solcher Ruf nicht taugen!   30
Denn in mir ja steigt die grimme
Sündflut,[5] bricht aus meinen Augen.

Und dann scheinen bös Gezüchte[6]
Mir die bunten Lämmer[7] alle,
Die ich grüßte, süße Früchte,   35
Die mir reiften,[8] bittre Galle.

Herr, erbarme du dich meiner,
Daß mein Herz neu blühend werde!
Mein erbarmte sich noch keiner
Von den Frühlingen der Erde.   40

Meister, wenn dir alle Hände
Nahn mit süß erfüllten Schalen,
Kann ich mit der bittern Spende[9]
Meine Schuld dir nimmer zahlen.

Ach! wie ich auch tiefer wühle,   45
Wie ich schöpfe,[10] wie ich weine,
Nimmer ich den Schwall erspüle[11]
Zum Kristallgrund[12] fest und reine!

Immer stürzen mir die Wände,
Jede Schicht hat mich belogen,   50
Und die arbeitblut'gen Hände
Brennen in den bittern Wogen.

Weh! der Raum wird immer enger,
Wilder, wüster stets die Wogen;

---

[1]'deposited' [2]'timbered' [3]i.e., defenses of reason [4]'control' [5]'deluge' (Biblical)
[6]'(an) evil brood' [7]The 'motley lambs' apparently connote sensual delights. [8]Supply
scheinen mir. [9]'offering' (cf. 35f.) [10]'bail' [11]'wash away' [12]i.e., inner purity

Herr, o Herr! ich treib's nicht länger,[13]   55
Schlage deinen Regenbogen![14]

Herr, ich mahne dich: Verschone!
Herr, ich hört' in jungen Tagen,
Wunderbare Rettung wohne —
Ach! — in deinem Blute, sagen.   60

Und so muß ich zu dir schreien,
Schreien aus der bittern Tiefe,
Könntest du auch nie verzeihen,
Daß dein Knecht so kühnlich riefe.

Daß des Lichtes Quelle wieder   65
Rein und heilig in mir flute,
Träufle einen Tropfen nieder,
Jesus, mir von deinem Blute!

The two most striking features of Brentano's verse are its melodiousness and its wealth of metaphor. "Wiegenlied" shows his melodious magic at its most enchanting, while "Frühlingsschrei" depends for its effect mainly on metaphor. The principal metaphors are:

1) That of a miner in an unsafe shaft. The shaft is the life, the *Erdenlagen, wie die Zeit sie angeschwemmet,* the poet (=miner) has lived in up to now.

2) Another important metaphor derives from the 69th Psalm: "Save me, O God; for the waters are come in unto my soul. I sink in deep mire, where there is no standing. . . . I am weary of my crying: my throat is dried: mine eyes fail while I wait for my God."

3) The regenerative power of spring, the welling up of the waters of life, which for the miner in his poorly timbered shaft, that is, for the poet in his misspent life, become the waters of death.*

4) Darkness and light, which come to stand for damnation and redemption.

The only salvation from the waters that "are come in unto his soul" is the blood of the Saviour. The poem was written shortly before Brentano's return to the Roman Catholic Church (1816).

---

[13]'can go on no longer' [14]i.e., the rainbow of promise (cf. 31f.)

*Cf. the first lines of T. S. Eliot's *Waste Land*: "April is the cruellest month, breeding / Lilacs out of the dead land, mixing / Memory and desire, stirring / Dull roots with spring rain. / Winter kept us warm, covering / Earth in forgetful snow, feeding / A little life with dried tubers."

Towards Interpretation

1. The poetical harvest of the years after Brentano's return to Catholicism is rather meagre. Do you see any possible connection between this fact and the striving of Romanticism to fuse the real with the ideal? Base your answer on an analysis of *Frühlingsschrei*.

Karoline von Günderode (1780-1806)

Liebe

O reiche Armut! Gebend, seliges Empfangen!
In Zagheit Mut! in Freiheit doch gefangen.
    In Stummheit Sprache —
    Schüchtern bei Tage —
Siegend mit zaghaftem Bangen.   5

Lebendiger Tod, im Einen sel'ges Leben
Schwelgend in Not, im Widerstand ergeben,
    Genießend schmachten,
    Nie satt betrachten
Leben im Traum und doppelt Leben.   10

Towards Interpretation

1. Stanza 1 refers to daytime existence, stanza 2, to the world of dreams. Why is there real happiness only in the latter?

Love — or rather disappointed love — and death are the two main themes of Günderode's poetry. Her reputation as a poet has suffered from the fact that it is almost impossible to separate Günderode the poet from Günderode the person. Unfortunately, the poetry itself encourages us to do this, since it is clear that when the poet reveals intense emotions, these are Günderode's emotions and no one else's: where truly great poets transform their own emotions through poetry into universals, Günderode's poetry never seems to transcend the raw imminence of personal experience. What is unusual about these poems, however, is that the restraints placed upon expression by meter and rime leave her intense passions undiminished. Poetic form seems to heighten their intensity almost to the limit of bearability.

Günderode's life story leaves little doubt that the intensity of her poetic voice was an accurate reflection of her existence, and her suicide at the age of twenty-six would suggest that eventually she herself could no longer bear that existence. The love she sought remained elusive: the legal historian Karl von Savigny, who is believed to have been put off by the intensity of her love for him, broke off with her; Clemens Brentano forsook her to marry Sophie Mereau, and the married classics professor Friedrich Creuzer eventually rejected her in favor of his wife. It was this final rejection that brought on her suicide. While some literary historians have deprecated Günderode's poetry as the work of an obsessive, "Romantic" personality with a sentimental fixation on death, it is perhaps above all the authenticity of her poetic voice that makes her poetry genuinely memorable.

"Die eine Klage" was printed in a volume of poetry which she dedicated to Creuzer, *Melete*; but after she took her life, he suppressed its publication.

Die eine Klage

Wer die tiefste aller Wunden
Hat in Geist und Sinn empfunden
Bittrer Trennung Schmerz;
Wer geliebt was er verloren,
Lassen muß was er erkoren,   5
Das geliebte Herz,

Der[1] versteht in Lust die Tränen
Und der Liebe ewig Sehnen
Eins in Zwei zu sein,
Eins im Andern sich zu finden,   10
Daß der Zweiheit Grenzen schwinden
Und des Daseins Pein.

Wer so ganz in Herz und Sinnen
Konnt' ein Wesen liebgewinnen
O! den tröstet's nicht,   15
Daß für Freuden, die verloren,
Neue werden neu geboren:
Jene sind's doch nicht.

Das geliebte, süße Leben,
Dieses Nehmen und dies Geben,   20

---

[1]Lines 1-6 are dependent clauses preceding the main clause beginning with line 7, *Der. . . .*

Wort und Sinn und Blick,
Dieses Suchen und dies Finden,
Dieses Denken und Empfinden
Giebt kein Gott zurück.

Towards Interpretation
 1. What is *die eine Klage*?
 2. What proffered consolation is rejected as vain in lines 13ff.?

Der Kuß im Traume

Es hat ein Kuß mir Leben eingehaucht,
Gestillet meines Busens tiefstes Schmachten,
Komm, Dunkelheit! mich traulich zu umnachten,
Daß neue Wonne meine Lippe saugt.

In Träume war solch Leben eingetaucht,   5
Drum leb' ich, ewig Träume zu betrachten,
Kann aller andern Freuden Glanz verachten,
Weil nur die Nacht so süßen Balsam haucht.

Der Tag ist karg an liebesüßen Wonnen,
Es schmerzt mich seines Lichtes eitles Prangen   10
Und mich verzehren seiner Sonne Gluten.
Drum birg dich Aug' dem Glanze ird'scher Sonnen!
Hüll' dich in Nacht, sie stillet dein Verlangen
Und heilt den Schmerz, wie Lethes kühle Fluten.

Towards Interpretation
 1. How does "Der Kuß im Traume" serve as a commentary on "Liebe"?

Ludwig Uhland (1787-1862)

Frühlingsglaube

Die linden Lüfte sind erwacht,
Sie säuseln und weben Tag und Nacht,
Sie schaffen[1] an allen Enden.
O frischer Duft, o neuer Klang!
Nun, armes Herze, sei nicht bang!   5
Nun muß sich alles, alles wenden.

Die Welt wird schöner mit jedem Tag,
Man weiß nicht, was noch werden mag,
Das Blühen will nicht enden.
Es blüht das fernste, tiefste Tal: 10
Nun, armes Herz, vergiß der[2] Qual!
Nun muß sich alles, alles wenden.

Der gute Kamerad

Ich hatt' einen Kameraden,
Einen bessern find'st du nit.
Die Trommel schlug zum Streite,
Er ging an meiner Seite
In gleichem Schritt und Tritt.   5

Eine Kugel kam geflogen,
Gilt's mir oder gilt es dir?
Ihn hat es weggerissen,
Er liegt mir vor den Füßen,
Als wär's ein Stück von mir.   10

Will mir die Hand noch reichen,
Derweil ich eben lad':[1]
„Kann dir die Hand nicht geben,
Bleib' du im ew'gen Leben
Mein guter Kamerad!"   5

---

[1]'are busy' [2]genitive with *vergessen*

[1]'just as I'm loading my gun'

In this poem Uhland presents a deeply ethical message with complete plasticity by means of a series of gestures and tableaux, without a word of overt moralizing.

Towards Interpretation

1. How is the *statement* in lines 1-2 translated into *gesture* in lines 4-5? What element of possible separation enters in the first stanza? How is it overcome?
2. Does the outside force that enters in the second stanza succeed in destroying the comradeship of the two soldiers? How is this expressed in gestic language?
3. In the last stanza, how does the gesture that shows the separation between the living and the dying also show their true union?
4. Why is the speaker's loading his rifle instead of giving his hand to his dying friend not a betrayal of their friendship?

Ludwig Uhland

Joseph v. Eichendorff

Friedrich Rückert

Joseph Freiherr v. Eichendorff (1788-1857)

Frische Fahrt

Laue Luft kommt blau geflossen,
Frühling, Frühling soll es sein!
Waldwärts Hörnerklang geschossen,[1]
Mut'ger Augen lichter Schein;
Und das Wirren bunt und bunter   5
Wird ein magisch wilder Fluß,
In die schöne Welt hinunter
Lockt dich dieses Stromes Gruß.

Und ich mag mich nicht bewahren![2]
Weit von euch treibt mich der Wind,   10
Auf dem Strome will ich fahren,
Von dem Glanze selig blind!
Tausend Stimmen lockend schlagen,[3]
Hoch Aurora[4] flammend weht,
Fahre zu! ich mag nicht fragen,   15
Wo die Fahrt zu Ende geht!

Towards Interpretation

1. Is *dieser Strom* (line 8) an actual river?
2. How do the syntax and imagery of lines 3-4 bring out the *Wirren* of line 5?
3. "Frische Fahrt" treats one of Eichendorff's central themes: the attraction of the world of appearances, *die schöne Welt*. Do the modals and such words as *locken, blind, Wirren, magisch wild* suggest any ethical overtones in the presentation of this world?

---

[1]'woodwards rings the sound of hunting horns'   [2]*bewahren* 'keep myself intact,' 'resist the influence'   [3]'call' (as a bird)   [4]goddess of the dawn

222

Schöne Fremde[1]

Es rauschen die Wipfel und schauern,[2]
Als machten zu dieser Stund'
Um die halbversunkenen Mauern
Die alten Götter[3] die Rund'.

Hier hinter den Myrtenbäumen   5
In heimlich dämmernder Pracht,
Was sprichst du wirr wie in Träumen
Zu mir, phantastische Nacht?

Es funkeln auf mich alle Sterne   10
Mit glühendem Liebesblick,
Es redet trunken die Ferne
Wie von künftigem, großem Glück! —

Towards Interpretation

1. The myrtle was sacred to Venus. What does this add to our appreciation of this poem?
2. The title is intentionally ambiguous. What may it refer to besides Italy (to the singer a strange and foreign land)?
3. Compare the attraction here exercised by night with that exercised by morning in "Frische Fahrt." What is the common denominator, i.e., what makes the attraction irresistible in both instances? What feeling is especially appealed to?

Nachtzauber

Hörst du nicht die Quellen gehen
Zwischen Stein und Blumen weit
Nach den stillen Waldes-Seen,
Wo die Marmorbilder stehen
In der schönen Einsamkeit?   5
Von den Bergen sacht hernieder,
Weckend die uralten Lieder,
Steigt die wunderbare Nacht,
Und die Gründe[1] glänzen wieder,
Wie du's oft im Traum gedacht.   10

---

[1]*die Fremde =unbekanntes, unheimisches Land*; these verses are sung by a young German, Fortunat, in Italy in Eichendorff's novel *Dichter und ihre Gesellen* (chapter 15). [2]'be seized with a slight tremor' [3]In the novel, statues of the gods stand in the park outisde Fortunat's window.

[1]'hollows,' 'valleys'

Kennst die Blume du, entsprossen
In dem mondbeglänzten Grund?
Aus der Knospe, halb erschlossen,
Junge Glieder blühend sprossen,
Weiße Arme, roter Mund,   15
Und die Nachtigallen schlagen,[2]
Und rings hebt es an[3] zu klagen,
Ach, vor Liebe todeswund,
Von versunknen schönen Tagen —
Komm', o komm' zum stillen Grund!   20

These lines are found in Eichendorff's epic poem *Julian*, in which a Christian knight, Octavian, is seduced to apostasy through the wiles of a demonic female, Fausta, a kind of Venus and Valkyrie incarnate. Octavian hears her singing *Hörst du nicht die Quellen gehen* and

Hat dem Klange folgen müssen
In den duftberauschten Grund —
Dort seitdem vor glüh'nden Küssen
War verstummt der Liedermund.

Auf einer Burg

Eingeschlafen auf der Lauer[1]
Oben ist der alte Ritter;
Drüben gehen Regenschauer,
Und der Wald rauscht durch das Gitter.

Eingewachsen Bart und Haare,   5
Und versteinert Brust und Krause,[2]
Sitzt er viele hundert Jahre
Oben in der stillen Klause.

Draußen ist es still und friedlich,
Alle sind ins Tal gezogen,   10
Waldesvögel einsam singen
In den leeren Fensterbogen.

Eine Hochzeit fährt da unten
Auf dem Rhein im Sonnenscheine,
Musikanten spielen munter,   15
Und die schöne Braut die weinet.

---

[2]'sing' (as bird) [3]*anheben* = *anfangen*

[1]'on the lookout' [2]'ruff'

Towards Interpretation

1. *Formally*, how does Eichendorff distinguish the world of the old knight from that of the bride?
2. What is the physical position of the speaker?
3. What adjectives describe the world surrounding the old knight? the speaker? the bride?
4. What does the old knight seem to symbolize? Preterity (past-ness)? Death? Futurity? Something else?
5. Why do you think the bride is weeping?

Waldgespräch

Es ist schon spät, es wird schon kalt,
Was reit'st du einsam durch den Wald?
Der Wald ist lang, du bist allein,
Du schöne Braut! Ich führ' dich heim!

„Groß ist der Männer Trug und List,   5
Vor Schmerz mein Herz gebrochen ist,
Wohl irrt das Waldhorn her und hin,
O flieh! Du weißt nicht, wer ich bin."

So reich geschmückt ist Roß und Weib,
So wunderschön der junge Leib,   10
Jetzt kenn' ich dich — Gott steh mir bei!
Du bist die Hexe Lorelei.

„Du kennst mich wohl — von hohem Stein
Schaut still mein Schloß tief in den Rhein.
Es ist schon spät, es wird schon kalt,   15
Kommst nimmermehr aus diesem Wald!"

Towards Interpretation

1. The first and the next to the last line of this poem are identical. Do they have the same emotional tone? Explain.
2. The *Waldhorn* in line 7 seems to have no connection with the context (except that we are in a forest); why do you think it is brought in?
3. How does the Lorelei's mentioning her castle above the Rhine add to the "legendary" atmosphere of the poem?
4. Eichendorff includes this poem among his *Romanzen*, i.e., his ballads. What is balladesque about it? Compare it with Goethe's "Erlkönig" and Brentano's "Lore Lay."
5. Has Eichendorff's Lorelei always been a "Hexe"? Why did she become one? Why did Brentano's Lore Lay become one?

6. What change has Eichendorff made in the setting of the story as compared with Brentano?

Der Umkehrende

Du sollst mich doch nicht fangen,
Duftschwüle Zaubernacht!
Es stehn mit goldnem Prangen
Die Stern' auf stiller Wacht,
Und machen überm Grunde,   5
Wo du verirret bist,
Getreu die alte Runde —
Gelobt sei Jesus Christ!

Wie bald in allen Bäumen
Geht nun die Morgenluft,   10
Sie schütteln sich in Träumen,
Und durch den roten Duft
Eine fromme Lerche[1] steiget,
Wenn alles still noch ist,
Den rechten Weg dir zeiget —   15
Gelobt sei Jesus Christ!

Eichendorff was a devout Catholic, who, unlike Brentano, never strayed from the Church, and, unlike the Protestant Novalis, never intellectualized his religion. "Der Umkehrende" he included among his *Geistliche Lieder* (Sacred Songs); there can be no doubt about its complete sincerity. By the same token, however, there can also be no doubt about the strength of the demonic attraction of those *id*-like forces which he symbolizes as *Nachtzauber, Wirrung,* Life's wild and magic stream, the call from the depths, Frau Venus, the Lorelei and so on. Much of his work lives from this ethical tension. Eichendorff is not so much the poet of romantic longing as the poet of the *dangers* of romantic longing. To these dangers he gives poetic embodiment again and again — they, and overcoming them, form the chief theme of his work.*

[1]The lark often symbolizes the spirit in Eichendorff.

*Cf. Johannes Hoffmeister, *Nachgoethesche Lyrik: Eichendorff, Lenau, Mörike* (Bonn: Bouvier, 1948), xv.

Der Sänger

Und zu den Felsengängen
Der nächt'ge Sänger flieht,
Denn wie mit Wahnsinns Klängen
Treibt ihn sein eig'nes Lied.

Bei leuchtenden Gewittern   5
Schreckt ihn das stille Land,
Ein wunderbar Erschüttern
Hat ihm das Herz gewandt.[1]

Bereuend sinkt sein Auge —
Da blickt durch Nacht und Schmerz   10
Ein unsichtbares Auge
Ihm klar ins tiefe Herz.

Sein Saitenspiel[2] zur Stunde[3]
Wirft er in tiefsten Schlund,
Und weint aus Herzensgrunde,   15
Und ewig schweigt sein Mund.

Towards Interpretation
1. What is meant by *der nächt'ge Sänger?* Is he merely a singer who sings at night?
2. Why does the singer throw away his harp?

Die Heimat
An meinen Bruder

Denkst du des Schlosses[1] noch auf stiller Höh'?
Das Horn lockt nächtlich dort, als ob's dich riefe,
Am Abgrund grast das Reh,
Es rauscht der Wald verwirrend aus der Tiefe —
O stille, wecke nicht! es war als schliefe   5
Da drunten unnennbares Weh. —

Kennst du den Garten? — Wenn sich Lenz[2] erneut,
Geht dort ein Mädchen auf den kühlen Gängen
Still durch die Einsamkeit

---

[1]'caused him to have a change of heart' [2]'stringed instrument' [3]=*sofort*

[1]Schloss Lubowitz, near Ratibor, where the Eichendorff brothers grew up. The family was subsequently forced to sell the property at auction. [2]=*Frühling*

Und weckt den leisen Strom von Zauberklängen,   10
Als ob die Bäume und die Blumen sängen
Rings von der alten schönen Zeit.

Ihr Wipfel und ihr Brunnen, rauscht nur zu!
Wohin du auch in wilder Flucht magst dringen,
Du findest nirgends Ruh,   15
Erreichen wird dich das geheime Singen, —
Ach, dieses Bannes[3] zauberischen Ringen
Entfliehn wir nimmer, ich und du!

The attraction exerted by the memory of home in this poem is certainly magical, though it can hardly be called demonic. The *unnennbares Weh* that seems
to be sleeping in the forest is not to be aroused, while an innocent girl, not
Frau Venus, walks through the garden in the spring awakening the *leisen
Strom von Zauberklängen* (perhaps this girl is meant as an embodiment of
spring itself). Nonetheless, the magic of home, "das geheime Singen," haunts
the poet wherever he may be and however desperately he may try to drown it
out. By extension and analogy, what may it be that the protagonists in Eichendorff's work are basically seeking when they succumb to (or are strongly
attracted by) the lure of the *duftschwüle Zaubernacht?*

Das zerbrochene Ringlein[1]

In einem kühlen Grunde
Da geht ein Mühlenrad,
Mein' Liebste ist verschwunden,
Die dort gewohnet hat.

Sie hat mir Treu' versprochen,   5
Gab mir ein'n Ring dabei,
Sie hat die Treu' gebrochen,
Mein Ringlein sprang entzwei.

Ich möcht' als Spielmann[2] reisen
Weit in die Welt hinaus,   10
Und singen meine Weisen,[3]
Und gehn von Haus zu Haus.

---

[3]'of this spell'

[1]Like Goethe's "Heidenröslein" and Uhland's "Der gute Kamerad," this poem has
become a folksong. [2]'itinerant musician' [3]'melodies'

Ich möcht' als Reiter fliegen
Wohl in die blut'ge Schlacht,
Um stille Feuer liegen   15
Im Feld bei dunkler Nacht.
Hör' ich das Mühlrad gehen:
Ich weiß nicht, was ich will —
Ich möcht' am liebsten sterben,
Da wär's auf einmal still!   20

Towards Interpretation

1. What does the turning of the millwheel come to symbolize here?
2. Why is the rime-scheme broken in the last stanza?
3. Why does the life of a *Spielmann* or a *Reiter* appeal to the speaker?
4. How does the theme of this poem resemble that of "Die Heimat"?
5. What is the stanzaic form of this poem called?
6. Eichendorff's poem is based on the following (authentic) *Volkslied*:

> Dort hoch auf jenem Berge,
> Da geht ein Mühlenrad,
> Das mahlet nichts denn Liebe
> Die Nacht bis an den Tag.
>
> Die Mühle ist zerbrochen,
> Die Liebe hat ein End.   5
> So g'segn' dich Gott, mein feines Lieb!
> Jetzt fahr' ich ins Elend.*

What changes does Eichendorff make that seem especially character-istic of him? (What about his putting the mill *in einem kühlen Grunde?* What does *Grund* signify in his vocabulary?† Does the *Volkslied* appeal to any one sense? How about Eichendorff's poem?)
7. The motif of the broken ring is absent in the *Volkslied*. Why do you think Eichendorff added it?
8. Eichendorff greatly expands the motif contained in the last two lines of the folksong. Explain how.

Mondnacht

> Es war, als hätt' der Himmel
> Die Erde still geküßt,
> Daß sie im Blütenschimmer
> Von ihm nun träumen müßt'.

---

*ins Elend = in die Fremde

†In another version of this song the mill is "da unten in jenem *Tale*," but even so we might ask why Eichendorff should change *Tal* to *Grund*.

Die Luft ging durch die Felder,   5
Die Ähren wogten sacht,
Es rauschten leis die Wälder,
So sternklar war die Nacht.

Und meine Seele spannte
Weit ihre Flügel aus,   10
Flog durch die stillen Lande,
Als flöge sie nach Haus.

In "Mondnacht" the fateful attraction so often associated with a nocturnal landscape in Eichendorff is completely absent, or, more accurately: it is translated into positive terms. The first stanza tells of a moment of perfect harmony between heaven and earth, the second shows earth's reaction to this harmony (to heaven's embrace), the third man's. Even in this moment of earthly perfection the soul of man longs for something higher: it spreads its wings as if to fly "home." The soul's home, heaven, the bosom of the father, the absolute, is the final goal of Romantic longing (i.e., the longing of the Romantics, most of whom take a Platonistic view of existence), and, for Eichendorff at any rate, to long for anything else is fundamentally an aberration.

Towards Interpretation

1. It is interesting to observe that in this "undemonic" night poem there is only one image that appeals to the sense of hearing (line 7), the others being tactual, visual, and motory. Compare "Mondnacht" in this respect with "Nachtzauber," "Schöne Fremde," "Das zerbrochene Ringlein," "Denkst du des Schlosses noch," and "Der Umkehrende." Does there seem to be a connection between the theme and auditory imagery?

2. Read the following poem and make the same comparison as above.

Die Lerche

Ich kann hier nicht singen,
Aus dieser Mauern dunklen Ringen
Muß ich mich schwingen
Vor Lust und tiefem Weh.
O Freude, in klarer Höh'   5
Zu sinken und sich zu heben,
In Gesang
Über die grüne Erde dahin zu schweben,
Wie unten die licht' und dunkeln Streifen
Wechselnd im Fluge vorüberschweifen,   10
Aus der Tiefe ein Wirren und Rauschen und
                                        Hämmern,

Die Erde aufschimmernd im Frühlingsdämmern,
Wie ist die Welt so voller Klang!
Herz, was bist du bang?
Mußt aufwärts dringen!   15
Die Sonne tritt hervor,
Wie glänzen mir Brust und Schwingen,[1]
Wie still und weit ist's droben am Himmelstor!

Towards Interpretation
1. Why is the lark full of *Lust u n d Weh* in line 4?
2. Trace out and comment upon the significance of the images of darkness and light in this poem.
3. Does God=Nature in this poem? How does Eichendorff compare with Brentano and Novalis in this respect? With Goethe?
4. How does the metrical form of this poem relate to the subject matter?

Der Einsiedler

Komm', Trost der Welt, du stille Nacht!
Wie steigst du von den Bergen sacht,
Die Lüfte alle schlafen,
Ein Schiffer nur noch, wandermüd,
Singt übers Meer sein Abendlied   5
Zu Gottes Lob im Hafen.

Die Jahre wie die Wolken gehn
Und lassen mich hier einsam stehn,
Die Welt hat mich vergessen,
Da tratst du wunderbar zu mir,   10
Wenn ich beim Waldesrauschen hier
Gedankenvoll gesessen.

O Trost der Welt, du stille Nacht!
Der Tag hat mich so müd gemacht,
Das weite Meer schon dunkelt,
Laß ausruhn mich von Lust und Not,
Bis daß das ew'ge Morgenrot   15
Den stillen Wald durchfunkelt.

---

[1] =*Flügel*

Todeslust

Bevor er in die blaue Flut gesunken,
Träumt noch der Schwan und singet todestrunken;
Die sommermüde Erde im Verblühen
Läßt all' ihr Feuer in den Trauben glühen;
Die Sonne, Funken sprühend, im Versinken,   5
Gibt noch einmal der Erde Glut zu trinken,
Bis, Stern auf Stern, die Trunkne zu umfangen,
Die wunderbare Nacht ist aufgegangen.

Towards Interpretation

1. In both "Der Einsiedler" and "Todeslust" night symbolizes death.
   What is the speaker's attitude towards death?
2. Is there an equivalency between swan and earth? If so, how does the
   imagery express this?
3. Is Eichendorff here *der nächt'ge Sänger* of whom he speaks in the
   poem "Der Sänger"?

Friedrich Rückert (1788-1866)

Aus der Jugendzeit

Aus der Jugendzeit, aus der Jugendzeit,
Klingt ein Lied mir immerdar;
O wie liegt so weit, o wie liegt so weit,
Was mein einst war!

Was die Schwalbe sang, was die Schwalbe sang,   5
Die den Herbst und Frühling bringt;
Ob[1] das Dorf entlang, ob das Dorf entlang,
Das jetzt noch klingt?

„Als ich Abschied nahm, als ich Abschied nahm,
Waren Kisten und Kasten schwer;   10
Als ich wieder kam, als ich wieder kam,
War alles leer."

O du Kindermund, o du Kindermund,
Unbewußter Weisheit froh,

---

[1]'I wonder if'

Vogelsprachekund, vogelsprachekund,   15
Wie Salomo![2]

O du Heimatflur, o du Heimatflur,
Laß zu deinem heil'gen Raum
Mich noch einmal nur, mich noch einmal nur,
Entfliehn im Traum!   20

Als ich Abschied nahm, als ich Abschied nahm,
War die Welt mir voll so sehr;
Als ich wieder kam, als ich wieder kam,
War alles leer.

Wohl[3] die Schwalbe kehrt, wohl die Schwalbe   25
Und der leere Kasten schwoll,   [kehrt,
Ist das Herz geleert, ist das Herz geleert,
Wird's nie mehr voll.

Keine Schwalbe bringt, keine Schwalbe bringt
Dir zurück, wonach du weinst;   30
Doch die Schwalbe singt, doch die Schwalbe singt
Im Dorf wie einst:

„Als ich Abschied nahm, als ich Abschied nahm,
Waren Kisten und Kasten schwer;
Als ich wieder kam, als ich wieder kam,   35
War alles leer."

Towards Interpretation

1. With what feeling does the speaker associate the song of the swallow
   at the beginning of the poem?
2. How does this feeling change towards the end of the poem? Can you
   point to the place where the change is indicated?

Barbarossa[1]

Der alte Barbarossa,
Der Kaiser Friederich,
Im unterird'schen Schlosse
Hält er verzaubert sich.

---

[2]King Solomon [3]'It's true'

[1]Friedrich I. Barbarossa ('red beard'), Holy Roman Emperor, 1152-1190. The legend
of Barbarossa, related in this poem, is one of the many legends of a great ruler returning to save his people in time of need, like King Arthur.

Er ist niemals gestorben,   35
Er lebt darin noch jetzt;
Er hat im Schloß verborgen
Zum Schlaf sich hingesetzt.

Er hat hinab genommen
Des Reiches Herrlichkeit,   10
Und wird einst wiederkommen
Mit ihr zu seiner Zeit.[2]

Der Stuhl ist elfenbeinern,
Darauf der Kaiser sitzt;
Der Tisch ist marmelsteinern,   15
Worauf sein Haupt er stützt.

Sein Bart ist nicht von Flachse,
Er ist von Feuersglut,
Ist durch den Tisch gewachsen,
Worauf sein Kinn ausruht.   20

Er nickt als wie im Traume,
Sein Aug' halb offen zwinkt;
Und je nach langem Raume
Er einem Knaben winkt.

Er spricht im Schlaf zum Knaben: 25
„Geh hin vors Schloß, o Zwerg,
Und sieh, ob noch die Raben
Herfliegen um den Berg.

Und wenn die alten Raben
Noch fliegen immerdar,   30
So muß ich auch noch schlafen
Verzaubert hundert Jahr."

„Kehr' ein bei mir"

Du bist die Ruh',
Der Friede mild,
Die Sehnsucht du,
Und was sie stillt.

Ich weihe dir   5
Voll Lust und Schmerz
Zur Wohnung hier
Mein Aug' und Herz.

---

[2] 'when the time is ripe'

Kehr' ein bei mir
Und schließe du   10
Still hinter dir
Die Pforten zu.

Treib andern Schmerz
Aus dieser Brust!
Voll sei dies Herz   15
Von deiner Lust.

Dies Augenzelt,[1]
Von deinem Glanz
Allein erhellt,
O füll' es ganz!   20

August Graf von Platen-Hallermünde
(1796-1835)

Tristan

Wer die Schönheit angeschaut mit Augen,
Ist dem Tode schon anheimgegeben,[1]
Wird für keinen Dienst auf Erden taugen,
Und doch wird er vor dem Tode beben,
Wer die Schönheit angeschaut mit Augen!   5

Ewig währt für ihn der Schmerz der Liebe,
Denn ein Tor nur kann auf Erden hoffen
Zu genügen einem solchen Triebe:
Wen der Pfeil des Schönen je getroffen,
Ewig währt für ihn der Schmerz der Liebe!   10

Ach, er möchte wie ein Quell versiechen,[2]
Jedem Hauch der Luft ein Gift entsaugen
Und den Tod aus jeder Blume riechen:
Wer die Schönheit angeschaut mit Augen,
Ach, er möchte wie ein Quell versiechen!   15

---

[1]Cf. *Himmelszelt*

[1]'delivered up to' [2]*versiechen*: cf. *versiegen* 'run dry' and (*dahin-*)*siechen* 'langsam
sterben'; Platen's neologism significantly combines both.

Towards Interpretation

1. Why is this poem called "Tristan"?
2. If you have read Plato's *Phaedrus,* explain its connection with the thought expressed in this poem.
3. If you know that Platen was a homosexual, might that allow a different reading of this poem?
4. Thomas Mann wrote an essay on Platen in his *Leiden und Größe der Meister.* If you are acquainted with Mann's work (especially *Der Tod in Venedig*), explain why Platen must be of particular interest to Mann.

„Die Liebe hat gelogen"

Die Liebe hat gelogen,
Die Sorge lastet schwer,
Betrogen, ach, betrogen,
Hat alles mich umher!

Es rinnen heiße Tropfen   5
Die Wange stets herab,
Laß ab, laß ab, zu klopfen,
Laß ab, mein Herz, laß ab!

Towards Interpretation

1. Show the way the "how" of this poem reflects the "what." (Note especially the regularity of the rhythm, the repetition of certain vowels, and above all the last two lines.)

Ghasel[1]

Im Wasser wogt die Lilie, die blanke, hin und her,
Doch irrst du, Freund, sobald du sagst, sie schwanke hin und her!
Es wurzelt ja so fest ihr Fuß im tiefen Meeresgrund,
Ihr Haupt nur wiegt ein lieblicher Gedanke hin und her!

---

[1]Persian verse form cultivated in German by Platen and Rückert. After the first couplet, the even lines show identical rime, the uneven lines remain rimeless. Some of Platen's ghasels contain as many as sixteen lines. The present example is a short ghasel on the nature of the ghasel, symbolized by the undulating lily.

Der Pilgrim vor St. Just[1]

Nacht ist's und Stürme sausen für und für,[2]
Hispanische Mönche, schließt mir auf die Tür!

Laßt hier mich ruhn, bis Glockenton mich weckt,
Der zum Gebet euch in die Kirche schreckt!

Bereitet mir, was euer Haus vermag,   5
Ein Ordenskleid und einen Sarkophag!

Gönnt mir die kleine Zelle, weiht mich ein,[3]
Mehr als die Hälfte dieser Welt war mein.

Das Haupt, das nun der Schere sich bequemt,[4]
Mit mancher Krone ward's bediademt.   10

Die Schulter, die der Kutte nun sich bückt;
Hat kaiserlicher Hermelin geschmückt.

Nun bin ich vor dem Tod den Toten gleich,
Und fall' in Trümmer, wie das alte Reich.

"Der Pilgrim vor St. Just" is an historical ballad consisting of a series of symbolic situations presented in the form of a monologue. The first stanza shows the "pilgrim" standing before the monastery gate demanding entrance, in the second he has been admitted, in the third he asks to be taken into the order. Up to this point the tone is that of a man of strong will, used to giving orders and to seeing them obeyed — each stanza contains a command and the three exclamation points are like three vigorous knocks. The fourth, axial, stanza — the poem is constructed with strict symmetry — also contains a command (in fact, two), but the tone, which has from stanza to stanza grown ever a shade less imperious, is now not peremptory at all (no exclamation point!). Indeed, the command is more a plea, the emperor lays off his imperial mien, secular authority submits to spiritual. The days of wordly power are past and their preterity, their "pastness," is shown forth in a series of contrasting pairs: *Zelle -(Hälfte dieser) Welt; Schere-Krone; Kutte-Hermelin,* in which the first member of each pair is associated with the present (in stanza four with the immediate future), while the second member is connected with a verb in the past. With each stanza another step is taken that separates past from present. In the final stanza, though, there is no contrast but rather complete correspondence: what may have seemed an unreasonable act, namely, that an emperor should enter a monastery, turns out to have a deep reason, the emperor identifies him-

---

[1]Charles V, Holy Roman Emperor, on whose realms the sun never set, abdicated in 1556 after reigning 37 years and entered the monastery of San Geronimo de Yuste.
[2]=*ohne Unterlaß*   [3]'initiate'   [4]'submits to'

self with his empire. The tone is one of utter resignation, suggesting silent decay, and stands in stark contrast to the stormy night and the hammer-like order of the first stanza: *sic transit gloria mundi.*

"Die meisten Menschen," Friedrich Hebbel noted in his diary (1. März 1861), "werden sich darüber wundern, daß Carl der Fünfte in's Kloster ging, *obgleich* er Kaiser war. Einige aber werden denken, daß er es tat, *weil* er Kaiser war." Platen's ballad presents a turning-point in history: "Das Ende Karls V. ist das Ende einer Epoche,"* the monarch's determination to enter a monastery is not merely a private affair but submission to a fate that controls the destiny of empires.

„Mein Auge ließ das hohe Meer zurücke"

Mein Auge ließ das hohe Meer zurücke,
Als aus der Flut Palladios[1] Tempel stiegen,
An deren Staffeln[2] sich die Wellen schmiegen,
Die uns getragen ohne Falsch und Tücke.[3]

Wir landen an, wir danken es dem Glücke,   5
Und die Lagune scheint zurück zu fliegen,
Der Dogen alte Säulengänge[4] liegen
Vor uns gigantisch mit der Seufzerbrücke.[5]

Venedigs Löwen, sonst Venedigs Wonne,[6]
Mit ehrnen[7] Flügeln sehen wir ihn ragen   10
Auf seiner kolossalischen Kolonne.

Ich steig'ans Land, nicht ohne Furcht und Zagen,
Da glänzt der Markusplatz[8] im Licht der Sonne:
Soll ich ihn wirklich zu betreten wagen?

Platen's *Sonette aus Venedig,* of which this is the first, are one of the most successful sonnet cycles in German literature. Platen was a master, as no German before or since, of the *eigentümlich kunstgeläutertes Parlando* (Thomas Mann) so characteristic of this genre. It is fascinating to observe to just what

---

*Wolfgang Kayser, *Geschichte der deutschen Ballade*, 188.

[1]Famous Italian architect, who built some of Venice's finest churches.   [2]=*Stufen*
[3]'treachery' [4]'arcades' (of the Doge's Palace) [5]Bridge of Sighs, connecting the Palazzo ducale (Doges's Palace) with the prison behind it. [6]A winged lion was the heraldic beast of the Venetian Republic. In 1824, when Platen first visited Venice, the Republic had fallen (occupied by Napoleon 1797) and was in Austrian hands. [7]'brazen' [8]Piazza San Marco (Saint Mark's Square), onto which face the Palazzo ducale and the great Byzantine church of St. Mark.

degree both the language and the experience on which this sonnet is based have been "purified by art" (*kunstgeläutert*). The *first* version of this poem reads:

Der Morgen lächelte zu meinem Glücke,
Als aus der Flut Palladios Tempel stiegen:
Die Säulengänge sah ich vor mir liegen,
Die Signoria[1] mit der Seufzerbrücke.

Geflügelt steht, doch ohne Falsch und Tücke,   5
Venedigs Löwe, sonst gewohnt zu siegen,
Entgegen scheint er unserm Schiff zu fliegen,
Und die Lagune weicht im Flug zurücke.

Ich steig' ans Land, wo zwo Kolonnen ragen
Wie Riesen an des Markusplatzes Schwellen:[2]   10
Soll ich ihn wirklich zu betreten wagen?

Mit mir im Haupte trag' ich aus den Wellen
Des Schiffes Schwindel noch und Mißbehagen,
Und diese Massen drohn mich zu zerschellen.[3]

The meter (iambic pentameter) and, with one exception, the rimes are the same in both versions, and on a first reading we may even feel that the tone is also essentially the same, except that perhaps the wonder and admiration come through more clearly in the later version. But it soon becomes evident that the changes are many — the skeleton of the poem, the experience of landing for the first time at the Piazetta (the "little square") in Venice, has been clothed in new flesh. It is clear that Platen changed his conception of what the sonnet means to say in the second version, but one could argue that not all the changes are happy ones.

In the first quatrain, it is undoubtedly a gain to place Venice in its setting and at the same time to contrast the trackless sea with Palladio's churches, nature with art, as the waves that lap (*schmiegen*) against the steps again contrast with *das hohe Meer*. All this is missing in the first version, which instead at once overwhelms us with an architectural maze: churches, arcades, the Signoria, the Bridge of Sighs. The clarity and *Übersichtlichkeit* of the revision are a definite improvement. Although the winged lion flying toward the approaching ship is marvelously seen, the main fault of the first eight lines of the original version lies in the unclear space-time relation: first we see the buildings lying directly before us (lines 2-4), then we approach them from a distance (lines 7-8). The revision sets this straight: first we approach, seeing only what is clearly visible from the sea, then we enter the canal to land (*landen an* implies a gradual process) and now see what is immediately in front of us.

---

[1]=Palazzo ducale   [2]'threshold(s)'   [3]'smash'

After reading "Mein Auge ließ," the last three lines of "Der Morgen lächelte" must, when we think about them, strike us as strange indeed. Why this sudden concern with such a purely private and inconsequential matter as a feeling of queasiness (*Schwindel, Mißbehagen*)? Is *this* the reason Platen doesn't know whether he dare pass the columns to enter the square? Perhaps not, but such an interpretation is certainly not excluded, and the reader has an unpleasant sense of letdown. But we now begin to see that in the original version all is on a different plane, the plane of experience not yet completely purified by art. The last tercet puzzles us because we expected art, not life. To find out why Platen originally wrote the last tercet as he did we need only go back one step further, namely, to his diary, which, since it makes no pretense to art (at least not to "great" art), contents itself with an unvarnished record of facts, feelings, impressions. The passage in question reads: "Das erste Anlanden unseres Dampfboots an der Piazetta war imposant genug. Die Aussicht auf die Seufzerbrücke und die schöne Brücke vor ihr auf den Palazzo ducale, auf die beiden Säulen der Piazzetta, sowie auf den jetzigen Palazzo reale mit seinen Gärten ist kein geringer Vorschmack von Venedig. Ich ging über den Markusplatz, aber noch immer *den Schwindel des Schiffs im Kopf.*" Undeniably, Platen did feel dizzy when he first landed in Venice, and this embarrassing fact, inseparably associated in his mind with his first impression of the city, the subject of the sonnet, crept into the realm of art.

In the final, "purified" version of his arrival in Venice, now reconceived as an ideal landscape, such human weaknesses have no place. From this single, but unusually revealing, instance we can perceive what the poet was striving to do when he revised the poem, namely, to raise the real to the ideal, so that that which *is* may become that which *signifies*. For Platen the ideal is the truly real, and ordinary reality only a confused half-truth.

We have already remarked that in the final version Platen has, so to speak, weeded out his art collection. Things are no longer piled and jumbled together but have space around them. This alone lends grandeur and significance. The arcades of the Doges' Palace "liegen vor uns *gigantisch*"; the Venetian lion, supreme symbol of the city (note how the name "Venedig" now flanks the lion), is given the whole first tercet, where he towers in isolated majesty with "brazen" wings upon his "colossal" column. Alliteration, instead of the outworn comparison *wie Riesen*, now enforces the sense of immensity, and whereas in the first version we are not even aware that the lion is on a column, he now seems to occupy the only one in sight, for the second has disappeared. We note, too, that, though winged, the lion no longer seems to fly — all intimations of movement have been eliminated from this stanza (all the others imply movement), for the lion is now the eternal, *unchanging* symbol of Venice, not just one object among others.

But the greatest triumph of the revised version comes in the last tercet. As we saw, in the original version the poet left room for speculation as to just

why he hesitated to enter the Piazza; *now* his "Furcht und Zagen" is owing
solely and indubitably to the thrill of awe he feels in the presence of Venice;
he pauses fearfully before the nobility and grandeur of the scene, hardly daring
to take possession of his dream.

Towards Interpretation
1. Compare the passage from Platen's diary with the two sonnets based
   upon the experience recorded there. What is in the sonnets that is not
   in the diary and vice versa? What about the relative level of language
   in the diary and the poems? Note in the diary such turns as *imposant*
   genug, kein geringer Vorschmack, and the free use of Italian names.)

„Venedig liegt nur noch im Land der Träume"

Venedig liegt nur noch im Land der Träume
Und wirft nur Schatten her aus alten Tagen,
Es liegt der Leu der Republik erschlagen,
Und öde feiern seines Kerkers Räume.[1]

Die ehrnen Hengste, die, durch salz'ge Schäume   5
Dahergeschleppt, auf jener Kirche ragen,[2]
Nicht mehr dieselben sind sie, ach! sie tragen
Des korsikan'schen Überwinders[3] Zäume.

Wo ist das Volk von Königen geblieben,
Das diese Marmorhäuser durfte bauen,   10
Die nun verfallen und gemach zerstieben?

Nur selten finden auf des Enkels Brauen
Der Ahnen große Züge sich geschrieben,
An Dogengräbern in den Stein gehauen.[4]

Towards Interpretation
1. What aspect(s) of Venice do the first eight lines deal with? The last
   six? What is the connection between the octet and the sestet?
2. How is the motif of the past casting shadows on the present (first
   stanza) resumed later in the sonnet?
3. How do its empty prisons show the impotence of Venice?
4. How would you translate *durfte* in line 10?

---

[1]Lines 2-4: 'The lion of the Republic lies slain, and the rooms of his prison lie idle and
desolate.' [2]The horses on St. Mark's were brought from Constantinople. [3]i.e., Napoleon [4]Lines 12-14: 'Only rarely does one find (written) on the grandchild's brow the
noble features of his ancestors [as one sees them] hewn in stone on the graves of
Doges.' *Züge* contains a play on words, since it can mean both 'features' and 'signa-
tures' (cf. Namens*zug*), and hence goes with both *schreiben* and *hauen*.

„Es scheint ein langes, ew'ges Ach zu wohnen"

Es scheint ein langes, ew'ges Ach zu wohnen
In diesen Lüften, die sich leise regen,
Aus jenen Hallen weht es mir entgegen,
Wo Scherz und Jubel sonst gepflegt zu thronen.

Venedig fiel, wiewohl's getrotzt Äonen,   5
Das Rad des Glücks kann nichts zurückbewegen:
Öd' ist der Hafen, wen'ge Schiffe legen
Sich an die schöne Riva der Sklavonen.[1]

Wie hast du sonst, Venetia, geprahlet
Als stolzes Weib mit goldenen Gewändern,   10
So wie dich Paolo Veronese[2] malet!

Nun steht ein Dichter an den Prachtgeländern
Der Riesentreppe staunend und bezahlet
Den Tränenzoll,[3] der nichts vermag zu ändern!

Towards Interpretation

1. Like many others, this poem is based on a platitude. What platitude?
2. The tension between *Einst* and *Jetzt* gives this poem life and at the same time lends it its air of melancholy. Show how this tension is achieved.
3. Who is the poet spoken of in the final tercet?
4. Read the second quatrain again (aloud) and point out how the sense of irrevocable loss is brought out by the rhythm in line 6 and by the change of metrical pattern in line 7.

The following sonnet describes a painting by Titian, "John the Baptist in the Wilderness," which Platen saw in Venice. Like much later poems by C. F. Meyer and R. M. Rilke, it is a *Dinggedicht,* i.e., a poem interpreting the essence of a thing.

---

[1]the Riva degli Schiavoni, a quay beside the Palazzo ducale at the entrance to St. Mark's Square [2]The painter Veronese (1528-1588) was born in Verona but spent his adult life in Venice. [3]'tribute of tears'

„Zur Wüste fliehend vor dem Menschenschwarme"

Zur Wüste fliehend vor dem Menschenschwarme,
Steht hier Johannes, um zu reinern Sphären
Durch Einsamkeit die Seele zu verklären,
Die hohe, großgestimmte,[1] gotteswarme.

Voll von Begeisterung, von heil'gem Harme[2]   5
Erglänzt sein ew'ger, ernster Blick von Zähren,[3]
Nach Jenem, den Maria soll gebären,
Scheint er zu deuten mit erhobnem Arme.

Wer kann sich weg von diesem Bilde kehren,
Und möchte nicht, mit brünstigen[4] Gebärden,   10
Den Gott im Busen Tizians verehren?

O goldne Zeit, die nicht mehr ist im Werden,[5]
Als noch die Kunst vermocht der Welt zu lehren,
Und nur das Schöne heilig war auf Erden!

Towards Interpretation

1. Tell as precisely as possible what Platen describes for us in the first eight lines of this sonnet.
2. What, *in general terms*, does the poet speak of in the sestet?
3. Indicate the inner connection between the sestet and the octet. (Whom or what does the *poet* seem to be pointing to *mit erhobnem Arme?*)
4. The painting here described has a religious subject. Is Platen's ideal religious in the usual sense of the word? What kind of ideal is it?
5. Why might a devout Christian well consider this poem blasphemous?
6. The *Schwermut* so characteristic of Platen springs largely from his conviction that the ideal is no longer realizable; in other words, he suffers from the age in which he lives. Show how the present sonnet exemplifies this.

„Anstimmen darf ich ungewohnte Töne"

Anstimmen darf ich ungewohnte[1] Töne,
Da nie dem Halben ich mein Herz ergeben:
Der Kunst gelobt'[2] ich ganz ein ganzes Leben,
Und wenn ich sterbe, sterb' ich für das Schöne.

---

[1]'attuned to great things'   [2]'melancholy,' 'affliction'   [3]'tears'   [4]=*leidenschaftlich*   [5]*die ... Werden*: 'which is no longer in the process of becoming,' but has come and gone

[1]'unaccustomed'   [2]'vowed'

Doch wünsch' ich, daß man Bessere bekröne,[3]   5
Mich aber ziehen lasse, wo ich neben
Dem Höchsten lernen kann, nach Hohem streben,
Ja, daß man mir mein Vaterland verpöne![4]

Ich lieb' es drum in keinem Sinne minder,
Da stets ich mich in seinem Dienst verzehre,   10
Doch wär' ich gern das fernste seiner Kinder.

Geschieht's, daß je den innern Schatz ich mehre,[5]
So bleibt der Fund, wenn längst dahin der Finder,
Ein sichres Eigentum der deutschen Ehre.

Towards Interpretation

1. Why does the poet wish to be forbidden his native land?
2. In what sense is he "continually consuming himself" in the service of his country?
3. What is meant by the *innern Schatz* (line 12)?

August v. Platen

Heinrich Heine

---

[3]Platen is thinking of the ancient custom of crowning poets. [4]'forbid' [5]'increase'

Heinrich Heine (1797-1856)

In der Fremde (III)

Ich hatte einst ein schönes Vaterland.
Der Eichenbaum
Wuchs dort so hoch, die Veilchen nickten sanft.
Es war ein Traum.

Das küßte mich auf deutsch, und sprach auf deutsch   5
(Man glaubt es kaum
Wie gut es klang) das Wort: „Ich liebe dich!"
Es war ein Traum.

„Ein Fichtenbaum steht einsam"

Ein Fichtenbaum steht einsam
Im Norden auf kahler Höh'.
Ihn schläfert; mit weißer Decke
Umhüllen ihn Eis und Schnee.

Er träumt von einer Palme,   5
Die fern im Morgenland
Einsam und schweigend trauert
Auf brennender Felsenwand.

Towards Interpretation

1. What is the spruce's "dream"? Can such a thing ever be realized?
2. Heine was a German and a Jew. How may the poem about the pine tree and the palm be taken as a symbolic statement of his situation?
3. Concerning the rhythm of this poem a critic has written:

Genial ist der Gebrauch des Rhythmus, um das Seelische zu ver-sinnbildlichen. Die erste Strophe besteht aus zwei Sätzen, die aber in Wirklichkeit drei sind, denn es gibt eine volle Pause nach *schläfert* sowohl also nach *Höh'* und *Schnee*. Jeder Ansatz zur Ausdehnung wird aufgehalten: der Fichtenbaum steht völlig isoliert auf seiner *kahlen Höh'*. Die zweite Strophe dagegen besteht aus nur einem Satz und hat zweimal Brechung (die Brechung zwischen Vv. 6 und 7 ist besonders expressiv). Durch die Traumgegenwart der Palme scheint die Einsamkeit des Fichtenbaumes gelindert und getröstet. Die Ausdehnung im Rhythmus bringt förmlich die Ausdehnung der Sehnsucht, ja das Sehnen selbst zum Ausdruck.*

---

*Robert M. Browning, *Umgang mit Gedichten* (New York: McGraw-Hill, 1969), 52.

„*Der Tod, das ist die kühle Nacht*"

Der Tod, das ist die kühle Nacht,
Das Leben ist der schwüle Tag.
Es dunkelt schon, mich schläfert,
Der Tag hat mich müd' gemacht.

Über mein Bett erhebt sich ein Baum,   5
Drin singt die junge Nachtigall;
Sie singt von lauter[1] Liebe,
Ich hör' es sogar im Traum.

"Der Tod, das ist die kühle Nacht" consists of a series of independent statements, whose relationship to each other is hinted at rather than expressed.
Such an arrangement is known as *parataxis*. Parataxis is very common in lyric
poetry; it is a way of making us read between the lines and so figure out the
connection for ourselves. Thus this objectively least involved of forms subjec-
tively involves the reader most. Since we do not ordinarily arrive at the connection by cold analysis but more by a process of instinctive association,
parataxis is especially effective when the poet wishes to arouse mood, *Stimmung*, and Heine wrote no more perfect mood poem than "Der Tod, das ist die
kühle Nacht."

In many ways, of course, such as through rhythm, rime, and vowel quality, the poet guides the associations we make, so that these are not really
"free"; he is concerned not with *our* inner life but with the objectification of
his.

„*Ein Jüngling liebt ein Mädchen*"

Ein Jüngling liebt ein Mädchen,
Die hat einen andern erwählt;
Der andre liebt eine andre
Und hat sich mit dieser vermählt.

Das Mädchen heiratet aus Ärger   5
Den ersten besten Mann,
Der ihr in den Weg gelaufen;
Der Jüngling ist übel dran.[1]

Es ist eine alte Geschichte,
Doch bleibt sie immer neu;   10

---

[1]'nothing but'

[1]'in a bad way'

Und wem sie just passieret,
Dem bricht das Herz entzwei.

Towards Interpretation
1. How is the power of love portrayed here, especially in comparison to the preceding poem?
2. The metrical form of "Ein Jüngling" is strongly influenced by that of the *Volkslied*. Is the meter appropriate to the subject matter?

„Als ich auf der Reise zufällig"

Als ich, auf der Reise, zufällig
Der Liebsten Familie fand,
Schwesterchen, Vater und Mutter
Sie haben mich freudig erkannt.

Sie fragten nach meinem Befinden,   5
Und sagten selber sogleich:
Ich hätte mich gar nicht verändert,
Nur mein Gesicht sei bleich.

Ich fragte nach Muhmen und Basen,
Nach manchem langweil'gen Gesell'n,   10
Und nach dem kleinen Hündchen
Mit seinem sanften Bell'n.

Auch nach der vermählten Geliebten
Fragte ich nebenbei;
Und freundlich gab man zur Antwort,   15
Daß sie in den Wochen sei.[1]

Und freundlich gratulier' ich,
Und lispelte liebevoll:
Daß man sie von mir recht herzlich
Viel tausendmal grüßen soll.   20

Schwesterchen rief dazwischen:
„Das Hündchen, sanft und klein,
Ist groß und toll geworden,
Und ward ertränkt,[2] im Rhein."

Die Kleine gleicht der Geliebten,   25
Besonders wenn sie lacht;

---

[1]*in der Wochen sein* 'be confined', i.e., 'just had a baby'   [2]*ward ertränkt* 'was drowned'

Sie hat dieselben Augen,
Die mich so elend gemacht.

Towards Interpretation
1. Why is the dog brought into this poem?
2. How does the end of the poem connect with the beginning? What is likely to happen next?
3. From what basic tension does the irony of this poem spring?
4. What is the thematic connection between this poem and the preceding one?

Der Asra

Täglich ging die wunderschöne
Sultanstochter auf und nieder
Um die Abendzeit am Springbrunn,
Wo die weißen Wasser plätschern.

Täglich stand der junge Sklave   5
Um die Abendzeit am Springbrunn,
Wo die weißen Wasser plätschern;
Täglich ward er bleich und bleicher.

Eines Abends trat die Fürstin
Auf ihn zu mit raschen Worten: 10
„Deinen Namen will ich wissen,
Deine Heimat, deine Sippschaft!"

Und der Sklave sprach: „Ich heiße
Mohamet, ich bin aus Jemen,
Und mein Stamm sind jene Asra,   15
Welche sterben, wenn sie lieben."

Towards Interpretation
1. Explain the significance of *ging . . . auf und nieder, trat . . . mit raschen Worten*, associated with the sultan's daughter, as opposed to *stand* and *sprach*, associated with the slave.
2. "Der Asra" we might call Heine's version of "Wer die Schönheit angeschaut mit Augen, / Ist dem Tode schon anheimgegeben." Compare the two poems and point out differences in the treatment of the theme.

„Wir saßen am Fischerhause"

Wir saßen am Fischerhause
Und schauten nach der See;
Die Abendnebel kamen
Und stiegen in die Höh'.

Im Leuchtturm wurden die Lichter   5
Allmählich angesteckt,
Und in der weiten Ferne
Ward noch ein Schiff entdeckt.

Wir sprachen von Sturm und Schiffbruch,
Vom Seemann, und wie er lebt   10
Und zwischen Himmel und Wasser
Und Angst und Freude schwebt.

Wir sprachen von fernen Küsten,
Vom Süden und vom Nord,
Und von den seltsamen Völkern   15
Und seltsamen Sitten dort.

Am Ganges duftet's und leuchtet's
Und Riesenbäume blüh'n
Und schöne, stille Menschen
Vor Lotusblumen knie'n.   20

In Lappland sind schmutzige Leute,
Plattköpfig, breitmäulig und klein;
Sie kauern ums Feuer und backen
Sich Fische und quäken und schrei'n.

Die Mädchen horchten ernsthaft,   25
Und endlich sprach niemand mehr;
Das Schiff war nicht mehr sichtbar,
Es dunkelte gar zu sehr.

Towards Interpretation

1. Who is telling these stories? Who is listening?
2. What would you call the theme of this poem as distinct from its literal subject?
3. Explain why lines 17-20 are easy to read aloud, while lines 21-24 require effort. Why this difference between the two stanzas?

„Die Lotosblume ängstigt"

Die Lotusblume ängstigt
Sich vor der Sonne Pracht,
Und mit gesenktem Haupte
Erwartet sie träumend die Nacht.

Der Mond, der ist ihr Buhle,   5
Er weckt sie mit seinem Licht,
Und ihm entschleiert sie freundlich
Ihr frommes[1] Blumengesicht.

Sie blüht und glüht und leuchtet,
Und starret stumm in die Höh';   10
Sie duftet und weinet und zittert
Vor Liebe und Liebesweh'.

Towards Interpretation

1. Why is the lotusflower's reaction to her beloved a mixture of joy and
   sadness?

„Mein Herz, mein Herz ist traurig"

Mein Herz, mein Herz ist traurig,
Doch lustig leuchtet der Mai;
Ich stehe, gelehnt an der Linde,
Hoch auf der alten Bastei.

Da drunten fließt der blaue   5
Stadtgraben[1] in stiller Ruh';
Ein Knabe fährt im Kahne
Und angelt und pfeift dazu.

Jenseits erheben sich freundlich,
In winziger, bunter Gestalt,   10
Lusthäuser,[2] und Gärten, und Menschen,
Und Ochsen, und Wiesen, und Wald.

Die Mägde bleichen Wäsche,[3]
Und springen im Gras herum;
Das Mühlrad stäubt Diamanten,   15
Ich höre sein fernes Gesumm.

---

[1] 'modest'

[1] 'city moat' [2] 'villas' [3] spread linen on grass to bleach

Am alten grauen Turme
Ein Schilderhäuschen⁴ steht;
Ein rotgeröckter Bursche
Dort auf und nieder geht.   20

Er spielt mit seiner Flinte,⁵
Die funkelt im Sonnnenrot,
Er präsentiert und schultert —
Ich wollt', er schösse mich tot.

Towards Interpretation

1. Unlike most of the poems we have read up to now, this poem pays considerable attention to minute detail — in a quite realistic fashion we see the landscape and the figures beheld by the poet from his post high above the scene. What is the relation of all this "realism," the outer world, to the inner world of strophe 1? Is Heine perhaps interested in these details for their own sake?
2. In Eichendorff's "Das zerbrochene Ringlein" it was at once evident that the millwheel had symbolic significance. Do any of the many objects (including the millwheel) in Heine's poem have such significance?
3. How do the images common to everyday life contribute to the surprising resolution of the poem?
4. In general terms, what is the speaker's problem?

„Es war ein alter König"

Es war ein alter König,
Sein Herz war schwer, sein Haupt war grau;
Der arme alte König,
Er nahm eine junge Frau.

Es war ein schöner Page,   5
Blond war sein Haupt, leicht war sein Sinn;
Er trug die seidne Schleppe
Der jungen Königin.

Kennst du das alte Liedchen?
Es klingt so süß, es klingt so trüb!   10
Sie mußten beide sterben,
Sie hatten sich viel zu lieb.

---

⁴'sentry-box' ⁵'rifle'

Towards Interpretation

1. Scan the first two stanzas and account for the change in meter in line 6.
2. How does the vocalism (vowel quality) of line 2 make the king's heart heavier and his head grayer?

Pfalzgräfin Jutta

Pfalzgräfin Jutta fuhr über den Rhein,
Im leichten Kahn, bei Mondenschein.
Die Zofe rudert, die Gräfin spricht:
„Siehst du die sieben Leichen nicht,
Die hinter uns kommen   5
Einhergeschwommen? —
So traurig schwimmen die Toten!

Das waren Ritter voll Jugendlust —
Sie sanken zärtlich an meine Brust
Und schwuren mir Treue. — Zur Sicherheit,   10
Daß sie nicht brächen ihren Eid,
Ließ ich sie ergreifen
Sogleich und ersäufen —
So traurig schwimmen die Toten!"

Die Zofe rudert, die Gräfin lacht.   15
Das hallt so höhnisch durch die Nacht!
Bis an die Hüfte tauchen hervor
Die Leichen und strecken die Finger empor,
Wie schwörend — Sie nicken
Mit gläsernen Blicken —   20
So traurig schwimmen die Toten!

"Pfalzgräfin Jutta" is a fairly subtle example of Heine's ironical treatment of "romantic" themes* — not too subtle, to be sure, for Heine never likes his readers to miss the point. The macabre subject is exposed to light raillery by the contrast between form and content. The first six verses of each stanza bound along in positively jolly fashion while they tell their tale of horror; only the slower tempo of the refrain introduces a note of pity for the hapless lovers. The "quick" rimes of the fifth and sixth lines of each stanza have an almost comical effect, as does the use of the vulgarism *ersäufen* for *ertränken* (line 13). Yet while thus making fun of his own poem, so to speak, Heine makes the same verses that cause a wry smile at their unsuitability for their overt content

---

*The poet was inspired here by a ballad in *Des Knaben Wunderhorn*.

also characterize in a vivid and masterly way the heartlessness of the Pfalzgräfin — for this, the true subject of the poem, the form fits like a glove. The
total effect is twice as gruesome as any "serious" treatment could have rendered it and twice as convincing — Heine has outromanticized the Romantics.

Karl I.[1]

Im Wald, in der Köhlerhütte[2] sitzt
Trübsinnig allein der König;
Er sitzt an der Wiege des Köhlerkinds
Und wiegt und singt eintönig:

Eiapopeia, was raschelt im Stroh?   5
Es blöken im Stalle die Schafe[3] —
Du trägst das Zeichen an der Stirn[4]
Und lächelst so furchtbar im Schlafe.

Eiapopeia, das Kätzchen ist tot —
Du trägst auf der Stirne das Zeichen —   10
Du wirst ein Mann und schwingst das Beil,
Schon zittern im Walde die Eichen.

Der alte Köhlerglaube[5] verschwand,
Es glauben die Köhlerkinder —
Eiapopeia — nicht mehr an Gott   15
Und an den König noch minder.

Das Kätzchen ist tot, die Mäuschen sind froh —
Wir müssen zuschanden werden[6] —
Eiapopeia — im Himmel der Gott
Und ich, der König auf Erden.   20

Mein Mut erlischt, mein Herz ist krank,
Und täglich wird es kränker —
Eiapopeia — du Köhlerkind,
Ich weiß es, du bist mein Henker.

Mein Todesgesang ist dein Wiegenlied —   25
Eiapopeia — die greisen[7]
Haarlocken schneidest du ab zuvor —
Im Nacken klirrt mir das Eisen.

---

[1]Charles I of England, beheaded in 1649 [2]'charcoal burner's hut' [3]Line 5 is part of a
folk-rime, line 6 probably only imitates such a rime. [4]i.e., the mark of Cain [5]=Aber-
glaube [6]=zugrunde gehen [7]'gray (with age)'

Eiapopeia, was raschelt im Stroh? —
Du hast das Reich erworben,[8]   30
Und schlägst mir das Haupt vom Rumpf herab —
Das Kätzchen ist gestorben.

Eiapopeia, was raschelt im Stroh?
Es blöken im Stalle die Schafe.
Das Kätzchen ist tot, die Mäuschen sind froh —   35
Schlafe, mein Henkerchen, schlafe!

Die schlesischen Weber[1]

Im düstern Auge keine Träne,
Sie sitzen am Webstuhl und fletschen die Zähne:
Deutschland, wir weben dein Leichentuch,
Wir weben hinein den dreifachen Fluch —
    Wir weben, wir weben!   5

Ein Fluch dem Gotte, zu dem wir gebeten
in Winterskälte und Hungersnöten;
Wir haben vergebens gehofft und geharrt,
Er hat uns geäfft und gefoppt und genarrt —
    Wir weben, wir weben!   10

Ein Fluch dem König, dem König der Reichen,
Den unser Elend nicht konnte erweichen,
Der den letzten Groschen von uns erpreßt,
Und uns wie Hunde erschießen läßt —
    Wir weben, wir weben!   15

Ein Fluch dem falschen Vaterlande,
Wo nur gedeihen Schmach und Schande,
Wo jede Blume früh geknickt,
Wo Fäulnis und Moder den Wurm erquickt —
    Wir weben, wir weben!   20

Das Schiffchen[2] fliegt, der Webstuhl kracht,
Wir weben emsig Tag und Nacht —

---

[8]Probably a bitterly ironical allusion to Matthew 25:34: "Da [on the Day of Judgement] wird der König sagen zu denen zu seiner Rechten: Kommt her, ... ererbet das Reich, das euch bereitet ist von Anbeginn der Welt!"

[1]A *Zeitgedicht*; the uprising of the Silesian weavers in 1844 came about as a result of the Industrial Revolution. Gehart Hauptmann treated the theme in his epoch-making drama, *Die Weber* (1892). [2]'shuttle'

Altdeutschland, wir weben dein Leichentuch,
Wir weben hinein den dreifachen Fluch,
Wir weben, wir weben!   25

„Es ragt ins Meer der Runenstein"

Es ragt ins Meer der Runenstein,
Da sitz' ich mit meinen Träumen.
Es pfeift der Wind, die Möwen schrei'n,
Die Wellen, die wandern und schäumen.

Ich habe geliebt manch schönes Kind[1]   5
Und manchen guten Gesellen —
Wo sind sie hin? Es pfeift der Wind,
Es schäumen und wandern die Wellen.

Towards Interpretation
1. Is the name of the rock on which the poet sits significant?
2. Line 8 is merely line 4 inverted. What is implied by this inversion?

„Ich wandle unter Blumen"

Ich wandle unter Blumen
Und blühe selber mit;
Ich wandle wie im Traume
Und schwanke bei jedem Schritt.

O, halt mich fest, Geliebte!   5
Vor Liebestrunkenheit
Fall' ich dir sonst zu Füßen,
Und der Garten ist voller Leut'.

Towards Interpretation
1. What choice does the beloved have in stanza 2?

„Das Fräulein stand am Meere"

Das Fräulein stand am Meere
Und seufzte lang und bang,
Es rührte sie so sehre
Der Sonnenuntergang.

---

[1] = Mädchen

„Mein Fräulein! sei'n Sie munter,   5
Das ist ein altes Stück;
Hier vorne geht sie unter
Und kehrt von hinten zurück."

Very possibly Heine might have become a genuine Romantic, if he could
have.* He shares the romantic aversion to reality. But around 1830 Romanticism was suffering from inflation; there were so many poetasters and epigones
grinding out verse in the romantic vein that Romanticism itself seemed cheap-
ened, and Heine felt compelled (as did Platen) to distance himself from it. To
be sure, much of his verse is thoroughly romantic — it could have been written
by Brentano — but side by side with this, and often even within it, we find a
tendency to "expose" romanticism, lay bare the vacuity of its now threadbare
conventions, point up its inability to cope with reality. Not always is this the
whole story, however. There is often a "double take" in Heine's wit, as for
example in "Ein Jüngling liebt ein Mädchen," where the last two lines reaf-
firm the rights of feeling after we have just laughed at the youth who is "in a
bad way." "Ich wandle unter Blumen" does not so much ridicule feeling, the
"romantic" attitude, as reveal its inappropriateness as a mode of social behav-
ior. Such is the world and we have to accept it. And while "Das Fräulein stand
am Meere" definitely does ridicule feeling, its target is pseudo-feeling. The
Fräulein is a second-rate Romantic, who finds a sunset by the sea touching.

Heine's wit is based on the confrontation of the ideal with ordinary reality. The two, each justified in itself, are made to cut across each other so that
the ideal, as the more finely organized and less protected, comes to appear
ridiculous. The true Romantics did exactly the opposite: they made everyday
reality appear blind and pitiable when compared with the ideal. Novalis's
"Hymnen an die Nacht" illustrate this perfectly.

Schöpfungslieder[1]
„Sprach der Herr am sechsten Tage"

Sprach der Herr am sechsten Tage:
Hab' am Ende nun vollbracht
Diese große, schöne Schöpfung,
Und hab' alles gut gemacht.

---

*Cf. Ursula Jaspersen, "Heinrich Heine," in *Die deutsche Lyrik* (Düsseldorf:
Schwann-Bagel, ²1981), 2:144-149, to whom these remarks are much indebted.

[1]*Schöpfung* 'Creation' The following four poems belong to this cycle.

Wie die Sonne rosengoldig   5
In dem Meere widerstrahlt!
Wie die Bäume grün und glänzend!
Ist nicht alles wie gemalt?

Sind nicht weiß wie Alabaster
Dort die Lämmchen auf der Flur?   10
Ist sie nicht so schön vollendet
Und natürlich die Natur?

Erd' und Himmel sind erfüllet
Ganz von meiner Herrlichkeit,
Und der Mensch, er wird mich loben   15
Bis in alle Ewigkeit!

Towards Interpretation

1. By what standard is God evaluating Creation? Where might we hear similar evaluative expressions?
2. Compare this poem with Goethe's "Es ist gut," especially in regard to the tone.

„Der Stoff, das Material des Gedichts"

Der Stoff, das Material des Gedichts,
Das saugt sich nicht aus dem Finger;
Kein Gott erschafft die Welt aus nichts,
So wenig wie irdische Singer.

Aus vorgefundenem[1] Urweltsdreck   5
Erschuf ich die Männerleiber,
Und aus dem Männerrippenspeck
Erschuf ich die schönen Weiber.

Den Himmel erschuf ich aus der Erd'
Und Engel aus Weiberentfaltung;[2]   10
Der Stoff gewinnt erst seinen Wert
Durch künstlerische Gestaltung.

---

[1]'already present' [2]'female development' (the angels are 'superwomen')

„*Warum ich eigentlich erschuf*"

Warum ich eigentlich erschuf
Die Welt, ich will es gern bekennen:
Ich fühlte in der Seele brennen,
Wie Flammenwahnsinn, den Beruf.

Krankheit ist wohl der letzte Grund   5
Des ganzen Schöpferdrangs gewesen;
Erschaffend konnte ich genesen,
Erschaffend wurde ich gesund.

Towards Interpretation
1. What is the basic metaphor underlying these three *Schöpfungslieder?*
2. Why did God create the world?

„*Laß die heil'gen Parabolen*"

Laß die heil'gen Parabolen,[1]
Laß die frommen Hypothesen —
Suche die verdammten Fragen
Ohne Umschweif uns zu lösen.

Warum schleppt sich, blutend, elend,   5
Unter Kreuzlast der Gerechte,
Während glücklich als ein Sieger
Trabt auf hohem Roß der Schlechte?

Woran liegt die Schuld? Ist etwa
Unser Herr nicht ganz allmächtig?   10
Oder treibt er selbst den Unfug?
Ach, das wäre niederträchtig.

Also fragen wir beständig,
Bis man uns mit einer Handvoll
Erde endlich stopft die Mäuler —   15
Aber ist das eine Antwort?

Towards Interpretation
1. Why does the poet need to go beyond parables?
2. Why is the final stanza rimeless?
3. Is this poem atheistic? Can one find such questions asked in the Bible?

---

[1] = *Parabeln, Gleichnisreden*

Gedächtnisfeier

Keine Messe wird man singen,
Keinen Kadosch[1] wird man sagen,
Nichts gesagt und nichts gesungen
Wird an meinen Sterbetagen.[2]

Doch vielleicht an solchem Tage   5
Wenn das Wetter schön und milde,
Geht spazieren auf Montmartre[3]
Mit Paulinen Frau Mathilde.[4]

Mit dem Kranz von Immortellen[5]
Kommt sie, mir das Grab zu schmücken,   10
Und sie seufzet: Pauvre homme!
Feuchte Wehmut in den Blicken.

Leider wohn' ich viel zu hoch,
Und ich habe meiner Süßen
Keinen Stuhl hier anzubieten;   15
Ach! sie schwankt mit müden Füßen.

Süßes, dickes Kind, du darfst
Nicht zu Fuß nach Hause gehen;
An dem Barriere-Gitter
Siehst du die Fiaker[6] stehen.   20

Towards Interpretation
1. What might be deduced here about the relationship of Heine and Mathilde? What does he expect from her after his death?

Sie erlischt

Der Vorhang fällt, das Stück ist aus,
Und Herrn und Damen gehn nach Haus.
Ob ihnen auch das Stück gefallen?
Ich glaub', ich hörte Beifall schallen.
Ein hochverehrtes Publikum   5
Beklatschte dankbar seinen Dichter.
Jetzt aber ist das Haus so stumm,
Und sind verschwunden Lust und Lichter.

---

[1]The Mourner's Kaddish is a five-part Jewish prayer for the dead. [2]The Jewish rites for the dead last several days. [3]Large hill in Paris; near the top is a cemetery where many writers and artists, including Heine, lie buried. [4]Mathilde was Heine's wife, Pauline her friend. [5]the everlasting flower (*Helychrysum*) [6]'carriages for hire'

Doch horch! ein schollernd schnöder Klang
Ertönt unfern der öden Bühne; —   10
Vielleicht daß eine Saite sprang
An einer alten Violine.
Verdrießlich rascheln im Parterr'
Etweiche Ratten hin und her,
Und alles riecht nach ranz'gem Öle.   15
Die letzte Lampe ächzt und zischt
Verzweiflungsvoll, und sie erlischt.
Das arme Licht war meine Seele.

Towards Interpretation

1. A critic has called this poem "one of Heine's most moving poems."*
   How would you differentiate the imagery in stanzas 1 and 2? What
   does this suggest?

Nikolaus Lenau* (1802-1850)

Bitte

Weil'[1] auf mir, du dunkles Auge,
Übe deine ganze Macht,
Ernste, milde, träumerische,
Unergründlich süße Nacht!

Nimm mit deinem Zauberdunkel   5
Diese Welt von hinnen mir,
Daß du über meinem Leben
Einsam schwebest für und für.

---

*Jeffrey L. Sammons, *Heinrich Heine: The Elusive Poet* (New Haven: Yale University
Press, 1969), 386.

*Pseudonym of Nikolaus Franz Niembsch, Edler von Strehlenau.

[1]'linger'

Die drei Zigeuner

Drei Zigeuner fand ich einmal
Liegen an einer Weide,
Als mein Fuhrwerk mit müder Qual
Schlich durch sandige Heide.

Hielt der eine für sich allein   5
In den Händen die Fiedel,
Spielte, umglüht vom Abendschein,
Sich ein feuriges Liedel.[1]

Hielt der zweite die Pfeif' im Mund,
Blickte nach seinem Rauche,   10
Froh, als ob er vom Erdenrund
Nichts zum Glücke mehr brauche.

Und der dritte behaglich schlief,
Und sein Zimbal[2] am Baum hing,
Über die Saiten der Windhauch lief,   15
Über sein Herz ein Traum ging.

An den Kleidern trugen die drei
Löcher und bunte Flicken,
Aber sie boten trotzig frei
Spott den Erdengeschicken.[3]   20

Dreifach haben sie mir gezeigt,
Wenn das Leben uns nachtet,
Wie man's verraucht, verschläft, vergeigt,
Und es dreimal verachtet.

Nach den Zigeunern lang noch schaun   25
Mußt' ich im Weiterfahren,
Nach den Gesichtern dunkelbraun,
Den schwarzlockigen Haaren.

Towards Interpretation
1. What is the underlying metaphor of this poem?
2. Is the imagery of "Die drei Zigeuner" principally visual or auditory? Where does the imagery attain its greatest poignancy?
3. What "trick" does Lenau use to make us *hear* the wind in the dulcimer?
4. Is the speaker's attitude towards the gypsies unproblematic? Support your view by reference to the text.

---

[1] =*Lied(chen)* [2]'dulcimer' (played by striking the strings) [3]'earthly fates'

Die Drei

Drei Reiter nach verlorner Schlacht,
Wie reiten sie so sacht, so sacht!

Aus tiefen Wunden quillt das Blut,
Es spürt das Roß die warme Flut.

Vom Sattel tropft das Blut, vom Zaum,   5
Und spült hinunter Staub und Schaum.

Die Rosse schreiten sanft und weich,
Sonst flöss' das Blut zu rasch, zu reich.

Die Reiter reiten dicht gesellt,
Und einer sich am andern hält.   10

Sie sehn sich traurig ins Gesicht,
Und einer um den andern spricht:

„Mir blüht daheim die schönste Maid,
Drum tut mein früher Tod mir leid."

„Hab' Haus und Hof und grünen Wald,   15
Und sterben muß ich hier so bald!"

„Den Blick hab' ich in Gottes Welt,
Sonst nichts, doch schwer mir 's Sterben fällt."

Und lauernd auf den Todesritt
Ziehn durch die Luft drei Geier mit.   20

Sie teilen kreischend unter sich:
„Den speisest du, den du, den ich."

Towards Interpretation

1. How does the stanzaic structure contribute to the meaning of the poem?
2. What are these cavalrymen dying for? Does patriotism play a role?
3. Why don't the vultures say: *Den f r i s s e s t du, den du, den ich?*

Welke Rose

In einem Buche blätternd, fand
Ich eine Rose welk, zerdrückt,
Und weiß auch nicht mehr, wessen Hand
Sie einst für mich gepflückt.

Ach, mehr und mehr im Abendhauch   5
Verweht Erinn'rung; bald zerstiebt

Mein Erdenlos,[1] dann weiß ich auch
Nicht mehr, wer mich geliebt.

Towards Interpretation

1. The cola (pauses) in this poem are placed in such a way as to make all but the *b*-rimes (*zerdrückt* – *gepflückt*) of the first stanza very light. How do the unemphatic rimes reflect the content of the poem?
2. Try scanning this poem. Are you certain of the stresses? How does the scansion reflect the content?

„Der Nachtwind hat in den Bäumen"

Der Nachtwind hat in den Bäumen
Sein Rauschen eingestellt,[1]
Die Vögel sitzen und träumen
Am Aste traut gesellt.

Die ferne schmächtige[2] Quelle,   5
Weil[3] alles andre ruht,
Läßt hörbar nun Welle auf Welle
Hinflüstern ihre Flut.

Und wenn die Nähe verklungen,[4]
Dann kommen an die Reih'   10
Die leisen Erinnerungen,
Und weinen fern vorbei.

Daß alles vorübersterbe,
Ist alt und allbekannt;
Doch diese Wehmut, die herbe,   15
Hat niemand noch gebannt.

A critic has written of this poem:

> Die Darstellung hebt an mit einem stillen und friedlichen Bilde, in welchem die verklungene Bewegung des Nachtwindes gleichsam noch nachzittert. In der zweiten Strophe öffnet sich das ruhende Bild durch das nun hörbar werdende Flüstern der fernen Quelle. Indem die dritte Strophe diesem weiterweisenden Eindruck nachgibt, öffnet sich eine neue und andere Ferne, eine Ferne in unanschaulicher, in übertragener Bedeutung: das Flüstern der Quelle wird zum Vorbeiweinen der Erinnerungen. . . . Über solche Sinnbildlichkeit hinaus führt die vierte Strophe zu einer Aussage, in der die

---

[1]'earthly lot'

[1]'ceased' [2]'meager' [3]'since' [4]'when nearby things have fallen silent'

einmalige Anschauung nun völlig verlassen ist um einer Quintessenz willen, die als allgemeine Einsicht aus dem erlebten Augenblicke aufsteigt.*

„Schläfrig hangen die sonnenmüden Blätter"

Schläfrig hangen die sonnenmüden Blätter,
Alles schweigt im Walde, nur eine Biene
Summt dort an der Blüte mit mattem Eifer;
Sie auch ließ vom sommerlichen Getöne,
Eingeschlafen vielleicht im Schoß der Blume.   5
Hier, noch Frühlings,[1] rauschte die muntre Quelle;
Still versiegend, ist in die Luft zergangen
All ihr frisches Geplauder, helles Schimmern.
Traurig kahlt[2] die Stätte, wo einst ein Quell floß;
Horchen muß ich noch dem gewohnten Rauschen,   10
Ich vermisse den Bach, wie liebe Grüße,
Die sonst fernher kamen, nun ausgeblieben.
Alles still, einschläfernd, des dichten Mooses
Sanft nachgiebige Schwellung ist so ruhlich;[3]
Möge hier mich holder Schlummer beschleichen,   15
Mir die Schlüssel zu meinen Schätzen stehlen
Und die Waffen entwenden meines Zornes,
Daß die Seele, rings nach außen vergessen,
Sich in ihre Tiefen hinein erinn're,
Preisen will ich den Schlummer, bis er leise   20
Naht in diesem Dunkel und mir das Aug' schließt.

Schlaf, du kindlicher Gott, du Gott der Kindheit!
Du Verjünger der Welt, die, dein entbehrend,
Rasch in wenig Stunden wäre gealtert.
Wundertätiger Freund, Erlöser des Herzens!   25
Rings umstellt und bewacht am hellen Tage
Ist das Herz in der Brust und unzugänglich
Für die leiseren Genien des Lebens,
Denn ihm wandeln voran auf allen Wegen
Die Gedanken, bewaffnet, als Liktoren,[4]   30
Schreckend und verscheuchend lieblichen Zauber.
Aber in der Stille der Nacht, des Schlummers,
Wacht die Seele heimlich und lauscht wie Hero,

---

*Johannes Pfeiffer, *Wege zur Dichtung* (Hamburg: Wittig, ⁷1969), 22f.

[1]'when it was still spring' [2]from *kahl* 'barren' [3]'inviting rest' [4]Look up "lictor" in a dictionary.

Bis verborgen ihr Gott ihr naht, herüber
Schwimmend durch das wallende Meer der Träume.[5] 35

Eine Flöte klang mir im Schlaf zuweilen,
Wie ein Gesang der Urwelt, Sehnsucht weckend,
Daß ich süß erschüttert erwacht' in Tränen,
Und noch lange hörte den Ruf der Heimat;
Bliebe davon ein Hauch in meinen Liedern!   40

Schlaf, melodischer Freund, woher die Flöte?
Ist sie ein Ast des Walds, durchhaucht vom Gotte,
Hört' ich im Traum des heiligen Pan Syringe[6]?

Towards Interpretation

1. "Pan's hour" is the "faunal noon," when all is silent in wood and meadow. How does the end of this poem return to its beginning? Do we now see the beginning in the same light?
2. *What* "Heimat" does the sleeper hear calling in line 39?
3. If you are familiar with modern theories of the dream, point out ways in which Lenau's poem (1842) anticipates and confirms them.

„Rings ein Verstummen, ein Entfärben"

Rings ein Verstummen, ein Entfärben:
Wie sanft den Wald die Lüfte streicheln,
Sein welkes Laub ihm abzuschmeicheln;
Ich liebe dieses milde Sterben.

Von hinnen geht die stille Reise,   5
Die Zeit der Liebe ist verklungen,
Die Vögel haben ausgesungen,
Und dürre Blätter sinken leise.

Die Vögel zogen nach dem Süden,
Aus dem Verfall des Laubes tauchen   10
Die Nester, die nicht Schutz mehr brauchen,
Die Blätter fallen stets, die müden.

In dieses Waldes leisem Rauschen
Ist mir, als hör' ich Kunde wehen,

---

[5]Leander swam the Hellespont at night to visit the beautiful priestess of Venus, Hero. She directed his course by holding a torch at the top of a tower. [6]The stem of the reed (syringa) was used to make Panpipes; cf. *syrinx.*

Daß alles Sterben und Vergehen   15
Nur heimlich still vergnügtes[1] Tauschen.

Towards Interpretation
1. Why didn't Lenau use masculine rimes in this poem?
2. How does Lenau employ prefixes like *ab-*, *aus-*, *ent-* and *ver-* to convey the underlying idea of the poem?
3. The Romantic philosopher Schelling postulated that "Natur soll der sichtbare Geist, der Geist die unsichtbare Natur sein." Do you see any connection between this idea and the present poem? How about Romantic poetry in general?

Nikolaus Lenau

Annette von Droste-Hülshoff

Annette von Droste-Hülshoff (1797-1848)

With Goethe there came into being a distinctively new kind of lyric poetry which the Germans still have in mind when they speak of verse as "lyrical."* The characteristic quality of this poetry is "inwardness" (*Innigkeit*), a mingling of nature and soul in one mood, so that, as in Goethe's "Mailied," the heart of

---

[1]'happily satisfied'

*The following remarks are in part a direct translation, in part an adaptation of a section of Emil Staiger, "Annette von Droste-Hülshoff: Festrede bei der Jahrhundertfeier am 24. Mai 1948 in Meersburg," *Jahrbuch der Droste-Gesellschaft* 2 (1948-50): 58ff.

the lover feels at one with the sprays of blossoms and the golden clouds of morning. If we look at the lyrical poetry of Goethe's day and at the same time keep in mind contemporary ideological developments, we see that this mingling of nature and soul becomes more and more intense, more "inward," and that the human ego disappears more and more *in* nature, surrendering itself to the stream of transient phenomena. For the Enlightment of the 18th century nature was still something outside man, and man stood over it as its master. In the classical period, with Goethe, the scales hung in equilibrium. Love joined the "I" of the poet with the "Thou" of the cosmos. The poets we call Romantics often seem to be the victims of nature, Merlins enchanted by their own too powerful magic. A giddiness has seized them, and a sense of self-loss, of impotence, begins to manifest itself. The spirit no longer rises free but is pulled to the earth and an unconquerable melancholy possesses it: *Die ganze Welt ist zum Verzweifeln traurig* (Lenau). Man is abandoned, isolated, and no longer capable of managing his own life. The awareness of our intimate union with nature has become a torment.

Annette von Droste-Hülshoff is one of the last of these figures. She is sensitive as no one before her to the lower forms of life, to atmospheric change, and to the demonic undercurrent in all existence, to all those things that seem to draw man, in his longing for abundance and immediacy, toward the earth until this longing turns to fear and horror. But at the same time she is one of the first figures of an epoch just emerging: poetic realism. Wolfgang Kayser has said of Droste's poetry:

> [Ihr] Werk ergreift nicht durch die Fülle tiefer und großer Gedanken unseren Geist, ergreift nicht durch den Zauber klanglicher und rhythmischer Schönheit unser Gefühl, aber sie ergreift und bestimmt durch ihre Gestaltung des Seins unser Verhältnis zum Sein, und das so stark, wie es nur großer Dichtung möglich ist.*

The double vision of the following poem, "Der Heidemann," is almost a textbook example of poetry in transition, with romantic and realistic points of view presented in alternate stanzas.

---

*Annette v. Droste-Hülshoff, *Sämtliche Werke* (Leipzig: Insel, 1939), 973.

Der Heidemann[1]

„Geht, Kinder, nicht zu weit ins Bruch,[2]
Die Sonne sinkt, schon surrt[3] den Flug
Die Biene matter, schlafgehemmt,
Am Grunde schwimmt ein blasses Tuch,
Der Heidemann kömmt!" —   5

Die Knaben spielen fort am Raine,[4]
Sie rupfen Gräser, schnellen[5] Steine,
Sie plätschern in des Teiches Rinne,[6]
Erhaschen die Phalän'[7] am Ried
Und freun sich, wenn die Wasserspinne   10
Langbeinig in die Binsen[8] flieht.

„Ihr Kinder, legt euch nicht ins Gras! —
Seht, wo noch grad die Biene saß,
Wie weißer Rauch die Glocken[9] füllt.
Scheu aus dem Busche glotzt der Has',   15
Der Heidemann schwillt!" —

Kaum hebt ihr schweres Haupt die Schmele[10]
Noch aus dem Dunst, in seine Höhle
Schiebt sich der Käfer, und am Halme
Die träge Motte höher kreucht,[11]   20
Sich flüchtend vor dem feuchten Qualme,
Der unter ihre Flügel steigt.

„Ihr Kinder, haltet euch bei Haus!
Lauft ja nicht in das Bruch hinaus;
Seht, wie bereits der Dorn ergraut,   25
Die Drossel[12] ächzt zum Nest hinaus,
Der Heidemann braut!" —

Man sieht des Hirten Pfeife glimmen
Und vor ihm her die Herde schwimmen,
Wie Proteus seine Robbenscharen   30
Heimschwemmt im grauen Ozean.[13]
Am Dach die Schwalben zwitschernd fahren,
Und melancholisch kräht der Hahn.

---

[1]*Der Heidemann* is "... die Nebelschicht, die sich zur Herbst- und Frühlingszeit über den Heidegrund legt" (Droste). [2]'moor' [3]'whirrs' (here transitive) [4]'edge' (of field; here, moor) [5]'flip,' 'toss' [6]'outlet' [7]night-flying moth [8]'long-bladed grass' [9]'bells' (of flowers) [10]a long-bladed grass [11]=*kriecht* [12]'thrush' [13]Proteus: sea deity, lord of the seals (*Robben*) and other marine animals; *heimschwemmt* 'drives swimming home'

„Ihr Kinder, bleibt am Hofe dicht!
Seht, wie die feuchte Nebelschicht   35
Schon an des Pförtchens Klinke[14] reicht;
Am Grunde schwimmt ein falsches Licht,
Der Heidemann steigt!" —

Nun strecken nur der Föhren[15] Wipfel
Noch aus dem Dunste grüne Gipfel,   40
Wie übern Schnee Wacholderbüsche;
Ein leises Brodeln[16] quillt im Moor,
Ein schwaches Schrillen, ein Gezische
Dringt aus der Niederung hervor.

„Ihr Kinder, kommt, kommt schnell herein!   45
Das Irrlicht[17] zündet seinen Schein,
Die Kröte schwillt, die Schlang' im Ried;
Jetzt ist's unheimlich draußen sein,
Der Heidemann zieht!" —

Nun sinkt die letzte Nadel, rauchend   50
Zergeht die Fichte, langsam tauchend
Steigt Nebelschemen[18] aus dem Moore,
Mit Hünenschritten[19] gleitet's fort;
Ein irres Leuchten zuckt im Rohre,
Der Krötenchor beginnt am Bord.[20]   55

Und plötzlich scheint ein schwaches Glühen
Des Hünen Glieder zu durchziehen;
Es siedet auf,[21] es färbt die Wellen,
Der Nord, der Nord entzündet sich —
Glutpfeile, Feuerspeere schnellen,[22]   60
Der Horizont ein Lavastrich![23]

„Gott gnad' uns! wie es zuckt und dräut,[24]
Wie's schwelet[25] an der Dünenscheid'![26]
Ihr Kinder, faltet eure Händ',
Das bringt uns Pest und teure Zeit[27] —   65
Der Heidemann brennt!" —

Towards Interpretation

1. How would you characterize the speaker's attitude in the 5-line
   stanzas? In the 6-line stanzas?

---

[14]'latch' (of the wicket leading into the farmyard) [15]'Scotch pine tree' [16]'bubbling,'
'boiling' [17]'will-o'-the-wisp' [18]'mist phantom' [19]'giant steps' (*der Hüne* 'giant')
[20]'edge' (of pond) [21]'seethes up' [22]'dart' [23]Lines 59-61 describe the northern lights.
[24]=*droht* [25]'smolders' [26]'brow of the dune' [27]'famine'

2. What formal or stylistic devices does Droste use to convey the attitudes?
3. Would you say that the poet takes sides with either party?

Das öde Haus

Tiefab im Tobel[1] liegt ein Haus,
Zerfallen nach des Försters Tode,
Dort ruh' ich manche Stunde aus,
Vergraben unter Rank' und Lode;[2]
's ist eine Wildnis, wo der Tag   5
Nur halb die schweren Wimpern lichtet;
Der Felsen tiefe Kluft verdichtet
Ergrauter Äste Schattenhag.[3]

Ich horche träumend, wie im Spalt[4]
Die schwarzen Fliegen taumelnd summen,   10
Wie Seufzer streifen durch den Wald,
Am Strauche irre Käfer brummen:
Wenn sich die Abendröte drängt
An sickernden Geschiefers Lauge,[5]
Dann ist's, als ob ein trübes Auge,   15
Ein rotgeweintes, drüberhängt.

Das Dach, vom Moose überschwellt,
Läßt wirre Schober[6] niederragen,
Und eine Spinne hat ihr Zelt
Im Fensterloche aufgeschlagen;   20
Da hängt, ein Blatt von zartem Flor,[7]
Der schillernden Libelle[8] Flügel,
Und ihres Panzers goldner Spiegel[9]
Ragt kopflos am Gesims[10] hervor.

Wo an zerrißner Laube Joch[11]   25
Die langen magern Schossen[12] streichen,[13]
An wildverwachsner Hecke noch
Im Moose Nelkensprossen schleichen,

---

[1]'forest ravine' [2]'tendrils and shoots' [3]Lines 7-8: 'Grayed branches' shady hedge darkens the rocks' deep ravine.' [4]=*Kluft*, line 7 [5]'on oozing slate's alkaline puddle' (alkali water that has oozed out of the slate deposit) [6]= *einzelne Strohbündel* (the house has a thatch roof) [7]'gauze' [8]'dragonfly,' genitive singular [9]'its armor's golden mirror,' i.e., the chitonous exoskeleton of the dragonfly's thorax [10]'sill' [11]'torn arbor's arch' [12]'shoots' [13]'wave'

Dort hat vom tröpfelnden Gestein[14]
Das dunkle Naß sich durchgesogen,   30
Kreucht um den Buchs[15] in trägen Bogen
Und sinkt am Fenchelstrauche[16] ein.

Zuweilen hat ein Schmetterling
Sich gaukelnd in der Schluft[17] gefangen
Und bleibt sekundenlang am Ring   35
Der kränkelnden Narzisse hangen;
Streicht[18] eine Taube durch den Hain,
So schweigt am Tobelrand ihr Girren,
Man höret nur die Flügel schwirren
Und sieht den Schatten am Gestein.   40

Und auf dem Herde, wo der Schnee
Seit Jahren durch den Schlot[19] geflogen,
Liegt Aschenmoder feucht and zäh,
Von Pilzes Glocken überzogen;[20]
Noch hängt am Mauerpflock[21] ein Rest   45
Verwirrten Wergs,[22] das Seil zu spinnen,
Wie halbvermorschtes Haar, und drinnen
Der Schwalbe überjährig[23] Nest.

Und von des Balkens Haken nickt
Ein Schellenband[24] an Schnall' und Riemen,   50
Mit grober Wolle ist gestickt
„Diana" auf dem Lederstriemen;[25]
Ein Pfeifchen[26] auch vergaß man hier,
Als man den Tannensarg geschlossen;
Den Mann begrub man, tot geschossen   55
Hat man das alte treue Tier.[27]

Sitz' ich so einsam am Gesträuch
Und hör' die Maus im Laube schrillen,
Das Eichorn blafft[28] von Zweig zu Zweig,
Am Sumpfe läuten Unk' und Grillen,[29] —   60
Wie Schauer überläuft's mich dann,
Als hör' ich klingeln noch die Schellen,
Im Walde die Diana bellen
Und pfeifen noch den toten Mann.

---

[14]The 'dripping rock' is the *sickerndes Geschiefer* of line 14.   [15]'boxwood' (plant)
[16]'fennel plant'   [17]=*Kluft*, line 7, and *Spalt*, l. 9.   [18]'flies low,' 'darts'   [19]'chimney'
[20]'covered with bell-shaped fungi'   [21]'wall-peg'   [22]'tow,' fiber prepared for rope-making   [23]'last year's'   [24]'(dog) harness with bells'   [25]'leather strap'   [26]'little whistle'
[27]i.e., "Diana"   [28]'leaps noisily'   [29]*Unke* 'orange-speckled toad'; *Grille* 'cricket'

Towards Interpretation

1. The underlying idea of this poem has been said to be *Dauer ohne Zukunft* (Emil Staiger), i.e., permanence without purpose or meaningless continuance. The deserted house itself of course symbolizes this. As another imaged exemplification of this idea we might take verses 21-24, which describe the remains of the dragonfly hanging in the spider's web. Find other examples pointing in the same direction.
2. How is the basic idea brought out *by contrast* in lines 33-40?
3. Does the language of this poem tend toward the concrete and specific or the general and abstract? Cite examples. Compare "Das öde Haus" in this regard with Lenau's "Schläfrig hangen die sonnenmüden Blätter." In which poem is the language more concrete?
4. How does the theme of this poem compare with that of Lenau's "Rings ein Verstummen. . ."?

Im Grase

Süße Ruh', süßer Taumel¹ im Gras,
Von des Krautes² Arome umhaucht,
Tiefe Flut, tief, tief trunkne Flut,
Wenn die Wolk' am Azure verraucht,
Wenn aufs müde, schwimmende Haupt   5
Süßes Lachen gaukelt herab,³
Liebe Stimme säuselt und träuft
Wie die Lindenblüt' auf ein Grab.

Wenn im Busen die Toten dann,
Jede Leiche sich streckt und regt,   10
Leise, leise den Odem⁴ zieht,
Die geschloßne Wimper bewegt,
Tote Lieb', tote Lust, tote Zeit,
All die Schätze, im Schutt verwühlt,⁵
Sich berühren mit schüchternem Klang   15
Gleich den Glöckchen, vom Winde umspielt.

Stunden, flücht'ger ihr als⁶ der Kuß
Eines Strahls auf den trauernden See,
Als des ziehenden Vogels Lied,
Das mir niederperlt⁷ aus der Höh',   20

---

¹'transport,' 'rapture' ²'herb's' ³'floats waywardly down' (the source of the laughter seems uncertain) ⁴=*Atem* ⁵'carelessly buried' ⁶'Hours, you who are more fleeting than' ⁷'ripples down'

Als des schillernden Käfers Blitz,
Wenn den Sonnenpfad er durcheilt,
Als der heiße Druck einer Hand,
Die zum letzten Male verweilt.

Dennoch, Himmel, immer mir nur   25
Dieses eine mir:[8] für das Lied
Jedes freien Vogels im Blau
Eine Seele, die mit ihm zieht,
Nur für jeden kärglichen Strahl
Meinen farbig schillernden Saum,[9]   30
Jeder warmen Hand meinen Druck,
Und für jedes Glück meinen Traum.

Towards Interpretation

1. Tell precisely what happens in the first two stanzas of "Im Grase."
2. Where are *die Toten* buried?
3. What exactly does the poet ask of heaven in the last stanza?
4. What is the connection between the fourth stanza and the third?
5. It might be maintained that this poem breaks in two in the middle, in other words, that there is no necessary connection between the first two stanzas and the last two. Take a stand on this question and adduce as much proof as possible in support of your argument.

Die Taxuswand[1]

Ich stehe gern vor dir,[2]
Du Fläche schwarz und rauh,
Du schartiges Visier[3]
Vor meines Liebsten Brau,
Gern mag ich vor dir stehen,   5
Wie vor grundiertem Tuch,
Und drüber gleiten sehen
Den bleichen Krönungszug;[4]

---

[8]*Dennoch ... mir* 'Yet, heaven, all I'll ever ask is this one thing' [9]'hem' (of garment)

[1]'yew hedge' [2]The hedge is addressed. [3]'slotted visor (of a helmet)' [4]Lines 6-8: As the speaker stands before the hedge, which is compared to a primed canvas (*grundiertes Tuch*), she sees in her mind's eye a pale coronation procession glide across it, like a sketched-in painting. A wedding procession, in which the bride wears a crown, is probably meant.

Als mein die Krone hier,
Von Händen, die nun kalt;[5]   10
Als man gesungen mir
In Weisen,[6] die nun alt;
Vorhang am Heiligtume,[7]
Mein Paradiesestor,
Dahinter alles Blume,   15
Und alles Dorn davor!

Denn jenseits weiß ich sie,
Die grüne Gartenbank,
Wo ich das Leben früh
Mit glühen[8] Lippen trank,   20
Als mich mein Haar umwallte
Noch golden wie ein Strahl,
Als noch mein Ruf erschallte,
Ein Hornstoß, durch das Tal.

Das zarte Efeureis,[9]   25
So[10] Liebe pflegte dort,
Sechs Schritte — und ich weiß,
Ich weiß dann, daß es fort.
So will ich immer schleichen
Nur an dein dunkles Tuch   30
Und achtzehn Jahre streichen
Aus meinem Lebensbuch.

Du starrtest[11] damals schon
So düster treu[12] wie heut',
Du, unsrer Liebe Thron   35
Und Wächter[13] manche Zeit:
Man sagt, daß Schlaf, ein schlimmer,
Dir aus den Nadeln raucht[14] —
Ach, wacher war ich nimmer,
Als rings von dir umhaucht!   40

Nun aber bin ich matt
Und möcht' an deinem Saum
Vergleiten, wie ein Blatt,

---

[5]Lines 9-10: 'When mine was here (in the imagined painting?) the crown (I received) from hands now cold' [6]'tunes,' 'melodies' [7]as before the Ark of the Covenant [8]=glühenden [9]'ivy sprig' (emblem of faithfulness) [10]=das [11]'stood stiffly' [12]'mournfully, gloomily loyal' [13]Perhaps the hedge was a throne because love was "enthroned" there; it was of course a watchman because it kept out prying eyes. For Thron, cf. also line 8. [14]The needles (and wood) of the yew contain a poisonous narcotic.

Geweht vom nächsten Baum;
Du lockst mich wie ein Hafen,   45
Wo alle Stürme stumm:
O, schlafen möcht' ich, schlafen,
Bis meine Zeit herum!¹⁵

Towards Interpretation

1. The hedge is called eight different things. Explain how it can be each of them.
2. The hedge is obviously symbolic of concealment. How many of its metaphorical designations carry out this idea?
3. Nature is here a symbol of an inward state; the scene presented is interpreted. "Das öde Haus," on the other hand, makes us seek a meaning rather than offering one itself. It is not directly interpretive. How is this reflected in the use of metaphor in each poem? What other differences in language do you find in the two poems? What can you say about the speaker in each poem?

Am Turme

Ich steh' auf hohem Balkone am Turm,
Umstrichen vom schreienden Stare¹
Und laß gleich einer Mänade² den Sturm
Mir wühlen im flatternden Haare;
O wilder Geselle, o toller Fant,³   5
Ich möchte dich kräftig umschlingen,
Und, Sehne an Sehne, zwei Schritte vom Rand
Auf Tod und Leben dann ringen!

Und drunten seh' ich am Strand, so frisch
Wie spielende Doggen, die Wellen   10
Sich tummeln rings mit Geklaff und Gezisch
Und glänzende Flocken schnellen.
O, springen möcht' ich hinein alsbald,
Recht in die tobenden Meute,
Und jagen durch den korallenen Wald   15
Das Walroß, die lustige Beute!

---

¹⁵'past' (The line may also imply 'until the Judgment Day.')

¹'starling'   ²The Meanads were the female followers and priestesses of Bacchus.
³'braggart youth,' refers to *Sturm*

Und drüben seh' ich ein Wimpel⁴ wehn
So keck wie eine Standarte,
Seh' auf und nieder den Kiel sich drehn
Von meiner luftigen Warte;   20
O, sitzen möcht' ich im kämpfenden Schiff,
Das Steuerruder ergreifen
Und zischend über das brandende Riff
Wie eine Seemöwe streifen.

Wär' ich ein Jäger auf freier Flur⁵,   25
Ein Stück⁶ nur von einem Soldaten,
Wär' ich ein Mann doch mindestens nur,
So würde der Himmel mir raten;
Nun muß ich sitzen so fein und klar,
Gleich einem artigen Kinde,   30
Und darf nur heimlich lösen mein Haar
Und lassen es flattern im Winde!

Towards Interpretation

1. Categorize the adventures the speaker would undertake is she were a man? Where would they lead her?
2. How does the meaning of the image of loosened hair change from line 4 to line 32?
3. Does the speaker want to *be* a man (line 27) or rather only a free *woman*?

Das Spiegelbild

Schaust du mich an aus dem Kristall
Mit deiner Augen Nebelball,
Kometen gleich, die im Verbleichen;¹
Mit Zügen, worin wunderlich
Zwei Seelen wie Spione sich   5
Umschleichen, ja, dann flüstre ich:
Phantom, du bist nicht meinesgleichen!

Bist nur entschlüpft der Träume Hut,²
Zu eisen³ mir das warme Blut,
Die dunkle Locke mir zu blassen;   10
Und dennoch, dämmerndes Gesicht,

---

⁴'pennant' ⁵'open fields' ⁶'bit'

¹'waning' (supply *sind* after *Verbleichen*) ²'care,' 'keeping' ³verb

Drin seltsam spielt ein Doppellicht,
Trätest du vor, ich weiß es nicht,
Würd' ich dich lieben oder hassen?

Zu deiner Stirne Herrscherthron, 15
Wo die Gedanken leisten Fron[4]
Wie Knechte, würd' ich schüchtern blicken;
Doch von des Auges kaltem Glast,[5]
Voll toten Lichts, gebrochen[6] fast,
Gespenstig, würd', ein scheuer Gast, 20
Weit, weit ich meinen Schemel rücken.

Und was den Mund umspielt so lind,
So weich und hülflos wie ein Kind,
Das möcht' in treue Hut ich bergen;
Und wieder, wenn er[7] höhnend spielt, 25
Wie von gespanntem Bogen[8] zielt,
Wenn leis es durch die Züge wühlt,
Dann möcht' ich fliehen wie vor Schergen.[9]

Es ist gewiß, du bist nicht Ich,
Ein fremdes Dasein, dem ich mich 30
Wie Moses nahe, unbeschuhet,[10]
Voll Kräfte die mir nicht bewußt,
Voll fremden Leides, fremder Lust;
Gnade mir Gott, wenn in der Brust
Mir schlummernd deine Seele ruht! 35

Und dennoch fühl' ich, wie verwandt,
Zu deinen Schauern mich gebannt,[11]
Und Liebe muß der Furcht sich einen.
Ja, trätest aus Kristalles Rund,
Phantom, du lebend auf den Grund, 40
Nur leise zittern würd' ich, und
Mich dünkt — ich würde um dich weinen!

Towards Interpretation

1. Is the subject of this poem the reflection in the mirror or the person
   reflected? Speaking generally, what/whom does the beholder of the
   image discover in it?
2. The poem progresses by sets of clearly distinguished antitheses. What
   are they?

---

[4]'forced service' [5]= *Glanz* [6]'destroyed' [7]i.e., *Mund* [8]'drawn bow' [9]'hangmen' [10]Cf.
Exodus 3:5, where God commands Moses to remove his shoes before the burning
bush, a sign of reverence and humility. [11]Construe: *ich fühle wie verwandt [ich dir
bin, und wie ich] zu deinen Schauern gebannt [bin].*

3. Does the rime scheme (a a b c c c b) seem to have symbolic function? Explain, if you think it does.

Eduard Mörike (1804-1875)

In the judgment of most who have a deeper acquaintance with German literature, Eduard Mörike, rather than his so dissimilar brother in Apollo, Heinrich Heine, is accounted the greatest German lyric poet of the 19th century. If this judgment sounds strange to English and American ears, it is mainly because we are much less familiar with the quietly unhappy Lutheran minister, Mörike, than with that unhappy convert to Lutheranism, Heine. Comparisons are odious but inevitable. If Heine is the darling of those who love the deliciously witty turn of phrase and bitter-sweet irony, Mörike is the favorite of those who have "read all the books" and still find here that delicate, inexpressible thrill that only the greatest lyric poetry can give.

Like his fellow Swabian, Hölderlin, who, to be sure, surpasses him in pathos and grandeur and in sense of cultural mission, though not in depth, Mörike is a *Nur–Dichter*, one who waits for the hour, the epiphany of the god, that moment of *süßes Erschrecken* from which his being takes fire and his poetry is born.

Mörike is an embarrassment to historians of literature because he refuses to fit neatly into a category. Genius is hard to catalogue, and second-rate talents are generally the best "examples" of a literary movement. The current fashion is to place Mörike in the *Spätromantik*, though some have called him a late classicist because of his "secret" affinity with Goethe and his use of classical forms and themes. For others, he is a prime example of *Biedermeier*, which in Germany is a term applied to literature as well as furniture and is associated with the loving treatment of the everyday and unpretentious. Others, again (as also in the case of Droste-Hülshoff), have stressed the "impressionism" of his art, the subtle way he presents detail, especially in nature. This all amounts to saying that in Mörike many of the main tendencies of 19th-century poetry find expression.

An einem Wintermorgen, vor Sonnenaufgang

O flaumenleichte Zeit der dunkeln Frühe!
Welch neue Welt bewegest du in mir?
Was ist's, daß ich auf einmal nun in dir
Von sanfter Wollust meines Daseins glühe?

Einem Kristall gleicht meine Seele nun,   5
Den noch kein falscher Strahl des Lichts getroffen;
Zu fluten scheint mein Geist, er scheint zu ruhn,
Dem Eindruck naher Wunderkräfte offen,
Die aus dem klaren Gürtel blauer Luft
Zuletzt ein Zauberwort vor meine Sinne ruft.   10

Bei hellen Augen glaub' ich doch zu schwanken;
Ich schließe sie, daß nicht der Traum entweiche.
Seh' ich hinab in lichte Feenreiche?[1]
Wer hat den bunten Schwarm von Bildern und Gedanken
Zur Pforte meines Herzens hergeladen,   15
Die glänzend sich in diesem Busen baden,
Goldfarb'gen Fischlein gleich im Gartenteiche?

Ich höre bald der Hirtenflöten Klänge,
Wie um die Krippe jener Wundernacht,[2]
Bald weinbekränzter Jugend Lustgesänge;[3]   20
Wer hat das friedenselige[4] Gedränge
In meine traurigen Wände hergebracht?

Und welch Gefühl entzückter Stärke,
Indem mein Sinn sich frisch zur Ferne lenkt!
Vom ersten Mark des heut'gen Tags getränkt,[5]   25
Fühl' ich mir Mut zu jedem frommen Werke.
Die Seele fliegt, soweit der Himmel reicht,
Der Genius jauchzt in mir! Doch sage,
Warum wird jetzt der Blick von Wehmut feucht?
Ist's ein verloren Glück, was mich erweicht?   30
Ist es ein werdendes, was ich im Herzen trage?
— Hinweg, mein Geist! hier gilt kein Stillestehn:
Es ist ein Augenblick, und alles wird verwehn!

Dort, sieh! am Horizont lüpft sich[6] der Vorhang schon!
Es träumt der Tag, nun sei die Nacht entflohn;   35
Die Purpurlippe,[7] die geschlossen lag,

---

[1]'fairy realms'   [2]i.e., at the birth of Christ   [3]'Now the voluptuous chants of vine-crowned youths'   [4]'peaceable'   [5]'Strengthened (lit. 'watered') by the first marrow of this day'   [6]'rises'   [7]The dark red lip is the edge of color on the horizon.

Haucht, halb geöffnet, süße Atemzüge:
Auf einmal blitzt das Aug', und, wie ein Gott, der Tag
Beginnt im Sprung die königlichen Flüge!

"Wintermorgen" takes place in the in-between world of dawn — it begins just before daybreak and ends with the sunrise. Natural setting and inward state reflect and symbolize each other, as is especially evident in the second strophe, where we need only substitute *diese Stunde* for *meine Seele* (verse 5) and *die Luft* for *mein Geist* (verse 7) to obtain a description of a clear early morning in winter. But it is the symbolism of the hour that is of primary importance. Dawn is an hour of balance — no longer night and not yet day. Three times within the poem an inward balance — in the spirit of the poet — is achieved and then lost, just as the balance between night and day, which is the hour before sunrise, is lost with the break of day.

The *Zauberwort* at the end of the second strophe upsets the first inward balance and brings about an inner sunrise that anticipates the one in nature (the third stanza is full of light), destroying the equilibrium implied in verse 7: "*Zu f l u t e n scheint mein Geist, er scheint zu r u h n.*" To regain this balance and to hold the fleeting dream, the poet closes his eyes — as we do when we are dizzy — and looks within himself (verses 11-13). What he sees and hears there we shall speak of later.

In the fourth, and axial, stanza, perfect balance has been again attained, though the imagery in which it is expressed may at first surprise us: shepherds' pipes and voluptuaries' chants, the birth of the Saviour and the worship of Dionysus, Christianity and antiquity. One is not given more weight than the other: *Ich höre bald . . . Bald. . . .*

The images of expansion with which the fifth strophe begins are the counterpart of the images of concentration at the beginning of the third, and just as the latter helped establish the balance imaged in the axial strophe (4) so do the former bring about its dissolution. This is of course a structural, not an imaged, balance.

The exultant expansion ends in the middle of the fifth strophe (line 28) and the eye which was fixed on distant horizons again turns inward. Now a new pair of opposites is weighed: *Ist's ein v e r l o r e n Glück . . . Ist es ein w e r d e n d e s. . . ?* For the third and last time the inner balance is destroyed, this time by an act of will: *Hinweg, mein Geist! hier gilt kein Stillestehn: / Es ist ein Augenblick, und alles wird verwehn!*

This is the recognition and acceptance that man's every experience of *Sein*, being, must suffer dissolution in *Zeit*, time. Every balance must be destroyed, every day must dawn. This is the poem's "message" and the poem itself is an attempt, thrice undertaken, to hold a time-less moment, to preserve *Sein* from *Zeit*.

What the latter half of the fifth strophe presents as an inward state, the final strophe presents as an outward scene: nature and spirit are ciphers of each other. Here too, in nature, we find images of balance — the rising curtain, the half opened lip — with night and day as the counterparts in nature of *verlorenes* and *werdendes Glück* in the human breast and the sudden awakening of Day, emphatically personified as a strong-willed being (god, king), as the outward referent of the inner resolve.

We now turn to the question of the meaning of what the poet sees when he looks into his own bosom. It must be admitted that this is not a matter that can be resolved with absolute certainty. Above all, it remains a mystery how the "motley swarm of images and ideas" got there in the first place. They are there, within him, that is all we know — at first only as inward movement (verses 2-4), then called into sight and sound by a *Zauberwort*, which likewise remains unexplained. But their very mysteriousness may offer us a clue to their meaning. "Wintermorgen," the astounding production of a youth of twenty-one, was placed by a friend, but with the poet's sanction, at the head of Mörike's collected poems, so that it constitutes a kind of prelude to his lyric. It is therefore quite possible, indeed very likely, that it is a poem about poetry and the nature of the poet. If such is the case, then we might think of the *bunten Schwarm* as something like poetic ideas, images, and figures awaiting transformation into works, unborn poems that have been called "to the gate of [the poet's] heart" in an hour of poetic grace. Where they come from the poet knows no more than we. But their mysteriousness is "natural" — it is the mystery of poetic inspiration. Beyond that, it is the mystery of genius, which no psychology can solve. All the unanswered questions in the first half of the poem are cries of wonderment and half-unbelief, which are our deepest expression of joy, here the joy of genius at the revelation of its own nature. Such an interpretation seems confirmed by verses 23ff., with their *Mut zu jedem frommen Werke*.

The middle stanza, with its reference to Christ and Dionysus, perhaps hints at two possible evaluations, two cultural patterns, as it were, that may be imposed — for all *poiesis*, all "making," is the imposition of a pattern — upon the yet unformed "swarm." Both the Christian pattern and the antique are sympathetic to Mörike, who was in this respect a typical product of Swabian humanism and brother of Hölderlin. The pipes of the shepherds rejoicing at the birth of Christ and the songs of the Dionysian revelers are messages that he, unlike Faust, not only hears but also believes (cf. *Faust*, line 765). It is a "*f r i e d e n s e l i g e s Gedränge*," not a *feindseliges*. The poet is not so much a man of "either - or" as of "not only - but also," which is only the positive expression of the "no longer and not yet" of dawn.

Um Mitternacht

Gelassen[1] stieg die Nacht ans Land,
Lehnt träumend an der Berge Wand,
Ihr Auge sieht die goldne Waage nun
Der Zeit in gleichen Schalen stille ruhn;
    Und kecker rauschen die Quellen hervor,   5
    Sie singen der Mutter, der Nacht, ins Ohr
        Vom Tage,
Vom heute gewesenen Tage.[2]

Das uralt alte Schlummerlied,
Sie achtet's nicht, sie ist es müd';   10
Ihr klingt des Himmels Bläue süßer noch,
Der flücht'gen Stunden gleichgeschwung'nes Joch.
    Doch immer behalten die Quellen das Wort,
    Es singen die Wasser im Schlafe noch fort
        Vom Tage,   15
Vom heute gewesenen Tage.

Towards Interpretation

1. What system of balances prevails in this poem, in both imagery and meter? What is in each dish of the scales, what is the fulcrum?
2. Mothers often sing to children to put them to sleep. Who sings to whom in this poem, and why?
3. What is implied by calling the song of the springs a *Schlummerlied*? What do they sing about?

Früh im Wagen

Es graut vom Morgenreif[1]
In Dämmerung das Feld,
Da schon ein blasser Streif
Den fernen Ost erhellt;

Man sieht im Lichte bald   5
Den Morgenstern vergehn,
Und doch am Fichtenwald
Den vollen Mond noch stehn:

---

[1]'calmly' [2]'Of the day that was today'

[1]*Reif* 'frost'

So ist mein scheuer Blick,
Den schon die Ferne drängt,   10
Noch in das Schmerzensglück
Der Abschiedsnacht versenkt.

Dein blaues Auge steht,
Ein dunkler See, vor mir,
Dein Kuß, dein Hauch umweht,   15
Dein Flüstern mich noch hier.

An deinem Hals begräbt
Sich weinend mein Gesicht,
Und Purpurschwärze² webt
Mir vor dem Auge dicht.   20

Die Sonne kommt; — sie scheucht
Den Traum hinweg im Nu,
Und von den Bergen streicht
Ein Schauer auf mich zu.

Towards Interpretation
1. Explain precisely the *physical* situation in "Früh im Wagen."
2. *Schmerzensglück* (line 11) is an oxymoron. Explain how the word *Schmerzensglück* might be said to sum up the whole poem. What is the significance of the position of this word in the poem as a whole?
3. The *Schauer* in the last verse refers both outward and inward. Look up this word in a good dictionary, then explain both references.

September-Morgen

Im Nebel ruhet noch die Welt,
Noch träumen Wald und Wiesen:
Bald siehst du, wenn der Schleier fällt,
Den blauen Himmel unverstellt,
Herbstkräftig die gedämpfte Welt   5
In warmem Golde fließen.

---

²*Purpurschwärze* refers to her hair; it means something like 'deep velvety black with bluish red lights' (cf. Poe's "thy hyacinth hair")

Auf einer Wanderung

In ein freundliches Städtchen tret' ich ein,
In den Straßen liegt roter Abendschein.
Aus einem offnen Fenster eben,
Über den reichsten Blumenflor[1]
Hinweg, hört man Goldglockentöne schweben   5
Und *eine* Stimme scheint ein Nachtigallenchor,
Daß die Blüten beben
Daß die Lüfte leben,
Daß in höherem Rot die Rosen leuchten vor.

Lang' hielt ich staunend, lustbeklommen.[2]   10
Wie ich hinaus vors Tor[3] gekommen,
Ich weiß es wahrlich selber nicht.
Ach hier, wie liegt die Welt so licht!
Der Himmel wogt in purpurnem Gewühle,
Rückwärts die Stadt in goldnem Rauch;   15
Wie rauscht der Erlenbach,[4] wie rauscht im Grund
Ich bin wie trunken, irrgeführt —   [die Mühle!
O Muse, du hast mein Herz berührt
Mit einem Liebeshauch!

A number of Mörike's poems capture and hold that moment of sudden over-powering excitement that seems to have been the kernel from which the poem sprang. In "Wintermorgen," for example, we can pinpoint this moment in the lines: *Was ist's, daß ich a u f e i n m a l nun in dir / Von sanfter Wollust meines Daseins g l ü h e?* In "Früh im Wagen," the moment must have been that in which the *Schauer* descends from the mountains with the morning breeze upon the poet's heart. (Cf. also "Neue Liebe," line 6, and "Die schöne Buche," line 19.)

In *Die Geburt der Tragödie aus dem Geiste der Musik*, Nietzsche postu-lates that the truly "Apollonian" work of art arises only from a "Dionysian" upheaval; in other words, clear form is born out of dark formlessness. The essence of the Dionysian is *Rausch*, drunkenness, delirium, transport; the essence of the Apollonian is *Traum*, dream, in the sense of interpretation of dark, primal urges. Such an hypothesis — for whatever its worth as scholar-ship, it is undoubtedly a profound psychological insight — may help us get below the surface of many poems. Its application to Mörike's "Auf einer Wan-derung" is obvious — Nietzsche could well have used this poem as an argu-ment for his thesis. It is also evident that Mörike must feel about the matter much as Nietzsche did:

---

[1]Perhaps flowers in a window box   [2]= *voller Lust und banger Sorge*   [3]i.e., the gate of the town   [4]'alder-lined brook'

O *Muse*, du hast mein Herz berührt
Mit einem Liebeshauch!

And the effect of the muse's "breath of love"? — Drunkenness: *Ich bin wie*
t r u n k e n,   i r r g e f ü h r t — And the Apollonian "dream" that arises from
the Dionysian delirium? — The poem itself. "Auf einer Wanderung" is a poem
about the nature of poetry.

Towards Interpretation

    1. Look at the first stanza and trace the poem's course from neutrality to
       Rausch.

Das verlassene Mägdlein

Früh, wann die Hähne krähn,
Eh' die Sternlein verschwinden,
Muß ich am Herde stehn,
Muß Feuer zünden.

Schön ist der Flammen Schein.   5
Es springen die Funken;
Ich schaue so drein,[1]
In Leid versunken.

Plötzlich, da kommt es mir,
Treuloser Knabe,   10
Daß ich die Nacht von dir
Geträumet habe.

Träne auf Träne dann
Stürzet hernieder;
So kommt der Tag heran —   15
O ging' er wieder!

Towards Interpretation

    1. In this poem inward motion (emotion) both coincides and contrasts
       with outward motion (movement). Work out this movement–emotion
       pattern.
    2. In the context of question 1, to what does the image of the fire cor-
       respond?
    3. Does the speaker long for dreams or dreamless sleep?

---

[1]'stare into space'

Agnes[1]

Rosenzeit! Wie schnell vorbei,
    Schnell vorbei
Bist du doch gegangen!
Wär' mein Lieb nur blieben[2] treu,
    Blieben treu,   5
Sollte mir nicht bangen.

Um die Ernte wohlgemut,[3]
    Wohlgemut
Schnitterinnen[4] singen.
Aber, ach! mir kranken Blut,[5]   10
    Mir kranken Blut
Will nichts mehr gelingen.

Schleiche[6] so durchs Wiesental,
    So durchs Tal,
Als im Traum verloren,   15
Nach dem Berg, da[7] tausendmal,
    Tausendmal
Er mir Treu' geschworen.

Oben auf des Hügels Rand,
    Abgewandt,   20
Wein' ich bei der Linde;
An dem Hut mein Rosenband,
    Von seiner Hand,
Spielet in dem Winde.

Towards Interpretation

1. How does the end of this poem return to its beginning? What remains of the "Rosenzeit" in the final stanza?

2. Why precisely are the "Schnitterinnen" brought in? Why not "Säerinnen," for example?

3. If the "echo" verses (2, 5, 8, etc.) in the first three stanzas hint at a former unity, what is the significance of their absence in the final stanza?

---

[1]A character in Mörike's novel *Maler Nolten*.   [2]=*geblieben*   [3]'happy and confident'
[4]*Schnitter* 'reaper'   [5]'thing' (person)   [6]Supply *ich.*   [7]=*wo*

Zitronenfalter¹ im April

Grausame Frühlingssonne,
Du weckst mich vor der Zeit,
Dem nur in Maienwonne
Die zarte Kost gedeiht!²
Ist nicht ein liebes Mädchen hier,   5
Das auf der Rosenlippe mir
Ein Tröpfchen Honig beut,³
So muß ich jämmerlich vergehn,
Und wird der Mai mich nimmer sehn
In meinem gelben Kleid.   10

Nixe Binsefuß¹

Des Wassermanns sein Töchterlein²
Tanzt auf dem Eis im Vollmondschein,
Sie singt und lachet sonder³ Scheu
Wohl an des Fischers Haus vorbei.

„Ich bin die Jungfer Binsefuß   5
Und meine Fisch' wohl hüten muß;
Meine Fisch', die sind im Kasten,
Sie haben kalte Fasten;
Von Böhmerglas mein Kasten ist,⁴
Da zähl' ich sie zu jeder Frist.⁵   10

Gelt, Fischermatz?⁶ gelt, alter Tropf,
Dir will der Winter nicht in Kopf?⁷
Komm mir mit deinen Netzen!
Die will ich schön zerfetzen!
Dein Mägdlein zwar ist fromm und gut,   15
Ihr Schatz ein braves Jägerblut.⁸

Drum häng' ich ihr, zum Hochzeitstrauß,⁹
Ein schilfen¹⁰ Kränzlein vor das Haus

---

¹'brimstone butterfly' ²Verses 3-4: 'Only in the rapture of May does my delicate food prosper' ³=*bietet*

¹*Nixe Binsefuß* (*Binse* 'rush') is the tutelary spirit of this stretch of water; the fish here are under her special protection and the fisherman her natural enemy. ²=*des Wassermanns Töchterlein*; the *Wassermann* is also a river spirit (nix), not a fisherman. ³=*ohne* ⁴The Bohemian glass of the cage is of course the ice. ⁵=*Zeit* ⁶*Matz*, a derogatory epithet ⁷'Can't you resign yourself to the winter?' ⁸=*Jägersmann* ⁹'wedding bouquet' ¹⁰'made of reeds'

Und einen Hecht,[11] von Silber schwer,
Er stammt von König Artus[12] her,   20
Ein Zwergen-Goldschmieds-Meisterstück,
Wer's hat, dem bringt es eitel[13] Glück:
Er läßt sich schuppen Jahr für Jahr,[14]
Da sind's fünfhundert Gröschlein bar.[15]

Ade, mein Kind! Ade für heut'!   25
Der Morgenhahn im Dorfe schreit. "

Auf ein altes Bild

In grüner Landschaft Sommerflor,[1]
Bei kühlem Wasser, Schilf und Rohr,
Schau, wie das Knäblein Sündelos[2]
Frei spielet auf der Jungfrau Schoß!
Und dort im Walde wonnesam,   5
Ach, grünet schon des Kreuzes Stamm!

Towards Interpretation
  1. What is the subject of the "old painting"?
  2. Each couplet of this poem deals with a different aspect of the divine
     plan for creation: the first, with timeless nature; the second, with God
     made temporal; the third, with redemption from time. Explain how
     the first and second are involved in the third.
  3. Comment on the juxtaposition of *wonnesam* and *ach*. Why should the
     tree of the Cross "blissfully" put forth foliage and why should man's
     reaction to this be a sigh?

Denk' es, o Seele![1]

Ein Tännlein grünet wo,[2]
Wer weiß, im Walde,
Ein Rosenstrauch, wer sagt,

---

[11]'pike' [12]Arthur [13]=*lauter* (nothing but) [14]'You can scale it (the pike) every year'
[15]'in cash'

[1]=*In dem Sommerflor* (summer luxuriance) *einer grünen Landschaft* [2]'the Child Sinless'

[1]This poem is sung by a character in Mörike's novella, "Mozart auf der Reise nach Prag." [2]=*irgendwo*

In welchem Garten?
Sie sind erlesen³ schon,   5
Denk' es, o Seele,
Auf deinem Grab zu wurzeln
Und zu wachsen.

Zwei schwarze Rößlein weiden
Auf der Wiese,   10
Sie kehren heim zur Stadt
In muntern Sprüngen.
Sie werden schrittweis gehn
Mit deiner Leiche;
Vielleicht, vielleicht noch eh'   15
An ihren Hufen
Das Eisen los wird,
Das ich blitzen sehe!

Towards Interpretation
  1. *Denk' es, o Seele!* — Was soll die Seele "denken"?

Verborgenheit

Laß, o Welt, o laß mich sein!
Locket nicht mit Liebesgaben,
Laßt dies Herz alleine haben
Seine Wonne, seine Pein!

Was ich traure, weiß ich nicht,   5
Es ist unbekanntes Wehe;
Immerdar durch Tränen sehe
Ich der Sonne liebes Licht.

Oft bin ich mir kaum bewußt,
Und die helle Freude zücket   10
Durch die Schwere, so mich drücket
Wonniglich in meiner Brust.

Laß, o Welt, o laß mich sein!
Locket nicht mit Liebesgaben,
Laßt dies Herz alleine haben   15
Seine Wonne, seine Pein!

---

³'chosen'

Towards Interpretation

1. Give a meaningful English translation of the title of this poem.
2. Note rime scheme and endings (masculine endings enclosing feminine). How does the form reflect the content, or: how does the poem answer its own prayer?

Gebet

Herr! schicke, was du willt,[1]
Ein Liebes oder Leides;
Ich bin vergnügt,[2] daß beides
Aus deinen Händen quillt.

Wollest mit Freuden   5
Und wollest mit Leiden
Mich nicht überschütten!
Doch in der Mitten
Liegt holdes Bescheiden.

Am Rheinfall

Halte dein Herz, o Wanderer, fest in gewaltigen Händen!
    Mir entstürzte vor Lust zitternd das meinige fast.
Rastlos donnernde Massen auf donnernde Massen geworfen,
    Ohr und Auge, wohin retten sie sich im Tumult?
Wahrlich, den eigenen Wutschrei hörete nicht der Gigant hier,   5
    Läg' er, vom Himmel gestürzt, unten am Felsen gekrümmt![1]
Rosse der Götter, im Schwung, eins über dem Rücken des andern,
    Stürmen herunter und streu'n silberne Mähnen umher;[2]
Herrliche Leiber, unzählbare, folgen sich, nimmer dieselben,
    Ewig dieselbigen — wer wartet das Ende wohl aus?   10
Angst umzieht dir den Busen mit eins,[3] und, *wie* du es denkest,
    Über das Haupt stürzt dir krachend das Himmelsgewölb'![4]

Towards Interpretation

1. The poet speaks of *Ohr und Auge* in verse four. What images appeal to each of these senses?

---

[1]=*willst* [2]'zufrieden'

[1]The Titans (here *Gigant*) took sides against Zeus in his struggle against Cronus and were cast down from Olympus. [2]The horse was sacred to the sea god, Poseidon. [3]=*auf einmal* [4]Zeus, the supreme Olympian deity, was the Thunderer. A clap of thunder was usually interpreted as a signal of his approval.

2. If the thunderclap signals the approval of Zeus, what is he approving
of here?

Die schöne Buche

Ganz verborgen im Wald kenn' ich ein Plätzchen, da stehet
  Eine Buche, man sieht schöner im Bilde sie nicht.
Rein und glatt, in gediegenem Wuchs erhebt sie sich einzeln,
  Keiner der Nachbarn rührt ihr an den seidenen Schmuck.
Rings, so weit sein Gezweig der stattliche Baum ausbreitet,   5
  Grünet der Rasen, das Aug' still zu erquicken, umher;
Gleich nach allen Seiten umzirkt er den Stamm in der Mitte;
  Kunstlos schuf die Natur selber dies liebliche Rund.
Zartes Gebüsch umkränzet es erst; hochstämmige Bäume,
  Folgend in dichtem Gedräng, wehren[1] dem himmlischen
                                Blau. 10
Neben der dunkleren Fülle des Eichbaums wieget die Birke
  Ihr jungfräuliches Haupt schüchtern im goldenen Licht.
Nur wo, verdeckt vom Felsen, der Fußsteig jäh sich hinab-
  Lässet die Hellung[2] mich ahnen das offene Feld.   [schlingt,
— Als ich unlängst einsam, von neuen Gestalten des Sommers[3] 15
  Ab dem Pfade gelockt, dort im Gebüsch mich verlor,
Führt' ein freundlicher Geist, des Hains auflauschende[4]
                                Gottheit,
  Hier mich zum ersten Mal, plötzlich, den Staunenden, ein.
Welch Entzücken! Es war um die hohe Stunde des Mittags,
  Lautlos alles, es schwieg selber der Vogel im Laub. 20
Und ich zauderte noch, auf den zierlichen Teppich[5] zu treten;
  Festlich empfing er den Fuß, leise beschritt ich ihn nur.
Jetzo, gelehnt an den Stamm (er trägt sein breites Gewölbe
  Nicht zu hoch), ließ ich rundum die Augen ergehn,
Wo den beschatteten Kreis die feurig strahlende Sonne, 25
  Fast gleich messend umher, säumte[6] mit blendendem Rand.
Aber ich stand und rührte mich nicht; dämonischer Stille,
  Unergründlicher Ruh' lauschte mein innerer Sinn.
Eingeschlossen mit dir in diesem sonnigen Zauber-
  Gürtel, o Einsamkeit, fühlt' ich und dachte nur dich! 30

---

[1] =*abhalten* [2] the thinning out of the trees [3] 'Summer's new forms' might well be such things as birds, insects, flowers. [4] 'attentive' *Auflauschen* implies a pricking up of the ears and so hints at the faun-like nature of the grove's tutelary divinity. [5] Cf. verses 5-7. [6] 'bordered'

"Die schöne Buche" contains fifteen distichs divided into two parts (note the dash at the beginning of line 15); there are seven distichs in the first, and eight in the second. The first part *describes* the scene, the second *experiences* it. So far as content goes, the two parts say much the same thing; the motifs of the first are repeated in the second. The difference lies in the tone. The first part shows the beech and its surroundings in themselves; the second embodies them in the life of the beholder, so that they attain new meaning and intensity.

All is ordered around the beech. The scene is a *liebliches Rund*, in the center of which stands the tree like a goddess in her temple. And, indeed, a temple — the word means etymologically "a space marked out" — is just what is here described. The theme, Nature as a temple, is not uncommon in the literature of the 19th century, but nowhere is it handled with such delicacy and subtle depth as in Mörike's "Schöne Buche." Beside this poem, Gottfried Keller's "Waldlieder," for example, which treat a like theme, sound almost as obvious as greeting-card verses. This is Keller lying among the ferns in a forest of firs:

> . . . Lieg' ich so im Farrenkraut,
> Schwindet jede Grille,
> Und es wird das Herz mir laut
> In der Föhrenstille.
>
> Weihrauchwolken ein und aus
> Durch die Räume wallen —
> Bin ich in ein Gotteshaus
> Etwan eingefallen?
>
> Doch der Unsichtbare läßt
> Lächelnd es geschehen,
> Wenn mein wildes Kirchenfest
> Hier ich will begehen!

Both "Die schöne Buche" and "Am Rheinfall" are written in classical, i.e., ancient, meters. It is fascinating to observe that both these poems also evoke ancient deities, though not by name; rather they recreate in terms of modern sensibility the emotional aura of polytheism. In "Am Rheinfall," it is Zeus, the god of thunder and the overthrower of the Titans (cf. verses 5-6!), who is evoked, together with his brother Poseidon, to whom the horse was sacred. In "Die schöne Buche" it is Pan and Pan's hour, "the faunal noon."

When we hold such poems as these up together with a poem such as "Auf ein altes Bild," Mörike's binocular vision appears in all its clarity. Let us recall the following lines from "An einem Wintermorgen . . ." and our discussion of that poem:

> Ich höre bald der Hirtenflöten Klänge,
> Wie um die Krippe jener Wundernacht,

Bald weinbekränzter Jugend Lustgesänge;
Wer hat das friedenselige Gedränge
In meine traurigen Wände hergebracht?

Towards Interpretation
1. Compare Lenau's "Schläfrig hangen die sonnenmüden Blätter" (p. 264), Droste's "Das öde Haus" (p. 270) and Mörike's "Die schöne Buche" from the standpoint a) of the central experience in each, and b) of structure and poetic economy.

Friedrich Hebbel (1813-1863)

Nachtlied

Quellende, schwellende Nacht,
Voll von Lichtern und Sternen;
In den ewigen Fernen,
Sage, was ist da erwacht?

Herz in der Brust wird beengt,   5
Steigendes, neigendes Leben,
Riesenhaft fühle ich's weben,
Welches das meine verdrängt.

Schlaf, da nahst du dich leis',
Wie dem Kinde die Amme,   10
Und um die dürftige Flamme
Ziehst du den schützenden Kreis.

Towards Interpretation
1. What is the "dürftige Flamme" (line 11)?

Sie seh'n sich nicht wieder

Von dunkelnden Wogen
Hinunter gezogen,
Zwei schimmernde Schwäne, sie schiffen daher.
Die Winde, sie schwellen
Allmählich die Wellen,   5
Die Nebel, sie senken sich finster und schwer.

Die Schwäne, sie meiden
Einander und leiden,
Nun tun sie es nicht mehr, sie können die Glut
Nicht länger verschließen,   10
Sie wollen genießen,
Verhüllt von den Nebeln, gewiegt von der Flut.

Sie schmeicheln, sie kosen,
Sie trotzen dem Tosen
Der Wellen, die Zweie in Eines verschränkt,   15
Wie die sich auch bäumen,
Sie[1] glühen und träumen,
In Liebe und Wonne zum Sterben versenkt.

Nach innigem Gatten[2]
Ein süßes Ermatten,   20
Da trennt sie die Woge, bevor sie's gedacht.
Laßt ruh'n das Gefieder!
Ihr seht euch nicht wieder,
Der Tag ist vorüber, es dämmert die Nacht.

Towards Interpretation

1. This poem offers an unusually clear example of rime symbolism. Study it carefully, and see what you can work out.
2. In Hugo von Hofmannsthal's *Gespräch über Gedichte*, one speaker ("Gabriel") has just quoted Hebbel's "Sie seh'n sich nicht wieder." He continues:

[*Gabriel:*] Mein Freund, auch dieses Gedicht drückt einen Zustand aus und nichts weiter, einen tiefen Zustand des Gemüts, voll banger Wollust, voll trauervoller Kühnheit.
Clemens: Und diese Schwäne? Sie sind ein Symbol? Sie bedeuten —
Gabriel: Laß mich dich unterbrechen. Ja, sie bedeuten, aber sprich es nicht aus, was sie bedeuten: was immer du sagen wolltest, es wäre unrichtig. Sie bedeuten hier nichts als sich selber: Schwäne. Schwäne, aber freilich gesehen mit den Augen der Poesie, die jedes Ding zum erstenmal sieht, die jedes Ding mit allen Wundern seines Daseins umgibt: dieses hier mit der Majestät seiner königlichen Flüge; mit der lautlosen Einsamkeit seines strahlenden weißen Leibes, auf schwarzem Wasser trauervoll verachtungsvoll kreisend; mit der wunderbaren Fabel* seiner Sterbestunde. . . . Gesehen mit diesen Augen sind die Tiere die eigentlichen Hieroglyphen, sie sind lebendige geheimnisvolle Chiffern, mit denen Gott unaussprechliche Dinge in die Welt geschrieben hat.

---

[1]*Wie die ... Sie ...* 'However much they (the waves) rear, they (the swans) ...' [2]'union'

*i.e., the 'fable' that swans sing only when they are dying

Sommerbild

Ich sah des Sommers letzte Rose stehn,
Sie war, als ob sie bluten könne, rot;
Da sprach ich schauernd im Vorübergehn:
So weit im Leben ist zu nah am Tod!

Es regte sich kein Hauch am heißen Tag,   5
Nur leise strich ein weißer Schmetterling;
Doch, ob auch kaum die Luft sein Flügelschlag
Bewegte, sie[1] empfand es und verging.

Betty Paoli* (1814-1894)

Wandlung

Willst du erschau'n, wie viel ein Herz kann tragen,
    O blick' in meins!
So reich an Wunden, vom Geschick geschlagen,
    War wohl noch keins.
Doch mitten in den wütendsten Orkanen   5
    Erhob ich mich,
Und schritt dahin auf meinen fernen Bahnen —
    Wie stark war ich!

Wie ward mir doch nun so mit einem Male
    Die Kraft geraubt?   10
Es trotzte mutig dem Gewitterstrahle
    Mein stolzes Haupt,
Doch als du zu mir sprachst mit leisem Grüßen:
    „Ich liebe dich!"
Da sank ich still und weinend dir zu Füßen —   15
    Wie schwach bin ich!

---

[1]i.e., the rose

*Pseudonym of Barbara Elisabeth Glück

Letztes Gedicht

Wenn quälend mich die Angst beschleicht,
Mein Teuerstes auf Erden,
Mein Liebstes könnte mir vielleicht
Einst noch entrissen werden;
Dann tröstet der Gedanke mich: 5
„Weshalb davor erbeben?
Dies große Leid vermöchte ich
Ja nicht zu überleben."

Die Hoffnung, die sich in dir regt,
Bevor du ihrer[1] dich entschlagen: 10
Daß keinem werde auferlegt
So viel als er kann tragen.
Wie groß das Leid, wie tief die Not,
Du wirst dich drein ergeben,
Und was dir bittrer als der Tod,   15
Du wirst es überleben.

Betty Paoli

Theodor Storm

---

[1]i.e., *Hoffnung*, genitive with *entschlagen*

Theodor Storm (1817-1888)

Hyazinthen[1]

Fern hallt Musik; doch hier ist stille Nacht,
Mit Schlummerduft anhauchen mich die Pflanzen;
Ich habe immer, immer dein[2] gedacht,
Ich möchte schlafen; aber du mußt tanzen.

Es hört nicht auf, es rast[3] ohn' Unterlaß;   5
Die Kerzen brennen und die Geigen schreien,
Es teilen und es schließen sich die Reihen,[4]
Und alle glühen; aber du bist blaß.

Und du mußt tanzen; fremde Arme schmiegen
Sich an dein Herz; o leide nicht Gewalt!   10
Ich seh' dein weißes Kleid vorüberfliegen
Und deine leichte, zärtliche Gestalt. — —

Und süßer strömend quillt der Duft der Nacht
Und träumerischer aus dem Kelch der Pflanzen.
Ich habe immer, immer dein gedacht;   15
Ich möchte schlafen; aber du mußt tanzen.

Towards Interpretation
1. This poem is structured around opposites. What are they?
2. . . . *alle g l ü h e n; aber du bist b l a ß*. Why is the beloved pale?

Die Nachtigall

Das macht,[1] es hat die Nachtigall
Die ganze Nacht gesungen;
Da sind von ihrem süßen Schall,
Da sind in Hall und Widerhall
Die Rosen aufgesprungen.   5

---

[1]S. S. Prawer offers a most interesting interpretation of this poem in his *German Lyric Poetry. A Critical Analysis of Selected Poems from Klopstock to Rilke* (London: Routledge and Paul, 1952), 177-181. [2]genitive with *gedenken* 'of you' [3]'rages' [4]'rows' of dancers

[1]'that's because'

Sie war doch sonst ein wildes Kind;
Nun geht sie tief in Sinnen,[2]
Trägt in der Hand den Sommerhut
Und duldet still der Sonne Glut
Und weiß nicht, was beginnen.[3]   10

Das macht, es hat die Nachtigall
Die ganze Nacht gesungen;
Da sind von ihrem süßen Schall,
Da sind in Hall und Widerhall
Die Rosen aufgesprungen.   15

Towards Interpretation
1. What is the connection between the first two stanzas of this poem?
2. Why this change in the girl?
3. Storm originally wrote *Blut* for *Kind* (line 6), but later changed it.
   Does this alter the meaning of the poem?
4. Why is the first stanza repeated?

Dämmerstunde

Im Nebenzimmer saßen ich und du;
Die Abendsonne fiel durch die Gardinen;[1]
Die fleißigen Hände fügten sich[2] der Ruh,
Von rotem Licht war deine Stirn beschienen.

Wir schwiegen beid'; ich wußte mir kein Wort,   5
Das in der Stunde Zauber mochte taugen;[3]
Nur nebenan die Alten schwatzten fort —
Du sahst mich an mit deinen Märchenaugen.

Im Walde

Hier an der Bergeshalde
Verstummet ganz der Wind;
Die Zweige hängen nieder,
Darunter sitzt das Kind.

Sie sitzt in Thymiane,   5
Sie sitzt in lauter Duft;

---

[2]'lost in thought' [3]'to do'

[1]'lace curtains' [2]'submitted themselves' (perhaps the woman has some kind of needle-work) [3]'That would suit the magic of this hour'

Die blauen Fliegen summen
Und blitzen durch die Luft.

Es steht der Wald so schweigend,
Sie schaut so klug darein;   10
Um ihre braunen Locken
Hinfließt der Sonnenschein.

Der Kuckuck lacht von ferne,
Es geht mir durch den Sinn:
Sie hat die goldnen Augen   15
Der Waldeskönigin.

Towards Interpretation

1. In the two preceding poems, what seems to move the poet to attribute
   "fairy-like" qualities to the maidens?

April

Das ist die Drossel,[1] die da schlägt,[2]
Der Frühling, der mein Herz bewegt;
Ich fühle, die sich hold bezeigen,
Die Geister aus der Erde steigen.[3]
Das Leben fließet wie ein Traum —   5
Mir ist wie Blume, Blatt und Baum.

Juli

Klingt im Wind ein Wiegenlied,
Sonne warm herniedersieht,
Seine Ähren[1] senkt das Korn,[2]
Rote Beere schwillt am Dorn,
Schwer von Segen ist die Flur —   5
Junge Frau, was sinnst du nur?

---

[1]'thrush' [2]'sings' [3]Verses 3-4: *Ich fühle die Geister, die ... aus der Erde steigen.*

[1]'tassles' [2]'grain'

Die Stadt[1]

Am grauen Strand, am grauen Meer
Und seitab liegt die Stadt;
Der Nebel drückt die Dächer schwer,
Und durch die Stille braust das Meer
Eintönig um die Stadt.   5

Es rauscht kein Wald, es schlägt im Mai
Kein Vogel ohn' Unterlaß;
Die Wandergans mit hartem Schrei
Nur fliegt in Herbstesnacht vorbei,
Am Strande weht das Gras.   10

Doch hängt mein ganzes Herz an dir,
Du graue Stadt am Meer;
Der Jugend Zauber für und für[2]
Ruht lächelnd doch auf dir, auf dir,
Du graue Stadt am Meer.   15

Towards Interpretation

1. This is a poem in praise of a town, to which no praise is offered. Why
   does the poet love it?

Meeresstrand

Ans Haff[1] nun fliegt die Möwe,
Und Dämmrung bricht herein;
Über die feuchten Watten[1]
Spiegelt der Abendschein.

Graues Geflügel huschet[2]   5
Neben dem Wasser her;
Wie Träume liegen die Inseln
Im Nebel auf dem Meer.

Ich höre des gärenden Schlammes
Geheimnisvollen Ton,   10

---

[1]Husum on the North Sea, Storm's birthplace [2]'for ever and ever'

[1]A *Haff* is an arm of the sea between the mainland and outlying islands, often so shallow that at ebb-tide the *Watten*, or mud flats, become visible (and audible); the *Gären* ('seething') in line 9 is caused by the decomposition of organic material in the mud deposit. [2]'flit'

Einsames Vogelrufen —
So war es immer schon.

Noch einmal schauert leise
Und schweiget dann der Wind;
Vernehmlich werden die Stimmen,   15
Die über der Tiefe sind.

Towards Interpretation

1. What kind of imagery (visual, auditory, tactual, etc.) do we find in the first two stanzas of "Meeresstrand"? in the last two?
2. What process, traceable through the imagery, takes place as we go from line 1 to line 8 and again from line 9 to line 16?

Abseits

Es ist so still; die Heide liegt
Im warmen Mittagssonnenstrahle,
Ein rosenroter Schimmer fliegt
Um ihre alten Gräbermale;[1]
Die Kräuter blühn; der Heideduft   5
Steigt in die blaue Sommerluft.

Laufkäfer[2] hasten durchs Gesträuch
In ihren goldnen Panzerröckchen,
Die Bienen hängen Zweig um Zweig
Sich an der Edelheide[3] Glöckchen,   10
Die Vögel schwirren aus dem Kraut[4] —
Die Luft ist voller Lerchenlaut.[5]

Ein halbverfallen niedrig Haus
Steht einsam hier und sonnbeschienen;
Der Kätner[6] lehnt zur Tür hinaus,   15
Behaglich blinzelnd nach den Bienen;
Sein Junge auf dem Stein davor
Schnitzt Pfeifen sich aus Kälberrohr.[7]

Kaum zittert durch die Mittagsruh
Ein Schlag der Dorfuhr, der entfernten;   20
Dem Alten fällt die Wimper zu,

---

[1]The so-called "giants' graves" (*Hünengräber*), round stone walls, often found in the North German lowlands. [2]'ground beetle' [3]a kind of heather [4]=*Heidekraut* (heather) [5]'lark song' [6]'cottager' [7]*Kerbel* 'wild chervil,' good for making flutes, pipes and whistles

Er träumt von seinen Honigernten.
— Kein Klang der aufgeregten Zeit
Drang noch in diese Einsamkeit.[8]

Towards Interpretation

1. How would you characterize the atmosphere of the first two stanzas?
2. If by "still" (line 1) Storm means lack of sound or activity, what about the nature description in stanza 2? What kind of "stillness" must then be implied?
3. What element enters in the second half of the poem that is absent from the first two stanzas? Are there hints that the *Kätner*'s situation is not as "*still*" as the opening of the poem seems to imply?
4. What stand would you take on the meaning of *drang noch* discussed in footnote 8?

Perhaps the best thing ever written on Storm is Thomas Mann's essay in *Leiden und Größe der Meister*, from which we quote the following:

> Ich muß von den Gedichten noch sprechen dürfen. . . . In dieser zehnmal gesichteten und geseihten Lyrik steht Perle fast neben Perle, und es ist darin, auf Schritt und Tritt, eine bebende Konzentrationskraft der Lebens- und Empfindungsaussage, eine Kunst der Formung zum Einfachen, die in bestimmten Fällen unfehlbar immer wieder, so alt man wird und sooft man etwas wieder liest oder sich vorspricht, dies Sichzusammenziehen der Kehle, dies Angepacktwerden von unerbittlich süß und wehem Lebensgefühl bewirkt, um dessentwillen man mit sechzehn, siebzehn diesem Tonfall so anhing.

„Geflüster der Nacht"

Es ist ein Flüstern in der Nacht,
Es hat mich ganz um den Schlaf gebracht;
Ich fühl's, es will sich was verkünden
Und kann den Weg nicht zu mir finden.

Sind's Liebesworte, vertrauet dem Wind,   5
Die unterwegs verwehet sind?
Oder ist's Unheil aus künftigen Tagen,
Das emsig drängt sich anzusagen?

---

[8]It is hard to say whether we should take *drang noch* to mean 'has yet penetrated' (=*ist noch gedrungen*) or 'ever penetrated.' If the latter, then we must regard the poem as reminiscence, and the scene as resting in the past; if the former, then even this idyllic *Abseits* is endangered.

Schlaflos

Aus Träumen in Ängsten bin ich erwacht;
Was[1] singt doch die Lerche so tief in der Nacht!

Der Tag ist gegangen, der Morgen ist fern,
Aufs Kissen hernieder scheinen die Stern'.

Und immer hör' ich den Lerchengesang,   5
O Stimme des Tages, mein Herz ist bang.

Über die Heide

Über die Heide hallet mein Schritt;
Dumpf aus der Erde wandert es mit.

Herbst ist gekommen, Frühling ist weit —
Gab es denn einmal selige Zeit?

Brauende Nebel geisten[1] umher;   5
Schwarz ist das Kraut[2] und der Himmel so leer.

Wär' ich hier nur nicht gegangen im Mai!
Leben und Liebe — wie flog es vorbei!

Towards Interpretation
1. What accompanies this wanderer on his walk over the heath? Where
   does it originate?

Geh nicht hinein[1]

Im Flügel[2] oben hinterm Korridor,
Wo es so jählings einsam worden ist,
— Nicht in dem ersten Zimmer, wo man sonst
Ihn finden mochte, in die blasse Hand
Das junge Haupt gestützt, die Augen träumend   5
Entlang den Wänden streifend, wo im Laub

---

[1] = warum

[1] 'float like ghosts'   [2] = Heidekraut

[1] This poem was inspired by the death of Theodor Reventlow, sixteen-year-old son of
Storm's friend, not Storm's own son. Theodor had shown great interest in becoming a
naturalist. [2] Cf. line 8: Flügel–Flügel

Von Tropenpflanzen ausgebälgt Getier[3]
Die Flügel spreizte und die Tatzen reckte,
Halb Wunder noch, halb Wissensrätsel ihm,
— Nicht dort; der Stuhl ist leer, die Pflanzen lassen   10
Verdürstend ihre schönen Blätter hängen;
Staub sinkt herab; — nein, nebenan die Tür,
In jenem hohen dämmrigen Gemach,
— Beklommne Schwüle[4] ist drin eingeschlossen —
Dort hinterm Wandschirm auf dem Bette liegt   15
Etwas — geh nicht hinein! Es schaut dich fremd
Und furchtbar an!
   Vor wenig Stunden noch
Auf jenen Kissen lag sein blondes Haupt;
Zwar bleich von Qualen, denn des Lebens Fäden
Zerrissen jäh; doch seine Augen sprachen   20
Noch zärtlich, und mitunter lächelt' er,
Als säh er noch in goldne Erdenferne.
Da plötzlich losch es aus; er wußt' es plötzlich,
— Und ein Entsetzen schrie aus seiner Brust,
Daß ratlos Mitleid, die[5] am Lager saßen,   25
In Stein verwandelte — er lag am Abgrund;
Bodenlos, ganz ohne Boden. — „Hilf!
Ach, Vater, lieber Vater!" Taumelnd schlug
Er um sich mit den Armen; ziellos griffen
In leere Luft die Hände; noch ein Schrei   30
Und dann verschwand er.
   Dort, wo er gelegen,
Dort hinterm Wandschirm, stumm und einsam liegt
Jetzt etwas — bleib ! Geh nicht hinein! Es schaut
Dich fremd und furchtbar an; für viele Tage
Kannst du nicht leben, wenn du es erblickt.[6]   35
„Und weiter — du, der du ihn liebtest — hast
Nichts weiter du zu sagen?"
   Weiter nichts.

---

[3]'stuffed or mounted animals'   [4]'oppressive atmosphere'   [5]'those who'   [6]supply *hast*

An Klaus Groth

Wenn't Abend ward,[1]
Un still de Welt un still dat Hart;
Wenn möd[2] upt Knee di liggt de Hand,
Un ut din Husklock[3] an de Wand
Du hörst den Parpendikelslag,[4]   5
De nich to Woort keem över Dag;
Wenn't Schummern[5] in de Ecken liggt,
Un buten[6] all de Nachtswulk[7] flüggt;

Wenn denn noch eenmal kiekt de Sünn
Mit golden Schiin to't Finster rin,   10
Un, ehr de Slap kümmt un de Nacht,
Noch eenmal allens lävt[8] un lacht, —
Dat is so wat vör't Minschenhart,
Wenn't Abend ward.

Klaus Groth* (1819-1899)

Aflohnt[1]

De Sæn de haar ęr banni leef, se weer so week un fee.
De Ole schull int Hus herum: wat se sik inbilln dę!

Se neem er Bündel ünnern Arm, vun Tran'n de Ogen blank,
Se sä de Ole sacht adüs, se sä de Sæn: heff Dank!

---

[1] 'When evening comes'; this poem is written in Storm's native *Plattdeutsch*. [2] = *müd*
[3] = *Hausuhr* [4] 'tick of the pendulum' [5] 'dusk' [6] = *draußen* [7] = *Abendnebel* [8] = *lebt*

*Klaus Groth's best verse is all in Low German. The dialect is Dithmarsisch (West Holstein).

[1] *Abgelohnt* ('Paid Off')
Der Sohn, der hatte sie sehr lieb, sie war so sanft und hold.
Der Alte schalt im Haus herum: was bildet sie sich ein!
Sie nahm ihr Bündel untern Arm, von Tränen die Augen blank,
Sie sagte dem Alten sacht adieu, sie sagte dem Sohn: hab Dank!
Sie ging bis um die Ecke am Zaun, und setzte sich auf den Stein.
Der Alte schalt im Haus herum, der Sohn, der stand und weinte.

Se gung bet um de Eck an Tun, un sett sik op den Steen.   5
De Ole schull int Hus herum, de Sæn de stunn un ween.

Matten Has'[1]

Lütt Matten de Has',
De mak sik en Spaß,
He weer bi't Studeern,
Dat Danzen to lehrn,
Un danz ganz alleen   5
Op de achtersten Been.

Keem Reinke de Voß
Un dach: das en Kost!
Un seggt: Lüttje Matten,
So flink oppe Padden?   10
Un danzst hier alleen
Oppe achtersten Been?

Kumm, lat uns tosam!
Ik kann as de Dam!
De Krei de spelt Fitel,   15
Denn geit dat canditel,
Denn geit dat mal schön;
Op de achtersten Been!

Lütt Matten gev Pot.
De Voß beet em dot   20
Un sett sik in Schatten,
Verspis' de lütt Matten:
De Krei de kreeg een
Vun de achtersten Been.

---

[1]*Martin Hare*
Little Martin the Hare thought he'd have some fun, he was studying to learn dancing and dancing all alone on his hind legs. / Came Reynard the Fox and thought: "That's a meal!" and says: "Little Martin, so nimble on your pads? And dancing here alone on your hind legs? / Come, let's dance together! I'll be the lady! The crow'll play the fiddle, then it'll go swell, then it'll really be fine; on the hind legs!" / Little Martin gave his foot. The fox bit him dead, sat down in the shade and made a meal of Little Martin: the crow got one of the hind legs.

Gottfried Keller (1819-1890)

Winternacht

Nicht ein Flügelschlag ging durch die Welt,
Still und blendend lag der weiße Schnee.
Nicht ein Wölklein hing am Sternenzelt,[1]
Keine Welle schlug im starren See.

Aus der Tiefe stieg der Seebaum auf,   5
Bis sein Wipfel in dem Eis gefror;
An den Ästen klomm die Nix'[2] herauf,
Schaute durch das grüne Eis empor.

Auf dem dünnen Glase stand ich da,
Das die schwarze Tiefe von mir schied;   10
Dicht ich unter meinen Füßen sah
Ihre weiße Schönheit, Glied um Glied.

Mit ersticktem Jammer tastet' sie
An der harten Decke her und hin,
Ich vergess' das dunkle Antlitz nie,   15
Immer, immer liegt es mir im Sinn!

Conrad Ferdinand Meyer (1825-1898)

The Swiss poet C. F. Meyer is now generally recognized as the initiator of the Symbolist manner in German literature. All poetry is of course symbolic (as is indeed all human communication), for all poetry expresses something inward by something outward; nonetheless, not all poetry is symbolistic, certainly not consciously so. In English literature we regard Yeats and Eliot, for example, as Symbolists; in French, Baudelaire, Verlaine, Mallarmé; in German — besides Meyer — Rilke, George, Hofmannsthal.* Creators of great symbols are not necessarily Symbolists in the narrower sense; neither Goethe, the creator of Faust, the most powerful symbolic figure in modern literature, nor Cervantes,

---

[1] i.e., the sky [2] 'water sprite'

*Perhaps it would be more exact to regard the English and German poets mentioned here (with the exception of Meyer) as the "inheritors" of Symbolism. (Cf. C. M. Bowra, *The Heritage of Symbolism* (London: Macmillan, 1967).

the creator of Don Quixote, is a Symbolist in the technical sense. From the standpoint of the literature of the German-speaking nations we can perhaps best understand what Symbolism implies by comparing it with Romanticism, from which it largely sprang. Romantic poetry — and here we can include most German poetry from Goethe through Storm — seeks an immediate expression of feeling, or rather: it seeks to express feeling with immediacy. It can do so of course only through symbols for such is the condition of all human expression, but the symbols are, as it were, consumed by the feeling they express. They hardly have independent life and, having been used once, are not likely to be used over and over again in a programmatic fashion in other contexts to say the same thing (or to remind us of the same thing) in a different setting.* Symbols as used

by the Symbolists, on the other hand, tend to have the value of a *leitmotiv* (it is no accident that Baudelaire was among the first to recognize Wagner's greatness) and the study of a Symbolist poet is thus to a considerable degree a matter of familiarizing oneself with his symbols and the meanings he attaches to them — only rarely does the poet tell us outright what a symbol is supposed to signify. This is another difference between the Romantic and the Symbolist manner: in romantic poetry the symbols are largely self-explanatory, insofar as they are (rationally) explicable at all, whereas some Symbolists (Mallarmé, for example) invest their symbolic motifs with meanings so private that none but they can understand them. Such is not the case with Meyer and Yeats, for instance. Still another difference between romantic and symbolistic poetry is the tendency of the former to glide rapidly from one symbol to another — probably an indication that the poet is not consciously employing the symbols as motifs — while the symbolistic poem tends to concentrate on a few symbols, sometimes even only one. In Meyer's work the chief symbol of a particular poem sometimes forms the title of the poem. As an example of a purely symbolistic poem employing only one motif, that of sails, we quote Meyer's "Zwei Segel."

---

*Eichendorff's work, which contains a clearly discernible body of symbolic motifs employed over and over in various contexts, would seem to offer a counterargument. Certainly Eichendorff is the most "symbolistic" of the German Romantics — a Symbolist before Baudelaire. See Oskar Seidlin, "Eichendorff's Symbolic Landscape," *PMLA* 72 (1957): 645-661, and Werner Kohlschmidt, "Die symbolische Formelhaftigkeit von Eichendorffs Prosastil," in: *Form und Innerlichkeit* (Bern: Francke, 1955), 177-209.

Zwei Segel

Zwei Segel erhellend
Die tiefblaue Bucht!
Zwei Segel sich schwellend
Zu ruhiger Flucht!

Wie eins in den Winden   5
Sich wölbt und bewegt,
Wird auch das Empfinden
Des andern erregt.

Begehrt eins zu hasten,
Das andre geht schnell,   10
Verlangt eins zu rasten,
Ruht auch sein Gesell.

The sail in Meyer's poetry is always a symbol of hope and assurance. This poem stands in a cycle of poems entitled "Liebe," and deals with harmonious marriage (or perhaps any harmonious relationship between two people in love). We deduce this both from what happens in the poem itself and from the place the poet assigned to it in his work. This does not mean that whenever a sail appears in Meyer's poetry we are to think of marriage. Rather, the *idea* of hope and assurance has here found embodiment in the *theme* of marriage and Meyer's *symbol* for this idea is a sail (or sails).

It is evident from the foregoing that symbolistic poetry bears some resemblance to allegorical: both require "interpretation." Symbolism differs from allegory, however, in that it strives for *con*notation rather than *de*notation. The symbols of symbolistic poetry are something of themselves and cannot be wholly thought away, whereas the emblems of pure allegory are in themselves nothing and their meaning everything. Thus the meaning of a good symbolistic poem can never be fully spelled out in discursive language any more than can that of a poem in the romantic manner, say Goethe's "Mailied" or Storm's "Meeresstrand."

Wetterleuchten[1]

Im Garten schritt ich durch die Lenzesnacht.[2]
Des Jahres erste Blitze loderten.
Die jungen Blüten glommen feuerrot
Und blichen[3] wieder dann. Ein schönes Spiel,
Davor ich stille hielt. Da sah ich *dich*!   5

---

[1] 'lightning below the horizon,' 'heat lightning'   [2] = *Frühlingsnacht*   [3] 'became pale'

Mit einem Blütenzweige spieltest du,
Die junggebliebne Tote! Durch die Hast
Und Flucht der Zeit zurück erkannt' ich dich,
Die just des Himmels Feuer überglomm.
Erglühend standest du, wie dazumal,   10
Da dich das erste Liebeswort erschreckt,
Du Ungebändigte, du Flüchtende!
Dann mit den Blüten wieder blichest du.

Towards Interpretation

1. Without studying Meyer's work fairly intensively it probably would not be possible for us to recognize that he associates blossoms at night with the idea of "sweet terror," though we may feel both the sweetness and terror of this poem. One learns to grasp the values assigned some motifs only gradually. It is easy to see, however, that lightning here acquires symbolic significance. The lightning makes the blossoms grow first red, then pale. The girl is identified with the blossoms (*Mit einem Blütenzweige spieltest du*) and she too grows first red, then pale. But it is not merely the physical lightning with which her change of color is associated. What does the lightning come to symbolize?

2. The central and most significant words in the poem are *die junggebliebne Tote*. Where do the dead remain young? Below *what* horizon does this lightning really play?

Stapfen

In jungen Jahren war's. Ich brachte dich
Zurück ins Nachbarhaus, wo du zu Gast,
Durch das Gehölz. Der Nebel rieselte,[1]
Du zogst des Reisekleids Kapuze[2] vor
Und blicktest traulich mit verhüllter Stirn.   5
Naß ward der Pfad. Die Sohlen prägten sich
Dem feuchten Waldesboden deutlich ein,
Die wandernden.[3] Du schrittest auf dem Bord,[4]
Von deiner Reise sprechend. Eine noch,
Die läng're, folge drauf, so sagtest du.   10
Dann scherzten wir, der nahen Trennung klug
Das Angesicht verhüllend,[5] und du schiedst,

[1] 'A fine rain was falling' [2] 'hood' [3] Modifies *Sohlen*, l. 6. [4] =*Rand* [5] *der nahen ... verhüllend* 'wisely covering our countenances before the coming separation'

Dort wo der First[6] sich über Ulmen hebt.
Ich ging denselben Pfad gemach zurück,
Leis' schwelgend[7] noch in deiner Lieblichkeit,   15
In deiner wilden Scheu, und wohlgemut
Vertrauend auf ein baldig Wiedersehn.
Vergnüglich schlendernd,[8] sah ich auf dem Rain
Den Umriß deiner Sohlen deutlich noch
Dem feuchten Waldesboden eingeprägt,   20
Die kleinste Spur von dir, die flüchtigste,
Und doch dein Wesen, wandernd, reisehaft,
Schlank, rein, walddunkel, aber o wie süß!
Die Stapfen schritten jetzt entgegen dem
Zurück dieselbe Strecke Wandernden:[9]   25
Aus deinen Stapfen hobst du dich empor
Vor meinem innern Auge. Deinen Wuchs
Erblickt' ich mit des Busens zartem Bug.[10]
Vorüber gingst du, eine Traumgestalt.
Die Stapfen wurden jetzt undeutlicher,   30
Vom Regen halb gelöscht, der stärker fiel.
Da überschlich mich eine Traurigkeit:
Fast unter meinem Blick verwischten sich
Die Spuren deines letzten Gangs mit mir.

"Stapfen"* is a story in verse. Like all stories, it may be divided into parts according to the development of the action:

    Verses   1-13 — the lovers walk together
    Verses 14-23 — he walks back alone and notices the footprints
    Verses 24-29 — the vision of the beloved
    Verses 30-34 — the footprints disappear

This schematisation of the action shows that the speaker alternately beholds the beloved herself, then her footprints. The divisions of the poem become ever shorter and the language more intense, as that which is to be communicated becomes ever more important and mysterious. First the lovers go the same way together; the mood is one of quiet happiness and sweet intimacy. He has hopes that they may some day go through life together as they now go together

[6]'roof ridge'; *Ulme* 'elm' [7]'quietly luxuriating' [8]'pleasureably strolling'; *Rain* 'edge of the path' [9]*entgegen ... Wandernden* 'toward the one returning by the same path' [10]'curve'

*These remarks are drawn from the analysis by Heinrich Henel, "Conrad Ferdinand Meyer," in *Die deutsche Lyrik*, ed. Benno v. Wiese (Düsseldorf: Schwann-Bagel, [2]1981), 2:230-242. See also Henel's *The Poetry of Conrad Ferdinand Meyer* (Madison: University of Wisconsin Press, 1954).

through the woods. But something about her seems to keep him from putting his hopes into words, and when it comes time to part they jest and speak of inconsequential things. Not until he is alone can he really be with her. Her footprints speak more clearly than her eyes and voice. Now he notices that they did not walk together but only beside each other. When she was with him he had only seen her look and heard her voice; now he becomes aware of her true being, her *Wesen*, her wild shyness and unattainableness. But these very qualities make her terribly desirable: *Wandernd, reisehaft, / Schlank, rein, walddunkel, aber o wie süß!* Out of his intense desire arises his vision. Now she comes toward him and he sees her as she really is, and seeing her thus, he recognizes their true relationship to each other. Their walk together was neither with nor beside each other; it was a mere passing of one another, only a meeting. She is a figure in a dream and only in his dreams does he understand and possess her. Did he not create her from his dreams? Even their fleeting moment together is now, as he looks back, like a dream — life is such stuff as dreams are made on. The poem reaches its highest intensity at this point and the language takes on for the first time the character of lyric incantation. Then the poem returns to reality. The lover awakens from his trance, notices that the rain is falling harder and the footprints are disappearing — the sad tenderness of the ending, as feeling fades away with the end of the poem, is hardly surpassed in the poetry of the nineteenth century.

We can also look at "Stapfen" in another way and so arrive at a different division: then the poem falls into two equal parts. The first ends with the lover's confident hope of reunion, the second with the intimation that no reunion can ever be. While the division into four parts articulates the action, that into two discloses a fine web of relationships between outward and inward, between that which meets the eye and that which is secret. The poem is meant to be read not only as a story but also as a symbolic configuration.

The beloved walks beside the speaker with covered brow: in the second half of the poem we realize that this is symbolic of his non-recognition of her in everyday life. She covers her face: she withdraws from him. Both cover their faces before the coming separation: one also covers the face of the dead, death will separate them. She speaks of a journey she has made and of a longer one she is to make: the journey of life lies behind her, the journey into the land of death will follow soon. They do not speak of their coming separation, just as one hesitates to speak of death. At first, journeying merely seems something she happens to do; later it becomes evident that it is a fundamental part of her: she is *wandernd, reisehaft*, one who will not remain long on this earth. The motif of journeying is concentrated in the basic symbol of the footprints. They *are* the beloved, her inmost nature (*Und doch dein Wesen*). She will leave but a fleeting trace of herself on earth. Even the scene, the woods, is significant, for the forest is her true home and she belongs to its darkness — she is *walddunkel, schlank, rein*, and "wildly shy," like a deer. She seems to have come from this darkness and to it she will return. Tender as the feeling in this poem is the atmosphere in which it is bathed: a fine rain envelops the poet's *leises Schwelgen*, his restrained happiness. Just as restrained is the sorrow at the end, the mood of inexplicable sadness at the sight of the disappearing footprints as the rain begins to fall faster. That it was to be their *letzter Gang* together he of course did not then know — this is added from much later knowledge as an old man looks back on his youth.

Towards Interpretation
1. What is the verse form of both "Wetterleuchtern" and "Stapfen"?
2. "The essence of all Meyer's later experiences is the penetration of a living present by a hidden past" (Henel). Show how "Wetterleuchten" and "Stapfen" treat essentially the same theme.

Die tote Liebe

Entgegen wandeln wir
Dem Dorf im Sonnenkuß,
Fast wie das Jüngerpaar
Nach Emmaus,[1]
Dazwischen[2] leise   5
Redend schritt
Der Meister, dem sie[3] folgten
Und der den Tod erlitt.
So wandelt zwischen uns
Im Abendlicht   10
Unsre tote Liebe,
Die leise spricht.
Sie weiß für das Geheimnis
Ein heimlich Wort,
Sie kennt der Seelen   15
Allertiefsten Hort.[4]
Sie deutet und erläutert
Uns jedes Ding,
Sie sagt, So ist's gekommen,
Daß ich am Holze[5] hing.   20
Ihr habet mich verleugnet
Und schlimm verhöhnt,
Ich saß im Purpur,

---

[1]Luke 24:13-32. *Emmaus* has three syllables: *Em-ma-us*. [2]'between whom' [3]i.e., the disciples [4]'treasure' [5]=*Kreuz*

Blutig, dorngekrönt,
Ich habe Tod erlitten,   25
Den Tod bezwang ich bald,
Und geh' in eurer Mitten
Als himmlische Gestalt —
Da ward die Weggesellin
Von uns erkannt,   30
Da hat uns wie den Jüngern
Das Herz gebrannt.[6]

Towards Interpretation

1. "Die tote Liebe" interprets its suffering in terms of the Passion. What
   gain accrues from this double vision? What risk does the poet run? Is
   the parallel true or is it forced?
2. With what does the heart burn at the end of the poem?

Im Spätboot

Aus der Schiffsbank mach' ich meinen Pfühl,[1]
Endlich wird die heiße Stirne kühl!
O wie süß erkaltet mir das Herz!
O wie weich verstummen Lust und Schmerz!
Über mir des Rohres[2] schwarzer Rauch   5
Wiegt und biegt sich in des Windes Hauch.
Hüben[3] hier und drüben wieder dort
Hält das Boot an manchem kleinen Port:
Bei der Schiffslaterne kargem Schein
Steigt ein Schatten aus und niemand ein.   10
Nur der Steurer noch, der wacht und steht!
Nur der Wind, der mir im Haare weht!
Schmerz und Lust erleiden sanften Tod.
Einen Schlummrer trägt das dunkle Boot.

Towards Interpretation

1. Outwardly, "Im Spätboot" is entirely realistic: a tired man takes the
   night boat home (on the Lake of Zürich), lies down on a bench on
   deck and drops off to sleep. No deeper meaning is urged on our attention. Yet this poem is usually interpreted as a *Todesfahrt* and the

---

[6]Luke 24:32. See Emil Staiger's interpretation of this poem in *Meisterwerke deutscher Sprache aus dem 19. Jahrhundert* (München: DTV, [2]1971), 202-222.

[1]'pillow' [2]'smokestack' [3]'on this side'

helmsman as Charon. Re-read the poem carefully and see what evidence you can find to support such an interpretation.

Eingelegte Ruder[1]

Meine eingelegten Ruder triefen,
Tropfen fallen langsam in die Tiefen.

Nichts, das mich verdroß! Nichts, das mich freute!
Niederrinnt ein schmerzenloses Heute!

Unter mir — ach, aus dem Licht verschwunden —   5
Träumen schon die schönern meiner Stunden.

Aus der blauen Tiefe ruft das Gestern:
Sind im Licht noch manche meiner Schwestern?

A critic has said of this poem:

Wie "Hälfte des Lebens" ist auch dies [wieder] ein Gedicht der Balance:
Die vier ersten Zeilen sprechen vom Heute, die vier letzten vom Gestern;
die vier ersten vom Oben, die vier letzten vom Unten; die vier ersten vom
Leben, die vier letzten vom Tod. Diese zwei Bereiche sind durch zwei
komplementäre Bilder symbolisch eng verbunden: in der ersten Strophe
durch die Tropfen, die von den Rudern in die Tiefe fallen; in der letzten
Strophe durch das Rufen des Gestern aus der Tiefe nach den *Schwestern*,
den noch im Lichte verweilenden Lebensstunden. Die zwei mittleren Strophen (Vv. 3-6) sprechen dann vom menschlichen Ich und dessen Verhältnis
zum Heute und Gestern, Leben und Tod, und zwar sind Vv. 2-4 nach
oben, an das Heute, verbunden, das aber *nieder*rinnt, während Vv. 5 und 6
nach unten, an das Gestern, verbunden sind, das aber *nach oben* ruft. Ein
schöneres Beispiel von Formsymbolismus wäre schwer zu finden.*

Towards Interpretation

1. Are the drops which drip into yesterday balanced psychologically with
   the call of yesterday from the depths? Do they overweigh or are they
   overweighed?
2. Is the speaker content with the *Schmerzlosigkeit* of today (*das Heute*)?
3. What happens to the *Stunden* in the depths when they disappear out of
   the light?

---

[1] 'shipped oars'

*Browning, *Umgang mit Gedichten*, 68.

Der römische Brunnen[1]

Aufsteigt der Strahl und fallend gießt
Er voll der Marmorschale Rund,
Die, sich verschleiernd,[2] überfließt
In einer zweiten Schale Grund;
Die zweite gibt, sie wird zu reich,   5
Der dritten wallend ihre Flut,
Und jede nimmt und gibt zugleich
    Und strömt und ruht.

Towards Interpretation

1. It has been poined out* that one of the most striking features of this
   poem is the alternation (in stressed syllables) of front and back
   vowels. (A front vowel is one that would be followed by *ch* = [ç], a
   back vowel by *ch* = [x].) Thus the first three lines show the following pattern:

   (B) F   B   B   F
   Aúfsteìgt der Stráhl und fállend gíeßt

         B   B   B   B
   Er vóll der Mármorschále Rúnd

         F   F   F   F
   Die, sích verschleíernd, úberflíeßt

   Continue this vowel analysis and state, in general terms, what this alternation of front and back vowels here symbolizes. (According to
   Ryder, the chances that the arrangement is accidental are only about 1
   in 350.)
2. What action is taking place in line 2? What kind of stressed vowels do
   we find here? What is taking place in line 5? What stressed vowels
   here?
   B vowels = ... F vowels = ...
3. On the basis of the above questions, explain changes from front to
   back vowels *within* lines 4 and 6.

---

[1]The fountain described here (probably inspired by the *fontana ovale* which stands near
the Villa Borghese in Rome) has three basins arranged about a central column. [2]'becoming veiled' (by the overflowing water)

*Frank G. Ryder, "'Der römische Brunnen' — Sound Pattern and Content," *Monats-
hefte* 52 (1960): 235ff.

Nicola Pesce[1]

Ein halbes Jährchen hab' ich nun geschwommen
Und noch behagt mir dieses kühle Gleiten,
Der Arme lässig Auseinanderbreiten[2] —
Die Fastenspeise[3] mag der Seele frommen!

Halb schlummernd lieg' ich stundenlang, umglommen   5
Von Wetterleuchten, bis auf allen Seiten
Sich Wogen türmen. Männlich gilt's zu streiten.
Ich freue mich. Stets bin ich durchgekommen.

Was machte mich zum Fisch? Ein Mißverständnis
Mit meinem Weib. Vermehrte Menschenkenntnis.   10
Mein Wanderdrang und meine Farbenlust.[4]

Die Furcht verlernt ich über Todestiefen,
Fast bis zum Frieren kühlt' ich mir die Brust —
Ich *bleib'* ein Fisch und meine Haare triefen!

Towards Interpretation

1. What does Pesce gain by his watery existence? What does he lose?
2. What connection do you find between *Nicola Pesce* and the three preceding poems?

Michelangelo und seine Statuen

Du öffnest, Sklave, deinen Mund,
Doch stöhnst du nicht. Die Lippe schweigt.
Nicht drückt, Gedankenvoller,[1] dich
Die Bürde der behelmten[2] Stirn.
Du packst mit nerv'ger Hand den Bart,   5
Doch springst du, Moses, nicht empor.
Maria mit dem toten Sohn,
Du weinst, doch rinnt die Träne nicht.
Ihr stellt des Leids Gebärde dar,
Ihr meine Kinder, ohne Leid!   10

[1]Legendary Sicilian swimmer and diver (Schiller also wrote a poem about him called *Der Taucher*), who stayed in water so long he became web-fingered. His name (pronounced *Pesche*) means 'the fish' in Italian. [2]=*das lässige Auseinanderbreiten der Arme* [3]Nicola of course lived on (raw) seafood: every day was meatless. [4]'delight in color'

[1]*Il Pensieroso*, a statue of Giuliano Medici. [2]'helmeted'

So sieht der freigewordne Geist
Des Lebens überwundne Qual.
Was martert die lebend'ge Brust,
Beseligt und ergötzt im Stein.
Den Augenblick verewigt ihr,   15
Und sterbt ihr, sterbt ihr ohne Tod.
Im Schilfe³ wartet Charon mein,
Der pfeifend sich die Zeit vertreibt.

"Michelangelo und seine Statuen" presents the contrast between art and life. In his book on Meyer's poetry, Henel points out that lines 11-12 contain the crucial passage, "Thus sees the liberated spirit life's vanquished torment."

The introductory 'thus' is ambiguous. Does it mean, 'As I look at you, the statues,' or, 'Like you'? In other words, does Meyer wish to say that men rise above life's torment by contemplating its presentation in the ideal figures of great art? Or does he mean that death liberates men, even as the artist creates figures which, while they show the gesture of suffering, do not feel it? Is art or is death the liberator? . . . The poem as a whole speaks of the contemplation of art, and especially the two lines following the ambiguous passage [*Was martert die lebend'ge Brust, / Beseligt und ergötzt im Stein*] favor the first alternative. To be enslaved, to weep over one's dead son, is terrible indeed; but it is blissful . . . to look at Michelangelo's *Slave* or *Pietà*. . . . Art . . . offers 'Leidlosigkeit.' It alone gives pure joy in a world of sorrow and horror; indeed it allows us to contemplate these sorrows and horrors unflinchingly and thus to master them. This is the main message of the poem. The thought of death . . . enters the poem only in its last four lines, as a postscript or afterthought. . . . The connection of these lines with the rest of the poem is thought of as an alternative to the aesthetic state, for in death that liberation from suffering will be permanent which is temporarily and precariously achieved by the mind absorbed in great works of art.*

Towards Interpretation

1. If you are familiar with Schopenhauer and if you agree with Henel's interpretation of this poem, point out the connection between the poem and Schopenhauer's philosophy of art.

---

³'among the reeds'; *mein* 'for me'

*Henel, *The Poetry of C. F. Meyer*, 165f.

Hussens Kerker[1]

Es geht mit mir zu Ende,
Mein Sach und Spruch[2] ist schon
Hoch über Menschenhände
Gerückt vor Gottes Thron,
Schon schwebt auf einer Wolke,   5
Umringt von seinem Volke,
Entgegen mir des Menschen Sohn.

Den Kerker will ich preisen,
Der Kerker, der ist gut!
Das Fensterkreuz[3] von Eisen   10
Blickt auf die frische Flut,
Und zwischen seinen Stäben
Seh ich ein Segel schweben,
Darob[4] im Blau die Firne[5] ruht.

Wie nah die Flut ich fühle,   15
Als läg' ich drein versenkt,
Mit wundesamer Kühle
Wird mir der Leib getränkt —
Auch seh' ich eine Traube
Mit einem roten Laube,   20
Die tief herab ins Fenster hängt.

Es ist die Zeit zu feiern![6]
Es kommt die große Ruh!
Dort lenkt ein Zug von Reihern[7]
Dem ew'gen Lenze zu,   25
Sie wissen Pfad' und Stege,
Sie kennen ihre Wege —
Was, meine Seele, fürchtest du?

"Men must endure
Their going hence, even as their coming hither:
Ripeness is all."

Hus, in Meyer's poem, seems to have made the sentiment expressed in these
words a part of himself, so much so in fact that his "going hence" is not merely something he must endure but something that he looks forward to with a
quiet mind, even with longing. A sense of euphoria pervades the poem. Tone

---

[1]Jan Hus, Bohemian reformer and Protestant martyr (a disciple of Wicliff), burned at
the stake in Konstanz am Bodensee in 1415. [2]*Sach und Spruch* 'my cause and its judgment' [3]"crossed" bars on windows [4]'above which' [5]"eternal" snows on the high
peaks [6]'rest from work' [7]'herons'

and mood are purposely reminiscent of Paul Gerhardt's "Abendlied" (*Nun ruhen alle Wälder*); the stanza used by Meyer is a variation of Gerhardt's. (Note especially the extra foot in the last line, indicative of expansion of feeling, and the framing of feminine rimes by masculine in both Gerhardt and Meyer.)

Each stanza speaks in symbols, most of them immediately comprehensible to any thoughtful person, as for example Christ's coming on a cloud (judgment), the cross (faith), the grape among red leaves ("Ripeness is all"), the migrating birds (return). Interwoven with these are the more private symbols of water (whose meaning we are already familiar with from "Im Spätboot," "Eingelegte Ruder," "Nicola Pesce"), sails (cf. "Zwei Segel"), distant snow-covered peaks. The second stanza particularly contains symbolic motifs more or less peculiar to Meyer. The cross made by the bars on the window looks upon the water: because of his faith Hus must suffer death. But on the water he sees a sail, Meyer's constant symbol of hope: death gives hope of God's just judgment (as opposed to man's). The eternal snow (*Firne*) against the blue sky toward which the sail seems to be moving is a fairly transparent symbol of "Himmelsnähe" (the title of one of Meyer's Alpine poems set among snow-covered peaks). The first four lines of the third stanza tell us that Hus has already died to this life, that he welcomes the thought of death, and the grapes among the red leaves of autumn tell us that the time of harvest, that is, death (which for the believer leads to true life) is near.

When we examine the symbolism in this rather pedantic way, we run the danger of making the poem seem contrived, and indeed in a sense it is. At any rate it is planned so that the symbols may be employed. Meyer could compose only in this fashion. His poetry is successful to the degree that he makes his symbolic motifs speak for themselves, and they speak for themselves to the extent that he succeeds in embodying them in a theme which suits them. Meyer wrote many quite bad poems, poems in which theme and motif are at odds, but "Hussens Kerker" is not one of them.

Towards Interpretation

1. Note the symbols mentioned in the second paragraph above. Describe how the theme of the poem is carried forward by the sequence of symbols.

Abendwolke

So stille ruht im Hafen
Das tiefe Wasser dort,
Die Ruder sind entschlafen,
Die Schifflein sind im Port.

Nur oben in dem Äther   5
Der lauen Maiennacht,
Dort segelt noch ein später
Friedfert'ger Ferge[1] sacht.

Die Barke still und dunkel
Fährt hin in Dämmerschein   10
Und leisem Sterngefunkel
Am Himmel und hinein.

Towards Interpretation

1. The title of this poem provides a key for the realistic identification of the "bark" in the sky, but what is the bark in non-realistic (symbolic) terms? What are the barks in the Harbor in symbolic terms? Support your answer by reference to other poems by Meyer.

Säerspruch[1]

Bemeßt den Schritt! Bemeßt den Schwung!
Die Erde bleibt noch lange jung!
Dort fällt ein Korn, das stirbt und ruht.
Die Ruh ist süß. Es hat es gut.
Hier eins, das durch die Scholle[2] bricht.   5
Es hat es gut. Süß ist das Licht.
Und keines fällt aus dieser Welt
Und jedes fällt, wie's Gott gefällt.

Towards Interpretation

1. It is obvious that this poem is constructed on the principles of 2's — one can trace this division into 2's even down to the caesuras, or pauses within the lines — but it is also obvious that the message of the poem is not duality but unity, i.e., 2=1. Point this out in detail. Note especially lines 4 and 6.

---

[1]'ferryman'

[1]Cf. Matthew 13:3-9, 18-23. To understand the poem one must think of someone sowing by hand, rhythmically casting seeds from a bag slung in front of him as he strides along. [2]'soil surface'

Marie von Ebner-Eschenbach (1830-1916)

Ebner-Eschenbach is known primarily for her prose works; however, as the friend of Betty Paoli and, with Paoli, a great admirer of Droste-Hülshoff, she coveted the ability to express herself in verse. Although she actually wrote very few poems, the two which follow make it clear that she understood what good poetry is. The irony is that in her attempt to express in verse her frustration at not being a born poet, she actually achieves her goal. "Ein kleines Lied" is a kind of poet's recipe for success.

Ein kleines Lied

Ein kleines Lied! Wie geht's nur an,
Daß man so lieb es haben kann,
Was liegt darin! erzähle!

Es liegt darin ein wenig Klang,
Ein wenig Wohllaut und Gesang   5
und eine ganze Seele.

Lebenszweck

Hilflos in die Welt gebannt,
Selbst ein Rätsel mir,
In dem schalen Unbestand,
        Ach, was soll ich hier?

— Leiden, armes Menschenkind,   5
Jede Erdennot,
Ringen, armes Menschenkind,
        Ringen um den Tod.

Friedrich Wilhelm Nietzsche (1844-1900)

Ecce Homo

Ja! ich weiß, woher ich stamme!
Ungesättigt gleich der Flamme
Glühe und verzehr ich mich.
Licht wird alles, was ich fasse,
Kohle alles, was ich lasse: 5
Flamme bin ich sicherlich.

Venedig

An der Brücke stand
jüngst ich in brauner Nacht.
Fernher kam Gesang;
goldener Tropfen quolls
über die zitternde Fläche weg.   5
Gondeln, Lichter, Musik —
trunken schwamms in die Dämmrung hinaus . . .

Meine Seele, ein Saitenspiel,
sang sich, unsichtbar berührt,
heimlich ein Gondellied dazu,   10
zitternd vor bunter Seligkeit.
— Hörte jemand ihr zu?

Vereinsamt

Die Krähen schrein
Und ziehen schwirren Flugs[1] zur Stadt:
Bald wird es schnein. —
Wohl dem, der jetzt noch — Heimat hat!

Nun stehst du starr,   5
Schaust rückwärts, ach! wie lange schon!
Was bist du Narr
Vor Winters in die Welt entflohn?

---

[1]adverbial genitive; *schwirren* 'whirr, whirl, be in moving confusion'

Die Welt — ein Tor
Zu tausend Wüsten stumm und kalt!   10
    Wer das verlor,
Was du verlorst, macht nirgends halt.

    Nun stehst du bleich,
Zur Winter-Wanderschaft verflucht,
    Dem Rauche gleich,   15
Der stets nach kältern Himmeln sucht.

    Flieg, Vogel, schnarr
Dein Lied im Wüstenvogel-Ton! —
    Versteck, du Narr,
Dein blutend Herz in Eis und Hohn!   20

    Die Krähen schrein
Und ziehen schwirren Flugs zur Stadt:
    Bald wird es schnein. —
Weh dem, der keine Heimat hat!

„Oh Mensch! Gib Acht!"

Oh Mensch! Gib Acht!
Was spricht die tiefe Mitternacht?
„Ich schlief, ich schlief —,
Aus tiefem Traum bin ich erwacht: —
Die Welt ist tief,   5
Und tiefer als der Tag gedacht.
Tief ist ihr Weh —,
Lust — tiefer noch als Herzeleid:
Weh spricht: Vergeh!
Doch alle Lust will Ewigkeit —,   10
— will tiefe, tiefe Ewigkeit!"

Sternen-Moral

Vorausbestimmt zur Sternenbahn,
Was geht dich, Stern, das Dunkel an?

Roll selig hin durch diese Zeit!
Ihr Elend sei dir fremd und weit!

Der fernsten Welt gehört dein Schein: 5
Mitleid soll Sünde für dich sein!

Nur *ein* Gebot gilt dir: sei rein!

Unverzagt

Wo du stehst, grab' tief hinein!
Drunten ist die Quelle!
Laß die dunklen Männer schrein:
"Stets ist drunten — Hölle!'

Friedrich Nietzsche

Ada Christen (1844-1901)

„Ich hab' in langen Tagen"

Ich hab' in langen Tagen
Gar oft an dich gedacht,
Ich hab' in langen Nächten
Gehofft, geweint, gewacht.

Wie einstmals sitz' ich wieder   5
Beim abgebrannten Licht;
Ich wache — aber hoffen
Und weinen kann ich nicht.

„Ich sehne mich nach wilden Küssen"

Ich sehne mich nach wilden Küssen,
Nach wollustheißen Fieberschauern;
Ich will die Nacht am hellen Tag
Nicht schon in banger Qual durchtrauern.

Noch schlägt mein Herz mit raschem Drang,   5
Noch brennt die Wang' in Jugendgluten —
Steh' still, lösch' aus mit einem Mal!
Nur nicht so tropfenweis verbluten.

Detlev von Liliencron (1844-1909)

Viererzug[1]

Vorne vier nickende Pferdeköpfe,
Neben mir zwei blonde Mädchenzöpfe,
Hinten der Groom mit wichtigen Mienen,
An den Rädern Gebell.

In den Dörfern windstillen Lebens Genüge,   5
Auf den Feldern fleißige Spaten und Pflüge,
Alles das von der Sonne beschienen
So hell, so hell.

"Viererzug" is one of the not very numerous German poems in the impressionistic manner that can be called nearly perfect.

> The condensation is unsurpassable: with a few sparse suggestions, with a
> minimum of words (there is not a single finite verb in the whole poem)
> Liliencron succeeds in evoking an intense atmosphere, in creating an entire
> picture — or rather, in forcing us to create it. How the situation comes to
> life through the adjective *nickend* and the phrase *mit wichtigen Mienen.* No
> elaboration of the relationship between the poet and the owner of the blond
> braids; but ever so indirectly, yet ever so deftly the mood of romance is
> indicated by the discrete gravity of the groom who refuses to hear and see.
> And then the vista opens up: the peaceful summery calm of the villages,
> broken only by the dogs as they dash forth from the farmyards (again: what
> economy of words), the brisk work in the fields, and over all this *plein air*
> picture the sun: *so hell, so hell**

In Erinnerung

Wilde Rosen überschlugen
Tiefer Wunden rotes Blut.
Windverwehte Klänge trugen
Siegesmarsch und Siegesflut.

Nacht. Entsetzen überspülte   5
Dorf und Dach in Lärm und Glut.

---

1 'four-in-hand,' a coach driven by one driver with four hourses in two teams

*Detlev W. Schumann, "Detlev von Liliencron: An Attempt at an Interpretation and
Evaluation," *Monatshefte* 37 (1945): 67.

„Wasser!" Und die Hand zerwühlte
Gras und Staub in Dursteswut.

Morgen. Gräbergraber. Grüfte.
Manch ein letzter Atemzug.   10
Weiter, witternd, durch die Lüfte
Braust und graust ein Geierflug.

Märztag

Wolkenschatten fliehen über Felder,
Blau umdunstet stehen ferne Wälder.

Kraniche, die hoch die Luft durchpflügen,
Kommen schreiend an in Wanderzügen.

Lerchen steigen schon in lauten Schwärmen,   5
Überall ein erstes Frühlingslärmen.

Lustig flattern, Mädchen, deine Bänder;
Kurzes Glück träumt durch die weiten Länder.

Kurzes Glück schwamm mit den Wolkenmassen;
Wollt es halten, mußt es schwimmen lassen.   10

Rosa Mayreder (1858-1938)

Erstes Begegnen

Was hält noch zögernd über Wald und Auen
Des Abends blassen Schimmer festgebannt,
Und läßt den Himmel über Strom und Land
In unerloschnem Glanze niederblauen?

Es will die Nacht mit ihrem Dämmergrauen   5
Nicht überschatten noch dein Angesicht;
Vom Tage borgt sie sich ein letztes Licht,
Um nimmersatt ins Auge dir zu schauen.

Dich liebt die Nacht. Sie raubt von deinem Munde
In liebesdurstgem Kuß den lauen Hauch   10
Und trägt ihn selig durch die weite Runde.

Da regt aus ihrer Ruhe traumversunken
Sich die entschlafne Flur, und Baum und Strauch
Erschauern leis mit mir, von Sehnsucht trunken.

Richard Dehmel (1863-1920)

Manche Nacht

Wenn die Felder sich verdunkeln,
Fühl ich, wird mein Auge heller;
Schon versucht ein Stern zu funkeln,
Und die Grillen wispern schneller.

Jeder Laut wird bilderreicher,   5
Das Gewohnte sonderbarer,
Hinterm Wald der Himmel bleicher,
Jeder Wipfel hebt sich klarer.

Und du merkst es nicht im Schreiten,
Wie das Licht verhundertfältigt   10
Sich entringt den Dunkelheiten.
Plötzlich stehst du überwältigt.

Towards Interpretation

1. In this poem the roles of light and dark are interchanged. Is this literally the case?
2. Why is one "plötzlich überwaltigt" (line 20)?

Christian Morgenstern (1871-1914)

Der Werwolf

Ein Werwolf eines Nachts entwich
von Weib und Kind und sich begab
an eines Dorfschullehrers Grab
und bat ihn: „Bitte, beuge mich!"[1]

Der Dorfschulmeister stieg hinauf   5
auf seines Blechschilds Messingknauf[2]
und sprach zum Wolf, der seine Pfoten
geduldig kreuzte vor dem Toten:

„Der Werwolf," sprach der gute Mann,
„des Weswolfs, Genitiv sodann,   10
dem Wemwolf, Dativ, wie man's nennt,
den Wenwolf, — damit hat's ein End."

Dem Werwolf schmeichelten die Fälle,[3]
er rollte seine Augenbälle.
„Indessen," bat er, „füge doch   15
zur Einzahl auch die Mehrzahl noch."

Der Dorfschulmeister aber mußte
gestehn, daß er von ihr nichts wußte.
Zwar Wölfe gäb's in großer Schar,
doch „Wer" gäb's nur im Singular.   20

Der Wolf erhob sich tränenblind —
er hatte ja doch Weib und Kind!!
Doch da er kein Gelehrter eben,
so schied er dankend und ergeben.

Vice Versa

Ein Hase sitzt auf einer Wiese,
des Glaubens, niemand sähe diese.

---

[1]"Please decline me!" [2]*Blechschilds Messingknauf*: brass knob on top of metal plate
set up as headstone. A *Dorfschullehrer* cannot afford real stone. [3]grammatical 'cases'

Doch, im Besitze eines Zeißes,[1]
betrachtet voll gehaltnen Fleißes[2]

vom vis-à-vis gelegnen Berg   5
ein Mensch den kleinen Löffelzwerg.[3]

Ihn aber blickt hinwiederum
ein Gott von fern an, mild und stumm.

Das Einhorn

Das Einhorn lebt von Ort zu Ort
    nur noch als Wirtshaus fort.[1]

Man geht hinein zur Abendstund'
    und sitzt den Stammtisch rund.[2]

Wer weiß! Nach Jahr und Tag sind wir   5
    auch ganz wie jenes Tier

Hotels nur noch, darin man speist —
    (so völlig wurden wir zu Geist).

Im „Goldnen Menschen" sitzt man dann
    und sagt sein Solo[3] an. . . .   10

Scholastikerproblem

I

Wieviel Engel sitzen können
auf der Spitze einer Nadel —
wolle dem[1] dein Denken gönnen,
Leser sonder[2] Furcht und Tadel!

„Alle!" wird's dein Hirn durchblitzen.   5
„Denn die Engel sind doch Geister!
Und ein ob auch noch so feister
Geist[3] bedarf schier nichts zum Sitzen."

---

[1]brand of binoculars [2]'full of restrained energy' [3]In hunters's language the hare's ears are called *Löffel* (spoons).

[1]'*Zum Einhorn*' is a popular name for German inns. [2]Pun: one sits *around* a table and so sits it *round*. [3]a hand in the German cardgame *Skat* (played in all *Wirtshäuser*)

[1]i.e., this matter [2]=*ohne* [3]lines 7-8: 'And a spirit no matter how plump'

Ich hingegen stell' den Satz[4] auf:
Keiner! — Denn die nie Erspähten
können einzig nehmen Platz auf
geistlichen Lokalitäten.

II

Kann ein Engel Berge steigen?
Nein. Er ist zu leicht dazu.
Menschenfuß und Menschenschuh
bleibt allein dies Können eigen.

Lockt ihn dennoch dieser Sport,   5
muß er wieder sich ver-erden
und ein Menschenfräulein werden
etwa namens Zuckertort.

Allerdings bemerkt man immer,
was darin[1] steckt und von wo —   10
denn ein solches Frauenzimmer
schreitet anders als nur so.

Towards Interpretation
1. Can you deduce from the content a reason for the changed rime scheme of the final stanza?

Stefan George (1868-1933)

With George modern poetry in the eminent sense begins in Germany. This poet was once extravagantly admired and even worshipped by a small inner circle and just as extravagantly rejected and vilified by the larger public; we can now appraise him more calmly and fairly, though the last word on him has not been said nor probably will be for some time to come.

George belongs to a distinct tradition in German poetry, a tradition that is composed of two main strands: the first, the concept of the poet as *vates* or seer, the second, the esthetic ideal, with emphasis on the one or the other aspect varying from poet to poet. To this tradition belong Klopstock, Hölderlin, Platen, Meyer. In Hölderlin we find the two strands combined in almost

[4]'proposition'

[1]i.e., in the *Menschenfräulein*

perfect union, nor can there be any doubt that he is the greatest of the poets of this tradition. In Klopstock, the main emphasis, especially from the reader's standpoint, is on the vatic nature of poetry, though he too was preoccupied with questions of form and theorized about them; in Platen and Meyer, it is the esthetic ideal that strikes one most. George's earlier work seems almost an apotheosis of the esthetic, whereas in his later poetry the seer and Jeremiah occupy the foreground.

These two aspects are of course not unrelated. The outward esthetic discipline is a manifestation of an inner ethical discipline. Formal strictness reflects spiritual sternness; one might even say it is symbolic of a will to power through the word. The almost exclusive condition of *poiesis* for George was the possibility of projecting that which is inward into something outward — he is a symbolist through and through. In this passion of his for complete objectivity lies the main stumbling-block for the uninitiated reader. To understand George one must first accustom oneself to his *Räume*, the atmosphere of his symbolical objectifications. Perhaps this is easier for us, who have been brought up on "modern" poetry, than it was for George's contemporaries.

In George's work objectification extends even to orthography, typography, and punctuation. Capitals are used only for emphasis and at the beginning of a line of verse; commas are omitted, but pauses are sometimes indicated by a vertical dash or by a dot placed on a line with the letters; the type used in the official edition, a kind of uncial, is derived from the poet's own stylized hand. (One should examine a volume of the *Gesamt-Ausgabe* to see precisely what is meant.) The general impression of a page of George's verse (or prose) is that of cool smoothness and hieratic aloofness. The sparse punctuation makes it almost impossible to read these poems silently — they must be read aloud, as indeed all poetry should be.*

---

*The translations by Cyril M. Scott, *Stefan George. Selections from his Works* (London: Mathews, 1910), and by Olga Marx and Ernst Morwitz (*The Works of Stefan George*, UNC Studies in the Germanic Languages and Literatures 78 (Chapel Hill: UNC Press, ²1974) may be of considerable help for obscure passages. Very helpful is also *George. Hofmannsthal. Rilke*, ed. Martin Sommerfeld (New York: W. W. Norton, 1938).

Vogelschau[1]

Weisse schwalben sah ich fliegen·
Schwalben schnee- und silberweiss·
Sah sie sich im winde wiegen·
In dem winde hell und heiss.

Bunte häher[2] sah ich hüpfen·   5
Papagei und kolibri
Durch die wunder-bäume schlüpfen
In dem wald der Tusferi.[3]

Grosse raben sah ich flattern·
Dohlen schwarz und dunkelgrau   10
Nah am grunde über nattern[4]
Im verzauberten gehau.[5]

Schwalben sah ich wieder fliegen·
Schnee- und silberweisse schar·
Wie sie sich im winde wiegen   15
In dem winde kalt und klar!

C. M. Bowra* writes of this poem:

In *Vogelschau* ('*Augury*'), the last poem of *Algabal*, George takes leave of
his exotic subjects and comes, as it were, home again. It is a summary of
his work and imaginative life up to date. In it George uses nothing but symbols, and his use of them is his own. They form a coherent whole. All the
imagery is taken from birds. There is no key, no explanation. All is trans-
lucid and brilliant, a real song. . . . The poet watches birds as an augur
may. He knows that they mean and foretell something if he can interpret it.
But these birds are different aspects of George's life: adventures and experiences through which he has passed. After sojourning in exotic and sinis-
ter regions he has returned to where he started and has found a change; a
cold wind blows where before the air was sultry. The young poet who felt
hampered in his own home [i.e., Germany] and tried strange experiments
in the mind, has returned refreshed and clear. . . . The symbols are all
taken from a single sphere and are maintained with complete consistency.
But they are presented with circumstances so vivid and so appropriate that
the primary and secondary meanings of the poem are transfused. There is
no gap between the symbols and what is symbolized. The birds have the
variety and qualities of George's adventures; his adventures are best

[1]'augury' (Look this word up in a good dictionary.) [2]'jays'; *Papagei* 'parrot'; *kolibri*
'hummingbird' [3]Tusferi will not be found in any atlas. [4]'vipers' [5]'enchanted cutting'
(Cyril Scott)

*C. M. Bowra, *The Heritage of Symbolism*, 103f.

understood as birds. The Symbolist method is mastered, and the poem gains by this double character which is not in the least ambiguous.

Towards Interpretation

1. Compare the technique of "Vogelschau" with that of Meyer's "Zwei Segel."

2. We find the key to the symbolism of both these poems in their *position* in the poet's work. Both Meyer and George arranged their poems in cycles. Why should this method of composition appeal to the Symbolist?

Der Herr der Insel

Die fischer überliefern[1] dass im süden
Auf einer insel reich an zimmt[2] und öl
Und edlen steinen die im sande glitzern
Ein vogel war der wenn am boden fussend
Mit seinem schnabel hoher stämme krone   5
Zerpflücken konnte· wenn er seine flügel
Gefärbt wie mit dem saft der Tyrer-schnecke[3]
Zu schwerem niedrem flug erhoben· habe
Er einer dunklen wolke gleichgesehn.
Des tages sei er im gehölz verschwunden·   10
Des abends aber an den strand gekommen·
Im kühlen windeshauch von salz und tang[4]
Die süsse stimme hebend dass delfine
Die freunde des gesanges näher schwammen[5]
In meer voll goldner federn goldner funken.[6]   15
So habe er seit urbeginn gelebt·
Gescheiterte[7] nur hätten ihn erblickt.
Denn als zum erstenmal die weissen segel
Der menschen sich mit günstigem geleit[8]
Dem eiland zugedreht sei er zum hügel   20
Die ganze teure stätte zu beschaun gestiegen·
Verbreitet habe er die grossen schwingen
Verscheidend[9] in gedämpften[10] schmerzeslauten.

---

[1]'pass on the story' Note that all the following verses depend from *überliefern dass*. [2]'cinnamon' [3]An extract derived from Tyrian snails was used to make the magnificent dye known as "royal purple." The secret of this dye has been lost. [4]'seaweed' [5]Cf. Herodotus, bk. I, ch. 23-24, for a famous story of dolphins' fondness for music. [6]Line 15: Either, 'In a sea full of the golden feathers of golden sparks' or, 'In a sea full of golden feathers (and) golden sparks.' [7]'the shipwrecked' [8]'with favoring winds' [9]'passing away' (purposely ambiguous) [10]'muted'

Der Teppich

Hier schlingen menschen mit gewächsen tieren
Sich fremd zum bund umrahmt von seidner franze
Und blaue sicheln weisse sterne zieren
Und queren sie in dem erstarrten tanze.

Und kahle linien ziehn in reich-gestickten   5
Und teil um teil ist wirr und gegenwendig
Und keiner ahnt das rätsel der verstrickten[1] . .
Da eines ebends wird das werk lebendig.

Da regen[2] schauernd sich die toten äste
Die wesen eng von strich und kreis umspannet[3]   10
Und treten klar vor die geknüpften quäste[4]
Die lösung bringend über die ihr sannet!

Sie[5] ist nach willen nicht : ist nicht für jede
Gewohne[6] stunde : ist kein schatz der gilde.
Sie wird den vielen nie und nie durch rede   15
Sie wird den seltnen selten im gebild.[7]

Modern poetry is characterized by its urge to talk about itself; it often becomes
its own obsessive theme. *Der Teppich des Lebens* (1900), George's fifth volume of verse, is even more a tapestry of art than of life, or of life as art. "Der
Teppich" is its programmatic poem. It is a symbolic description of George's
art and the way it may be understood. Most striking is the poet's insistence
upon the artificial nature of his work — this art is not life, he tells us, it is
something made, an artifact. It is a tapestry with figures of human beings,
plants, and animals caught in a complicated arabesque none can decipher: *Und
keiner ahnt das rätsel der verstricken.* Then "one evening" the tapestry comes
alive — the dead branches begin to move, the figures in the "frozen dance"
stand out against their background and the whole takes on meaning: the reader
sees the pattern. The poem describes a *kairos*, an opportune moment, a right
point of time (not *jede gewohne stunde*), experienced by us, the readers, when,
in a flash of intuition (not when we will, *nach willen nicht*) which comes only

---

[1]Lines 1-7: *Menschen, Gewächse und Tiere sind auf dem Teppich zum einem Bund
vereinigt; sie sind von seidenen Franzen* [fringes] *umrahmt; blaue, sichelförmige Figuren und weisse Sterne sind als Schmuck hineingewoben und unterbrechen den erstar-
ten Reigen der Figuren. Einfache, schmucklose ('kahle') Linien ziehen sich durch reich
gestickte, und die einzelnen Teile sind als Gegenbilder zu einander ('gegenwendig')
angeordnet; und niemand ahnt, wie sie mit einander verknüpft sind.* (Sommerfeld's
note) [2]verb [3]past participle [4]'tassels' [5]i.e., *die lösung* [6]=*gewöhnliche* [7]Lines 15-16:
The many will never find the answer and no one will ever arrive at it through talk, but
at rare hours the rare will grasp it as a work of art.

after long puzzling over the riddle, we see what is meant. But we do not see the meaning in a way that can be told, the poet insists — one cannot "tell" a tapestry — we see it *im gebilde*. Art can be comprehended only in its own terms. If we are capable of experiencing this *kairos*, we are among the *seltenen*. George's art is emphatically un-popular. But neither is it a *schatz der gilde*. It is not meant for a coterie, some little group on the "inside." Later, it is true, George does write some poetry that falls under this category, though the main line of his development is toward ever wider comprehensibility.

„Komm in den totgesagten park . . . "

Komm in den totgesagten park und schau :
Der schimmer ferner lächelnder gestade·
Der reinen wolken unverhofftes blau[1]
Erhellt die weiher und die bunten pfade.

Dort nimm das tiefe gelb· das weiche grau   5
Von birken und von buchs· der wind ist lau·
Die späten rosen welkten noch nicht ganz·
Erlese[2] küsse sie und flicht den kranz·

Vergiss auch diese lezten astern nicht·
Den purpur um die ranken wilder reben   10
Und auch was übrig blieb von grünem leben
Verwinde[3] leicht im herbstlichen gesicht.[4]

This poem comes from *Das Jahr der Seele* (1897), the cycle of poems preceding *Der Teppich des Lebens*. As the latter showed life as a tapestry, so the former shows the year as a *Jahr der Kunst* or *des Künstlers Jahr*. Our poem is the first of this "year," which begins not with spring but autumn, *Nach der Lese* (After the Harvest), and includes spring only by indirection as the end of winter.

Perhaps the first thing to strike one who has just read Goethe and his successors is the setting of this poem: a tended park, not *freie Natur*. Furthermore, it is a *totgesagter* park, an autumnal landscape "they say is dead." Is George going to show us that "they" are wrong? And who are "they"? One critic* suggests that "they" are the poets, those who, either directly or by implication, have seen parks only negatively, as constraint, and have regarded

[1]'Pure clouds with rifts of unexpected blue' (transl. Marx-Morwitz) [2]=*erlies* 'select,' 'gather' [3]'entwine,' but also with the secondary meaning 'overcome' (*überwinden*) [4]'vision' (Marx-Morwitz)

*Paul Gerhard Klußmann, "Stefan George," in *Die deutsche Lyrik*, ed. Benno von Wiese, (Düsseldorf: Schwann-Bagel, [2]1981), 2:269f.

autumn only from the standpoint of dying (cf. Lenau!). George, for his part, does not deny that autumn is a time of dying; on the contrary he insists upon it: the blue is "unexpected," the "late" roses are withering, these are the "last" asters, the grape leaves have turned red, nor does he deny that a park is a park and not open nature, but he finds something positive in all this. The tone of the poem is one of restrained joy. The second and third stanzas show us *im gebilde* why this is "his," the artist's, time. With autumn ("after the harvest") nature ceases, as it were, to be her own artist; she gives up forming things according to *her* will, so that now man, the artificer, can step in. This is precisely what happens in our poem: out of the "materials" of nature a wreath is wound, an artifact produced. Man's will — note the many imperatives! — replaces nature's. Within the park, itself a symbol of nature subjected to restraint, we witness the creation of another symbol of the imposition of man's will: the wreath.

Goethe chose the awakening of the world in spring as the symbol of his creative impulse (cf. end of "Mailed"), George's "spring" is the autumn, a dead world submissive to the will of the artist. Goethe's youthful lyric finds its most fitting emblem in the vigorously blossoming spray, George's in the man-made wreath, the artful tapestry. "Whatever remains of green life," the poet instructs the "you" in our poem — a "you" which is basically an aspect of himself — "*Verwinde* leicht im herbstlichen gesicht." The purposely ambiguous verb means both "entwine" and "overcome" (*einen Schmerz verwinden*). In other words, when the artist makes use of "green life" in his art, he overcomes it *as* life. This is by no means so far from Goethe's view as might at first appear; indeed, we may even say that it is only a restatement of his view in modern terms.

Towards Interpretation

1. Note carefully the unusual rime scheme of this poem and see if you can determine its significance. Remember always that "significant" form is form that shows forth content *im gebilde*.

2. If you are familiar with W. B. Yeats' "Sailing to Byzantium" (published thirty years after the *Jahr der Seele*), compare the ideal Yeats aspires to there with that of George in "Der Teppich" and the present poem. What larger conclusions can you draw from this comparison about the nature of Symbolism?

Die Fremde

Sie kam allein aus fernen gauen[1]
Ihr haus umging[2] das volk mit grauen
Sie sott[3] und buk[4] und sagte wahr[5]
Sie sang im mond mit offenem haar.

Am kirchtag trug sie bunten staat[6]   5
Damit[7] sie oft zur luke[8] trat . .
Dann ward ihr lächeln süss und herb
Gatten und brüdern zum verderb.

Und übers jahr als sie im dunkel
Einst attich suchte und ranunkel[9]   10
Da sah man wie sie sank im torf[10] —
Und andere schwuren dass vorm dorf

Sie auf dem mitten weg[11] verschwand . .
Sie liess das knäblein nur als pfand
So schwarz wie nacht so bleich wie lein[12]   15
Das sie gebar im hornungschein.[13]

Towards Interpretation

    1. How might this poem be interpreted as a "symbolical objectification"?

„*Einer stand auf . . .* "

Einer[1] stand auf der scharf wie blitz und stahl
Die klüfte aufriss und die lager schied[2]
Ein Drüben schuf durch umkehr eures Hier[3] . .
Der euren wahnsinn so lang in euch schrie
Mit solcher wucht dass ihm die kehle barst.[4]   5

---

[1]'cantons,' 'districts' [2]'gave a wide berth' [3]from *sieden* [4]from *backen* [5]'read palms,'
'prophesied' [6]'finery' [7]'in which' [8]Low German: =*Öffnung in der Tür* (Sommerfeld)
[9]Dwarf elder (*Attich*) and crowfoot (*Ranunkel*) may have magic properties, though it
seems more likely they are found here because of their vowel qualities. [10]'peat bog'
[11]=*mitten auf dem Weg* [12] The child had black hair and a very white skin (*lein* = *Lein-
wand*). [13]*Hornung* is the old German name of February. The word means 'bastard,'
i.e., one born in a 'horn' or *corner*, and was applied to February as the less favored
(because shortest) month.

[1]Nietzsche [2]'Tore open the abysses and divided the camps' [3]Nietzsche's central doctrine is the *Umwertung aller Werte*. [4]Nietzsche's whole work may be looked upon as a
single *Zeitgedicht*. He was not heeded and died insane.

Und ihr? ob dumpf ob klug ob falsch ob echt
Vernahmt und saht als wäre nichts geschehn . .
Ihr handelt weiter⁵ sprecht und lacht und heckt·⁶
Der warner ging . . dem rad das niederrollt
Zur leere greift kein arm mehr in die speiche.⁷   10

*Der Widerchrist*¹

„Dort kommt er vom berge· dort steht er im hain!
Wir sahen es selber· er wandelt in wein
Das wasser und spricht mit den toten. "

O könntet ihr hören mein lachen bei nacht :
Nun schlug meine stunde· nun füllt sich das garn·   5
Nun strömen die fische zum hamen.²

Die weisen die toren — toll wälzt sich das volk :
Entwurzelt die bäume· zerklittert³ das korn·
Macht bahn für den zug des Erstandnen.⁴

Kein werk ist des himmels das ich euch nicht tu.   10
Ein haarbreit nur fehlt und ihr merkt nicht den trug
Mit euren geschlagenen sinnen.⁵

Ich schaff euch für alles was selten und schwer
Das Leichte· ein ding das wie gold ist aus lehm·
Wie duft ist und saft ist und würze⁶ —   15

Und was sich der grosse profet nicht getraut :
Die kunst ohne roden und säen und baun
Zu saugen gespeicherte kräfte.⁷

Der Fürst des Geziefers⁸ verbreitet sein reich·
Kein Schatz der ihm mangelt· kein glück das ihm   20
Zu grund mit dem rest der empörer!   [weicht . .

---

⁵'go on behaving as usual' ⁶'breed,' 'fornicate' ⁷'spoke'

¹'Antichrist' Cf. 2 Thessalonians 2. Lines 1-3 are spoken by the people, 4-27 by the Antichrist. ²Low German: 'purse net' (*Sommerfeld*) ³'grinds to dust' ⁴'the risen one' ⁵Cf. *mit Wahnsinn (Blindheit) geschlagen*. ⁶Lines 14-15: *ein Ding aus Lehm* (clay), *das wie Duft, Saft und Würze ist* (Sommerfeld) ⁷Lines 16-18: What Christ himself (*der grosse profet*) dared not give you, I (the Anti-Christ) will, namely the art of drawing sustenance from nature (*saugen gespeicherte kräfte*) without clearing the land (*roden*) or sowing or planting (*baun*). ⁸'The prince of vermin' is Satan.

Ihr jauchzet· entzückt von dem teuflischen schein·[9]
Verprasset was blieb von dem früheren seim[10]
Und fühlt erst die not vor dem ende.

Dann hängt ihr die zunge am trocknenden trog·   25
Irrt ratlos wie vieh durch den brennenden hof . .
Und schrecklich erschallt die posaune.[11]

Towards Interpretation

1. The only rime in this poem is in lines 1-2, when the people are speaking. In place of rime, we find assonance in all other stanzas. Why is
   this?

„Wer je die flamme umschritt . . .“

Wer je die flamme umschritt
Bleibe[1] der flamme trabant!
Wie er auch wandert und kreist :
Wo noch ihr schein ihn erreicht
Irrt er zu weit nie vom ziel.   5
Nur wenn sein blick sie verlor
Eigener schimmer ihn trügt :[2]
Fehlt ihm der mitte gesetz[3]
Treibt er zerstiebend ins all.

Hehre Harfe[1]

Sucht ihr neben noch das übel
Greift ihr aussen nach dem heile :[2]
Giesst ihr noch in lecke kübel·[3]
Müht ihr euch noch um das feile.[4]

Alles seid ihr selbst und drinne :   5
Des gebets entzückter laut

---

[9]'seeming' (opposed to *Sein* 'being') [10]'thick juice,' 'syrup' [11]i.e., trumpet of doom

[1]hortatory subjunctive [2]*Wenn der Adept die Flamme aus den Augen verliert, wird er von dem Glanz des eigenen Selbst getäuscht* (Sommerfeld) [3]=*das Gesetz der Mitte* (symbolized by the flame)

[1]'Sacred Lyre' [2]The colon is George's way if indicating *dann* or *so*. [3]'leaky pails'
[4]'that which can be bought'

Schmilzt in eins mit jeder minne·[5]
Nennt sie Gott und freund und braut !

Keine zeiten können borgen . .
Fegt der sturm die erde sauber :   10
Tretet ihr in euren morgen·[6]
Werfet euren blick voll zauber

Auf die euch verliehnen gaue
Auf das volk das euch umfahet[7]
Und das land das dämmergraue   15
Das ihr früh im brunnen[8] sahet.

Hegt den wahn nicht[9] : mehr zu lernen
Als aus staunen überschwang[10]
Holden blumen hohen sternen[11]
EINEN sonnigen lobgesang.   20

Towards Interpretation

1. Explain the title of this poem. What is the "harp"?
2. Explain what is meant by line 9.
3. Why is our glance *voll zauber* (line 12)?
4. Why are the *gaue* (line 13) said to be *verliehen* 'lent'?
5. Compare the idea expressed in "Hehre Harfe" with that of Goethe's "Das Göttliche."

„Kreuz der strasse . . ."

Kreuz der strasse[1] . .
Wir sind am end.
Abend sank schon . .
Dies ist das end.
Kurzes wallen[2]   5
Wen macht es müd?
Mir zu lang schon . .
Der schmerz macht müd.

---

[5]'(act of) love' *Minne* (cognate with English 'mind'), an old word for *Liebe*, recalls both troubadors (*Minnesinger*) and the mystics (cf. *Gottesminne*); used here to emphasize the spiritual aspect of love. [6]i.e., in the realm which is properly yours [7]=*umfängt* [8]The *brunnen* is of course within us; in it early intuitions are reflected. [9]'Don't cherish the illusion' [10]'enthusiasm' [11]Lines 18-19: There is a slight pause after each noun, which are all governed by *aus*, l. 18.

[1]'Lo, the crossways' (Cyril Scott) [2]'wandering,' 'making a pilgrimage'

Hände lockten :
Was³ nahmst du nicht?   10
Seufzer stockten :
Vernahmst du nicht?
Meine strasse
Du ziehst sie nicht.
Tränen fallen   15
Du siehst sie nicht.

„Die blume die ich mir am fenster hege"

Die blume die ich mir am fenster hege
Verwahrt vorm froste in der grauen scherbe¹
Betrübt mich nur trotz meiner guten pflege
Und hängt das haupt als ob sie langsam sterbe.

Um ihrer frühern blühenden geschicke
Erinnerung aus meinem sinn zu merzen
Erwähl ich scharfe waffen und ich knicke
Die blasse blume mit dem kranken herzen.

Was soll sie nur zur bitternis mir taugen?
Ich wünschte dass vom fenster sie verschwände . .
Nun heb ich wieder meine leeren augen
Und in die leere nacht die leeren hände.

Towards Interpretation

1. The relationship between the speaker and the flower is ambiguous, to say the least. What clues does the poem give to help us understand what the flower symbolizes to the speaker? What is the significance of the season?

---

³ = warum

¹ 'pot'

Das Wort

Wunder von ferne oder traum
Bracht ich an meines landes saum[1]

Und harrte bis die graue norn
Den namen fand in ihrem born[2] —

Drauf konnt ichs greifen dicht und stark   5
Nun blüht und glänzt es durch die mark[3] . .

Einst langt ich an[4] nach guter fahrt
Mit einem kleinod reich und zart

Sie suchte lang und gab mir kund :
„So schläft hier nichts auf tiefem grund"   10

Worauf es meiner hand entrann
Und nie mein land den schatz gewann . . .

So lernt ich traurig den verzicht :
Kein ding sei[5] wo das wort gebricht.[6]

Nichts, sagt George — so hat er erfahren — sei wirklich ohne das Wort
[lines 13-14]. Die wortlose Welt ist dem Dichter ein unwirklicher, schatten-
haft dunkler Bereich zahlloser Möglichkeiten [„Wunder von ferne oder
traum"], die sich immer erst im Wort verwirklichen. Deutlich sagen die
Verse 5-6, was die wortgeborene Welt auszeichnet. Das Wort ‚verdichtet'
ein Fernes, Unfaßliches, traumhaft Flüchtiges zum Ding, macht es ‚greif-
bar,' ‚blühend' und ‚glänzend'. . . . Das Wort stiftet das Sein [makes being
possible] als die sichtbare Welt. Woher aber sollte ihm [dem Wort] diese
einzigartige Kraft zuwachsen, wenn nicht aus seiner eigenen lebendigen
Wirklichkeit! Dem Dichter ist das Wort selbst ein Sichtbares, nicht Begriff,
sondern leibhafte Erscheinung.

Das Wort der Norn ist Georges eigenes Wort. Was der alte Mythos
jener Urd am Fuße des Weltbaums zuschrieb, das mutet George dem Dichter zu: Sein Wort erst begründet die Wirklichkeit des Seins und sein Spruch
bestimmt das Geschick der Erde. . . . Diese Botschaft . . . ist freilich ganz
nur zu verstehen auf dem Hintergrund der geschichtlichen Situation des
modernen Menschen, dem seit Nietzsche die überlieferten Glaubensinhalte
[traditional dogmas] fragwürdig geworden sind. . . . George glaubt nicht
mehr an einen vorgegebenen [preëstablished] Sinnzusammenhang der
Dinge. Dichterisches Wort und dichterisches Bild übernehmen bei ihm die
Funktion, die Ordnung und Wahrheit des Seins neu zu stiften.*

---

[1]'border' [2]In Germanic mythology the norn Urd lives at the foot of the world-ash Igg-
drasil and waters it from a spring (born), called the Urd-Well; she is thus a preserving
force. Her slighest word is law for men and gods alike. In one of the sagas a poet
drinks wisdom from her well. [3]=Land [4]anlangen 'arrive' [5]'may be' [6]'is lacking'

*Klußmann, Deutsche Lyrik, 2:289ff.

Hugo von Hofmannsthal (1874-1929)

To the larger public outside German speaking lands, Hugo von Hofmannsthal is known principally as the librettist of the operas of Richard Strauss (*Die Frau ohne Schatten, Elektra, Der Rosenkavalier* and others). To some he may also be known as the playwright of the perennially popular Salzburg *Jedermann*, to a few as an editor and essayist, to a handful as a lyric poet. Yet his lyrical output, though slim, is perhaps the most important part of his work, the part that has most definite *Unsterblichkeitscharakter*. It contains *in nuce* the whole Hofmannsthal. Though the peer of any of his famous contemporaries in Germany, France, and England as an artificer, Hofmannsthal does not believe that poetry can "take the place of belief in God" (Wallace Stevens), as George, for example, would seem to do (cf. "Das Wort"). His work looks forward to a time when all artifice can fall away and man can share in the spirit directly. He is more nearly akin to Novalis than to his one-time friend and brother in Apollo, George.

Vorfrühling

Es läuft der Frühlingswind
Durch kahle Alleen,
Seltsame Dinge sind
In seinem Wehn.

Er hat sich gewiegt,   5
Wo Weinen war,
Und hat sich geschmiegt
In zerrüttetes[1] Haar.

Er schüttelte nieder
Akazienblüten   10
Und kühlte die Glieder,
Die atmend glühten.

---

[1]'disheveled'

344

Lippen im Lachen
Hat er berührt,
Die weichen und wachen   15
Fluren² durchspürt.

Er glitt durch die Flöte
Als schluchzender Schrei,
An dämmernder Röte³
Flog er vorbei.   20

Er flog mit Schweigen
Durch flüsternde Zimmer⁴
Und löschte im Neigen⁵
Der Ampel Schimmer.

Es läuft der Frühlingswind   25
Durch kahle Alleen,
Seltsame Dinge sind
In seinem Wehn.

Durch die glatten
Kahlen Alleen   30
Treibt sein Wehn
Blasse Schatten.

Und den Duft,
Den er gebracht,
Von wo er gekommen   35
Seit gestern nacht.

Towards Interpretation
1. Why does Hofmannsthal repeat stanza 1 as stanza 7, instead of at the end of the poem? What is the tense in stanzas 2-6? Stanza 8?
2. What grammatical observations can you make about the last stanza?

Die Beiden

Sie trug den Becher in der Hand
— Ihr Kinn und Mund glich seinem Rand¹ —,
So leicht und sicher war ihr Gang,
Kein Tropfen aus dem Becher Sprang.

---

²'meadows'   ³=*Morgen-* oder *Abendröte*   ⁴=*Zimmer, worin geflüstert wird*   ⁵Whether it was the wind or the lamp that was *im Neigen*, cannot be determined.

¹'were like its (the cup's) brim'

So leicht und fest war seine Hand: 5
Er ritt auf einem jungen Pferde,
Und mit nachlässiger² Gebärde
Erzwang er, daß es zitternd stand.

Jedoch, wenn er aus ihrer Hand
Den leichten Becher nehmen sollte,   10
So war es beiden allzu schwer:
Denn beide bebten sie so sehr,
Daß keine Hand die andre fand
Und dunkler Wein am Boden rollte.

Reim ist bloss ein wortspiel
wenn zwischen den durch den reim verbundenen worten
keine innere verbindung besteht.

(George)

Although its rime scheme departs widely from the classical Italian form (as cultivated by Platen, for example), "Die Beiden" may still be regarded as a sonnet. As against the traditional *abba abba cdc dcd*, we find here *aabb acca ade ead*. The variety of Hofmannsthal's rimes thus seems at first to be greater — five instead of four — but closer examination renders this variety problematic, for the five are actually reduced to three by the use of assonance: H*a*nd – G*a*ng, Pf*erde* – schw*er*, so that we perhaps obtain a more accurate picture of the rime scheme if we use superscripts: *aaa¹a¹ abba acb¹ b¹ac*. The quartets are assigned respectively to a "he" and a "she" and are printed separately. The sestet is assigned to both and is printed as a block, so that the look of the poem on the page reflects the (imperfect) triad. In a sonnet we expect four parts, here we get what looks like three. We also expect four different rimes, and here we get what looks like five but turns out to be three! Even so, the quadruplicity of the poem cannot be denied. From the standpoint of what happens in it, it has a 3 + 1 structure (three acts and an accident), and to each of these parts a traditional sonnet section is devoted, the tercets being clearly indicated by *Jedoch* and *Denn* (lines 9 and 12). The subtle game the poet plays with a familiar form is a means of establishing tensions.

To turn now to the first quartet. As form and discursive content so clearly indicate, the girl is perfectly at one both with herself and the action she is performing. She herself is the cup she carries, filled to the brim and ready to be drunk: *Ihr Kinn und Mund g l i c h seinem Rand.* So harmonious is her being that the second couplet is merely an assonantic variant of the first. The couplets indicate absence of "in-betweenness"; no foreign element has yet entered this being to disturb her equanimity: the cup is in no danger. Each

---

²'nonchalant'

verse forms a sense unit with a marked pause at the end, reinforced by the weighty double consonants of the masculine rimes. This hand *is* what it holds.

If self-containment is the theme of the first quartet, self-restraint is the theme of the second. The new vocalic element (*-er-*) introduced in the feminine rimes is associated first with a transparent symbol of energy, the horse, and then in the word *Gebärde* with the energy of the human will. This element is contained by the *-and* rimes already established in the first stanza as a sign of control and self-possession. But the control here, despite the rider's nonchalance, is somewhat precarious. This is most clearly seen in lines 7-8, where the energy symbol, *-er-*, quite literally trembles almost to the end of the line before it is contained by *-and*. Note the interplay of *er, ng, nd,* in verse 8: *Erzwang er, daß es zitternd stand.* This hand is engaged in a dubious struggle with that which holds it.

Perfectly self-controlled (because not yet endangered) femininity (cup, "*leicht und sicher*") and gracefully but tensely controlled (because inwardly endangered) masculinity (horse, "*leicht und fest*") are then the contrasting motifs of the octet. The sestet reveals what happens when these two meet, when the rider attempts to take the cup from the girl.

As in the foregoing stanza the new vocalic element (soll*te* – roll*te*) is the feminine rimes, but this time it cannot be contained by the firm masculine endings (here, as above, *-and*): *Und dunkler Wein am Boden* roll*te*. Conscious human purposes are frustrated. *Dem Soll ist etwas entrollt.* (Normally, *rollen* is not used to describe the activity of a liquid — the "correct" word would be *fließen* or *strömen*. The "incorrectness" of the term draws attention to the more-than-winelike density of that which escapes control, as well of course as carrying the dark vowel quality out beyond the containing element.) Masterful is the use of interior rime in verse 13, where the controlling *-and* flutters vainly in an attempt to encompass something and finds nothing but thin air: *Daß keine H a n d die andre f a n d. . . .* That the uncontrollable is not merely the cup but something much more mysterious and significant the poet has already hinted in verse 11: *So war es* (not *er!*) *beiden allzu schwer. . . .* The *oll*-sound may be said to represent this mysterious "es," this sound being the third element *and* the third member of the vocalic triad (*-and (-ang)* | *-er (-är)* | *-oll*) arising out of the meeting of the masculine and feminine principles. We note that the energy symbol (*schwer* – *sehr*), though contained by the *-and*, is so to speak contained imperfectly, for that which causes the cup to spill — symbolized by the *oll*-sound — has inserted itself between the containing *-and* and the *-er*. The perfect balance of the first quartet and the tense balance of the second has been upset, and a new, inexorably forward-rolling something has taken its place. The heavy, regular rhythm of the last line shows that this something moves forward according to a law of its own. These hands have lost what they attempted to hold.

In "Die Beiden" Hofmannsthal gives form to the essence of a fateful human situation: the destined meeting. In one of his essays we read: "Mich dünkt, es ist nicht die Umarmung, sondern die Begegnung die eigentlich

entscheidende erotische Pantomine. Es ist in keinem Augenblick das Sinnliche
so seelenhaft, das Seelenhafte so sinnlich als in der Begegnung."

Manche freilich . . .

Manche freilich müssen drunten sterben,
Wo die schweren Ruder der Schiffe streifen,[1]
Andre wohnen bei dem Steuer droben,
Kennen Vogelflug und die Länder der Sterne.[2]

Manche liegen immer mit schweren Gliedern   5
Bei den Wurzeln des verworrenen Lebens,
Andern sind die Stühle gerichtet
Bei den Sibyllen, den Königinnen,
Und da sitzen sie wie zu Hause,
Leichten Hauptes und leichter Hände.[3]   10

Doch ein Schatten fällt von jenen Leben
In die anderen Leben hinüber,
Und die leichten sind an die schweren
Wie an Luft und Erde[4] gebunden:

Ganz vergessener Völker Müdigkeiten   15
Kann ich nicht abtun von meinen Lidern,[5]
Noch weghalten von der erschrockenen Seele
Stummes Niederfallen ferner Sterne.

Viele Geschicke weben neben dem meinen,
Durcheinander spielt sie alle das Dasein,   20
Und mein Teil ist mehr als dieses Lebens
Schlanke Flamme oder schmale Leier.[6]

Antithetisch stehen sich die Bilder in den ersten beiden Strophen gegenüber
(drunten – droben; schwer – leicht). Die entsprechenden Paare binden sich
noch durch die Anaphern: manche – andere. Die beiden Antithesen kehren
wörtlich in der dritten Strophe wieder, die nun die Verbindung zwischen
den bisher so gesonderten Bezirken gestaltet bzw. aussagt. Die vierte
Strophe spricht die Erfahrung der Verbundenheit als parallele Erlebnisse
des eigenen Ich aus. Die letzte Strophe wendet sich von den Erlebnissen
des Ich zu seinem Sein [being]. Zwei Teile lassen sich also unterscheiden,

---

[1]'sweep' (the water) The image is that of a galley. [2]i.e., think they know the future
through augery and the stars [3]genitives of manner (cf. Goethe's *Iphigenie*, Act IV, sc.
5, "Parzenlied," for the imagery.) [4]two things essential to life [5]'eyelids' [6]The
"slender flame" and "narrow lyre" are emblems of life and art and, at the same time,
of *Leichtigkeit* (see line 13).

und der Doppelpunkt ist die Stelle des Umschlagens. Der erste Teil spricht über die Welt der anderen, der zweite über die des Ich. In jedem Teil vollzieht sich eine gedankliche Bewegung zum Schluß hin.*

Lebenslied

Den Erben[1] laß verschwenden
An Adler, Lamm und Pfau
Das Salböl[2] aus den Händen
Der toten alten Frau!
Die Toten, die entgleiten,   5
Die Wipfel in dem Weiten —
Ihm[3] sind sie wie das Schreiten
Der Tänzerinnen wert!

Er geht wie den[4] kein Walten[5]
Vom Rücken her bedroht.   10
Er lächelt, wenn die Falten
Des Lebens flüstern: Tod!
Ihm bietet jede Stelle
Geheimnisvoll die Schwelle,[6]
Es gibt sich jeder Welle   15
Der Heimatlose hin.

Der Schwarm von wilden Bienen
Nimmt seine Seele mit,
Das Singen der Delphinen
Beflügelt seinen Schritt: 20
Ihn tragen alle Erden[7]
Mit mächtigen Gebärden.
Der Flüsse Dunkelwerden
Begrenzt den Hirtentag![8]

Das Salböl aus den Händen   25
Der toten alten Frau
Laß lächelnd ihn verschwenden
An Adler, Lamm und Pfau:

---

*Wolgang Kayser, *Das sprachliche Kunstwerk* (Bern: Francke, [18]1978), 318f. One should read Kayser's fascinating *Stilbestimmung* of this poem in its entirety.

[1]'heir' [2]'oinment' (such as that used to annoint a king) [3]i.e., *dem Erben* [4]=*wie einer, den* [5]'superior might' [6]The implication of lines 13-14 is made clearer by lines 15-16 and the next strophe. [7]i.e., all spheres of being (exemplified by bees and dolphins) [8]'pastoral day'

Er lächelt der Gefährten.[9] —
Die schwebend unbeschwerten   30
Abgründe und die Gärten
Des Lebens tragen ihn.

Towards Interpretation

1. What might the *tote alte Frau* stand for?
2. What associations are aroused by *Adler, Lamm und Pfau*?
3. Hofmannsthal was a Viennese of patrician birth who began writing poetry that was to become famous while he was still in the *Gymnasium*. What connection might this have with "Lebenslied"? Can you imagine Walt Whitman or Robert Burns writing in this vein? How about Oscar Wilde?
4. What aspect of existence of primary importance in "Manche freilich . . ." is excluded from this poem?

Despite the immediacy of its appeal, "Lebenslied" is one of the most hermetic poems in modern German literature, and hermetic in both senses of the word: magical and perfectly closed. It would be presumptuous to try to offer an interpretation here. Rather, let us follow the advice Gabriel gives Clemens in Hofmannsthal's own "Gespräch über Gedichte" (see p. 295) and restrain for once our urge to ascertain precise meanings.*

Ballade des äußeren Lebens

Und Kinder wachsen auf mit tiefen Augen,
Die von nichts wissen,[1] wachsen auf und sterben,
Und alle Menschen gehen ihre Wege.

Und süße Früchte werden aus den herben
Und fallen nachts wie tote Vögel nieder   5
Und liegen wenig Tage und verderben.

---

[9]'smiles at his companions'

*Those who may wish to pursue the matter further are directed to Richard Exner, *Hugo von Hofmannsthals "Lebenslied": eine Studie* (Heidelberg: Winter, 1964), and "Zu Hugo von Hofmannsthals 'Lebenslied': Einige Addenda und Hinweise zum Verständnis des Gedichts," *Hofmannsthal-Blätter* 12 (1974): 439-453, as well as Jost Schneider, *Alte und neue Sprechweisen: Untersuchungen zur Sprachthematik in den Gedichten Hugo von Hofmannsthals*, Bochumer Schriften 18 (Frankfurt a. M.: Lang, 1989), 338-362.

[1]*Die Augen der Kinder w i s s e n von nichts, aber sie a h n e n viel; sie sind "tief."*

Und immer weht der Wind, und immer wieder
Vernehmen[2] wir und reden viele Worte
Und spüren Lust und Müdigkeit der Glieder.

Und Straßen laufen durch das Gras, und Orte   10
Sind da und dort, voll Fackeln, Bäumen, Teichen,
Und drohende, und totenhaft verdorrte[3] . . .

Wozu sind diese[4] aufgebaut? und gleichen
Einander nie? und sind unzählig viele?
Was wechselt Lachen, Weinen und Erbleichen?[5]   15

Was frommt das alles uns[6] und diese Spiele,
Die wir[7] doch groß[8] und ewig einsam sind
Und wandernd nimmer suchen irgend Ziele?[9]

Was frommt's, dergleichen viel gesehen haben?
Und dennoch sagt der viel, der „Abend" sagt,   20
Ein Wort, daraus Tiefsinn und Trauer rinnt

Wie schwerer Honig aus den hohlen Waben.[10]

Hofmannsthal's "Ballade des äußeren Lebens" is "modern" poetry with a vengeance. One should neither expect nor be satisfied with a facile explanation. We can refer here only to a few central aspects.

First of all, what is implied by calling such a completely non-narrative poem a "ballad"? Perhaps this: A ballad concerns itself with externals; at most, it interprets an inward state (typically heroism) by overt acts; in our poem life is seen from the outside — it is a "ballad of external life." "External" of course implies "internal." Here, that which is outward is passed in review before an inner court of judgment, thus establishing a tension which determines the poem's structure. This is the "ballad" life sings to us. Even more important, however, is the following consideration. "Ballad" comes from *balar* 'to dance' (the word is of Provençal origin).* Originally, ballads

---

[2]The object of *vernehmen* is *Worte*. [3]It is not certain what *drohende* and *verdorrte* modify, perhaps *Orte*, but not necessarily. [4]The referent of *diese* is also uncertain; probably *all* the phenomena enumerated in the preceding stanzas are meant, not just the *Orte*, for seen "outwardly" all forms have a mechanical aspect, seem *aufgebaut*. [5]At least two renderings of this line are possible: either, 'What is it that keeps changing from laughing to weeping to blanching?' or, 'Why this constant change from ... ?' The second rendering seems to fit the context. [6]'What good's all that to us ... ?' [7]'We who' [8]= *erwachsen, reif* [9]'And without ever expecting to find any goal wander on' [10]'honeycombs'

*It is not improbable that "Ballade des äußeren Lebens" (*Ballade=Tanzlied*) is Hofmannsthal's answer to Nietzsche's "Tanzlieder" in *Zarathustra* (II and III), both of which end, like "Ballade," with the highly significant word *Abend*.

were songs sung to be danced to. Here something inward must dance to something outward. *Das äußere Leben* provides the dance song, the ballad, for *das innere Leben*.

Certain to strike our attention immediately is the use of the conjunction *und* in this poem. *Und* is the most primitive of conjunctons — it adds one thing to another, nothing more. It is the conjunction of children. But one realizes that Hofmannsthal uses it in a very unnaive fashion as soon as one sees that the poem *begins* with *und*, thereby implying that those things specifically mentioned are merely links in an endless chain of things that might have been mentioned (which is hardly a naive idea). Only some of the phenomena of "external life" are singled out. The points of suspension at the end of the fourth tercet show that the chain (*und - und - und*) could be continued indefinitely. The verse form, *terza rima*, is by nature unending, and of course points to the same thing.

The enumeration of aspects of "outward life" ends (or is dropped) with the fourth tercet. With the fifth there is a change of key. Some "I" or "We," some inner seat of judgment, poses a series of impatient, almost despairing, questions about the meaning of all these externalities. The questions seem to imply that outward life *has* no meaning, or is at any rate unfathomable and profitless to try to fathom. What is the sense of individuation ("manyness")? Why all these masks, these "games"? Are we not "grown up" and "eternally lonely," incapable of being amused by this play with its countless roles whose end is always death and decay (*wachsen auf und sterben; fallen nieder und verderben; spüren Müdigkeit der Glieder; totenhaft verdorrte*)? Why this "and – and – and"? And yet . . .

> *Und dennoch sagt der viel, der „Abend" sagt. . . .*

Though this verse may sound precious on first reading, Hofmannsthal is not trying to palm off on us some mystique of the word. He who says "evening" in the way of the poem has found the positive aspect of all this seemingly senseless, marionette-like outwardness presented in such eerie foreshortening in the first tercets (with nothing between growing up and dying, ripening and rotting). To put it in theological language (but not in language ungermane to Hofmannsthal, who in his prose speaks of *der Abend als Erfüllung: etwas Millenarisches*), the eschatology of the first six tercets receives a chiliastic interpretation in the last three lines. That is, the doctrine of last things (eschatology) — and here all externals are seen as "last things" — is now viewed from the standpoint of the fulfillment of time, the end is seen as the millenium (chiliasm) and "evening,"* even the evenings of this life of and-and-and,

---

*The many poems of evening in the literature of the West (several included in this book) certainly contribute to the emotional aura of the word, even if they do not interpret it in the sense of our poem.

becomes a symbol of fulfillment. To "say" evening in this way is to sense a oneness at the core of all this manyness. The *Tiefsinn und Trauer* that flows from this word is our deep melancholy over life's "outwardness." Yet this melancholy flows like "heavy honey." It is heavy with the insight that an evening without "and" will finally come. The honey flows from the hollow cells of "external life." Without this life there would be nowhere for us to store the honey of our insight, and "evening" would be without meaning.

Reiselied

Wasser stürzt, uns zu verschlingen,
Rollt der Fels, uns zu erschlagen,
Kommen schon auf starken Schwingen
Vögel her, uns fortzutragen.

Aber unten liegt ein Land,   5
Früchte spiegelnd ohne Ende
In den alterslosen Seen.

Marmorstirn und Brunnenrand
Steigt aus blumigem Gelände,
Und die leichten Winde wehn.   10

Towards Interpretation
1. Read this poem aloud several times, then, *disregarding the imagery,* try to determine how the effect of two completely different worlds is achieved here.

Verse zum Gedächtnis des Schauspielers Josef Kainz

O hätt ich seine Stimme, hier um ihn
Zu klagen! Seinen königlichen Anstand,[1]
Mit meiner Klage dazustehn vor euch!
Dann wahrlich wäre diese Stunde groß
Und Glanz und Königtum auf mir, und mehr   5
Als Trauer: denn dem Tun der Könige
Ist Herrlichkeit und Jubel beigemengt,
Auch wo sie klagen und ein Totenfest begehn.

O seine Stimme, daß sie unter uns
Die Flügel schlüge! — Woher tönte sie?   10

---

[1]'dignity'

Woher drang dies an unser Ohr? Wer sprach
Mit solcher Zunge? Welcher Fürst und Dämon
Sprach da zu uns? Wer sprach von diesen Brettern[2]
Herab? Wer redete da aus dem Leib
Des Jünglings Romeo, wer aus dem Leib   15
Des unglückseligen Richard Plantagenet[3]
Oder des Tasso?[4] Wer?
Ein Unverwandelter in viel Verwandlungen,
Ein niebezauberter Bezauberer,
Ein Ungerührter, der uns rührte, einer,   20
Der fern war, da wir meinten, er sei nah,
Ein Fremdling über allen Fremdlingen,
Einsamer über allen Einsamen,
Der Bote aller Boten, namenlos
Und Bote eines namenlosen Herrn.   25

Er ist an uns vorüber. Seine Seele
War eine allzu schnelle Seele, und
Sein Aug glich allzusehr dem Aug des Vogels.
Dies Haus[5] hat ihn gehabt — doch hielt es ihn?
Wir haben ihn gehabt — er fiel dahin,   30
Wie unsre eigne Jugend uns entfällt,
Grausam und prangend gleich dem Wassersturz.

O Unrast! O Geheimnis, offenkundiges
Geheimnis menschlicher Natur! O Wesen,
Wer warest du? O Schweifender! O Fremdling!   35
O nächtlicher Gespräche Einsamkeit
Mit deinen höchst zufälligen Genossen!
O starrend[6] tiefe Herzenseinsamkeit!
O ruheloser Geist! Geist ohne Schlaf!
O Geist! O Stimme! Wundervolles Licht!   40
Wie du hinliefest, weißes Licht, und rings
Ins Dunkel aus den Worten dir Paläste
Hinbautest, drin für eines Herzschlags Frist[7]
Wir mit dir wohnten — Stimme, die wir nie
Vergessen werden — o Geschick — o Ende —   45
Geheimnisvolles Leben! Dunkler Tod!

O wie das Leben um ihn rang und niemals
Ihn ganz verstricken konnte ins Geheimnis

---

[2]"these boards" are the stage of the Wiener Hofburg-Theater. [3]in Shakespeare's *Richard II* [4]in Goethe's play by the same name [5]i.e., the *Burg-Theater*, but also of course life itself [6]'trance-like' [7]'for the space of a heartbeat'

Wollüstiger Verwandlung! Wie er *blieb*!
Wie königlich er standhielt! Wie er schmal,[8]   50
Gleich einem Knaben, *stand*! O kleine Hand
Voll Kraft, o kleines Haupt auf feinen Schultern,
O vogelhaftes Auge, das verschmähte,[9]
Jung oder alt zu sein, schlafloses Aug,
O Aug des Sperbers,[10] der auch vor der Sonne   55
Den Blick nicht niederschlägt, o kühnes Aug,
Das beiderlei Abgrund[11] gemessen hat,
Des Lebens wie des Todes — Aug des *Boten*!
O Bote aller Boten, Geist! Du Geist!
Dein Bleiben unter uns war ein Verschmähen,   60
Fortwollender! Enteilter! Aufgeflogener!

Ich klage nicht um dich. Ich weiß jetzt, wer du warst,
Schauspieler ohne Maske du, Vergeistiger,[12]
Du bist empor, und wo mein Auge dich
Nicht sieht, dort kreisest du dem Sperber gleich,   65
Dem Unzerstörbaren,[13] und hältst in Fängen[14]
Den Spiegel, der ein weißes Licht herabwirft,
Weißer als Licht der Sterne: dieses Lichtes
Bote und Träger bist du immerdar,
Und als des[15] Schwebend-Unzerstörbaren   70
Gedenken wir des Geistes, der du bist.

O Stimme! Seele! aufgeflogene!

Towards Interpretation

1. Trace the use of bird imagery in this poem, noting the other images with which it is associated. (Remember that bird *imagery* may be present even if there is no specific mention of a bird.)
2. Angels are usually thought of as winged beings. Look up the etymology of the word "angel."
3. The basic theme of these verses is the same as that of "Ballade des äußeren Lebens," namely, the problem of individuation. Point this out in detail. (What is at the core of all *Verwandlungen*?)
4. In eulogizing Kainz does Hofmannsthal euologize a man?

---

[8]'slim' [9]'disdained' [10]'sparrow-hawk' [11]'both abysses' [12]'enspiriter' [13]cf. lines 55f.
[14]'claws' [15]genitive with *gedenken* 'remember,' 'think of')

Alfred Mombert (1872-1942)

„Einsames Land! Einsamer Baum darinnen!"

Einsames Land! Einsamer Baum darinnen!
Süß ist das Stehn und Sinnen
unter deinen Zweigen.
Aus deinen Wipfeln sinkt es nieder,
das Selig-Dämmernde und Schweigende.   5
Die Hände strecke ich aus, und sie füllen sich
mit unsichtbaren Blättern, und ich fühle das ganz
im reifgewordenen Herzen.
O Baum, an deinem Stamm, unter deinen Zweigen
ward ich ein blinder Mann, und sammle ein   10
die Gaben, die aus deinen Wipfeln niedersinken.
Das Herrlichste, es sinkt mir auf das Haupt,
und auf die Schultern, liegt zu meinen Füßen.
Es verschüttet mich.
Reicht eine Harfe! Das Tief-Ewige   15
umschauert mich.

Es dringt ein Glanz herein in meine Nacht.
Das muß die Träne sein, die draußen auf der Schwelle
des Hauses lagert und den Mond anblickt.
Reicht mir die Harfe! Glänzender war ich nie!   20
Schließt die Pforten auf! öffnet die Fenster!
Ihr Alle, Alle, kommt zum großen Fest!

During the campaign in the Balkans in World War I the poet Hans Carossa had no other reading material than a volume of Mombert's verse. In *Führung und Geleit* he relates the following incident:

Mein Exemplar des Mombertschen Werkes war nur geheftet [paperback] und fiel allmählich in einzelne Bogen auseinander. Einen verlor ich beim Lesen am Biwakfeuer; ein Feldwebelleutnant [first sergeant] bemerkte es, hob ihn auf, sah hinein, schüttelte den Kopf und fragte, was denn das wäre. Schon wollte ich Auskunft geben, besann mich aber und sagte, dies seien Übersetzungen aus dem Sanskrit, uralte indische Gedichte, vor etwa zweitausend Jahren geschrieben. Der einselbige Mann, ein Buchbinder aus Würzburg, nahm nunmehr die Blätter, die er schon zurückgeben wollte, ehrfürchtig noch einmal an sich und studierte mit krauser Stirn die geheimnisvollen Zeilen. — „Das waren noch Kerle, diese Sanskritiker", meinte er schließlich, „die haben mehr von der Welt gewußt als wir." Ich gab ihm recht, und er erbot sich, mir in seinem nächsten Urlaub das ganze Buch in Pergament oder Leder zu binden; doch fand er drei Wochen später am Berg Runkulmare den Tod.

Rainer Maria Rilke (1875-1926)

Perhaps no modern poet, certainly no modern German poet, has extended the boundaries of human consciousness through the resources inherent in language as has Rilke. For those who have read Rilke the world is different from the way it was before. This remains true even if we reject what are sometimes called his "false ideas," such as *besitzlose Liebe*, and *der eigene Tod*. It remains true even if we reject the religious implications of such a central idea as the singer-god.

Rilke as the founder of a religion — for it is as hardly less than this that he is revered in some circles — is indeed a dubious figure. Since the decay of faith (brought into the open by Nietzsche, but not of course brought about by him) great and compelling poets of unorthodox belief have again and again been regarded as *Religionsstifter*. Rilke does not seem to have been averse to the role.

Central to understanding Rilke is the recognition of the unheard-of emphasis he places on feeling as a transmuting force. For him, feeling *c'est le propre de l'homme*. Through feeling we can transform the world into spirit, in Rilke's language, make it "invisible," and thus, paradoxically, save it, keep it from slipping away, for it will then be in a realm beyond space and time, *aufgehoben* forever. (The parallel with Hegel and German Idealism will be apparent to every student of philosophy.) For Rilke (as for Fichte), the world is man's "task." The world is here to be felt and we are in the world to feel it. We *can* feel because of our awareness of transiency, that is, because we know death. Death is therefore Rilke's theme of themes. But for the poet feeling is not enough — he must also "say." In saying he shows the rest of mankind what is to be felt. Goethe would say, the poet *fühlt uns v o r*. In this way he extends the limits of our consciousness. And this is the poet's age-old mission.

From: *Das Buch der Bilder*

Der Schauende (1901)

Ich sehe den Bäumen die Stürme an,
die aus laugewordenen Tagen
an meine ängstlichen Fenster[1] schlagen,
und höre die Fernen Dinge sagen,
die ich nicht ohne Freund ertragen,   5
nicht ohne Schwester[2] lieben kann.

Da geht der Sturm, ein Umgestalter,
geht durch den Wald und durch die Zeit,
und alles ist wie ohne Alter:
die Landschaft, wie ein Vers im Psalter,   10
ist Ernst und Wucht und Ewigkeit.[3]

Wie ist das klein, womit wir ringen,
was mit uns ringt, wie ist das groß;
ließen wir, ähnlicher den Dingen,
uns *so* vom großen Sturm bezwingen, —   15
wir würden weit und namenlos.[4]

Was wir besiegen, ist das Kleine,
und der Erfolg selbst macht uns klein.
Das Ewige und Ungemeine
will nicht von uns gebogen sein.   20
Das ist der Engel, der den Ringern
des Alten Testaments erschien:[5]
wenn seiner Wiedersacher Sehnen
im Kampfe sich metallen dehnen,
fühlt er sie unter seinen Fingern   25
wie Saiten tiefer Melodien.[6]

Wen dieser Engel überwand,
welcher so oft auf Kampf verzichtet,[7]
der geht gerecht und aufgerichtet
und groß aus jener harten Hand,   30
die sich, wie formend, an ihn schmiegte.

---

[1]i.e., the *Angst* of the poet at the window is attributed to the window [2]Not necessarily a sibling. [3]The wind transforms the landscape, rendering it unfamiliar and "ageless." [4]As the landscape becomes ageless, so would we become "nameless," no longer subsumed under a name; we would exceed ourselves. [5]Genesis 32:24-32. [6]The strings are the sinews, deep beneath the skin and deep within the wrestler, who becomes the instrument on which the angel plays. [7]Many the angel disdains to wrestle with.

Die Siege laden ihn nicht ein.
Sein Wachstum ist: der Tiefbesiegte
von immer Größerem zu sein.

Herbst (1902)

Die Blätter fallen, fallen wie von weit,
als welkten in den Himmeln ferne Gärten;
sie fallen mit verneinender Gebärde.

Und in den Nächten fällt die schwere Erde
aus allen Sternen in die Einsamkeit.   5

Wir alle fallen. Diese Hand da fällt.
Und sieh dir andre an: es ist in allen.

Und doch ist Einer, welcher dieses Fallen
unendlich sanft in seinen Händen hält.

Herbsttag (1902)

Herr: es ist Zeit. Der Sommer war sehr groß.
Leg deinen Schatten auf die Sonnenuhren,
und auf den Fluren laß die Winde los.

Befiehl den letzten Früchten voll zu sein;
gieb ihnen noch zwei südlichere Tage,   5
dränge sie zur Vollendung hin und jage
die letzte Süße in den schweren Wein.

Wer jetzt kein Haus hat, baut sich keines mehr.
Wer jetzt allein ist, wird es lange bleiben,
wird wachen, lesen, lange Briefe schreiben   10
und wird in den Alleen hin und her
unruhig wandern, wenn die Blätter treiben.

Der Einsame (1903)

Wie einer, der auf fremden Meeren fuhr,
so bin ich bei den ewig Einheimischen;[1]
die vollen Tage stehn auf ihren Tischen,
mir aber ist die Ferne voll Figur.

---

[1]'those eternally at home, native everywhere'

In mein Gesicht reicht eine Welt herein,   5
die vielleicht unbewohnt ist wie ein Mond,
sie aber lassen kein Gefühl allein,
und alle ihre Worte sind bewohnt.

Die Dinge, die ich weither mit mir nahm,
sehn selten aus, gehalten an² das Ihre — :   10
in ihrer³ großen Heimat sind sie Tiere,
hier halten sie den Atem an vor Scham.

Towards Interpretation

1. What criticism is implied in saying that "the full days stand on the tables" of the "ewig Einheimischen" and that "all their words are inhabited"?

2. Is an animal that "holds its breath in shame" an animal? What happens to the things the Solitary brings with him from afar? What do you take these things to be?

3. In the three preceding poems, show how the rime schemes contribute to the sense of the poems.

From: *Neue Gedichte* (1907-08)

Adam

Staunend steht er an der Kathedrale
steilem Aufstieg, nah der Fensterrose,¹
wie erschreckt von der Apotheose,
welche wuchs und ihn mit einem Male

niederstellte über die und die.   5
Und er ragt und freut sich seiner Dauer
schlicht entschlossen;² als der Ackerbauer
der begann, und der nicht wußte, wie

aus dem fertig-vollen Garten Eden
einen Ausweg in die neue Erde   10
finden. Gott war schwer zu überreden;

und er drohte ihm,³ statt zu gewähren,
immer wieder, daß er sterben werde,
doch der Mensch bestand:⁴ sie⁵ wird gebären.

---

²'compared to' ³refers to *Dinge*

¹Flanking the great rose window of Notre Dame de Paris are the statues of Adam and Eve. ²'determined, like the plain man that he is' ³Adam ⁴'refused to give in' ⁵=*die neue Erde* (but also Eve)

Eva

Einfach steht sie an der Kathedrale
großem Aufstieg, nah der Fensterrose,
mit dem Apfel in der Apfelpose,[1]
schuldlos-schuldig ein für alle Male

an dem Wachsenden, das sie gebar,   5
seit sie aus dem Kreis der Ewigkeiten
liebend fortging, um sich durchzustreiten
durch die Erde, wie ein junges Jahr.[2]

Ach, sie hätte gern in jenem Land
noch ein wenig weilen mögen, achtend   10
auf der Tiere Eintracht und Verstand.

Doch da sie den Mann entschlossen fand,
ging sie mit ihm, nach dem Tode trachtend,[3]
und sie hatte Gott noch kaum gekannt.

Towards Interpretation

1. Is Adam, as Rilke sees him, one of the *ewig Einheimischen*? If Adam
   is *d e r Mensch*, what does this imply about Rilke's conception of
   man?
2. What reasons can you suggest for the changes Rilke makes in the
   story of man's expulsion from the Garden?

Liebes-Lied

Wie soll ich meine Seele halten, daß
sie nicht an deine rührt? Wie soll ich sie
hinheben über dich zu andern Dingen?
Ach gerne möcht ich sie bei irgendwas
Verlorenem im Dunkel unterbringen   5
an einer fremden Stelle, die
nicht weiterschwingt,[1] wenn deine Tiefen schwingen.
Doch alles, was uns anrührt, dich und mich,

---

[1]The traditional way Eve holds the apple is the "apple pose." [2]The year is subject to
change; Eve leaves the *Kreis der Ewigkeiten* to enter the realm of time. [3]*trachten* (fr.
Lat. *tractare*) 'strive,' 'seek'; cf. *trächtig* (fr. *tragen*) 'pregnant,' 'fertile.' Though the
two words are not etymologically related, Rilke probably intends that we hear overtones of *trächtig* in *trachten*: Eve must die to give life.

[1]'continues to vibrate'

nimmt uns zusammen wie ein Bogenstrich,[2]
der aus zwei Saiten *eine* Stimme zieht.   10
Auf welches Instrument sind wir gespannt?
Und welcher Geiger hat uns in der Hand?
O süßes Lied.

Towards Interpretation

1. Note the unobstrusiveness of the rimes in the first seven lines of this poem. How is this effect achieved?
2. Note how definite and immediately noticeable are the rimes of the last six lines. How is this achieved? Account for this formal difference on the basis of the content.

Der Tod der Geliebten

Er wußte nur vom Tod was alle wissen:
daß er uns nimmt und in das Stumme stößt.
Als aber sie,[1] nicht von ihm fortgerissen,
nein, leis aus seinen Augen ausgelöst,

hinüberglitt zu unbekannten Schatten,   5
und als er fühlte, daß sie drüben[2] nun
wie einen Mond ihr Mädchenlächeln hatten
und ihre Weise wohlzutun:[3]

da wurden ihm die Toten so bekannt,
als wäre er durch sie[4] mit einem jeden   10
ganz nah verwandt; er ließ die andern reden

und glaubte nicht und nannte jenes Land
das gutgelegene, das immersüße —
Und tastete es ab für ihre[4] Füße.

---

[2]'stroke of a violin bow'

[1]=*die Geliebte* [2]'those over on the other side' (the shades) [3]'her way of making one feel good' [4]refers to *die Geliebte*

Die Spitze[1]

I

Menschlichkeit: Namen schwankender Besitze,
noch unbestätigter Bestand von Glück:
ist das unmenschlich, daß zu dieser Spitze,
zu diesem kleinen dichten Spitzenstück
zwei Augen wurden? — Willst du sie zurück?   5

Du Langvergangene und schließlich Blinde,
ist deine Seligkeit in diesem Ding,
zu welcher hin, wie zwischen Stamm und Rinde,
dein großes Fühlen, kleinverwandelt, ging?

Durch einen Riß im Schicksal, eine Lücke   10
entzogst du deine Seele deiner Zeit;
und sie ist so in diesem lichten Stücke,
daß es mich lächeln macht vor Nützlichkeit.

II

Und wenn uns eines Tages dieses Tun[2]
und was an uns geschieht gering erschiene
und uns so fremd, als ob es nicht verdiene,
daß wir so mühsam aus den Kinderschuhn
um seinetwillen wachsen — : Ob die Bahn[3]   5
vergilbter Spitze, diese dichtgefügte
blumige Spitzenbahn, dann nicht genügte,
uns hier zu halten? Sieh: sie ward *getan*.

Ein Leben ward vielleicht verschmäht, wer weiß?
Ein Glück war da und wurde hingegeben,   10
und endlich wurde doch, um jeden Preis,
dies Ding daraus, nicht leichter als das Leben
und doch vollendet und so schön als sei's
nicht mehr zu früh, zu lächeln und zu schweben.

Towards Interpretation
1. What specifically is meant by saying that two eyes became a piece of lace?
2. What gives the poet the right to speak of the lace-maker's *großes Fühlen*? What is meant by calling it *kleinverwandelt*?

---

[1] '(piece of) lace'

[2] all human activity   [3] 'length'

3. In what sense was the lace-maker a poet even if she wrote no poetry? (Compare introductory remarks on Rilke.)
4. Why does this piece of lace make Rilke so happy?

Früher Apollo

Wie manches Mal durch das noch unbelaubte
Gezweig ein Morgen durchsieht, der schon ganz
im Frühling ist: so ist in seinem[1] Haupte
nichts was verhindern könnte, daß der Glanz

aller Gedichte uns fast tödlich träfe;   5
denn noch kein Schatten ist in seinem Schaun,
zu kühl für Lorbeer sind noch seine Schläfe[2]
und später erst wird aus den Augenbraun

hochstämmig sich der Rosengarten heben,
aus welchem Blätter, einzeln, ausgelöst   10
hintreiben werden auf des Mundes Beben,

der jetzt noch still ist, niegebraucht und blinkend
und nur mit seinem Lächeln[3] etwas trinkend
als würde ihm sein Singen eingeflößt.[4]

Towards Interpretation

1. This poem concerns something in a state of becoming. What in the *structure* of the poem reinforces and illustrates the theme? How is this shown in the *imagery*?
2. Who is the implied speaker of the poem? Where does he seem to be?

---

[1]Apollo's [2]'temples' [3]The famous "archaic smile" of early Greek statues. [4]*jemandem etwas einflößen* 'administer something to someone' and 'inspire someone with something' Both meanings are active here. (Understanding this poem is mainly a matter of carefully following the metaphor: an early representation of Apollo, the god of song, is compared to bare branches in early spring; as we sometimes feel in early spring that the season is more advanced than the foliage shows [full spring through bare branches], so do we feel before this early statue of the god the spring of song that he portends.)

Der Panther
Im Jardin des Plantes, Paris

Sein Blick ist vom Vorübergehn der Stäbe
so müd geworden, daß er[1] nichts mehr hält.
Ihm ist, als ob es tausend Stäbe gäbe
und hinter tausend Stäben keine Welt.

Der weiche Gang geschmeidig starker Schritte,   5
der sich im allerkleinsten Kreise dreht,
ist wie ein Tanz von Kraft um eine Mitte,
in der betäubt ein großer Wille steht.

Nur manchmal schiebt der Vorhang der Pupille
sich lautlos auf —. Dann geht ein Bild hinein,   10
geht durch der Glieder angespannte Stille —
und hört im Herzen auf zu sein.

Towards Interpretation

1. See if you can show coincidence of rhythm and situation in this poem. What about vowel symbolism? alliteration?
2. Could the situation in this poem be applied to other creatures? To the human condition?

Römische Fontäne
Borghese

Zwei Becken, eins das andre übersteigend
aus einem alten runden Marmorrand,
und aus dem oberen Wasser leis sich neigend
zum Wasser, welches unten wartend stand,

dem leise redenden entgegenschweigend   5
und heimlich, gleichsam in der hohlen Hand,
ihm Himmel hinter Grün und Dunkel zeigend
wie einen unbekannten Gegenstand;

sich selber ruhig in der schönen Schale
verbreitend ohne Heimweh, Kreis aus Kreis,   10
nur manchmal träumerisch und tropfenweis

sich niederlassend an den Moosehängen
zum letzten Spiegel, der sein Becken leis
von unten lächeln macht mit Übergängen.

---

[1] i.e., *Blick*

Towards Interpretation

1. Look at the rimes in the octet and explain the function of the *end*-rimes as compared to the *and*-rimes?
2. Compare this poem to Meyer's "Der römische Brunnen." How does the identical poetic object result in different poetic visions? In which poem does one sense the speaker's presence more?

Archäischer Torso Apollos

Wir kannten nicht sein unerhörtes Haupt,
darin die Augenäpfel[1] reiften. Aber
sein Torso glüht noch wie ein Kandelaber,
in dem sein Schauen, nur zurückgeschraubt,[2]

sich hält und glänzt. Sonst könnte nicht der Bug[3]   5
der Brust dich blenden, und im leisen Drehen
der Lenden könnte nicht ein Lächeln gehen
zu jener Mitte, die die Zeugung[4] trug.

Sonst stünde dieser Stein entstellt[5] und kurz
unter der Schultern durchsichtigem Sturz[6]   10
und flimmerte nicht so wie Raubtierfelle;

und bräche nicht aus allen seinen Rändern
aus wie ein Stern: denn da ist keine Stelle,
die dich nicht sieht. Du mußt dein Leben ändern.

Towards Interpretation

1. One might say that the whole poem is a justification of the adjective *unerhört* ('incredible') in line 1. The argumentation is built up almost like a syllogism. Trace the development of the argument in the clauses beginning with *Aber* . . ., *Sonst*. . ., *Sonst*. . ., and *denn*. . . .
2. What is missing from this torso besides the head? Why then isn't this torso "entstellt" (line 9)?
3. The poem purports to be about the *Torso*, but it could well be about us. *Why* must we change our lives?
4. How does Rilke reverse the normal relationship between the work of art and the viewer of art?

---

[1]'eyeballs' [2]*zurückschrauben* 'turn down (a light)' [3]'curve' [4]'organ of procreation'
[5]'disfigured' [6]perhaps a play on words: *Sturz* 'plunge' – *Glassturz* 'glass bell jar'

Das Karussell
Jardin du Luxembourg

Mit einem Dach und seinem Schatten dreht
sich eine kleine Weile der Bestand
von bunten Pferden, alle aus dem Land,
das lange zögert, eh es untergeht.
Zwar manche sind an Wagen angespannt,   5
doch alle haben Mut in ihren Mienen;
ein böser roter Löwe geht mit ihnen
und dann und wann ein weißer Elefant.

Sogar ein Hirsch ist da, ganz wie im Wald,
nur daß er einen Sattel trägt und drüber   10
ein kleines blaues Mädchen aufgeschnallt.

Und auf dem Löwen reitet weiß ein Junge
und hält sich mit der kleinen heißen Hand,
dieweil der Löwe Zähne zeigt und Zunge.

Und dann und wann ein weißer Elefant.   15

Und auf den Pferden kommen sie vorüber,
auch Mädchen, helle, diesem Pferdesprunge
fast schon entwachsen; mitten in dem Schwunge
schauen sie auf, irgendwohin, herüber —

Und dann und wann ein weißer Elefant.   20

Und das geht hin und eilt sich, daß es endet,
und kreist und dreht sich nur und hat kein Ziel.
Ein Rot, ein Grün, ein Grau vorbeigesendet,
ein kleines kaum begonnenes Profil — .
Und manchesmal ein Lächeln, hergewendet,   25
ein seliges, das blendet und verschwendet,
an dieses atemlose blinde Spiel . . .

Poems such as these and many others in the *Neue Gedichte* are often called
Dinggedichte (the term is not Rilke's). Obviously, a "thing" in this sense is
not quite what we usually designate by the term. It is anything that is not us. It
may be a person in a certain capacity (beggar, nun), an animal, plant, city. The
Dinggedicht strives to regard such "things" in their quiddity or "whatness,"
i.e., their essence. What *is* a merry-go-round, a caged panther, a statue of
Apollo, Venice, a blind beggar? Complete bracketing out of any subjective element seems to be Rilke's aim, though it may be doubtful whether he achieves
it. Nor do his *Dinggedichte* seem to be meant symbolically, though a symbolical interpretation sometimes forces itself upon us (it is hard not to see "Das
Karussell," for example, as an image of childhood.) In the language of the

Duino Elegies (composed some time after the poems in the *Neue Gedichte*), what the *Dinggedichte* attempt is to "say" things with such fervor and meaning that these things are changed (*verwandelt*) into us (and we into them), so that the earth may come into being "invisibly within us."

> . . . Sind wir vielleicht *hier*, um zu sagen: Haus,
> Brücke, Brunnen, Tor, Krug, Obstbaum, Fenster, —
> höchstens: Säule, Turm . . . . aber zu *sagen*, verstehs,
> oh zu sagen *so*, wie selber die Dinge niemals
> innig meinten zu sein. . . .

When he wrote the poems in the *Neue Gedichte*, Rilke may not have been as fully conscious of the metaphysical import of "saying" things as he is in these lines from the Ninth Elegy, but there can be little doubt that in many of the *Dinggedichte* a "*Verwandlung*" *is* achieved and that the things of this earth take on a new dimension within us through his poetry, that is, through his having "said" them.

Spätherbst in Venedig

Nun treibt[1] die Stadt schon nicht mehr wie ein Köder,[2]
der alle aufgetauchten Tage fängt.
Die gläsernen Paläste klingen spröder[3]
an deinen Blick. Und aus den Gärten hängt

der Sommer wie ein Haufen Marionetten   5
kopfüber, müde, umgebracht.[4]
Aber vom Grund aus alten Waldskeletten
steigt Willen auf:[5] als sollte über Nacht

der General des Meeres die Galeeren
verdoppeln in dem wachen Arsenal,   10
um schon die nächste Morgenluft zu teeren[6]

mit einer Flotte, welche ruderschlagend
sich drängt und jäh, mit allen Flaggen tagend,[7]
den großen Wind hat, strahlend und fatal.

Towards Interpretation
1. Compare Venice as seen in this sonnet with the Venice of Platen's "Venedig liegt nur noch im Land der Träume."

---

[1]'drifts' [2]'bait' [3]*spröde* =*abweisend, gefühlskalt*, but also *leicht zerbrechlich* (the palaces are "glassy"). The image combines hearing, touch, and sound. [4]'done in' [5]Venice is built on a swamp. The *Waldskeletten* may be the sunken trees beneath it or the wooden piles on which the buildings rest or both. [6]'tar,' 'give a tarry smell' [7]*tagen* 'dawn,' 'rise' and 'assemble' (cf. *Reichstag*). Both meanings are active here.

From: *Das Marien-Leben* (1912)

Argwohn Josephs

Und der Engel sprach und gab sich Müh
an dem Mann, der seine Fäuste ballte:
Aber siehst du nicht an jeder Falte,
daß sie kühl ist wie die Gottesfrüh.[1]

Doch der andre sah ihn finster an,   5
murmelnd nur: Was hat sie so verwandelt?
Doch da schrie der Engel: Zimmermann,
merkst du's noch nicht, daß der Herrgott handelt?

Weil du Bretter machst, in deinem Stolze,
willst du wirklich *den* zur Rede stelln,   10
der bescheiden aus dem gleichen Holze
Blätter treiben macht und Knospen schwelln?

Er begriff. Und wie er jetzt die Blicke,
recht erschrocken, zu dem Engel hob,
war der fort. Da schob er seine dicke   15
Mütze langsam ab.[2] Dann sang er lob.

Pietà[1]

Jetzt wird mein Elend voll, und namenlos
erfüllt es mich. Ich starre wie des Steins
Inneres starrt.
Hart wie ich bin, weiß ich nur Eins:
Du wurdest groß —   5
. . . . . . und wurdest groß,
um als zu großer Schmerz
ganz über meines Herzens Fassung
hinauszustehn.
Jetzt liegst du quer durch meinen Schooß,[2]   10
jetzt kann ich dich nicht mehr
gebären.

---

[1]'God's early morn'; *sie* is Mary.   [2]A Jew would normally *cover* his head to pray!

[1]A *pietà* is a representation of Mary holding the body of the crucified Christ.
[2]Remember that *Scho(o)ß* means both 'lap' and 'womb.'

Towards Interpretation
1. Mary is again pregnant. What is she pregnant with? Why can she not give birth?

From: *Gedichte aus den Jahren 1906 bis 1926*

Christi Höllenfahrt[1] (1913)

Endlich verlitten,[2] entging sein Wesen dem schrecklichen
Leibe der Leiden. Oben. Ließ ihn.
Und die Finsternis fürchtete sich allein
und warf an das Bleiche[3]
Fledermäuse heran, — immer noch schwankt abends   5
in ihrem Flattern die Angst vor dem Anprall
an die erkaltete Qual.[4] Dunkle ruhlose Luft
entmutigte sich an dem Leichnam; und in den starken
wachsamen Tieren der Nacht war Dumpfheit und Unlust.
Sein entlassener[5] Geist gedachte vielleicht in der Landschaft   10
anzustehen, unhandelnd. Denn seiner Leidung[6] Ereignis
war noch genug. Maßvoll[7]
schien ihm der Dinge nächtliches Dastehn,
und wie ein trauriger Raum griff er darüber um sich.[8]
Aber die Erde, vertrocknet im Durst seiner Wunden,[9]   15
aber die Erde riß auf,[10] und es rufte[11] im Abgrund.
Er, Kenner der Martern, hörte die Hölle
herheulend, begehrend Bewußtsein
seiner vollendeten Not: daß über dem Ende der seinen

---

[1]'Harrowing of Hell' After the crucifixion Christ descended into Hell and took from Limbus the souls of the worthy people of the Old Testament. Allusions to this event are found in Ephesians 4:9; I Peter 3:19 and 4:6. Rilke's version hardly follows Church doctrine. [2]i.e., *nachdem das Endliche ausgelitten war.* [3]=*das Bleiche des Leichnams* [4]Verses 5-7: Rilke here creates a myth explaining the erratic darting flight of bats. The "agony grown cold" is the body on the cross. [5]The spirit was both 'freed' and 'dismissed,' for it had done its task (of taking on flesh). [6]*Leidung* is Rilke's coinage making a verbal noun out of *Leid.* [7]Not 'moderate' but 'measure-full' (*das Maß*). In the Passion creation's measure was fulfilled; hence the early Christians momentarily awaited the end of the world. [8]The spirit of the Crucified begins to include everything about it; in much less expressive language: all is filled with sadness at this death. [9]The earth is here identified with Christ's body. [10]Matthew 27:51. [11]=*rief* (Rilke wants *u* — why?)

(unendlichen) ihre, währende Pein erschrecke, ahne.[12]   20
Und er stürzte, der Geist, mit der völligen Schwere
seiner Erschöpfung[13] herein: schritt als ein Eilender
durch das befremdete Nachschaun weidender[14] Schatten,
hob zu Adam den Aufblick, eilig,
eilte hinab, schwand, schien und verging in dem Stürzen   25
wilderer Tiefen.[15] Plötzlich (höher höher) über der Mitte
aufschäumender Schreie, auf dem langen[16]
Turm seines Duldens trat er hervor: ohne Atem,
stand, ohne Geländer, Eigentümer der Schmerzen. Schwieg.

„Tränen, Tränen, die aus mir brechen" (1913)

Tränen, Tränen, die aus mir brechen.
Mein Tod,[1] Mohr, Träger
meines Herzens, halte mich schräger,[2]
daß sie abfließen. Ich will sprechen.

Schwarzer, riesiger Herzhalter.   5
Wenn ich auch spräche,
glaubst du denn, daß das Schweigen bräche?

Wiege mich, Alter.[3]

---

[12]Verses 19-20: Christ's suffering is *vollendet* in the double sense of 'perfect' and 'completed'; it is *unendlich* (though ended) because of its eternal meaning, whereas the suffering of those in Hell is neither: it is only a *währende Pein*. They, whose lot is constant suffering, want to know about perfect suffering. [13]*Erschöpfung* has multiple layers of meaning: the god incarnate is now *er-schöpft*, i.e., a) 'exhausted,' b) 'no longer in the flesh' (no longer a *Ge-schöpf*), c) in a state of having fulfilled the *Schöpfung* (er- indicating outcome or completion), this in turn being the cause of his *Erschöpfung*. Such plays on words are one of Rilke's chief stylistic devices. [14]Look up both *weiden* and *Augenweide*. [15]We are in a Dantesque Hell with circles ranged around the inside of a funnel-shaped crater; as one descends the depths grow ever "wilder." [16] Why not *hohen* or *großen*?

[1]vocative [2]*schräg* 'at an angle' [3]'old fellow'

„*Ausgesetzt auf den Bergen des Herzens*" (1914)

Ausgesetzt[1] auf den Bergen des Herzens. Siehe, wie klein
siehe: die letzte Ortschaft der Worte, und höher,[2]   [dort,
aber wie klein auch, noch ein letztes
Gehöft[3] von Gefühl. Erkennst du's?
Ausgesetzt auf den Bergen des Herzens. Steingrund   5
unter den Händen. Hier blüht wohl
einiges auf; aus stummem Absturz[4]
blüht ein unwissendes Kraut singend hervor.
Aber der Wissende? Ach, der zu wissen begann
und schweigt nun, ausgesetzt auf den Bergen des Herzens.   10
Da geht wohl, heilen Bewußtseins,[5]
manches umher, manches gesicherte Bergtier,
wechselt[6] und weilt. Und der große geborgene[7] Vogel
kreist um der Gipfel reine Verweigerung.[8] — Aber
ungeborgen, hier auf den Bergen des Herzens. . . .   15

This poem evokes an "inner landscape," the topography of the spirit in an
hour of crisis. The crisis seems to consist in this: how to sing though *wissend?*
(Note lines 8-10.) Though in Rilke's own case the crisis is probably of an artistic nature, its application is nonetheless general: how can we (how can
modern human beings) live with full heart and undivided mind knowing what
we do? As so often in Rilke — especially in his later work (this poem was
written in 1914) — the abstract is given in terms of the concrete: "mountains
of the heart" ("heart" is here shorthand for all things of the spirit), "last village of words," "farm of feeling." Thus the invisible is made visible, is discovered. Once the method has been established in the first part of the poem, it
is left to the reader to imagine what aspects of inwardness may be represented
by the *unwissendes Kraut*, the *gesichertes Bergtier*, the *großer, geborgner
Vogel* — all we are sure of is that these things refer inward, not outward. Here
the poet has not correlated the concrete and the abstract but simply left us with
not completely interpretable "real" things. Despite their cryptic nature, these
lines remain among the most unforgettable and most dismaying Rilke ever
wrote.

---

[1]'exposed,' 'left to die'   [2]Above the *Ortschaft der Worte* but below the speaker.
[3]'farmstead' [4]'(steep) declivity' [5]'with undivided (whole) consciousness' [6]'crosses'
(cf. deer-crossing) [7]=*sicher, behütet, nicht ausgesetzt* [8]'the pure denial of the peaks'

From: *Sonette an Orpheus* (1922)

„*Ist er ein Hiesiger?*"

Ist er ein Hiesiger?[1] Nein, aus beiden
Reichen[2] erwuchs seine weite Natur.
Kundiger böge die Zweige der Weiden,
wer die Wurzeln der Weiden erfuhr.[3]

Geht ihr zu Bette, so laßt auf dem Tische   5
Brot nicht und Milch nicht; die Toten ziehts[4] —.
Aber er, der Beschwörende,[5] mische[6]
unter der Milde des Augenlids

ihre[7] Erscheinung in alles Geschaute;
und der Zauber von Erdrauch und Raute[8]   10
sei ihm so wahr wie der klarste Bezug.[9]

Nichts kann das gültige Bild ihm verschlimmern;
sei es[10] aus Gräbern, sei es aus Zimmern,
rühme er[11] Fingerring, Spange und Krug.[12]

This sonnet is a meditation on Orpheus, the singer-god, the poet of poets. It is addressed to those who would participate in his worship. Through his song Orpheus confirms the oneness of all that is, especially the oneness of life and death, and so cancels out time, the realm of successiveness and hence of separation. Orpheus celebrates pure Being, "is-ness." He is related to the angel of the Duino Elegies, who, so the poet tells us, often does not know whether he is in the land of the dead or the living. But Orpheus differs from the angel in being a "sayer," that is a poet, whereas the angel is mute. Though a god, Orpheus is still more human than the angel. He is the poet in his highest potentiality.

Towards Interpretation
   1. The theme of this sonnet is the unity of all being. This is *das gültige Bild* (line 12). How many times (in how many different images) is this theme brought forth?

---

[1]"Is he a native of this place?' (i.e., of our life as we commonly conceive it) [2]'both realms,' Life *and* Death [3]'He who has experienced the roots of the willows would bend their withes more cunningly.' The image is from basket-weaving. [4]It is an old superstition that bread and milk left on the table attract the dead. [5]Orpheus [6]'let him mix / may he mingle' [7]refers to *die Toten* [8]Earth-smoke (fumitory) and rue are both *Totenpflanzen*. Rue is often buried with the dead, fumitory is used in conjuring them up. [9]'link,' 'relation' *Bezug* is a key word in Rilke. [10]'whether it be' [11]'whether he praise' [12]Objects often buried with the dead, but also found in *Zimmern*.

2. Why is the novice in Orphic mysteries admonished *not* to leave bread and milk on the table? Isn't the whole point communication with the dead?

3. Look up the word *Erscheinung* (line 9) and explain its double meaning here.

„Rühmen, das ists!"

Rühmen, das ists! Ein zum Rühmen Bestellter,
ging er hervor wie das Erz aus des Steins
Schweigen.[1] Sein Herz, o vergängliche Kelter[2]
eines den Menschen unendlichen Weins.

Nie versagt ihm die Stimme am Staube,   5
wenn ihn das göttliche Beispiel[3] ergreift.
Alles wird Weinberg, alles wird Traube,
in seinem fühlenden Süden gereift.

Nicht in den Grüften der Könige Moder
straft ihm die Rühmung lügen,[4] oder   10
daß von den Göttern ein Schatten fällt.

Er ist einer der bleibenden Boten,[5]
der noch weit in die Türen der Toten
Schalen mit rühmlichen Früchten[6] hält.

---

[1]The image of ore issuing from the silence of the stone recalls Orpheus' return from the Underworld. [2]'wine-press' [3]The "sacred example" is that of Orpheus. In this sonnet *er* is the mortal poet who takes Orpheus as his model: *imitatio Orphei*. [4]*Nicht ... lügen =Der Moder* (mold, decay) *in den Grüften* (crypts) *der Könige straft seine Rühmung nicht lügen* (doesn't make his praise a lie). [5]The poet is always there to remind us that Being is one; as a "messenger" between the "two realms" he establishes an unfailing *Bezug*. [6]*Rühmliche Früchte* are fruits both praiseworthy and praised; they are here also both the fruits of the poet's effort and those of a funeral offering.

„Ein Gott vermags"

Ein Gott vermags.[1] Wie aber, sag mir, soll
ein Mann ihm folgen durch die schmale Leier?
Sein[2] Sinn ist Zwiespalt. An der Kreuzung zweier
Herzwege steht kein Tempel für Apoll.[3]

Gesang, wie du ihn lehrst, ist nicht Begehr,   5
nicht Werbung um ein endlich noch Erreichtes;
Gesang ist Dasein. Für den Gott ein Leichtes.
Wann aber *sind* wir?[4] Und wann wendet *er*

an unser Sein die Erde und die Sterne?[5]
Dies *ists* nicht, Jüngling, daß du liebst, wenn auch   10
die Stimme dann den Mund dir aufstößt,[6] — lerne

vergessen, daß du aufsangst. Das verrinnt.
In Wahrheit singen, ist ein andrer Hauch.
Ein Hauch um nichts.[7] Ein Wehn im Gott. Ein Wind.

„Nur wer die Leier schon hob"

Nur wer die Leier schon hob
auch unter Schatten,
darf das unendliche Lob
ahnend erstatten.

Nur wer mit Toten vom Mohn   5
aß, von dem ihren,
wird nicht den leisesten Ton
wieder verlieren.

Mag auch die Spieglung im Teich
oft uns verschwimmen: 10
Wisse das Bild.

---

[1]'A god (like Orpheus) can do it,' i.e., celebrate the oneness of all being without regard for personal considerations. Lines 1-9 are spoken by the *Jüngling* (line 10), a neophyte in the worship of Orpheus; lines 10-14 by a mystagogue, or "priest" of Orpheus. [2]a man's [3]'Where two hearts cross can stand no temple to Apollo.' The song a *man* sings when in love has a personal reference, is not *pure* celebration. [4]When *are* we without being *something*? How can we mortals ever experience pure being? [5]When does the god ever establish a relation between us and the rest of creation? Doesn't the celebration of pure being leave out the very thing that matters to us: our individuality? [6]'even if then (when you're in love) your voice forces open your mouth' [7]'A breath (that sues) for nothing,' *pure* song as in verses 5-7. The mystagogue's answer tells the youth nothing he does not know; its purpose is to exhort and impress rather than instruct.

> Erst in dem Doppelbereich
> werden die Stimmen
> ewig und mild.

Towards Interpretation

1. How might *Der Tod der Geliebten* (p. 362) serve as a commentary on this sonnet?
2. What "Bild" is meant in line 11?

„*Heil dem Geist, der uns verbinden mag*"

> Heil dem Geist, der uns verbinden mag;[1]
> denn wir leben wahrhaft in Figuren.[2]
> Und mit kleinen Schritten gehn die Uhren
> neben unserm eigentlichen Tag.[3]
>
> Ohne unsern wahren Platz zu kennen,   5
> handeln wir aus wirklichem Bezug.
> Die Antennen fühlen die Antennen,
> und die leere Ferne trug[4] . . .
>
> Reine Spannung. O Musik der Kräfte!
> Ist nicht durch die läßlichen Geschäfte[5]   10
> jede Störung von dir abgelenkt?
>
> Selbst wenn sich der Bauer sorgt und handelt,
> wo die Saat in Sommer sich verwandelt,
> reicht er niemals hin. Die Erde *schenkt*.

---

[1]*mag* =*will und kann* [2]The emphasis is on *wahrhaft*. The *Figuren* are formed by the *Verbindungen* established by the *Geist*. Look up *figürlich*. [3]*Durch den Geist wird die Zeit überwunden.* [4]"We do not know what we are or where we are, and yet our half-conscious application of uncomprehended laws somehow leads to results that are right. There is a mysterious contact between us and the unseen powers, like that between the aerials (*Antennen*) on the lonely, isolated masts of a receiving station and those of a distant transmitter. . . ." (*Sonnets to Orpheus*, trans. J. B. Leishman [London: Hogarth Press, 1957], 154) [5]*die läßlichen Geschäfte*: In German one speaks of *läßliche Sünden* (venial sins) but hardly of *läßliche Geschäfte*. The final tercet, which varies the image of the aerials, shows what is meant: The work the farmer does, does not finally accomplish the miracle of "turning the seed into summer" (summer = fruition), it merely helps make the miracle possible, for the earth *bestows*. In the same way, our *läßliche Geschäfte* merely keep down the static (*Störung*), so that "empty distance" may "carry." Our *läßliche Geschäfte* are hardly more than "busy work": *sie sind Geschäfte, die man l a s s e n könnte, obwohl verzeihlich.*

„Frühling ist wiedergekommen"

Frühling ist wiedergekommen. Die Erde
ist wie ein Kind, das Gedichte weiß;
viele, o viele. . . Für die Beschwerde
langen Lernens bekommt sie den Preis.

Streng war ihr Lehrer. Wir mochten das Weiße   5
an dem Barte des alten Manns.
Nun, wie das Grüne, das Blaue heiße,
dürfen wir fragen: sie kanns, sie kanns!

Erde, die frei hat, du glückliche, spiele
nun mit den Kindern. Wir wollen dich fangen,   10
fröhliche Erde. Dem Frohsten gelingts.

O, was der Lehrer sie lehrte, das Viele,
und was gedruckt steht in Wurzeln und langen
schwierigen Stämmen[1]: sie singts, sie singts!

„O dieses ist das Tier, das es nicht giebt"

O dieses ist das Tier, das es nicht giebt.
Sie wußtens nicht und habens jeden Falls
— sein Wandeln, seine Haltung, seinen Hals,
bis in des stillen Blickes Licht — geliebt.

Zwar *war* es nicht. Doch weil sie's liebten, ward   5
ein reines Tier. Sie ließen immer Raum.
Und in dem Raume, klar und ausgespart,
erhob es leicht sein Haupt und brauchte kaum

zu sein. Sie nährten es mit keinem Korn,
nur immer mit der Möglichkeit, es sei.[1]   10
Und die gab solche Stärke an das Tier,

daß es aus sich ein Stirnhorn trieb. Ein Horn.
Zu einer Jungfrau kam es weiß herbei —
und war im Silber-Spiegel und in ihr.[2]

[1]'Roots' and 'stems' are both horticultural and grammatical terms.

[1]'They fed it with no grain of any kind, only with the possibility of its being.' [2]The virgin with the silver mirror and the unicorn (*das Einhorn*): allusion to the famous tapestries of *La Dame à la Licorne* in the Musée de Cluny, Paris. Described by Rilke in his novel *Malte Laurids Brigge*.

Towards Interpretation

1. Who is the *sie* (lines 2ff.) in this poem?

„*Rose, du thronende, denen im Altertume*"

Rose, du thronende, denen im Altertume
warst du ein Kelch mit einfachem Rand.[1]
Uns aber bist du die volle zahllose Blume,
der unerschöpfliche Gegenstand.

In deinem Reichtum scheinst du wie Kleidung um   5
um einen Leib aus nichts als Glanz;   [Kleidung
aber dein einzelnes Blatt ist zugleich die Vermeidung
und die Verleugnung jedes Gewands.[2]

Seit Jahrhunderten ruft uns dein Duft
seine süßesten Namen herüber;[3]   10
plötzlich liegt er wie Ruhm in der Luft.

Dennoch, wir wissen ihn nicht zu nennen, wir raten . . .
Und Erinnerung geht zu ihm über,
die wir von rufbaren Stunden erbaten.[4]

From: *Gedichte aus den Jahren 1906 bis 1926*

Eros (1924)

Masken! Masken! Daß man Eros blende.
Wer erträgt sein strahlendes Gesicht,
wenn er wie die Sommersonnenwende[1]
frühlingliches Vorspiel unterbricht.

Wie es unversehens im Geplauder   5
anders wird und ernsthaft . . . Etwas schrie . . .
Und er wirft den namenlosen Schauder
wie ein Tempelinnres über sie.[2]

---

[1]'for those in antiquity you were a calyx with a single rim,' i.e., with one series of petals, like the wild rose today.   [2]In his *Grabspruch* Rilke calls the rose a "pure contradiction."   [3]For centuries the rose has been praised as the flower of flowers.   [4]We can re-call the hours in which the rose became meaningful to us, but we cannot "call" the fragrance of the rose: *wir wissen ihn nicht zu nennen.* . . .

[1]'summer solstice'   [2]*sie*: Those who suddenly realize the power of Eros. The most famous example in world literature of what this stanza describes is the story of Paolo and Francesca in Canto V of Dante's *Inferno*.

Oh verloren, plötzlich, oh verloren!
Göttliche umarmen schnell.   10
Leben wand sich,³ Schicksal ward geboren.
Und im Innern weint ein Quell.

„*Nichts blieb so schön*" (1924)

Nichts blieb so schön. Ich war damals zu klein.
Ein Nachmittag. Sie wollten plötzlich tanzen
und rollten rasch den alten Teppich ein.
(Was für ein Schimmer liegt noch auf dem Ganzen.)

Sie tanzte dann. Man sah nur sie allein.   5
Und manchesmal verlor man sie sogar,
weil ihr Geruch die Welt geworden war,
in der man unterging. Ich war zu klein.

Wann aber war ich jemals groß genug,
um solchen Duftes Herr zu sein?   10
Um aus dem unbeschreiblichen Bezug
herauszufallen wie ein Stein? —

Nein, dies blieb schön! Ihr blumiger Geruch
in diesem Gartensaal an jenem Tag.
Wie ist er heil. Nie kam ein Widerspruch.   15
Wie ist er mein. Unendlicher Ertrag.

Vorfrühling (1924)

Härte schwand. Auf einmal legt sich Schonung
auf der Wiesen aufgedecktes Grau.
Kleine Wasser ändern die Betonung.
Zärtlichkeiten, ungenau,

greifen nach der Erde aus dem Raum.   5
Wege gehen weit ins Land und zeigens.¹
Unvermutet siehst du seines² Steigens
Ausdruck in dem leeren Baum.

---

³*sich winden* 'be in throes (of childbirth)'

¹=*Die Wege zeigen das Land, denn ohne Wege kann ein Land nicht „gezeigt" werden.*
²i.e., *des Landes*

Vollmacht (1926)

Ach entzögen wir uns Zählern und Stundenschlägern.
Einen Morgen hinaus, heißes Jungsein mit Jägern,
    Rufen im Hundegekläff.[1]
Daß im durchdrängten Gebüsch Kühle uns fröhlich besprühe,
und wir im Neuen und Frein — in den Lüften der Frühe   5
    fühlten den graden Betreff![2]

Solches war uns bestimmt. Leichte beschwingte Erscheinung.
Nicht, im starren Gelaß,[3] nach einer Nacht voll Verneinung,
    ein verneinender Tag.
Diese sind ewig im Recht: dringend dem Leben Genahte;[4]   10
weil sie Lebendige sind, tritt das unendlich bejahte
    Tier in den tödlichen Schlag.[5]

Rilkes Grabschrift

Rose, oh reiner Widerspruch, Lust,
Niemandes Schlaf zu sein unter soviel Lidern.[1]

General Exercises on Rilke

1. Compile a list of rimes from the Rilke poems given here. Does Rilke have a leaning toward unusual, perhaps even eccentric, rimes? Do Rilke's rimes tend to be *sinntragend* or *rein klanglich*? Compare Rilke's rimes with Goethe's, Mörike's, and Heine's.

2. Certainly one of the most striking features of Rilke's style is his extensive use of enjambement (run-over lines). Study a number of Rilke poems from this point of view and see if you can suggest reasons for the enjambement. Compare Rilke's practice with that of Goethe, Hölderlin, Eichendorff, Heine, and Meyer.

3. Study Rilke's use of alliteration (*Jungsein mit Jägern* / *Ferne voll Figur* / *wecken wir Gegengewicht*, and so forth) and try to determine under what circumstances and in order to achieve what ends it is used.

---

[1]'yapping and barking of dogs' [2]Cf. *Es betrifft mich* 'It concerns me.' [3]'room' The word is not very common; Rilke wants to remind us a) of *lassen* (a place where one is left), b) of *Gelassenheit* 'calm,' 'resignation.' *Heißes Jungsein mit Jägern* is the opposite of this. [4]'those who insistently press up against life' [5]*Schlag*: The first level of meaning is here 'path of a projectile.' *Der tödliche Schlag* is, as it were, *der grade Betreff* turned around. If we feel *den graden Betreff*, our "game" will step into *den tödlichen Schlag*. This *Schlag* is the opposite of the *Schlag* of the *Stundenschläger* (line 1), which "kills" *us* with its oppressive sense of separateness and successiveness.

[1]Even here there is perhaps a pun: *Lider* 'lids' – *Lieder* 'songs'

Compare Rilke's practice with that of Klopstock, Hölderlin, Platen, Heine, and Storm.

4. Perhaps no German poet since Brentano is such a magician with vowels as Rilke. Examine the vowelling of the sonnet "Rose, du thronende. . . ." Note especially the use of *o - a - u* in the first quartet, *ei - u(ng) - a* in the second, and *u - ü - a* in the sestet. Study other Rilke poems from this standpoint — "Christi Höllenfahrt," "Herbst," "Vollmacht," and the sonnet "O dieses ist das Tier . . ." are particularly rewarding. Suggest a symbolic significance of some of the vowelling.

August Stramm (1874-1915)

Patrouille[1]

Die Steine feinden
Fenster grinst Verrat
Äste würgen
Berge Sträucher blättern raschlig
Gellen   5
Tod.

Verzweifelt

Droben schmettert ein greller Stein
Nacht grant[1] Glas
Die Zeiten stehn
Ich
Steine.[2]   5
Weit
Glast[2]
Du!

---

[1] French for "military patrol"

[1]'granulates' [2]verb

Else Lasker-Schüler (1876-1945)

Ein alter Tibetteppich

Deine Seele, die die meine liebet,
Ist verwirkt[1] mit ihr im Teppichtibet.

Strahl in Strahl, verliebte Farben,
Sterne, die sich himmellang umwarben.

Unsere Füße ruhen auf der Kostbarkeit,   5
Maschentausendabertausendweit.[2]

Süßer Lamasohn auf Moschuspflanzenthron,[3]
Wie lange küßt dein Mund den meinen wohl
Und Wang die Wange buntgeknüpfte Zeiten[4] schon?

Towards Interpretation
    1. Show how each succeeding stanza develops linguistically the state-
    ment in the first stanza.

Ein Liebeslied

Komm zu mir in der Nacht — wir schlafen engverschlungen.
Müde bin ich sehr, vom Wachen einsam.
Ein fremder Vogel hat in dunkler Frühe schon gesungen,
Als noch mein Traum mit sich und mir gerungen.

Es öffnen Blumen sich vor allen Quellen   5
Und färben sich mit deiner Augen Immortellen[1] .....

Komm zu mir in der Nacht auf Siebensternenschuhen[2]
Und Liebe eingehüllt spät in mein Zelt.
Es steigen Monde aus verstaubten Himmelstruhen.

Wir wollen wie zwei seltene Tiere liebesruhen   10
Im hohen Rohre[3] hinter dieser Welt.

---

[1]'interwoven' (probably also with the secondary sense of 'consumed,' 'used up')
[2]'thousands and thousands of meshes broad' [3]*Moschus* 'musk' [4]'brightly knotted
times' The play on words, *Zeiten* instead of *Male*, is untranslatable. As in *himmellang*
(coined on the model of *himmelhoch*) spatial and temporal concepts are combined.

[1]'the immortal flower' (Helychrysum) [2]cf. *Siebenmeilenstiefel* [3]'cane-brake'

Mein Volk[1]

Der Fels wird morsch,
Dem ich entspringe
Und meine Gotteslieder singe . . .
Jäh stürz ich vom Weg
Und riesele ganz in mir   5
Fernab, allein über Klagegestein
Dem Meer zu.

Hab mich so abgeströmt
Von meines Blutes
Mostvergorenheit.[2]   10
Und immer, immer noch der Widerhall
In mir,
Wenn schauerlich gen Ost
Das morsche Felsgebein,
Mein Volk,   15
Zu Gott schreit.

Towards Interpretation

1. How does the poet see herself in relation to the Jewish people (*der Fels*)?

O Gott

Überall nur kurzer Schlaf
Im Mensch, im Grün, im Kelch der Winde.
Jeder kehrt in sein totes Herz heim.

— Ich wollt die Welt wär noch ein Kind —
Und wüßte mir vom ersten Atem zu erzählen.   5

Früher war eine große Frömmigkeit am Himmel,
Gaben sich die Sterne die Bibel zu lesen.
Könnte ich einmal Gottes Hand fassen
Oder den Mond an seinem Finger sehn.

O Gott, o Gott, wie weit bin ich von dir!   10

---

[1] i.e., the Jews. [2] 'over-fermentation of new wine (must)'

Else Lasker-Schüler

Theodor Däubler

Theodor Däubler (1876-1934)

Die Buche

Die Buche sagt: Mein Walten[1] bleibt das Laub.
Ich bin kein Baum mit sprechenden Gedanken,
Mein Ausdruck wird ein Ästeüberranken,
Ich bin das Laub, die Krone[2] überm Staub.

Dem warmen Aufruf mag ich rasch vertraun,   5
Ich fang im Frühling selig an zu reden,
Ich wende mich in schlichter Art an jeden.
Du staunst, denn ich beginne rostigbraun!

Mein Waldgehaben[3] zeigt sich sommerfroh.
Ich will, daß Nebel sich um Äste legen,   10
Ich mag das Naß, ich selber bin der Regen.
Die Hitze stirbt: ich grüne lichterloh!

Die Winterpflicht erfüll ich ernst und grau.
Doch schütt ich erst den Herbst aus meinem Wesen.

---

[1]'command,' 'power' [2]'treetop' as well as 'crown' [3]'forest activity'

Er[4] ist noch niemals ohne mich gewesen.   15
Da werd ich Teppich, sammetrote[5] Au.

Kalte Nacht

Der Schnee auf den Bergen ist kindlich und heilig.
Er scheint mir des Flutens-verzücktes Erschaudern.
Die flüchtigen Vögel berühren ihn eilig;
Ihr Ruhen auf Schnee ist ein fiebriges Zaudern.

Es darf bloß der Mond solche Reinheit betasten.   5
Mit silbernen Launen verziert er die Hänge.
Dort oben, wo eisbehaucht Mondseelen rasten,
Besinnt sich die Nacht alter Totengesänge.

Ich nahe euch nicht, o verhaltene Geister!
Ich mag den Vernunftturm am Gletscherrand bauen.   10
Von dort können Traumkäuzchen angstloser, dreister
Hinab auf Gespensterverschwörungen schauen.

Sie fliegen zu Fichten in nebelnden Furchen,
Zu Tauhauchen, die in den Windecken frieren,
Ins Dickicht zu mondtollen Finsternislurchen[1]:   15
Zu plötzlichen eisgrellen Schneerätseltieren.

Towards Interpretation
1. This poem is about the effects of the wind on a snowfield in the mountains. What images are said to be created by the blowing snow?
2. What do you take the *Vernunftturm* (line 10) to signify? What are the *Traumkäuzchen* (dream owls) that fly from it?

---

[4]i.e., *Herbst* [5]'velvet-red'

[1]*der Lurch* 'amphibian'

Gertrud von Le Fort (1876-1971)

Heimweg zur Kirche

IV

Ich bin in das Gesetz deines[1] Glaubens gefallen
    wie in ein nackendes Schwert!
Mitten durch meinen Verstand ging seine Schärfe,
    mitten durch die Leuchte meiner Erkenntnis!
Nie wieder werde ich wandeln unter dem Stern
    und am Stabe meiner Kraft!   [meiner Augen
Du hast meine Ufer weggerissen
    und hast Gewalt angetan der Erde zu meinen Füßen!
Meine Schiffe treiben im Meer:
    alle meine Anker hast du gelichtet![2]   5
Die Ketten meiner Gedanken sind zerbrochen,
    sie hängen wie Wildnis im Abgrund.
Ich irre wie ein Vogel um meines Vaters Haus,
    ob ein Spalt ist, der dein fremdes Licht einläßt,
Aber es ist keiner auf Erden,
    außer der Wunde in meinem Geist —
Ich bin in das Gesetz deines Glaubens gefallen
    wie in ein nackendes Schwert!

V

Aber es geht noch Kraft aus von deinen Dornen,
    und aus deinen Abgründen tönt Gesang.
Deine Schatten liegen auf meinem Herzen wie Rosen,
    und deine Nächte sind wie starker Wein:
Ich will dich noch lieben, wo meine Liebe zu dir endet.
Ich will dich noch wollen, wo ich dich nicht mehr will.
Wo ich selbst anfange, da will ich aufhören,
    und wo ich aufhöre, da will ich ewiglich bleiben.   5
Wo meine Füße sich weigern, mit mir zu gehen,
    da will ich mich einknien,
Und wo meine Hände versagen, da will ich sie falten.
Ich will zu Hauch werden in Herbsten des Stolzes
    und zu Schnee in Wintern der Zweifel,
Ja, wie in Gräbern von Schnee soll alle Frucht
    in mir schlafen

---

[1]i.e., of the Church   [2]'weighed,' 'raised'

Ich will Staub werden vor dem Fels deiner Lehre
   und Asche vor der Flamme deines Gebots —   10
Ich will meine Arme zerbrechen,
   ob¹ ich dich mit ihren Schatten umfange.

Corpus Christi Mysticum

II

Denn Überall auf Erden wehet der Wind des Verlassens:
   lausche, wie es in den Fluren der Welt klagt!
Überall ist einer und niemals zwei!
Überall ist ein Schrei im Gefängnis
   und ist eine Hand hinter vermauerten Toren;
Überall ist einer lebendig begraben!
Unsre Mütter weinen, und unsre Geliebten verstummen;
   denn keiner kann dem andern helfen:
   sie sind alle allein!   5
Sie rufen sich von Schweigen zu Schweigen,
   sie küssen sich von Einsamkeit zu Einsamkeit.
   Sie lieben sich tausend Schmerzen weit von ihren
Denn alle Nähe der Menschen ist wie Blumen, [Seelen.
   die auf Grüften welken,
   und aller Trost ist wie eine Stimme von außen. —
Aber du bist wie eine Stimme mitten in der Seele.

Hermann Hesse (1877-1962)

Im Nebel

Seltsam, im Nebel zu wandern!
Einsam ist jeder Busch und Stein,
Kein Baum sieht den andern,
Jeder ist allein.

Voll von Freunden war mir die Welt,
Als noch mein Leben licht war;

----

¹'to see whether'

Nun, da der Nebel fällt,
Ist keiner mehr sichtbar.

Wahrlich, keiner ist weise,
Der nicht das Dunkel kennt,
Das unentrinnbar und leise
Von allen ihn trennt.

Seltsam, im Nebel zu wandern!
Leben ist Einsamsein.
Kein Mensch kennt den andern,
Jeder ist allein.

Heimweg vom Wirtshaus

Wunderliches Wehgefühl,
Wenn ich meinen Tisch verlassen
Und die Nacht so still und kühl
Wandelt durch die leeren Gassen!

Müde und vom Wein berauscht   5
Hab ich oft dem bangen Winde
Durch die Straßen nachgelauscht,
Traumbewegt gleich einem Kinde.

Irgendein geheimer Gruß,
Irdendein geheimes Singen,   10
Irgendeine Liebe muß
In dem leisen Brausen klingen.

Eine stille Güte auch
Hat der Ton in mir beschworen —
Ist es jener Jugend Hauch,   15
Die ich schon so lang verloren?

Rudolf Borchardt (1877-1945)

Auf eine angeschossene Schwalbe,
die der Dichter fand

Da liegst du nun, gebrochner kleiner Pfeil;
Die Sehne ist dir durchgeschlagen
Und keine Schwinge mehr ist heil,
Denn eine Schwinge taugt nicht, dich zu tragen.

Du richtest meinem ungeheuren Nahn   5
Den Blick der Todesangst entgegen:
Mein Stutzen heißt dir Fang und Zahn,
Mein Niederbeugen Hunger deinetwegen,

Und keine Flucht mehr; denn du bist nicht schnell;
Das Leben könnt ihr nur gewinnen,   10
Weil du und weil dein Nestgesell
Den überholen mögt,[1] und dem entrinnen:

Feindselig durch die Wüste eurer Welt
Hinschießend, immer vor dem Feinde,
Im Rufe nur, der gellt und gellt,   15
Hängt ihr zusammen, einsame Gemeinde!

Wie sich in meiner Hand, die Wärme flößt,[2]
Das lebenschwarze Auge wundert!
Ich bin nicht Gott, der dich verstößt
Wie hundert jeden Tag und aberhundert,[3] —   20

Es gab dir Flug, und was dich fristen mag,[4]
Er, deines Feinds gleichmütiger Frister,
Dem Fleck, wo deine Ohnmacht lag,
Vorüber fuhr dein Gott, flog dein Geschwister,[5]

Und die du nie gewürdigt deines Raubs,[6]   25
Wenn du im Blau die Bahn gerundet,
Schon kroch an dir Geburt des Staubs,[6]
Ihr bist du Aas, sieht sie dich kaum verwundet! —

---

[1] =könnt [2]'puts forth' [3]*hundert ... und aberhundert* 'hundreds and hundreds' [4]'whatever can keep you alive' [5]*Dem Fleck ... Geschwister* =*An dem Fleck vorüber, wo du in deiner Ohnmacht lagst, fuhr dein Gott und flog dein Geschwister* [6]The swallow never considered the worm, *die Geburt des Staubs,* worthy of being its prey.

Zünglein, das mir schon dreist vom Finger schmaust,
Du bist voll Botschaft ohne Sprechen;   30
Damit du ein Mal Stärkern traust,
Muß Gott den Ring der eigenen Fügung brechen, —

Sich einzulenken, wo ihn selbst des Hohns
Im eigenen Werk, der Unbill jammert,
Bedarf er seines großen Sohns,   35
Den das gemeine Reich nicht ganz unklammert.[7]

Hier dankt er mir, was er mir zugewandt:[8]
Daß er mir seine Seele gönnte,
Hat zwischen dir und ihm entspannt
Die Brücke, die er selbst nicht bauen könnte.   40

Der jeden Leib in Todes Schranken wies,
Läßt sich die eigne nicht verwetten:[9]
Er schuf, der das Geschöpf verstieß,
Noch das Geschöpf, Verstoßnes zu erretten.

Grabschrift der Schwalbe

Ich, die verwundete Schwalbe, drei Tage des Menschen Genossin,
   Sahe den schrecklichen Tod freundlicher werden und starb:
Schwetern im Blau, fliegt schweigend hier überhin, who sich das
                                                        Geistlein
   Schüttelt und ringt nach Ruf, wenn es euch Rufende hört.
Gönnt mir Schweigen und singt, singt anderswo, wenn ihr das
                                                     Meer wagt: 5
   Nicht ganz, nicht ganz stumm flattert' ich eine[1] beiseit.

Towards Interpretation
   1. What does man learn about himself from sharing in the fate of the
      swallow?

---

[7]Lines 33-36: that God may intercede in His own creation He has need of man ('his great son') who is not completely subject to physical drives. [8]'gave,' 'granted' [9]'Does not risk losing his own bounds on a bet' (God's bounds are His creation; cf. Goethe's "Es ist gut.")

[1]'one alone'

Rudolf Alexander Schröder (1878-1962)

Schotteck[1]

Wer weiß nun im Grünen die vielerlei Namen
Der Blumen, der Bäume, der Kräuter, der Samen?
   Sie nannten dich alt; aber alt ist nicht alt,
   Und das Ende der Weisheit kommt immer zu bald.

Wer will nun im Hause die vielen, die Gäste   5
Bewirten, beschmausen, befreunden aufs beste?
   Sie nannten dich alt; aber alt ist nicht alt,
   Und das Ende der Freundschaft kommt immer zu bald.

Wer trägt nun die Tücher, die seidenen, feinen,
Gehäng und Gebräme[2] von Perlen und Steinen?   10
   Sie nannten dich alt; aber alt ist nicht alt,
   Und das Ende der Anmut kommt immer zu bald.

Wann war es? Da sind wir noch einmal inmitten
Von Primeln und Veilchen selbander[3] geschritten.
   Doch der Frühling ward alt, und der Sommer   15
                        ward kalt. —
   Ach Sommer, dein Ende kommt immer zu bald!

Ja, grüßt euch, und herzt euch, und haltet die Hände!
Mit Lieben und Leiden kommt alles zum Ende.
   Das Leben träumt: Ewig; die Zeit lächelt: Bald;
   Und es altert die Treue. — Doch alt ist nicht alt.   20

Towards Interpretation
1. What seems to be the relationship between the speaker and the other person in the poem? In what three spheres is the other person imagined?
2. Read the poem aloud. Comment on the relation between meter and subject matter.
3. Reread Nietzsche's "Das trunkene Lied" and address the time theme treated here.

---

[1]Apparently a place name. [2]*Gehäng und Gebräme* =*Schmuck* (That which hangs down and that which forms a border) [3]'together'

Nachts

Im bangen Zimmer entschlief ich kaum
    Und war kaum wieder erwacht:
Kühl blickte der Stern, kühl hauchte der Baum,
    Kühl wehte der Wind in der Nacht.

Und immer der Bronnen, der rauscht und quillt,   5
    Als wären, geschehn und vollbracht,
Dein Tag ein Traum und dein Traum ein Bild,
    Ein Bild und ein Wind in der Nacht.

Towards Interpretation

1. Using Mörike's "Um Mitternacht" as a model of comparison, discuss the time theme in this poem.
2. What can the speaker learn from nature?
3. Read the next poem, "Der alte Brunnen," and compare the role of the fountains.

R. A. Schröder   *Hans Carossa*

Hans Carossa (1878-1956)

Der alte Brunnen

Lösch aus dein Licht und schlaf! Das immer wache
Geplätscher nur vom alten Brunnen tönt.
Wer aber Gast war unter meinem Dache,
Hat stets sich bald an diesen Ton gewöhnt.

Zwar kann es einmal sein, wenn du schon mitten   5
Im Traume bist, daß Unruh geht ums Haus,
Der Kies beim Brunnen knirscht von harten Tritten,
Das helle Plätschern setzt auf einmal aus,

Und du erwachst, — dann mußt du nicht erschrecken!
Die Sterne stehn vollzählig überm Land,   10
Und nur ein Wandrer trat ans Marmorbecken,
Der schöpft vom Brunnen mit der hohlen Hand.

Er geht gleich weiter, und es rauscht wie immer.
O freue dich, du bleibst nicht einsam hier.
Viel Wandrer gehen fern im Sternenschimmer,   15
Und mancher noch ist auf dem Weg zu dir.

An eine Katze

Katze, stolze Gefangene,
Lange kamst du nicht mehr.
Nun, über dämmerverhangene
Tische zögerst du her,[1]

Feierabendbote,[2]   5
Feindlich dem emsigen Stift[3]
Legst mir die Vorderpfote
Leicht auf begonnene Schrift,

Mahnst mich zu neuem Besinnen,
Du so gelassen[4] und schön!   10
Leise schon hör ich dich spinnen[5]
Heimliches Orgeltön.

---

[1] = *kommst du zögernd her* [2] 'messenger of quitting time' [3] = *Bleistift* [4] 'calm' [5] *spinnen* 'to purr'

Lautlos geht eine Türe.
Alles wird ungewohnt.[6]
Wenn ich die Stirn dir berühre,   15
Fühl ich auf einmal den Mond.

Woran denkst du nun? An dein Heute?
Was du verfehlt und erreicht?
An dein Spiel? Deine Jagd? Deine Beute?
Oder träumst du vielleicht,   20

Frei von versuchenden Schemen[7]
Grausamer Gegenwart,
Milde teilzunehmen
An der menschlichen Art,

Selig in großem Verzichte[8]   25
Welten entgegen zu gehn,
Wandelnd in einem Lichte,
Das wir beide nicht sehn?

Towards Interpretation

1. Do you think the cat is tempting the man to cat-ness or the man tempting the cat to human-ness? Or is this a poem about the utter difference between cat and man?

„Unzugänglich schien der Gipfel"

Unzugänglich schien der Gipfel;
Nun begehn wir ihn so leicht.
Fern verdämmern erste Wege,
Neue Himmel sind erreicht.

Urgebirg und offne Länder   5
Schweben weit, in Eins verspielt.
Städte, die wir nachts durchzogen,
Sind ein einfach-lichtes Bild.

Helle Wolke streift herüber;
Uns umweht ihr Schattenlauf.   10
Große blaue Falter[1] schlagen
Sich wie Bücher vor uns auf.

---

[6]'strange'   [7]'tempter phantoms'   [8]If the cat dreams of "gently sharing in humankind," then it must give up cat-kind, its own *grausame Gegenwart*.

[1] = *Schmetterlinge*

Towards Interpretation

1. The underlying idea of this delightful and perfect poem in the symbolist manner is the synthesis of polar opposites to produce some third, still unknown, but certainly higher form of existence. Point out the polarities.
2. What image signifies their unification in stanza 2? Is this a perfect union? Can you account for the impure rime *verspielt – Bild* on the basis of the idea expressed?
3. Compare this poem with the two preceding from the standpoint of the underlying idea.

„Ja, wir sind Widerhall ewigen Halls"

Ja, wir sind Widerhall ewigen Halls.
Was man das Nichts nennt, ist Wurzel des Alls.
Aber das wollen wir mutig vergessen,
Wollen die Kreise des Da-Seins durchmessen!
Was hier nicht gebunden wird, ist nirgends gebannt.[1]   5
Wie weit eine Liebe sich spannt
In die Zeit, in die Tat, in das Glück ihrer Erde,
So tief wird sie zeugen im ewigen Werde.

Konrad Weiss (1880-1940)

Morgen-Leis[1]

Nach einer schlaflos langen Nacht
den Sinn dumpf, müd und überwacht
weckt quirlend[2] eine Vogelstimme,
das klingt so rein im frühen Schein,
und über jedem dunklen Grimme   5
schläft Unrast ein und Eigenpein.

Da irgendwo, wo ich nicht weiß,
singt nun das Kehlchen wirbelleis

---

[1]'fixed'

[1]*der Leis* =*kirchlicher Bittgesang; geistliches Volkslied* [from the Greek: *kyrie eleison*, 'Lord have mercy upon us']   [2]'whirling'

und steht auf seinen zarten Füßen,
es ringt sein Mund, ihm selbst nicht kund,   10
als müsse doppelt es begrüßen
zu dieser Stund den Erdenrund.

Mein Sinn und mein Gedankenspiel
sucht neu erquickt das alte Ziel:
so will ich meine Seele schreiben,   15
so rein und nicht verdroßner Pflicht,[3]
daß nirgendwo die Füße bleiben,
daß mein Gesicht vergeht im Licht.

„Ich erstaune tief in Scheu"

Ich erstaune tief in Scheu,
wie sich alles fügt,
nicht gewollt und nur getreu
mich kein Ding betrügt,

wie ich einen Willen tun   5
in Entfernung muß,
doch der Wille hüllt mich nun
wie in Baumes Nuß.

Immer in Bewegung ich
war doch immer Ruh,   10
wie ich dachte, regend mich,
handeltest nur du.

Wirf die Nuß ins Ackerland,
wenn der Baum erbebt,
ich bin nicht, in deiner Hand   15
sieh die Schöpfung lebt,

ich bin alles, Mensch auch ich,
wandelirrer Stern,
ihn gebar die Jungfrau sich
und ich harre gern.   20

Unerschütterlich erblüht
wird dies Herz in Gott,[1]

---

[3]genitive of manner, 'peevishly, grudgingly dutiful'

[1]Lines 21-22: The heart is continually *being* brought to bloom in God, "unshakeably,"
even if the nut is thrown to the ground *wenn der Baum erbebt.*

singe mir das Wiegenlied,
Jungfrau Kummernot.

The work of Konrad Weiss, *poeta christianissimus*, is as difficult as any in modern literature. "Ich erstaune tief in Scheu" sees man (Adam) as the son of earth, *Jungfrau Kummernot*, even as Christ (the second Adam) is the son of the Blessed Virgin. (We find the earth as a symbol for the Virgin in the Church Fathers, e.g., in Augustine and Tertullian.) The earth is our mother, but the earth is God's. In our way we and all other things do the divine will just as the Savior did. The poem presents the moment of sudden insight into the divine plan: *Ich e r s t a u n e tief in Scheu.* . . .

Mann aus Erde

Dem[1] alles nur im Geist geschah,
du meinst, die Grenze sei so nah,
dein armes Sein in Gottes Licht zu zücken,[2]
du unlösbarer Zeitvertreib,[3]
du mußt, o unverklärter Leib,   5
den Stein erst überm Grabe rücken.

Nun überfällt die Seelenangst
dich wieder, daß du stockst und bangst,
zurückwillst zu der Markverwesung[4] Schmerzen,
Verjüngter du in dem Gericht   10
des Wortes, werde Fleisch, dann bricht
die Ader ein zum ewgen Herzen.[5]

---

[1]'you, for whom' [2]'transport' (cf. *entzückt*) [3]*unlösbarer Zeitvertreib*: Through time man is and through him time passes, he is a "pass-time" (*Zeit-Vertreib*). Time is man's mode of being and he cannot be dissolved (*gelöst*) from it. [4]'decomposition of the spinal marrow' [5]Lines 10-12: Probably, 'you (who are to be / would be) rejuvenated in the Last Judgment (judgment of the Word = Logos = Christ), become flesh, then the vein to the eternal heart will form.' The figure is from embryology.

Wilhelm Lehmann (1882-1968)

Ahnung im Januar

Münchhausens Horn ist aufgetaut,[1]
Zerbrochene Gefangenschaft!
Erstarrter Ton wird leise laut,
In Holz und Stengel treibt der Saft.

Dem Anruf als ein Widerhall,   5
Aus Lehmesklumpen, eisig, kahl,
Steigt Ammernleib,[2] ein Federball,
Schon viele Male, erstes Mal.

Ob Juniluft den Stier umblaut,
Den Winterstall ein Wald durchlaubt?   10
Ist es Europa,[3] die ihn kraut?
Leicht richtet er das schwere Haupt.

So warmen Fußes, Sommergeist,
Daß unter dir das Eis zerreißt —
Verheißung, und schon brenne ich,   15
Erfüllung, wie ertrag ich dich?

Klage ohne Trauer

Die Spinne wirft ihr Silberseil.
Der Wind schläft ein. So bleibt es heil.

Wie schnell flog meine Zeit vorbei,
Aus jeder Hecke Vogelschrei.

Die Erde spricht, Heuschreck[1] ihr Mund,   5
Blaugrüne Diemen,[2] wigwamrund.

Die Pappel samt.[3] Die Wolle[4] schneit,
Als Polster meinem Kopf bereit.

---

[1]According to Baron von Münchhausen a particular winter was so severe the notes froze in a postillion's horn. [2]*die Ammer* 'bunting' [3]Princess with whom Jupiter fell in love; the better to seduce her he assumed the shape of a bull and mingled with her father's herds; *krauen* 'scratch or rub gently'

[1]'grasshopper' [2]'hay stacks' [3]'releases its seeds' [4]'wool' from the poplars

Ein Seufzer seufzt: „Vergeh, vergeh";
Die Pappel rauscht: „Es tut nicht weh. "   10

Fliehender Sommer

Marguerite, Marguerite,[1]
Weiße Frau in goldener Haube —
Erstes Heu wölbt sich zum Schaube.[2]
Kuckuck reist, als er es sieht.

Pappel braust wie ein Prophet.   5
Aus dem vielgezüngten[3] Munde
Stößt sie[4] orgelnd ihre Kunde.
Elster[5] hüpft, die sie versteht.

Pappel, du, in Weisheit grau,
Diene ich dir erst zur Speise,   10
Fall ich ein in eure Weise,[6]
Kuckuck, Elster, weiße Frau.

Oberon[1]

Durch den warmen Lehm geschnitten
Zieht der Weg. Inmitten
Wachsen Lolch und Bibernell.[2]
Oberon ist ihn geritten,
Heuschreckschnell.   5

Oberon ist längst die Sagenzeit hinabgeglitten.
Nur ein Klirren
Wie von goldnen Reitgeschirren
Bleibt,
Wenn der Wind die Haferkörner[3] reibt.   10

---

[1]'daisy' [2]'bundle (of hay)' [3]'many-tongued' [4]i.e., *die Pappel* [5]'magpie' [6]'I'll join in your melody'

[1]King of the Fairies (see *A Midsummer-Night's Dream*) [2]'darnel and saxifrage' [3]*Hafer* 'oats'

Oskar Loerke (1884-1941)

Strom

Du rinnst wie melodische Zeit, entrückst mich den Zeiten,
Fern schlafen mir Fuß und Hand, sie schlafen an meinem
Phantom.
Doch die Seele wächst hinab, beginnt schon zu gleiten,
Zu fahren, zu tragen, — und nun ist sie der Strom,
Beginnt schon im Grundsand, im grauen,   5
Zu tasten mit schwebend gedrängtem Gewicht,
Beginnt schon die Ufer, die auf sie schauen,
Spiegelnd zu haben[1] und weiß es nicht.

In mir werden Eschen mit langen Haaren,
Voll mönchischer Windlitanei,   10
Und Felder mit Rindern, die sich paaren,
Und balzender Vögel Geschrei.[2]
Und über Gehöft, Wiese, Baum
Ist viel hoher Raum;
Fische und Wasserratten und Lurche[3]   15
Ziehn, seine[4] Träume, durch ihn hin —.
So rausch ich in wärmender Erdenfurche,[5]
Ich spüre schon fast, daß ich bin:

Wie messe ich, ohne zu messen, den Flug der Tauben,
So hoch und tief er blitzt, so tief und hoch mir ein!   20
Alles ist an ein Jenseits nur Glauben,
Und Du ist Ich, gewiß und rein.[6]

Zuletzt steigen Nebel- und Wolkenzinnen[7]
In mir auf wie die göttliche Kaiserpfalz.[8]
Ich ahne, die Ewigkeit will beginnen   25
Mit einem Duft von Salz.

---

[1]By reflecting them the soul-stream "has" the banks that look upon it. [2]*Ein Vogel balzt*, i.e., gives the mating cry and carries out certain dance-like movements. [3]'amphibians' [4]i.e., *des Raumes* [5]The 'furrow' is the river bed. [6]Lines 19-22: Approximately: 'How I measure without measuring the pigeons' flight / As high and deep as it flashes, as deep and high within me! / Everything is only belief in a Beyond, / And You is I, certainly and purely.' The stanza is a statement of utter identification of man and nature. [7]*Zinnen* 'battlements' [8]'imperial palace' (of the Holy Roman Emperors)

An die Grundmächte[1]

Es zählt vor euch nicht, daß ich Schmerzen leide.
Es schweigt die Weide,[2]
Wenn man zur Flöte sie schneidet und schält.
Doch daß ich leide und nicht meutere,[3]
Und was ich mir draus läutere[4]   5
Zum Zwiegespräch mit euch, es zählt.

Pompeji: Grab des Dichters

Früh sah ich vorne
Vorm Tor, wo der Bauer im Kühlen harkt,[1]
Die feurigen Dorne
Des Morgens zu maßlosem Licht erstarkt.[2]

Der Gott hat Muße.[3]   5
Andern verblieb es, ein Tagwerk zu tun,
Mir,[4] unter dem Fuße
Der trauernd geschwätzigen Winde zu ruhn.

Wenn die uralte Traube,
Die schwarze, wiederkehrt staubig und warm,   10
Weckt mich immer der Glaube:
Du sollst nicht schluchzen, der Gott wird nicht arm.

Towards Interpretation
1. Who is the speaker in this poem?
2. Why is the grape *uralt*? Can a grape be that? What god is particularly associated with the grape(vine)?
3. What kind of poems does the dead poet seem to be (have been) especially known for?
4. What is meant by saying, *der Gott wird nicht arm*?

---

[1]'basic forces of nature' [2]'willow' [3]'mutiny,' 'rebel' [4]'purify'

[1]'rakes' [2]Lines 3-4 are an image of the sunrise. [3]'leisure' [4]Supply *verblieb es*

Ernst Stadler (1883-1914)

Around 1912, poetry in a distinctly new key began to appear in Germany, poetry that was neither impressionistic nor symbolistic, neither realistic nor romantic. This poetry came to be known as "expressionistic" and the years between 1910 and 1920, when the most characteristic works in this vein were produced, as the expressionistic decade or period of Expressionism. Expressionism was Germany's last great artistic movement. It affected not only lyric poetry but also drama, painting, and sculpture.* Of the poets represented here — though their poems have not been specially chosen to illustrate this aspect of their work — Stramm, Loerke, Stadler, Heym, Trakl, Benn, Werfel, Goll, and Brecht were, for at least part of their productive years, Expressionists, while Mombert and Lasker-Schüler are often accounted forerunners of the movement.

Though it is hardly possible to state in a few words what Expressionism is, it is not too difficult to recognize a work done in the expressionistic manner. Probably it is most fruitful not to try to confine Expressionism to precise historical limits but to regard it as a mode of artistic expression that may come into being any time inward and outward circumstances demand or permit. Viewed thus, the German "expressionistic decade" is only an exemplary case of a fundamental direction art may take, and one can think of the works of Matthias Grünewald, El Greco, many artists of the Baroque, the writers of the *Sturm und Drang*, Heinrich von Kleist, Georg Büchner, and van Gogh as expressionistic in a larger sense. It is immediately apparent that these artists and writers have at least two important traits in common: 1) they strive for a dynamic effect rather than a harmonious one; 2) they treat outward reality in a supercharged, non-realistic (or ultra-realistic) fashion. The latter is of course only a means of attaining the former.

The reasons for wanting to achieve a dynamic effect differ. The German Expressionists, especially the lyric poets, were revolutionary in spirit, antibourgeois, and above all inordinately desirous of the ecstatic. They wanted to

---

*Some representative names in fields other than lyrical poetry: in the drama, Carl Sternheim, Georg Kaiser, and the early Bertolt Brecht; in painting, Oskar Kokoschka, Wassily Kandinsky, Franz Marc, and a number of others; in sculpture, Wilhelm Lehmbruck and Ernst Barlach. Arnold Schönberg and Alban Berg might be considered expressionistic composers, though the term is not often applied to music.

lift man out of himself, to transform him and his world. They sought to warn and waken, crying like Angelus Silesius, *Mensch, werde wesentlich!* The tones in which this cry resounded varied widely, but behind most Expressionistic utterances, whether cynical, grotesque, prayerful, or prophetic, lies the longing for the new man, the man who will exceed himself. In this the Expressionists were the direct heirs of Nietzsche. In its pronounced ethical emphasis, as also in its comparative disinterest in artistic theory, German Expressionism differs radically from other modernist movements in art, such as imagism, futurism, and surrealism, though it often employs similar techniques.

The term Expressionism itself of course implies a contrast with Impressionism (which was very unproductive of good lyric poetry in Germany) — *Ausdruckskunst* versus *Eindruckskunst*, the inner vision versus the outward impression, Dostoevski versus Flaubert, Strindberg versus Ibsen, Cézanne versus Renoir. The Expressionists strove to externalize something within, to bring to germination the seed of the soul. The resulting plants were not infrequently merely rank weeds, but sometimes they were strange, strong trees.

Kleine Stadt

Die vielen kleinen Gassen,
    die die langgestreckte Hauptstraße überqueren,
Laufen alle ins Grüne.
    Überall fängt Land an.
Überall strömt Himmel ein und Geruch von Bäumen
    und der starke Duft der Äcker.
Überall erlischt die Stadt
    in einer feuchten Herrlichkeit von Wiesen,
Und durch den grauen Ausschnitt
    niedrer Dächer schwankt   5
Gebirge, über das die Reben klettern,
    die mit hellen Stützen in die Sonne leuchten.
Darüber aber schließt sich Kiefernwald:
    der stößt
Wie eine breite dunkle Mauer an die rote Fröhlichkeit
    der Sandsteinkirche.

Am Abend, wenn die Fabriken schließen,
    ist die große Straße mit Menschen gefüllt.
Sie gehen langsam
    oder bleiben mitten auf der Gasse stehn.   10
Sie sind geschwärzt von Arbeit und Maschinenruß.
    Aber ihre Augen tragen
Noch Scholle, zähe Kraft des Bodens
    und das feierliche Licht der Felder.

Typisch für den ganzen Expressionismus ist . . . die von Stadler konse-
quent [consistently] durchgeführte *Verbalisierung des Stils*. . . . Ein wahres
Musterbeispiel expressionistischer Landschaftsdarstellung gab Stadler mit
dem Gedicht ‚Kleine Stadt'. . . . Hier ist alles statische Sein der Landschaft
in Dynamik umgesetzt. Das Bild wird dem Leser nicht fertig gegeben, sondern seine Bestandteile arrangieren sich gewissermaßen erst unter den
Augen des Betrachters zum Bilde. Gebirge ‚schwankt' durch den Dächer-
ausschnitt, wird von Reben ‚überklettert,' und über diesen ‚schließt sich'
Wald, der an die rote Fröhlichkeit der Sandsteinkirche ‚stößt.' Die gleich-
zeitige Gegenwart der Erscheinungen ist in eine dramatische Abfolge des
In-Erscheinung-Tretens verwandelt, Landschaft zum Spiegelbild innerer
Bewegung geworden. . . .*

Towards Interpretation

1. It is characteristic of Expressionism to regard the great modern city as
   an instrument of dehumanization and the most striking symptom of
   the sickness of modern man. Does this attitude find expression in
   "Kleine Stadt"? Is a counterweight indicated? Is it threatened?
2. Suppose this were a *große* Stadt. What then? Would a counterweight
   be apparent?

Fahrt über die Kölner Rheinbrücke bei Nacht

Der Schnellzug tastet sich
    und stößt die Dunkelheit entlang.[1]
Kein Stern will vor. Die ganze Welt ist nur ein enger,
    nachtumschienter Minengang,[2]
Darein zuweilen Förderstellen[3]
    blauen Lichts jähe Horizonte reißen: Feuerkreis
Von Kugellampen, Dächern, Schloten,
    dampfend, strömend . . nur sekundenweis . .
Und wieder alles schwarz.
    Als führen wir ins Eingeweid der Nacht zur Schicht.[4]   5
Nun taumeln Lichter her . . verirrt, trostlos vereinsamt . .
    mehr . . und sammeln sich . . und werden dicht.
Gerippe grauer Häuserfronten liegen bloß,[5]
    im Zwielicht bleichend, tot —
    etwas muß kommen . . o, ich fühl es schwer

---

*Ernst Stadler, *Dichtungen*, ed. Karl Ludwig Schneider (Hamburg: Ellermann, 1954),
1:96f.

[1]*Entlang* goes with both *tastet* and *stößt*. [2]'mine gallery timbered with night' [3]mining
term: place where ore is hauled up [4]*zur Schicht fahren* 'go on shift' [5]'bare'

Im Hirn. Eine Beklemmung[6] singt im Blut.
    Dann dröhnt der Boden plötzlich wie ein Meer:
Wir fliegen, aufgehoben,
    königlich durch nachtentrissne Luft, hoch übern Strom.
    O Biegung der Millionen Lichter, stumme Wacht,
Vor deren blitzender Parade
    schwer die Wasser abwärts rollen.[7]
    Endloses Spalier,[8] zum Gruß gestellt bei Nacht!   10
Wie Fackeln stürmend! Freudiges![9]
    Salut von Schiffen über blauer See![10] Bestirntes[11] Fest!
Wimmelnd, mit hellen Augen hingedrängt![12]
    Bis wo die Stadt
    mit letzten Häusern ihren Gast entläßt.
Und dann die langen Einsamkeiten. Nackte Ufer.
    Stille. Nacht. Besinnung. Einkehr.[13] Kommunion.
    Und Glut und Drang
Zum Letzten, Segnenden. Zum Zeugungsfest.[14]
    Zur Wollust. Zum Gebet. Zum Meer.
    Zum Untergang.[15]

    . . . O Biegung der *Millionen Lichter, stumme Wacht,*
      Vor deren *blitzender Parade* schwer die Wasser abwärts rollen.
    Endloses Spalier, zum Gruß gestellt bei Nacht!
    Wie Fackeln stürmend! Freudiges!
      Salut von Schiffen über blauer See! *Bestirntes Fest!*
    Wimmelnd, mit hellen Augen hingedrängt!
      Bis wo die Stadt mit letzten Häusern ihren Gast entläßt.

Die Bildfolge beginnt mit dem optischen Befund ,Millionen Lichter.'
Diesem folgt in schnellem Wechsel eine Serie von Bildern, in der jedes
Bild neue Assoziationen heranträgt. Den Höhepunkt bringt . . . das Schluß-
bild, in dem sich die Szene als ,bestirntes Fest' und die Lichter als ,helle
Augen' darstellen. Wie wenig all diese Bilder auf die Erfassung des optischen Eindrucks ausgehen, ergibt sich aus der Ungenauigkeit des Gesamt-
bildes. Im Sinne der Deskription ist diese Darstellung durchaus unzuläng-
lich, denn sie besteht aus einem durchquirlten Brei von Wahrnehmungs-
fragmenten. Aber die äußere Wirklichkeit spielt hier nur noch insofern eine
Rolle, als sich an ihr das innere Erlebnis niederschlägt, das mit jedem Bild

---

[6]'sense of apprehension' [7]*O Biegung ... rollen:* the lights of Cologne along the banks
of the Rhine. [8]*Spalier stehen* 'form a lane' [9]Does not have to refer to *Spalier,* may be
taken absolutely. [10]This image refers to the lights, but also looks forward to the end of
the poem. [11]'starry' [12]Now the lights are the bright eyes of forward-pressing on-
lookers. [13]'meditation' [14]'festival of procreation' [15]*Und Glut ... Untergang:* These
words are meant positively, as an acceptance of all life. The student of *Faust* will be
reminded of the end of the *Klassische Walpurgisnacht.* Compare also Loerke's
"Strom": *Ich ahne die Ewigkeit will beginnen / Mit einem Duft von Salz.*

von einer anderen Seite berührt wird und am Ende mit erstaunlicher Leb-
haftigkeit gegenwärtig ist. Die Bilder sind hier das eilig hingeworfene
Stenogramm eines inneren Ablaufs. Die übergangslose Koordination der
Bilder und ihre Häufung spiegeln die Simultaneität der Empfindungen, aus
denen das Erlebnis sich zusammensetzt. Die Steigerung versinnbildlicht die
zunehmende Exaltation, die sich bis zum ekstatischen Taumel und Schwindel erhöht. Da das Bild . . . in allererster Linie der inneren Situation
angemessen sein soll, ist die Wahl der Bildvorstellung immer primär von
der jeweiligen Gefühlslage abhängig und nur sekundär von der objektiven
Beschaffenheit der Bezugssache [referent] mitbestimmt.*

To the series of images enumerated here, we may well add *Salut von Schiffen
über blauer See*, which Schneider seems indisposed to take as referring to the
primary "optical diagnosis," i.e., the lights. There is, however, no good
reason why it should not; and since this image is perhaps more strictly
determined by the inner emotional situation than any of the others, hence less
directly "descriptive" than any, it is the most revealing of all. In addition, it is
the structurally most important image in the poem, because it looks forward to
the end: *Meer, Untergang*.

Georg Heym (1887-1912)

Rußland[1]

Mit weißem Haar, in den verrufnen[2] Orten
Noch hinter Werchojansk,[3] in öden Steppen,
Da schmachten sie, die ihre Ketten schleppen
Tagaus, tagein, die düsteren Kohorten.

In Bergwerksnacht, wo ihre Beile klingen   5
Wie von Zyklopen. Doch ihr Mund ist stumm.
Und mit den Peitschen gehn die Wärter um.
Klatsch. — Daß klaffend[4] ihre Schultern springen.[5]

Der Mond schwenkt seine große Nachtlaterne
Auf ihren Weg, wenn sie zur Hürde[6] wanken,   10
Sie fallen schwer in Schlaf. Und sehen ferne

*K. L. Schneider, *Der bildhafte Ausdruck in den Dichtungen Georg Heyms, Georg
Trakls und Ernst Stadlers* (Heidelberg: Winter, ³1968), 158.

[1]Written March, 1911, six years before the Russian Revolution. [2]'infamous' [3]place
name [4]'gaping' [5]'spring open' [6]'sheep pen'

Die Nacht voll Feuer in den Traumgedanken
Und auf der Stange, rot, gleich einem Sterne,
Aus Aufruhrs Meer⁷ das Haupt des Zaren schwanken.

*Robespierre*¹

Er meckert vor sich hin. Die Augen starren
Ins Wagenstroh. Der Mund kaut weißen Schleim.
Er zieht ihn schluckend durch die Backen ein.
Sein Fuß hängt nackt heraus durch zwei der Sparren.²

Bei jedem Wagenstoß fliegt er nach oben.   5
Der Arme Ketten rasseln dann wie Schellen.
Man hört der Kinder frohes Lachen gellen,
Die ihre Mütter aus der Menge hoben.

Man kitzelt ihn am Bein, er merkt es nicht.
Da hält der Wagen. Er sieht auf und schaut   10
Am Straßenende schwarz das Hochgericht.

Die aschengraue Stirn wird schweißbetaut.
Der Mund verzerrt sich furchtbar im Gesicht.
Man harrt³ des Schreis. Doch hört man keinen Laut.

„*Spitzköpfig kommt er . . .*"

Spitzköpfig kommt er über die Dächer hoch
Und schleppt seine gelben Haare nach,
Der Zauberer, der still in die Himmelszimmer steigt,
In vieler Gestirne gewundenem Blumenpfad.

Alle Tiere in Wald und Gestrüpp   5
Liegen mit Häuptern sauber gekämmt,
Singend den Mond-Choral. Aber die Kinder
Knien in den Bettchen in weißem Hemd.

---

⁷'out of revolt's sea'

¹Maximilian Robespierre (1758-1794) was a moving force behind the "Reign of Terror" in the French Revolution and engineered the execution of Louis XVI, among
many others, on the guillotine. He himself met a similar end when his supporters
turned against him.   ²Robespierre is being transported in an open cart, a tumbril.
³*harren* 'await,' with genitive

Meiner Seele unendliche See
Ebbet langsam in sanfter Flut.   10
Ganz grün bin ich innen. Ich schwinde hinaus
Wie ein gläserner Luftballon.

Towards Interpretation

1. Who do you think *der Spitzköpfige* is?
2. How might the speaker be *ganz grün* on the inside? And how would he know that he is?

Ophelia[1]

Im Haar ein Nest von jungen Wasserratten,
Und die beringten Hände auf der Flut
Wie Flossen, also treibt sie durch den Schatten
Des großen Urwalds, der im Wasser ruht.

Die letzte Sonne, die im Dunkel irrt,   5
Versenkt sich tief in ihres Hirnes Schrein.
Warum sie starb? Warum sie so allein
Im Wasser treibt, das Farn und Kraut verwirrt?

Im dichten Röhricht steht der Wind. Er scheucht
Wie eine Hand die Fledermäuse auf.   10
Mit dunklem Fittich, von dem Wasser feucht
Stehn sie wie Rauch im dunklen Wasserlauf,

Wie Nachtgewölk. Ein langer, weißer Aal
Schlüpft über ihre Brust. Ein Glühwurm scheint
Auf ihrer Stirn. Und eine Weide weint   15
Das Laub auf sie und ihre stumme Qual.

Towards Interpretation

1. Does the poem answer the questions posed in lines 7-8?
2. After all the horrific images used to describe Ophelia's state, does the poem end on a note of horror? of disgust? Of sympathy? Of pity?

---

[1]i.e., the character in Shakespeare's *Hamlet*

Georg Trakl (1887-1914)

Verfall

Am Abend, wenn die Glocken Frieden läuten,
Folg ich der Vögel wundervollen Flügen,
Die lang geschart,[1] gleich frommen Pilgerzügen,[2]
Entschwinden in den herbstlich klaren Weiten.

Hinwandelnd durch den dämmervollen Garten   5
Träum ich nach ihren helleren Geschicken
Und fühl der Stunden Weiser[3] kaum mehr rücken.
So folg ich über Wolken ihren Fahrten.

Da macht ein Hauch mich von Verfall erzittern[4]
Die Amsel klagt in den entlaubten Zweigen.   10
Es schwankt der rote Wein[5] an rostigen Gittern,

Indes wie blasser Kinder Todesreigen[6]
Um dunkle Brunnenränder, die verwittern,
Im Wind sich fröstelnd blaue Astern neigen.

Die schöne Stadt[1]

Alte Plätze sonnig schweigen.
Tief in Blau und Gold versponnen
Traumhaft hasten sanfte Nonnen
Unter schwüler Buchen Schweigen.

Aus den braun erhellten Kirchen   5
Schaun des Todes reine Bilder,
Großer Fürsten schöne Schilder.[2]
Kronen schimmern in den Kirchen.

Rösser tauchen aus dem Brunnen.[3]
Blütenkrallen[4] drohn aus Bäumen.   10

---

[1]=*in langen Scharen* (flocks)   [2]'pilgrim processions'   [3]i.e., the hour hand   [4]=*ein Hauch von Verfall macht mich erzittern*   [5]'grape vine'   [6]*der Reigen =Ringelreihen* 'dance with joined hands'

[1]Salzburg, Trakl's native town.   [2]The coats-of-arms of princes whose memorials are placed in the churches.   [3]Reference to the magnificent *Pferdeschwemme* in the *Altstadt*, a great stone horse pond with figures of rearing horses. *Rösser=Rosse*.   [4]The *Blütenkrallen* are probably blossoms of the horse chestnut.

Knaben spielen wirr von Träumen
Abends leise dort am Brunnen.

Mädchen stehen an den Toren,
Schauen scheu ins farbige Leben.
Ihre feuchten Lippen beben   15
Und sie warten an den Toren.

Zitternd flattern Glockenklänge,
Marschtakt hallt und Wacherufen.[5]
Fremde lauschen auf den Stufen.
Hoch im Blau sind Orgelklänge.   20

Helle Instrumente singen.
Durch der Gärten Blätterrahmen
Schwirrt das Lachen schöner Damen.
Leise junge Mütter singen.

Heimlich haucht an blumigen Fenstern   25
Duft von Weihrauch, Teer und Flieder.
Silbern flimmern müde Lider[6]
Durch die Blumen an den Fenstern.

Towards Interpretation

1. One critic finds in this poem "ein letzlich beziehungsloses Nebenei-
   nander von vielfältigen Sinnesdaten [sense perceptions]."* Read the
   poem again and see if you agree.
2. What is the effect of such words as *schimmern* (8), *zitternd flattern*
   (17), *schwirrt* (23), *silbern flimmern* (27)?
3. Is there any "I" in this poem? If so, how is its presence felt?
4. Would you say this is a recognizable portrait of a specific town?
5. Examine the sentence structure. Are there any dependent clauses?
   How does this fit in with your answer to question 1?
6. Read the poem aloud. How would you characterize the rhythm?
7. "Das Faszinierende des Gedichts liegt in der wehmütig-weichen, im
   einzelnen sehr kunstvollen Melodie der Sprachklänge, vor allem der
   Reime; daß sie alle weiblich und zudem in dem umfassenden Reim
   der 1. und 4. Zeile jeder Strophe identisch sind, verstärkt den
   Eindruck des *Traumhaften* und *Müden*" (Hock). Compare this poem
   in the above respects with Hölderlin's "Heidelberg."

---

[5]'calls of the guard' [6]'eyelids'

*Erich Hock, *Motivgleiche Gedichte: Lehrerband*, Am Born der Weltliteratur A7L
(Bamberg: Bayer. Verlagsanstalt, [7]1963), 70f.

Im Winter

Der Acker leuchtet weiß und kalt.
Der Himmel ist einsam und ungeheuer.
Dohlen kreisen über dem Weiher
Und Jäger steigen nieder vom Wald.

Ein Schweigen in schwarzen Wipfeln wohnt.   5
Ein Feuerschein huscht aus den Hütten.
Bisweilen schellt sehr fern ein Schlitten[1]
Und langsam steigt der graue Mond.

Ein Wild[2] verblutet sanft am Rain[3]
Und Raben plätschern in blutigen Gossen.   10
Das Rohr[4] bebt gelb und aufgeschossen.
Frost, Rauch, ein Schritt im leeren Hain.

Sometimes we can most clearly perceive the characteristic qualities of a poem by comparing it with another poem on the same theme by a different author. For this purpose we quote here a poem by the "impressionist," Detlev von Liliencron:

Die Sonne leiht dem Schnee das Prachtgeschmeide,
Doch ach! wie kurz ist Schein und Licht.
Ein Nebel tropft, und traurig zieht im Leide
Die Landschaft ihren Schleier dicht.

Ein Häslein nur fühlt noch des Lebens Wärme,   5
Am Weidenstumpfe hockt es bang.
Doch kreischen hungrig schon die Rabenschwärme
Und hacken auf den sichern Fang.

Bis auf den schwarzen Schlammgrund sind gefroren
Die Wasserlöcher und der See.   10
Zuweilen geht ein Wimmern, wie veloren,
Dann stirbt im toten Wald ein Reh.

In a superficial way, these two poems are strikingly similar: both string together paratactically a series of wintery images and the images themselves even correspond to some extent. In both poems we see ravens engaged in bloody work, in both a dying deer. Yet the feeling engendered by the two poems is quite different; it is even of a different order.

Liliencron personifies his landscape, making it first a kind of great lady with glittering jewels (*Prachtgeschmeide*), then a widow in mourning: . . . *Und traurig zieht im Leide / Die Landschaft ihren Schleier dicht.* His attitude

---

[1]'Now and then sleighbells are heard afar' [2]'game,' 'deer' [3]'edge' [4]'reeds'

is outspokenly subjective, though the impressionist *qua* impressionist is usually thought of as being objective. His subjectivism is seen in the *Doch ach!* of line 2 and the sympathetic diminutive *Häslein* (5), as well as in the statement that only the hare still "feels life's warmth," though it is obvious that the ravens must be as "warm" as the hare. Compared with Trakl, Liliencron seems wordy. (By actual count, the poems contain respectively 72 and 78 words.) Trakl's poem is far more concentrated, the bleakness of the winter scene — which Liliencron also aims to convey — much more insistently present in the form itself. Overtly, at least, Trakl's poem contains no figurative language (though on another level it is much more figurative than Liliencron's), whereas Liliencron's begins with a rather elaborate metaphor. Trakl's poem is devoid of any connectives except *und* — each line is a self-contained statement — while Liliencron, though his language is comparatively spare, uses *doch* (twice), *nur noch*, and *dann*.

Very revealing is the use of adjectives and adverbs in the two poems. Liliencron's are used in a literal sense: the light *is* "short," the hare *is* "fearful," the ravens *are* "hungry," and a personfied landscape may even be "sad." Trakl's use of words of this class is to a considerable extent non-literal. (In later poems it sometimes becomes completely so.) To say that the sky is *einsam und ungeheuer* is not an objective statement; rather than describing the object it expresses an attitude toward it. Tree-tops may of course be "black" (line 5), but one immediately senses that this blackness is more than a color attribute. The same is true of the "gray" moon. Trakl's line, *Ein Wild verblutet s a n f t am Rain*, awakens a feeling of deep melancholy, the deer might seem some kind of sacrificial victim; Liliencron's animal is merely freezing to death.

In Liliencron's poem we have a desolate winter landscape with sentimental overtones (caused by the impressionist's objectivism slipping into subjectivism); in Trakl's we have the desolation of life itself expressed in terms of a winter landscape. His winter is the winter of the soul. The two poems offer a good illustration of the "outside in" versus "inside out" of Impressionism and Expressionism.*

Towards Interpretation

1. Note the frequency with which the sounds *eu* and *ei* (*ai*) occur in the Trakl poem (14 times). What may this be said to symbolize?
2. Does Liliencron use a similar technique?

---

*Analysis based on Erich Hock, *Motivgleiche Gedichte*: Lehrerband, 71f.

Untergang

Über den weißen Weiher
Sind die wilden Vögel fortgezogen.
Am Abend weht von unseren Sternen ein eisiger Wind.

Über unsere Gräber
Beugt sich die zerbrochene Stirne der Nacht.   5
Unter Eichen schaukeln wir auf einem silbernen Kahn. —

Immer klingen die weißen Mauern der Stadt.
Unter Dornenbogen
O mein Bruder klimmen wir blinde Zeiger[1] gen[2] Mitternacht.

This poem, from Trakl's middle period, is introduced as an example of the
abstract manner in lyric poetry. It is no more interpretable in the usual sense
(though of course it has been "interpreted") than an abstraction by Klee or
mobile by Calder. Yet it is undeniably powerful. One cannot read it without
being moved and without feeling a sense of impending doom. Its "difficulty,"
if one can speak of the poem in such terms, does not lie so much in the poem
itself as in our unwillingness to accept the word without being able to discover
a referent. All our habits demand that words mean *something*. This seems to be
a poem in which words simply *mean*. Pure expressiveness = pure abstraction.

Abendländisches Lied

O der Seele nächtlicher Flügelschlag:
Hirten gingen wir einst an dämmernden Wäldern hin
Und es folgte das rote Wild,[1] die grüne Blume und der lal-
Demutsvoll. O, der uralte Ton des Heimchens,[2]   [lende Quell
Blut blühend am Opferstein[3]   5
Und der Schrei des einsamen Vogels über der grünen Stille
                                                     des Teichs.

O ihr Kreuzzüge[4] und glühenden Martern
Des Fleisches, Fallen purpurner Früchte
Im Abendgarten, wo vor Zeiten die frommen Jünger[5] gegangen,
Kriegsleute nun, erwachend aus Wunden und Sternenträumen.   10
O, das sanfte Zyanenbündel[6] der Nacht.

---

[1]'hands of a clock' (*Zeiger* is in apposition to *wir*.)   [2]=*gegen*

[1]Reminiscent of *Rotwild* 'red deer.'   [2]=*Grille* 'cricket'   [3]'altar' (made of stone)
[4]'crusades'   [5]'disciples'   [6]*die Zyane* 'cornflower'

O, ihr Zeiten der Stille und goldener Herbste,
Da wir friedliche Mönche die purpurne Traube gekeltert;
Und rings erglänzten Hügel und Wald.
O, ihr Jagden und Schlösser; Ruh des Abends,   15
Da in seiner Kammer der Mensch Gerechtes sann,
In stummem Gebet um Gottes lebendiges Haupt rang.

O, die bittere Stunde des Untergangs,
Da wir ein steinernes Antlitz in schwarzen Wassern beschaun.
Aber strahlend heben die silbernen Lider die Liebenden: 20
Ein Geschlecht. Weihrauch strömt von rosigen Kissen
Und der süße Gesang der Auferstandenen.[7]

It is at once evident that the "difficulty" of this poem is of a different order
from that of "Untergang." Language is here used referentially, not abstractly,
or, at any rate, referentially as well as abstractly. First level orientation is
therefore a matter of understanding the references, much as it would be in a
poem by, say, Hölderlin, of whose tone "Abendländisches Lied" (like many
poems by Trakl) is so forcibly reminiscent.

The title means "Occidental Song" or "Song of the Occident." Knowing
that the poem refers to Western culture, many things take on a fairly definite
meaning — their referent is easily found.

O der Seele nächtlicher Flügelschlag, 'Oh, the nocturnal wing-beat of the
soul.' The soul lives not only in the past, present, and future of the individual,
but in the whole life of the race. With one beat of its wings it is back in a
pastoral economy: *Hirten gingen wir einst.* . . . And now each strophe evokes
an "hour" in the life of Western man. Our own hour is of course *die bittere
Stunde des Untergangs*; here the tense becomes present for the first time. The
stony face we see in the black waters is our own. (Like many modern poets —
among them Rilke and Valéry — Trakl finds the Narcissus motif significant.)
The poet sees a promise of redemption from the stony face in love. Obviously,
erotic love — in Trakl's poetry always sinful — cannot be meant; *E i n Geschlecht* excludes this interpretation. Rather, the reference would seem to be to
a final reconciliation of all opposites; in the words of the Bible: "The children
of this world marry, and are given in marriage: But they which shall be
accounted worthy to obtain that world, *and the resurrection from the dead*,
neither marry, nor are given in marriage . . . they are equal unto the angels,
and are the children of God, being the children of the resurrection" (Luke
20:34-36). As angels and children of God, the lovers are *one*, whether we take
Geschlecht to mean "sex," "race," or "family." Trakl, the Christian, could
look forward to an end of all time and all "hours."

---

[7]'the resurrected'

Georg Trakl

Gottfried Benn

Gottfried Benn (1886-1956)

„O daß wir unsere Ururahnen wären"

O daß wir unsere Ururahnen wären.
Ein Klümpchen Schleim in einem warmen Moor.
Leben und Tod, Befruchten und Gebären
glitte aus unseren stummen Säften vor.

Ein Algenblatt oder ein Dünenhügel,   5
vom Wind Geformtes und nach unten schwer.
Schon ein Libellenkopf, ein Möwenflügel
wäre zu weit[1] und litte schon zu sehr.

Verlorenes Ich

Verlorenes Ich, zersprengt von Stratosphären,
Opfer des Ion —: Gamma-Strahlen-Lamm —
Teilchen und Feld —: Unendlickeitchimären
auf deinem grauen Stein von Notre–Dame.[1]

---

[1]'too far developed'

[1]Benn introduces the terminology of modern science into his lyric poetry. The concepts of science, with the stratosphere at one extreme and the ion at the other, are the

Die Tage gehn dir ohne Nacht und Morgen,   5
die Jahre halten ohne Schnee und Frucht
bedrohend das Unendliche verborgen —
die Welt als Flucht.

Wo endest du, wo lagerst du, wo breiten
sich deine Sphären an — Verlust, Gewinn — :   10
ein Spiel von Bestien: Ewigkeiten,
an ihren Gittern fliehst du hin.[2]

Der Bestienblick: die Sterne als Kaldaunen,[3]
der Dschungeltod als Seins- und Schöpfungsgrund,[4]
Mensch, Völkerschlachten, Katalaunen[5]   15
hinab den Bestienschlund.

Die Welt zerdacht. Und Raum und Zeiten
und was die Menschheit wob und wog,
Funktion nur von Unendlichkeiten —
Die Mythe log.   20

Woher, wohin — nicht Nacht, nicht Morgen,
kein Evoë, kein Requiem,[6]
du möchtest dir ein Stichwort[7] borgen —
allein bei wem?

Ach, als sich alle einer Mitte neigten   25
und auch die Denker nur den Gott gedacht,
sie sich dem Hirten und dem Lamm verzweigten,[8]
wenn aus dem Kelch das Blut sie[9] rein gemacht,

---

modern "infinities" of which the ego is the "victim," the sacrificial "gamma-ray lamb." *Teilchen und Feld* 'particle and (magnetic) field' — the ego no longer has a will of its own but is merely a function of forces beyond the power of comprehension. The things referred to in the first two and a half lines are the *Unendlichkeitschimären* on the temple of modern man, *our* temple, as the gargoyles, dragons, cobolds, devils, and other grotesqueries were the *Unendlichkeitschimären* the man of the Middle Ages placed on the outside of his temple. (Look up "chimera.") *Our* Notre Dame is science. [2]The infinities (eternities) of science are beasts along whose cages (*Gitter*) man is forced to flee. Here he can find no place to be. What is gained or lost in modern life is all in the "beasts'" game, not man's. [3]=*Eingeweide* [4]Reference to Darwinism and the survival of the fittest. [5]A neologism referring to such great victories as that of the Romans and Goths over Attila the Hun at Chalons in 451 A.D., called in German *die Schlacht auf den Katalaunischen Gefilden* (*campi catalaunici*). [6]'no evoë, no requiem,' i.e., no religion, whether pagan or Christian [7]'cue' [8]i.e., joined like the limb of a tree to the Shepherd and the Lamb, i.e., Christ and the Church [9]accusative

und alle rannen aus der einen Wunde,[10]
brachen das Brot, das jeglicher genoß —   30
o ferne zwingende erfüllte Stunde,
die einst auch das verlorne Ich umschloß.[11]

In his introduction to an anthology of Expressionist poetry,* Benn says:

Wirklichkeit — Europas dämonischer Begriff: Glücklich nur jene Zeitalter und Generationen, in denen es eine unbezweifelbare [Wirklichkeit] gab, welch tiefes erstes Zittern des Mittelalters bei der Auflösung der religiösen [Wirklichkeit], welche fundamentale Erschütterung jetzt seit 1900 bei Zertrümmerung der naturwissenschaftlichen, der seit 400 Jahren ‚wirklich' gemachten. Ihre ältesten Restbestände lösten sich auf, und was übrigblieb, waren Beziehungen und Funktionen; irre, wurzellose Utopien; humanitäre, soziale oder pazifistische Makulaturen [pieces of waste paper], durch die lief ein Prozeß an sich, eine Wirtschaft als solche, Sinn und Ziel waren imaginär, gestaltlos, ideologisch . . . Auflösung der Natur, Auflösung der Geschichte. Die alten Realitäten Raum und Zeit: Funktionen von Formeln; Gesundheit und Krankheit: Funktionen vom Bewußtsein; selbst die konkrete Mächte wie Staat und Gesellschaft substantiell gar nicht mehr zu fassen, immer nur der Betrieb [=Prozeß] an sich, der Prozeß als solcher. . . .

This passage is the best possible commentary on "Verlorenes Ich." In "explaining" the universe, science leaves no room for man, for it leaves no reality. Without mankind, God is also meaningless, for meaning is being and lack of meaning nothingness. Thus modern man's central experience, *das Nichts*, is the paradoxial result of his being able to account for everything. This is the theme of Benn's poem. His answer is not a return to the "Mitte" of the last two stanzas, is not the Christian answer of some contemporary intellectuals, but rather an aesthetic, extreme *l'art pour l'art*. It is formulated in the next poem.

---

[10]i.e., from the wound in Christ's side [11]In the Middle Ages even *das verlorene Ich* (called by Oswald Spengler, one of Benn's favorite authors, *die faustische Seele*) was "enclosed" by the sacraments of the Church. This whole poem is indebted to a passage in Spengler's *Der Untergang des Abendlandes*, 2:354ff. There (358) Spengler calls the "Faustian soul" an *"Ich im Unendlichen verloren."*

Lyrik des expressionistischen Jahrzehnts (Wiesbaden: Limes, 1955), 14f.

Ein Wort

Ein Wort, ein Satz —: aus Chiffren steigen
erkanntes Leben, jäher Sinn,
die Sonne steht, die Sphären schweigen
und alles ballt sich zu ihm[1] hin.

Ein Wort — ein Glanz, ein Flug, ein Feuer,   5
ein Flammenwurf, ein Sternenstrich —
und wieder Dunkel, ungeheuer,
im leeren Raum um Welt und Ich.

Astern

Astern — schwelende Tage,
alte Beschwörung, Bann,
die Götter halten die Waage
eine zögernde Stunde an.

Noch einmal die goldenen Herden   5
der Himmel, das Licht, der Flor,
was brütet das alte Werden
unter den sterbenden Flügeln vor?

Noch einmal das Ersehnte,
Den Rausch, der Rosen Du[1] —   10
der Sommer stand und lehnte
und sah den Schwalben zu,

noch einmal ein Vermuten,
wo längst Gewißheit wacht:
die Schwalben streifen die Fluten   15
und trinken Fahrt und Nacht.

---

[1]i.e., *dem Wort*

[1]'the Thou of the roses'

Turin[1]

„Ich laufe auf zerrissenen Sohlen",
schrieb dieses große Weltgenie
in seinem letzten Brief — dann holen
sie ihn nach Jena — Psychiatrie.

Ich kann mir keine Bücher kaufen,   5
ich sitze in den Librairien:[2]
Notizen — dann nach Aufschnitt[3] laufen: —
das sind die Tage von Turin.

Indes Europas Edelfäule[4]
an Pau, Bayreuth und Epsom[5] sog,   5
unmarmte er zwei Droschkengäule
bis ihn sein Wirt nach Hause zog.

Franz Werfel (1890-1945)

Der Mensch ist stumm

Ich habe dir den Abschiedskuß gegeben
Und klammre mich nervös an deine Hand.
Schon mahn ich dich, auf Dies und Jenes Acht zu geben.
Der Mensch ist stumm.

Will denn der Zug, der Zug nicht endlich pfeifen?   5
Mir ist, als dürfte ich dich nie mehr wiedersehn.
Ich rede runde Sätze, ohne zu begreifen . . .
Der Mensch ist stumm.

Ich weiß, wenn ich dich nicht mehr hätte,
Das wär' der Tod, der Tod, der Tod!   10
Und dennoch möcht' ich fliehn. Gott, eine Zigarette!
Der Mensch ist stumm.

---

[1]In January, 1889, Nietzsche became hopelessly insane in Turin, Italy. His landlord found him in the street embracing a team of carriage horses. Then he was taken back to Germany (Jena, Naumburg) for treatment. He died in Weimar 10 years later. [2]'bookstores' (*not* 'libraries') [3]'cold cuts' [4]'decaying nobility,' a play on words: *Edelfäule* 'noble rot' (vintner's term) properly refers to the procedure of allowing grapes to rot on the vine for flavor. [5]Names of famous European resorts

Dahin! Jetzt auf der Straße würgt mich Weinen.
Verwundert blicke ich mich um.
Denn auch das Weinen sagt nicht, was wir meinen.   15
Der Mensch is stumm.

Veni creator spiritus

Komm heiliger Geist du, schöpferisch!
Den Marmor unsrer Form zerbrich!
Daß nicht mehr Mauer krank und hart
Den Brunnen dieser Welt umstarrt,[1]
Daß wir gemeinsam und nach oben   5
Wie Flammen in einander toben!

Tauch auf aus unsern Flächen wund,
Delphin von aller Wesen Grund,
Alt allgemein und heiliger Fisch![2]
Komm reiner Geist du, schöpferisch,   10
Nach dem wir ewig uns entfalten,[3]
Kristallgesetz der Weltgestalten!

Wie sind wir alle Fremde doch!
Wie unterm letzten Hemde noch
Die Schattengreise im Spital   15
Sich hassen bis zum letzten Mal,
Und jeder, eh' er ostwärts mündet,[4]
Allein sein Abendlicht entzündet,

So sind wir eitel eingespannt,
Und hocken bös an unserm Rand,   20
Und morden uns an jedem Tisch.
Komm heiliger Geist du, schöpferisch
Aus uns empor mit tausend Flügen!
Zerbrich das Eis in unsern Zügen,

Daß tränenhaft und gut und gut   25
Aufsiede die entzückte Flut,
Daß nicht mehr fern und unerreicht

---

[1] =*fest umzäunt* [2] The fish, especially the dolphin, stood for Christ in early Christian iconography. The Greeks connected the dolphin with a number of deities, especially Apollo, Dionysos, and Aphrodite. [3] Line 11: approximately, 'whose perfection we eternally strive to attain as we develop' [4] 'empties eastward,' i.e., returns to the source, dies

Ein Wesen um das andre schleicht,
Daß jauchzend wir in Blick, Hand, Mund und
Haaren,
Und in uns selbst dein Attribut erfahren! 30

Daß, wer dem Bruder in die Arme fällt,
Dein tiefes Schlagen süß am Herzen hält,
Daß, wer des armen Hundes Schaun empfängt,
Von deinem weisen Blicke wird beschenkt,
Daß alle wir in Küssens Überflüssen 35
Nur deine reine heilige Lippe küssen!

Der dicke Mann im Spiegel

Ach Gott, ich bin das nicht, der aus dem Spiegel stiert,[1]
Der Mensch mit wildbewachsner Brust und unrasiert.
Tag war heut so blau,
Mit der Kinderfrau
Wurde ja im Stadtpark promeniert. 5

Noch kein Matrosenanzug flatterte mir fort
Zu jenes strengverschlossenen Kastens Totenort.[2]
Eben abgelegt
Hängt er[3] unbewegt,
Klein und müde an der Türe dort. 10

Und ward nicht in die Küche nachmittags geblickt,
Kaffee roch winterlich, und Uhr hat laut getickt. —
Lieblich stand verwundert
Der vorher getschundert,
Übers Glatteis mit den Brüderchen geschickt.[4] 15

Auch hat die Frau mir heut wie immer Angst gemacht
Vor jenem Wächter Kakitz,[5] der den Park bewacht.
Oft zu schnöder Zeit
Hör' im Traum ich weit
Diesen Teufel säbelschleppen[6] in der Nacht. 20

Die treue Alte,[7] warum kommt sie denn noch nicht?
Von Schlafensnähe allzuschwer ist mein Gesicht.

---

[1]'stare' [2]'no sailor suit (had) yet fluttered away to the grave of that strictly closed trunk' [3]=der Matrosenanzug [4]"the boy who had just been sliding so skillfully (geschickt) over the ice with his little brothers" [5]personal name [6]'dragging his saber' [7]i.e., die Kinderfrau

Wenn sie doch schon käme
Und es mit sich nähme,
Das dort oben leise singt, das Licht!   25

Ach, abendlich besänftigt tönt kein stiller Schritt.
Und Babi[7] dreht das Licht nicht aus und nimmt es mit.
　　Nur der dicke Mann
　　Schaut mich hilflos an,
Bis er tieferschrocken aus dem Spiegel tritt.   30

Towards Interpretation
　1. What symbolic function can we ascribe to the striking difference in rhythm between the first two and the last three lines of each stanza?
　2. Why *Kaffee* and *Uhr* (line 12) instead of *der Kaffee* and *die Uhr*?
　3. How would you formulate in *general* terms the subject of this poem?

Yvan [Ywan] Goll (1891-1950)

Stunden

Wasserträgerinnen
Hochgeschürzte Töchter
Schreiten schwer herab die Totenstraße
Auf den Köpfen wiegend
Einen Krug voll Zeit   5
Eine Ernte ungepflückter Tropfen
Die schon reifen auf dem Weg hinab
Wasserfälle Flüsse Tränen Nebel Dampf
Immer geheimere Tropfen immer kargere Zeit
Schattenträgerinnen   10
Schon vergangen schon verhangen
Ewigkeit

Abendgesang[1]

Mit allen Farben die ich geblutet
Mit allen Vögeln die ich getötet
Letzten Gesang unsres Schicksals
Sing ich Geliebte in dein wissendes Ohr

Denn zusammen haben wir viel Rosen geliebt   5
Und beim Ruf der Amsel
Stieg ein Engel in dein Gesicht
Und verwandelte dich zu Natur

Schwalben bewunderten wir
Die sich von Larven nährten   10
Und den Lerchen warfen wir aus dem Klee
Unser Glück nach

Ölbaum von einst entwurzle ich[2]
Aus der Vergangenheit Traum[3]
Um dich zu beschatten   15
Während du kelterst den letzten Wein

„Dreißig Jahre"

Dreißig Jahre
Hab ich gewartet
Um dich am Himmel vorüberziehen
Und die Sonne verdunkeln zu sehen

In städtischen Gärten   5
Hab ich gewartet
Hinter eisernen Büschen
Eine vergebliche Jugend lang

An jeder Haltestelle
Sprang ich in den Autobus   10
Hoffend dein Lächeln zu überraschen
Und wohnte in möblierten Hotels
Um in blinden[1] Spiegeln dein Profil zu finden

---

[1]A love poem written by the poet to his wife during his last illness. He remembers and forms (that they may not perish) those things which shall shelter the beloved when he is gone. [2]*Ölbaum* is accusative [3]*Traum* is governed by *aus*.

[1]'tarnished'

Dreißig Jahre
Hab ich an Flüssen   15
Den weißen Schiffen gewinkt
Von Bergen das Dach deines Hauses gesucht

Dreißig verregnete Herbste
Hab ich gewartet
Mein Haar lichtet sich   20
Mein Augenlicht läßt nach

Komm schnell!
Denn heute wenn du nicht pünktlich bist
Warte ich nur noch bis zur nächsten Tram!

Yvan Goll

Georg Britting

Georg Britting (1891-1964)

Mondnacht auf dem Turm

In den Bäumen geht der Wind leis
Und das Horn des Mondes funkelt blaß.
Aus dem Garten, heiß vom Tage,
Auf zum Turme steigt der Duft vom Gras.

Dunkel schattet das Geäst   5
Und der Bach rauscht laut, wie ers gewohnt.

Die Brüstung glänzt, vom Abendtau genäßt.
Aus dem Kornfeld tritt das Reh und äst.[1]
Eine Wolke haucht der See zum Mond.

Das Grillenvolk[2] mit Silbernadlen näht,   10
Die schwarzen Bäume atmen mit Gebraus.
Morgen wird das erste Gras gemäht.

Die Nacht rückt vor, es ist schon spät,
Und das fromme Horn des Mondes steht,
Lautlos blasend, wie ein Wächter über Turm   15
                    und Haus.

Towards Interpretation

1. This poem, with its completely irregular rime scheme, its seemingly hit or miss way of presenting various features of the scene, looks as though it must fall into fragments. Yet it does not. See if you can discover why.
2. Would you call this an impressionistic or an expressionistic poem?

Unruhe

Immer wieder
Blühn die Gärten,
Singen Vögel
Ihre Lieder,
Jedes Jahr.   5

Und die Sterne
Stehn am Himmel,
Weiß und prächtig,
Und die Ferne
Tut wie Gold sich   10
Mächtig auf.

Wär der goldne
Mond nicht über
Deinem Vogelgarten,
Über deinem   15
Stillen Haus,
Hieltest du das
Lange Warten
Nicht mehr aus.

---

[1]'grazes' [2]'cricket folk'

Wespen-Sonett

Das Stroh ist gelb. Das ist Septembers Farbe.
Die fette Birne ist so gelb wie er,[1]
Und für die Wespe da, daß sie nicht darbe:[2]
Verspätete,[3] sonst flögen viele her!

Die goldne Sonne hängt am Himmel schwer,   5
Gelb wie die Birne, die zersprungen klafft.
Die Wespe trinkt bedächtig von dem Saft:
Die Birne, weiß sie, wird so schnell nicht leer

Und trocken sein, und nichts als dürre Haut!
Vom Himmel oben, der gewaltig blaut,   10
Strömt überreifes, süßes Licht hernieder.

Die Wespe trinkt. Bei jedem Zuge[4] rührt
Die Brust sich ihr, spannt sich das enge Mieder,[5]
Das ihre fräuleinshafte Hüfte schnürt.

Nelly Sachs (1891-1970)

Had she not survived the Second World War, Nelly Sachs, *Dichterin jüdischen Schicksals* (W. A. Berendsohn), would now be forgotten as a poet, since her early efforts were written under the influence of German Romanticism and showed little influence of or even familiarity with the development of literature since that time — this, although she lived in Berlin, to a great extent the center of German Expressionism and the avant garde. Sachs later recounted that on the same day in May, 1940, she received in the mail a summons to report to a so-called "work camp" and also a visa for herself and her mother to emigrate to Sweden, where she lived in exile for the rest of her life. Influenced by the language and images of the Psalms, the Jewish caballa and Hassidic mysticism, and of German mystics like Jakob Böhme on the one hand, and the incantatory-ecstatic tone of Hölderlin and Novalis, on the other, Sachs forged an idiosyncratic metaphorical language (*Staub, Finger, Stern, Rauch, Essenkehrer*) that allowed her to attempt to express the inexpressible. That she regarded the fate of the Jewish people as in a certain sense exemplary, that is, a metaphor for the potential fate of all those regarded as "strangers," is made clear in

---

[1]i.e., *der September* [2]The pear is there for the wasp, that it should not go without.
[3]supply *Wespe* [4]'sip' [5]'bodice'

the poem, "Kommt einer von ferne." The universality of this message gained wider public recognition for Sachs' work in the last years of her life, including the Nobel Prize for Literature in 1966.

„O die Schornsteine"

Und wenn diese meine Haut zerschlagen sein wird,
so werde ich ohne mein Fleisch Gott schauen.
(Hiob)[1]

O die Schornsteine
Auf den sinnreich erdachten Wohnungen des Todes,[2]
Als Israels Leib zog aufgelöst in Rauch
Durch die Luft —
Als Essenkehrer ihn ein Stern empfing[3]   5
Der schwarz wurde
Oder war es ein Sonnenstrahl?

O die Schornsteine!
Freiheitswege für Jeremias und Hiobs Staub —
Wer erdachte[4] euch und baute Stein auf Stein   10
Den Weg für Flüchtlinge aus Rauch?

O die Wohnungen des Todes,
Einladend hergerichtet
Für den Wirt des Hauses, der sonst Gast[5] war —
O ihr Finger,[6]   15
Die Eingangsschwelle legend
Wie ein Messer zwischen Leben und Tod —

O ihr Schornsteine,
O ihr Finger,
Und Israels Leib im Rauch durch die Luft!   20

Towards Interpretation
1. The poet employs everyday images to describe far from everyday events. What is her purpose in doing so?

---

[1]Job 19:26 [2]i.e., crematoria [3]=*ein Stern empfing ihn* (=*Rauch*=*Leib*) *als Essen-kehrer* ('chimney sweep') [4]cf. line 1 [5]*Einladend ... war* 'invitingly furnished for the owner/host of the house, who formerly was a guest' Some gas chambers were decorated on the outside to look inviting so as not to alert the victims; *Gast* denotes both 'guest' and 'stranger.' [6]i.e., *Schornsteine*

Chor der Ungeborenen

Wir Ungeborenen
Schon beginnt die Sehnsucht an uns zu schaffen
Die Ufer des Blutes weiten sich zu unserem Empfang
Wie Tau sinken wir in die Liebe hinein.
Noch liegen die Schatten der Zeit wie Fragen   5
Über unserem Geheimnis.

Ihr Liebenden,
Ihr Sehnsüchtigen,
Hört, ihr Abschiedskranken:
Wir sind es, die in euren Blicken zu leben beginnen,   10
In euren Händen, die suchende sind in der blauen Luft —
Wir sind es, die nach Morgen Duftenden.
Schon zieht uns euer Atem ein,
Nimmt uns hinab in euren Schlaf
In die Träume, die unser Erdreich sind   15
Wo unsere schwarze Amme, die Nacht
Uns wachsen läßt,
Bis wir uns spiegeln in euren Augen
Bis wir sprechen in euer Ohr.

Schmetterlingsgleich   20
Werden wir von den Häschern eurer Sehnsucht gefangen —
Wie Vogelstimmen an die Erde verkauft —
Wir Morgenduftenden,
Wir kommenden Lichter für eure Traurigkeit.

Towards Interpretation

  1. This poem is based upon a reversal of the roles of parents and child.
     Explain how this is developed.

„Kommt einer von ferne"

Kommt einer[1]
von ferne
mit einer Sprache
die vielleicht die Laute
verschließt   5
mit dem Wiehern der Stute[2]

---

[1]'If someone ...' Lines 1-18 are two 'if'-clauses, lines 19-25 contain the conclusion.
[2]'who ends his utterances with the neigh of a mare'

oder
dem Piepen
junger Schwarzamseln
oder   10
auch wie eine knirschende Säge
die alle Nähe zerschneidet —

Kommt einer
Von ferne
mit Bewegungen des Hundes   15
oder
vielleicht der Ratte
und es ist Winter
so kleide ihn warm
kann auch sein   20
er hat Feuer unter den Sohlen
(vielleicht ritt er
auf einem Meteor)
so schilt[3] ihn nicht
falls dein Teppich durchlöchert schreit —   25

Ein Fremder hat immer
seine Heimat im Arm
wie eine Waise
für die er vielleicht nichts
als ein Grab sucht.   30

Towards Interpretation

1. In what terms does the poet describe the stranger in the 'if'-clauses? In what terms should one show understanding?
2. Under what circumstances might a stranger be carrying his homeland like "an orphan in his arms?" Why might a stranger be seeking a grave for the orphan?

---

[3]imperative of *schelten*

Josef Weinheber (1892-1945)

„Der Schöpfer stirbt . . .“

Der Schöpfer stirbt . . . Geschaffnes kommt zu Jahren[1]
und löst sich ab vom Tag, dem es entstiegen.
Und anders als die ruhmreichen Fanfaren
geschlagner Schlachten wird *dies* Gleichnis siegen.

Das Dunkel Pindars,[2] die erhaben[3] klaren   5
Gebärden Dantes, Platons Tiefe: wiegen
sie nicht die Zeiten auf, die ihre waren,
und reden uns, wenn selbst die Steine schwiegen?

Altar den Späten,[4] heilig, fern und hoh,
wie mir der Schmerz des Michelangelo,   10
dem er die Herbheit seines Worts gegeben.

Und da ich es, das bittre, abermal
erfülle,[5] stark von meiner eignen Qual,
so siegt die Kunst — so unterliegt das Leben.

Alt-Ottakring[1]

Was noch lebt, ist Traum.
Ach, wie war es schön!
Jüngre werden kaum
jene Zeit verstehn,
wo das Kirchlein stand   5
und die Häuser blank

---

[1]'The creator dies, that which he created matures'   [2]Greek poet, known for his obscurity. [3]'sublimely' [4]dative plural [5]Weinheber is "again fulfilling" Michelangelo's "bitter word" in a double sense: Firstly, by writing in the same vein and by experiencing the same pain as the great Renaissance master; secondly, by translating his work. This sonnet stands in a 15-sonnet sequence, in which the first and last lines of each sonnet are a translation of two lines of a sonnet by Michelangelo (placed at the head of the sequence) and in which the last line of one sonnet furnishes the first line of the next. (So-called "master-sonnet.") Sonnet 15 is then a complete translation of the Italian original. Such intense concern with form and the solution of formal problems is characteristic of much of Weinheber's poetry.

[1]District (XVI. Bezirk) in Vienna.

unterm Giebelrand
hatten Weingerank.[2]

Und im Herbste gar,
wenn der Maische[3] Duft   10
hing im blauen Klar
der beschwingten Luft!
Von den Hügeln schlicht[4]
kam der Hauer[5] Sang,
da die Stadt noch nicht   15
grau ins Grüne drang.

Heut ein Steinbezirk
wie ein andrer auch,
und nur sanft Gebirg
schickt wie einst den Hauch,   20
Hauch von Obst und Wein
in die Gassen aus,
und der Sonnenschein
liegt auf altem Haus.

Da und dort ein Tor   25
hat noch breiten Schwung,
Buschen[6] grün davor
lädt wie einst zum Trunk,
und im Abend wird
längst Vergangnes nah,   30
spielt ein Bursch gerührt
Ziehharmonika.

Begegnung mit dem Melos[1]

Wie ein Geisterlaut
durch die Stille geht,
wie am Mittag Pan
in den Feldern steht:
Also unvertraut —   5
und ich stand und sann —
sah dein Auge mich
an.

---

[2]'grapevines' [3]*die Maische* 'young, unpurified wine' (mash) [4]'clearly' [5]'vintners'
[6]'bush' (green branches over gateway to indicate that the *Hauer* has new wine for sale
— the Viennese say: *Er hat ausg'steckt*)

[1]'(spirit of) song'

Da du kamst von fern,
aus verborgnem Land,   10
deine Sprache war
mir so unbekannt;
Deiner Stirne Stern
aber bot so klar
wie ein Spiegel dich   15
dar.

Eine Ewigkeit,
einen Augenblick
hat mein Herz gebebt
von dem großen Glück.   20
In die bittre Zeit
ist die Spur verschwebt,
wie ein Windhauch sich
hebt . .

Werner Bergengruen (1892-1964)

Auf ein Grab

Der hier begraben liegt, hat nicht viel Geld erworben
und außer dieser hier nie eine Liegenschaft.[1]
Er ist wie jedermann geboren und gestorben,
und niemand rühmte ihn um Tat- und Geisteskraft.

Da er nichts hinterließ, ist er wohl längst vergessen.   5
Du, Fremder, bleibe stehn und merk auf diese Schrift.
Dann sag mir, ob sein Lob nicht manches übertrifft,
das in der Leute Mund und ihrem Ohr gesessen.

Daß jedes Jahr geblüht, war seine größte Lust!
Da schritt er ohne Hut gemächlich über Land.   10
Und wenn zu Winterszeit er erstmals heizen mußt,
dann hat er wie den Schlaf den Ofen Freund genannt.

Er teilte brüderlich sein Brot mit Hund und Meise
und wer es sonst begehrt. Hat niemanden verdammt,

---

[1] 'a piece of real estate'

hat niemanden gehaßt als nur das Steueramt,   15
sprach nie vom Börsenkurs und selten über Preise.

Versichert[2] war er nicht und nicht im Sportvereine.
Er ging zu keiner Wahl,[3] er diente keinem Herrn,
sang nicht im Kirchenchor. Zeitungen hielt er keine.[4]
Doch daß ichs nicht vergeß: er hatte Rettich gern.   20

Er rauchte Caporal.[5] Ist wenig nur gereist.
Dafür hats ihn gefreut, in jungem Gras zu ruhn.
Dann war er noch bemüht, gar niemand wehzutun,
und lobte Gottes Treu und Zuger Kirschengeist.[6]

Du, Wandrer, bitt für ihn. Und bleibe eingedenk,   25
daß Gott dein Kämmrer ist, dein Truchseß und dein
                                                 Schenk.[7]

Towards Interpretation

1. Translate the title. Where might these lines of poetry be found written?
2. How would you characterize in modern slang the man buried here?

Gertrud Kolmar (1894-1943)

Charlotte Corday

*Keine gemeine, schändliche Hand schnitt seinen Lebensfaden ab, die Mörderin
war ein junges Mädchen voll weiblicher Tugend . . . Um sieben Uhr kam
Marie-Anne Charlotte Corday zu dem Bürger Marat . . .*
(Restif de la Bretonne)

Die in Schleiern schwebend und geweiht,
Eine aschenblonde Kerze, glomm:
Ihre Augen blühten klar und fromm,
Ihre Hände griffen Dunkelheit;

Dunkelheit umschmiegte, was sie barg,   5
Ihres Mordes streng erwählte Pflicht,

---

[2]'insured' [3]'He never voted' [4]'He took no newspapers' [5]cigarette brand name
[6]cherry schnaps made in Zug (Switzerland) [7]court offices: chamberlain, steward, and
butler

Da sie ohne Flackern ihr Gesicht
Leuchtend hinhob an den nahen Sarg.[1]

In den düstern Käfig stieg sie hell.
Ach, die Treppe war so schwer zu gehn!   10
Jede Stufe ward ihr zehnmal zehn,
Alle Stufen schwanden viel zu schnell.

Als ihr Mut die Glocke droben zog,
Schrie das Herz, schrie Wehe ob der Hand,[2]
Rief so tönend, daß sie nicht verstand,   15
Wie ihr Mund die Öffnende[3] belog,

Jenes ernste, ungeschmückte Weib,
Das den Dämon heilig liebte, ihn,
Der von Flammenkronen widerschien . . .
Und sie sah das Bad, den Männerleib,   20

Sah die Schulter nackt, die breite Brust,
Um sein Haupt ein wunderliches Tuch,
Spürte dünnen Arzeneigeruch,
Fand in falbem armutskranken Dust[4]

Linnen, Wanne, Brett[5] und Tintenfaß,   25
Federkiel, der winkte.[6] Und sie kam,
Warf vom Lid[7] die Röte ihrer Scham,
Riß ums Antlitz blendend ihren Haß,

Saß so stark und zitternd zu Gericht,[8]
Bot den Zettel, den er fiebrig griff,   30
Wiederholte schweigend dieses: „Triff!",
Fest sich fassend schon. Sie wußte nicht,

Daß er groß war. Aber sie war rein,
Stahl, der seine Feuerpranke[9] brach.
Sie erglänzte, zuckte auf und stach   35
Als ein Messer blitzend in ihn ein.

Werkzeug, gleich umklammert und zerschellt;
Heldin, die dem Glauben starb. Er ruht.
Aus der Wunde fließt sein Herz, sein Blut
Über Frankreich strömend in die Welt.   40

---

[1]Cf. lines 20ff. [2]'cried woe upon the hand' [3]i.e., woman who opens the door
[4]'atmosphere' [5]'writing board' [6]i.e., the movement of the quill as Marat writes
[7]'eyelid' [8]*zu Gericht sitzen* 'to sit in judgment' [9]'fiery paw'

Towards Interpretation

1. Trace the poet's use of light-dark imagery as a reflection of the heroine's inner state.
2. Compare the poet's description of the scene with David's famous depiction of it. Does the poet owe much of her vision to David?

Die alte Frau

Heut bin ich krank, nur heute, und morgen bin ich gesund.
Heut bin ich arm, nur heute, und morgen bin ich reich.
Einst aber werde ich immer so sitzen,
In dunkles Schultertuch frierend verkrochen, mit hüstelnder,
    rasselnder Kehle,
Mühsam hinschlurfen und an den Kachelofen knöchrige
    Hände tun.   5
Dann werde ich alt sein.

Meiner Haare finstere Amselschwingen[1] sind grau,
Meine Lippen bestaubte, verdorrte Blüten,
Und nichts weiß mein Leib mehr vom Fallen und Steigen der
    roten springenden Brunnen des Blutes.
Ich starb vielleicht   10
Lange schon vor meinem Tode.

Und doch war ich jung.
War lieb und recht einem Manne wie das braune nährende
    Brot seiner hungrigen Hand,
War süß wie ein Labetrunk seinem dürstenden Munde.
Ich lächelte,   15
Und meiner Arme weiche, schwellende Nattern[2] lockten
    umschlingend in Zauberwald.
Aus meiner Schulter sproßte rauchblauer Flügel,
Und ich lag an der breiteren buschigen Brust,
Abwärts rauschend, ein weißes Wasser, vom Herzen des
    Tannenfelsens.[3]

Aber es kam der Tag und die Stunde kam,   20
Da das bittere Korn in Reife stand, da ich ernten mußte.
Und die Sichel schnitt meine Seele.
„Geh", sprach ich, „Lieber, geh!
Siehe, mein Haar weht Altweiberfäden,[4]
Abendnebel näßt schon die Wange,   25

---

[1]'blackbird wings' [2]'vipers' [3]i.e., "die buschige Brust" [4]'filaments that float through the air in Indian summer (*Altweibersommer*)'

Und meine Blume schauert welkend in Frösten.
Furchen durchziehn mein Gesicht,
Schwarze Gräben die herbstliche Weide.
Geh; denn ich liebe dich sehr."

Still nahm ich die goldene Krone vom Haupt und verhüllte
    mein Antlitz.   30
Er ging,
Und seine heimatlosen Schritte trugen wohl anderem Rastort
    ihn zu unter helleren Augensternen.

Meine Augen sind trüb geworden und bringen Garn und
    Nadelöhr⁵ kaum noch zusammen.
Meine Augen tränen müde unter den faltig schweren,
    rotumränderten Lidern.
Selten   35
Dämmert wieder aus mattem Blick der schwache, fern-
    vergangene Schein
Eines Sommertages,
Da mein leichtes, rieselndes Kleid durch Schaumkrautwiesen⁶
    floß
Und meine Sehnsucht Lerchenjubel in den offenen Himmel
    warf.

Towards Interpretation
1. Carefully translate lines 1-3 of this poem. What temporal level in
    envisioned after line 3?
2. In terms of what imagery does the speaker describe her physical state?
    What image does not fit into this pattern? What does that signify?

Friedrich Georg Jünger (1898-1977)

Die Delphine

Sag, was ist's, das mich erheitert
Wie der Lorbeer, die Zitrone?
Warum muß ich lachen, ohne
Daß ein Widerspruch mich peinigt?

---

⁵'thread and eye of needle'   ⁶'meadows of cardamine'

Wie das Erz auf einer Scheibe[1]   5
Sanfter rundet sich im Gusse,[2]
Spielend sich erhöht im Flusse,
Wallt es in dem nassen Reiche.

Aus den glatten Wassern steigen
Die Delphine; von den feuchten   10
Flanken trieft es, und ein Leuchten
Fährt gleich Blitzen in die Weite.

Hebung sind und Senkung eines,
Und im Steigen wie im Fallen
Spüre ich: ein Maß ist allen   15
Dingen dieser Welt verliehen.

Seliges Erstaunen zwingt mich,
Und ich sehe mit Entzücken:
Von den runden, schwarzen Rücken
Rollt ein Kamm von Silber nieder.   20

Mit den Wassern sind sie einig,
Doch genügt nicht, wie den Fischen,
Diese Flut, sie zu erfrischen,
Kosten müssen sie vom Lichte.

Siehe nun, wie sie es treiben.   25
Duft und Feuer fährt zusammen,
Wenn die Leiber in den Flammen
Zarten Äthers lustvoll kreisen.

Und sie wiegen sich gewichtlos
Wie die geistigsten Gedichte,   30
Prismen sind's aus blauem Lichte,
Keines ihrer Teilchen lichtlos.

Towards Interpretation

1. Taking your cue from lines 21-24, see if you can find a symbolical explanation for the rimes within each stanza and for the assonance (e.g. *Scheibe - Reiche*) in several of the first and fourth lines enclosing these rimes. Can you, by taking the analogical relation between form and content a step further, say why there is perfect rime in lines 1 and 4 of the last stanza?
2. What is the answer to the question(s) asked in the first stanza?
3. What do *Hebung und Senkung* (l. 13) refer to in poetry? Is the com-

---

[1]Shaking table over which ore and water are fed to bring about gravity concentration of the ore.   [2] 'gush' (of water onto the *Scheibe*)

parison of the dolphins to poems (l. 30) a mere phrase or has it been
established beforehand?

Die Zukunft

Wie ein Fisch, der in der roten Pfanne
Aufschnellt, winden sie in harten Leiden
Sich verzweifelt, doch der roten Pfanne,
Prophezei' ich, ihr entfliehet keiner.

Wieder mehrt Verzweiflung ihre Qualen,   5
Feiges Dulden. Wie ein heißes Lager
Ist die Angst, und tiefes Todesgrauen
Schnauben sie wie schwarzen Dunst ins Blaue.

Gibt es Rettung? — Rettung? — Welche Stimmen
Hör' ich rufen? Kraftlos wilde Schreie!   10
Wie die Städte brausen! Doch die Wüsten
Und die großen, wilden Wälder schweigen.

Schön ist die Vernichtung, wo das Niedre
Übermächtig herrscht. Und nimmer lieben
Götter das Gemeine, nicht den Aufruhr.   15
Ordnung lieben sie und hohe Schönheit.

Bald nun werden ihre[1] weiten Hallen,
Ihre Säle hell voll Feuern leuchten.
Widerstrahlend von der Erde Flammen
Werden sie, das Auge blendend, leuchten.   20

Erz ist euer[2] Wagen, Flügel, Flosse.
In den Elementen hebt und senkt ihr
Euch wie Adler, seid dem schwarzen Löwen
Gleich und gleich den schnellen, kühnen Fischen.

Wie ein Hag[3] von Rosen blüht das Feuer.   25
Duftlos brennt es. Rote Flammen stürzen
Auf die Städte, eherne Geschosse.
Wie der Wind, wie Staub verwehn die Klagen.

Towards Interpretation

1. What kind of future is envisioned here? By whom is it imposed? Why
   is such a future looked upon as inevitably necessary?
2. The key stanza is the middle stanza (4). Translate it.

---

[1]i.e., the gods' [2]the gods are addressed [3]'hedge'

3. What is the speaker's attitude towards his own prophecy? Point out images that reveal this.

Bertolt Brecht (1898-1956)

Vom armen B.B.[1]

Ich, Bertolt Brecht, bin aus den schwarzen Wäldern.
Meine Mutter trug mich in die Städte hinein
Als ich in ihrem Leibe lag. Und die Kälte der Wälder
Wird in mir bis zu meinem Absterben sein.

In der Asphaltstadt bin ich daheim. Von allem Anfang   5
Versehen mit jedem Sterbsakrament:
Mit Zeitungen. Und Tabak. Und Branntwein.[2]
Mißtrauisch und faul und zufrieden am End.

Ich bin zu den Leuten freundlich. Ich setze
Einen steifen Hut auf nach ihrem Brauch.   10
Ich sage: Es sind ganz besonders riechende Tiere
Und ich sage: Es macht nichts, ich bin es auch.

In meine leeren Schaukelstühle vormittags
Setze ich mir mitunter ein paar Frauen
Und ich betrachte sie sorglos und sage ihnen: 15
In mir habt ihr einen, auf den könnt ihr nicht bauen.

Gegen Abend versammle ich um mich Männer
Wir reden uns da mit „Gentlemen" an.
Sie haben ihre Füße auf meinen Tischen
Und sagen: Es wird besser mit uns. Und ich frage nicht:
                                                   Wann?   20

Gegen Morgen in der grauen Frühe pissen die Tannen
Und ihr Ungeziefer, die Vögel, fängt an zu schrein.
Um die Stunde trink ich mein Glas in der Stadt aus und
                                                   schmeiße
Den Tabakstummel weg und schlafe beunruhigt ein.

---

[1]A pun may be intended: *B.B.* =*bébé* (baby) [2]Newspapers, tobacco, and brandy are good to make us forget reality: they take the sting out of the living death that is modern civilization, hence, *Sterbsakramente.*

Wir sind gesessen ein leichtes Geschlechte   25
In Häusern, die für unzerstörbare galten   [Manhatten
(So haben wir gebaut die langen Gehäuse des Eilands
Und die dünnen Antennen, die das Atlantische Meer unter-
                                                              halten).[3]

Von diesen Städten wird bleiben: der durch sie hindurchging:
                                              der Wind!
Fröhlich machet das Haus den Esser: er leert es.[4]   30
Wir wissen, daß wir Vorläufige sind
Und nach uns wird kommen: nichts Nennenswertes.

Bei den Erdbeben, die kommen werden, werde ich hoffentlich
Meine Virginia[5] nicht ausgehen lassen durch Bitterkeit
Ich, Bertolt Brecht, in die Asphaltstädte verschlagen   35
Aus den schwarzen Wäldern in meiner Mutter in früher Zeit.

Gegen Verführung

Laßt euch nicht verführen!
Es gibt keine Wiederkehr.
Der Tag steht in den Türen;[1]
Ihr könnt schon Nachtwind spüren:
Es kommt kein Morgen mehr.   5

Laßt euch nicht betrügen!
Das Leben wenig ist.
Schlürft es in vollen Zügen!
Es wird euch nicht genügen
Wenn ihr es lassen müßt!   10

Laßt euch nicht vertrösten![2]
Ihr habt nicht zu viel Zeit!
Laßt Moder den Erlösten![3]

---

[3]"Die Antennen 'unterhalten' das Atlantische Meer sicher nicht mit Musik und mit der gesprochenen Zeitung sondern mit Kurz- und Langwellen, mit den Molekularvorgängen, die den physikalischen Aspekt des Radios ausmachen. In dieser Zeile wird die Verwertung der technischen Mittel durch die heutigen Menschen mit einem Achselzukken abgetan" (Walter Benjamin, "Kommentare zu Gedichten von Brecht").   [4]The "eater" is apparently he who takes joy in the thought of destruction, the "house" modern civilization.   [5]'stogie'

[1]Day stands in the doors ready to leave, yet also still present.   [2]'be put off with promises'   [3]'leave mould to the redeemed'

Das Leben ist am größten:
Es steht nicht mehr bereit.[4]   15

Laßt euch nicht verführen!
Zu Fron und Ausgezehr![5]
Was kann euch Angst noch rühren?
Ihr sterbt mit allen Tieren
Und es kommt nichts nacher.   20

Towards Interpretation
  1. What does the *Verführung* consist of?

Legende vom toten Soldaten

Und als der Krieg im vierten Lenz
Keinen Ausblick auf Frieden bot
Da zog der Soldat seine Konsequenz[1]
Und starb den Heldentod.

Der Krieg war aber noch nicht gar[2]   5
Drum tat es dem Kaiser leid
Daß sein Soldat gestorben war:
Es schien ihm noch vor der Zeit.

Der Sommer zog über die Gräber her
Und der Soldat schlief schon   10
Da kam eines Nachts eine militär-
ische ärztliche Kommission.

Es zog die ärztliche Kommission
Zum Gottesacker hinaus
Und grub mit geweihtem[3] Spaten den   15
Gefallnen Soldaten aus.

Der Doktor besah den Soldaten genau
Oder was von ihm noch da war
Und der Doktor fand, der Soldat war k.v.[4]
Und er drücke sich vor der Gefahr.   20

---

[4]Life no longer stands "ready" since we have already begun to live it.   [5]*Fron* 'forced labor'; *auszehren* 'consume,' 'exploit'

[1]i.e., *die Konsequenz ziehen* 'draw one's own concusion'   [2]'done' (culinary image)
[3]'consecrated'   [4]=*kriegsverwendungsfähig* 'fit for military service'

Und sie nahmen sogleich den Soldaten mit
Die Nacht war blau und schön.
Man konnte, wenn man keinen Helm aufhatte
Die Sterne der Heimat sehn.

Sie schütteten ihm einen feurigen Schnaps   25
In den verwesten Leib
Und hängten zwei Schwestern[5] in seinen Arm
Und ein halb entblößtes Weib.

Und weil der Soldat nach Verwesung stinkt
Drum hinkt ein Pfaffe voran   30
Der über ihn ein Weihrauchfaß schwingt
Daß er nicht stinken kann.

Voran die Musik mit Tschindrara
Spielt einen flotten Marsch.
Und der Soldat, so wie er's gelernt   35
Schmeißt[6] seine Beine vom Arsch.

Und brüderlich den Arm um ihn
Zwei Sanitäter gehn
Sonst flög er noch in den Dreck ihnen hin
Und das darf nicht geschehn.   40

Sie malten auf sein Leichenhemd
Die Farben Schwarz-Weiß-Rot[7]
Und trugen's vor ihm her; man sah
Vor Farben nicht mehr den Kot.

Ein Herr im Frack schritt auch voran   45
Mit einer gestärkten Brust[8]
Der war sich als ein deutscher Mann
Seiner Pflicht genau bewußt.

So zogen sie mit Tschindrara
Hinab die dunkle Chaussee   50
Und der Soldat zog taumelnd mit
Wie im Sturm die Flocke Schnee.

Die Katzen und die Hunde schrein
Die Ratzen im Feld pfeifen wüst:
Sie wollen nicht französisch sein   55
Weil das eine Schande ist.

---

[5] = *Krankenschwestern* [6] 'flings,' i.e., goosesteps [7] colors of the Imperial German flag
[8] 'with a starched shirt front'

Und wenn sie durch die Dörfer ziehn
Waren alle Weiber da.
Die Bäume verneigten sich, Vollmond schien
Und alles schrie hurra.   60

Mit Tschindrara und Wiedersehn!
Und Weib und Hund und Pfaff!
Und mitten drin der tote Soldat
Wie ein besoffner Aff.

Und wenn sie durch die Dörfer ziehn   65
Kommt's, daß ihn keiner sah
So viele waren herum um ihn
Mit Tschindra und Hurra.

So viele tanzten und johlten um ihn
Daß ihn keiner sah.   70
Man konnte ihn einzig von oben noch sehn
Und da sind nur Sterne da.

Die Sterne sind nicht immer da
Es kommt ein Morgenrot.
Doch der Soldat, so wie er's gelernt   75
Zieht in den Heldentod.

Legende von der Entstehung des Buchs Taoteking auf dem Wege des Laotse in die Emigration[1]

Als er Siebzig war und war gebrechlich
Drängte es den Lehrer doch nach Ruh
Denn die Güte war im Lande wieder einmal schwächlich
Und die Bosheit nahm an Kräften wieder einmal zu.
Und er gürtete den Schuh.   5

Und er packte ein, was er so brauchte:
Wenig. Doch es wurde dies und das.
So die Pfeife, die er immer abends rauchte
Und das Büchlein, das er immer las.
Weißbrot nach dem Augenmaß.[2]   10

Freute sich des Tals noch einmal und vergaß es
Als er ins Gebirg den Weg einschlug.
Und sein Ochse freute sich des frischen Grases

---

[1]Lao-tse, Chinese philosopher, founder of Taoism, born 604 B.C. "Tao-te-king"
means "book of Tao and virtue." [2]'visual estimate'

Kauend, während er den Alten trug.
Denn dem ging es schnell genug.   15

Doch am vierten Tag im Felsgesteine
Hat ein Zöllner ihm den Weg verwehrt:
„Kostbarkeiten zu verzollen?" — „Keine."   [gelehrt."
Und der Knabe, der den Ochsen führte, sprach: „Er hat
Und so war auch das erklärt.   20

Doch der Mann, in einer heitren Regung³
Fragte noch: „Hat er was rausgekriegt?"⁴
Sprach der Knabe: „Daß das weiche Wasser in Bewegung
Mit der Zeit den mächtigen Stein besiegt.
Du verstehst, das Harte unterliegt."   25

Daß er nicht das letzte Tageslicht verlöre
Trieb der Knabe nun den Ochsen an.
Und die drei verschwanden schon um eine schwarze Föhre
Da kam plötzlich Fahrt in unsern Mann⁵
Und er schrie: „He, du! Halt an!   30

Was ist das mit diesem Wasser, Alter?"
Hielt der Alte: „Interessiert es dich?"
Sprach der Mann: „Ich bin nur Zollverwalter
Doch wer wen besiegt, das interessiert auch mich.
Wenn du's weißt, dann sprich!   35

Schreib mir's auf! Diktier es diesem Kinde!
So was nimmt man doch nicht mit sich fort.
Da gibt's doch Papier bei uns und Tinte
Und ein Nachtmahl gibt es auch: ich wohne dort.
Nun, ist das ein Wort?"⁶   40

Über seine Schulter sah der Alte
Auf den Mann: Flickjoppe.⁷ Keine Schuh.
Und die Stirne eine einzige Falte.
Ach, kein Sieger trat da auf ihn zu.
Und er murmelte: „Auch du?"   45

Eine höfliche Bitte abzuschlagen
War der Alte, wie es schien, zu alt.
Denn er sagte laut: „Die etwas fragen   [schon kalt."
Die verdienen Antwort." Sprach der Knabe: „Es wird auch
„Gut, ein kleiner Aufenthalt."   50

---

³'in a jolly mood' ⁴'Did he find out anything?' ⁵i.e., he was suddenly struck by an
idea and 'got a move on' ⁶'What do you say?' ⁷'jacket of patches'

Und von seinem Ochsen stieg der Weise.
Sieben Tage schrieben sie zu zweit.
Und der Zöllner brachte Essen (und er fluchte nur noch leise
Mit den Schmugglern in der ganzen Zeit).
Und dann war's so weit.[8]   55

Und dem Zöllner händigte der Knabe
Eines Morgens einundachtzig Sprüche ein
Und mit Dank für eine kleine Reisegabe
Bogen sie um jene Föhre ins Gestein.
Sagt jetzt: kann man höflicher sein?   60

Aber rühmen wir nicht nur den Weisen
Dessen Name auf dem Buche prangt!
Denn man muß dem Weisen seine Weisheit erst entreißen.
Darum sei der Zöllner auch bedankt:
Er hat sie ihm abverlangt.[9]   65

Towards Interpretation
1. Why does Lao-tse think "Auch du?" in line 45?
2. How does the poet view the teacher–pupil relationship?

Elisabeth Langgässer (1899-1950)

Frühlingsmond[1]
„. . . descendit ad inferos"

Abendhin färbt sich der Weiden
Purpurblau[2] bis auf den Grund,
Flut, nicht von Feuer zu scheiden,
Hebt sich das Strombett der Heiden,[3]
Öffnet sich Heraklits Mund.[4]   5

---

[8]'Then they were through' [9]'He was the one who demanded it of him'

[1]Easter is the first Sunday after the first full moon after the spring equinox; "...
descended into Hell" (from the Nicean Creed); cf. Rilke, "Christi Höllenfahrt."
[2]=*das Purpurblau der Weiden* (pastures) [3]*Heiden* means both 'heaths' and 'heathens.'
[4]The heath aglow in the evening light like a river of fire is "Heraclitus' mouth." Heraclitus taught that the universe is an eternal living fire that periodically flames up and
dies down; thus the world is for him ceaselessly becoming and passing away, and we
"never swim in the same river twice."

Kokusgrau dämmern die Lüfte
Hinter dem dunklen Gezweig . . .
Füllt sich des Sichelmonds Hüfte,
Flüstern die knospenden Grüfte:[5]
Schattenspiel,[6] steige! Oh, steig!   10

Unter der stygischen Stelle
Vogelhaft atmet Vergil.[7]
Wenn der Durchbohrte[8] die Welle
Lethes zerteilt, bricht die Schwelle,
Und ist Aeneas am Ziel.[9]   15

Samenzug

Nun peitscht mit leisen Ruten
September sie hinaus,
Die harten braunbeschuhten,
Im Duftkelch reif geruhten,
Die Samen aus dem Haus.   5

Die kleinen Karmeliter,
Die unbeschuhten, auch,[1]
Und an des Grases Gitter
Entlädt sich ein Gewitter
Von spelzgelöstem Rauch.[2]   10

Sandale und Cuculle[3]
So wandern sie dahin
Wie eines Schöpfers Schrulle[4]
Aus klaffender Schatulle
Von tief erschöpftem Grün.   15

Es formt sich zur Pagode
Der schießende Salat,[5]
In Todeslust zu Tode

---

[5]'budding crypts' (a significant oxymoron) [6]The "shadow play" is both the play of
shade and of the shades (of the dead), as the next stanza makes evident. [7]Vergil is of
course among the shades. It is significant that in the Middle Ages his Fourth Eclogue
was thought to prophesy the birth of Christ. [8]Christ [9]Aeneas = ancient man and, in a
wider sense, no doubt the quester of all times. Through Christ the eternal Heraclitian
Werden and *Vergehn* has a stop; the world is released from the wheel of process.

[1]The Carmelites (mendicant monks) are divided into the shod and the unshod. [2]*Spelze*
'glume' (seed-container) [3]'cucullus' (cowl) [4]'whim' [5]'lettuce going to seed'

Die plattgedrückte Hode
Mit der Akaziensaat.   20

Hinab aus Glanz und Bläue
Dringt auf geweihtem Weg
Die Mystenschar,[6] die scheue,
Damit sie sich erneue,
In orphisches Geheg.   25

Die Mütze deckt den Namen,
Der Name die Gestalt.[7]
Will schon das Licht erlahmen,
Birgt sich das Wort[8] im Samen —
So wird die Welt nicht alt.   30

So esoterisch der Sinn, so eingängig ist die Form der
Langgässerschen Lyrik. Die Melodie der Klänge, der
klar bestimmte Rhythmus, das Zusammenfall der
sprachlichen und metrischen Gliederung, die einfache
Syntax, der Kehrreim und ähnliches — das alles sind
liedhafte Elemente. Das Lied ist innerhalb der Gat-
tungen der Lyrik schlechthin Sprache der „Natur" (im
Gegensatz etwa zur Ode, zum Sonett, zur Elegie als
„Geist"-Ausdruck). „Natur" ist diese Lyrik nicht als
Gefäß der Stimmung, sondern gerade als Gefäß des
„Geistes," wobei „Geist" eines ist mit Mysterium.
Die lyrische Sprache dieser Dichterin ist betörender
Klang und mystische Chiffre zugleich; in ihr ist die
bedrängende Macht und Süße des Irdischen und die
befreiende Kraft des Logos; sie ist „Natur" im
Zeichen der Erlösung.*

---

[6]The seeds are now seen as a procession of *mystai* (those initiated in [Orphic] mysteries). [7]Reference to Orphic rites: *Mütze* = seed capsule and cap or veil worn by neophyte in Orphic initiation ceremony; *Name* = logos, more specifically, *logos spermati-
kos* (seed word), which contains within itself the future form (*Gestalt*). [8]i.e., the divine
Word, Logos

*Erich Hock, in *Wege zum Gedicht*, ed. Rupert Hirschenauer and Albrecht Weber
(München and Zürich: Schnell und Steiner, [8]1972), 1:383.

An den Leser

Leser, wie gefall ich dir?
Leser, wie gefällst du mir?
Friedrich von Logau

Freund, es ist genug. Im Fall du mehr willst lesen,
So geh und werde selbst die Schrift und selbst das Wesen.
Angelus Silesius

Appendix: German Literary Terms

Metrical Feet

*Iambus**	| ˘ – |	con-tról	her-béi
Trochäus	| – ˘ |	stú-pid	eín-zig
Anapest	| ˘ ˘ – |	con-tra-díct	Me-di-zín
Dactylus	| – ˘ ˘ |	clúm-si-ness	é-wi-ge
Spondäus	| – – |	snów-stòrm	Wélt-schmèrz
Amphibrachus	| ˘ – ˘ |	be-líeve me	Ge-heím-nis
Kretikus	| – ˘ – |	bóred to deáth	Quál und Leíd
Choriambus	| – ˘ ˘ – |	yeár after yeár	Mút-ter Na-túr

General Terms

Alliteration — English: Alliteration, head rime. The repetition of consonant sounds at the beginning of words.

> *S*ie *s*ang zu ihm, *s*ie *s*prach zu ihm:
> (Goethe)

Anakreonitik — English: Anacreontic poetry. Poetry in praise of wine, women and song, named after the Greek poet, Anacreon.

Auftakt — English: Anacrusis. One or more unaccented syllables before the first accented syllable that are not counted as part of the metrical scheme.

Ballade — See below, under "Strophic forms"

Dinggedicht — English: Dinggedicht. A poem consisting of a dispassionate and objective description of an object, often a work of visual art.

Encomium — A work which praises a person or thing by extolling inherent virtues.

Gelegenheitsgedicht — English: Occasional poem. A work composed to commemorate a particular event.

Hochzeitslied — or *Epithelamium*. English: Epithelamion. A joyous song in praise of marriage, often with bawdy elements.

Kadenz — English: cadence. Either macsuline (*männlich*) or feminine (*weiblich*), depending upon whether the last sylla-

---

*The English names for the metrical feet are: iamb, trochee, anapest, dactyl, spondee, amphibrach, cretic or amphimacer, and choriamb. Rarely used in German are the Pyrrhic/*Pyrrhichius* (˘ ˘) and the tribrach/*Tribrachys* (˘ ˘ ˘)

ble is accented (m.) or unaccented (f.). The Germans also distinguish, particularly in medieval poetry, between feminine and *klingend*, where the last linguistically unaccented syllable is accented for the sake of the meter (*wér-dè*). A line is called *stumpf* when the meter would demand another foot, but it is absent: this forces a pause for the duration of the absent foot.

Únd so- | láng du | dás nicht | hást,   *m*
díeses: | stírb und | wérde   *f*
(Goethe)

The last line above could also be scanned as *klingend* to achieve a four-foot line (tetrameter):

díeses: | stírb und | wér- | dè

or as *stumpf*:

díeses: | stírb und | wérde | ‿ |

Katalexe

English: Catalexis. Incomplete metrical foot (permissible at the end of a metrical line).

Laúe Lúft kommt blaú geflóssen,
Frǘhling, Frǘhling sóll es seín!
(Eichendorff)

Schwebende Betonung

English: Hovering accent. The formation of a spondee to resolve a conflict between natural accent and metrical constrictions in iambic or trochaic feet.

Sēhnsūcht | muß wách- | sen án | der Tié- | fe...
(Eichendorff)

Strophe

English: Stanza. A grouping of verses arranged together in a specific metrical pattern. See "Strophic Forms" below.

Totenklage

or *Threnodie*. English: Elegy, threnody. In classical times, a mournful poem in distichs recited during funeral processions or at feasts in honor of the dead; later, any poetic lament for the deceased.

Vers

English: Verse. Commonly referred to as a "line" of poetry.

Zäsur

English: Caesura. A slight pause in the verse occasioned either by the natural rhythm of the language (often indicated by punctuation) or by metrical constraints.

Du ungesehner Blitz, ‖ du dunkel-helles Licht
(Greiffenberg)

Zeilensprung

English: Enjambement, run-over line. A line of poetry that runs over into the next line without a grammatical break.

Auf den Canal Grande betten
Tief sich ein die Abendschatten.

(C. F. Meyer)

Rime Patterns

Assonanz   English: Assonance, vowel rime. Occurs when two words have the same vowels but different consonants. Not a pure rime: w*ei*ch – br*ei*t.

Binnenreim   English: Internal rime. A rhyme between two words in the same line.

Freud*voll* und leid*voll*
Gedankenvoll sein.

(Goethe)

Dreireim   English: Triplet. Three-line stanza with a single rime: a a a | b b b | c c c [...].

Identischer Reim   English: Identical rime. Two or more lines rime on the same word.

Zwischen Menschen, Göttern und *Heroen*
Knüpfte Amor einen schönen Bund,
Sterbliche mit Göttern und *Heroen*
Huldigten in Amathunt.

(Schiller)

Kreuzreim   English: Alternate or cross rime. Each pair of rhyming lines is split up by another of a pair of rhyming lines: a b a b c d c d [...].

Es ist ein Reis entsprungen	*a*
Aus einer Wurzel zart,	*b*
Als uns die Alten sungen;	*a*
Aus Jesse kam die Art.	*b*

(*Volkslied*)

A variation is the *Erweiterter* or *Verschränkter Reim*: a b c [...] a b c [...].

Männlicher Reim   See above under *Kadenz*.

Paarreim   English: Couplet. Two successive lines of poetry, of equal length, that rime with each other: a a b b c c [...].

Jetzund kömmt die Nacht herbei,	*a*
Vieh und Menschen werden frei,	*a*
Die gewünschte Ruh geht an,	*b*
Meine Sorge kömmt heran.	*b*

(Opitz)

Schweifreim   Also called *Zwischenreim*. English: Tail rime. Rime scheme in which a third line (in group of six rimes) with the sixth line, with lines 1 + 2, 4 + 5 forming couplets: a a b c c b.

	Der Mond ist aufgegangen, *a*
	Die goldnen Sternlein prangen *a*
	Am Himmel hell und klar; *b*
	Der Wald steht schwarz und schweiget, *c*
	Und aus den Wiesen steiget *c*
	Der weiße Nebel wunderbar. *b*
	(Claudius)

Terzine English: Tercet. Rime scheme in which the second line of a group of 3 lines (tercet) rimes with the first and third of the next tercet: a b a | b c b | c d c [...]. Also a strophic form (see *Terzarima*).

Umarmender Reim English: Enclosing rime. The rime scheme is: a b b a.

> Es sang vor langen Jahren *a*
> Wohl auch die Nachtigall, *b*
> Das war wohl süßer Schall, *b*
> Da wir zusammen waren. *a*
> (Brentano)

Waise Line that does not rime with any other in the stanza

Weiblicher Reim See above under *Kadenz*.

Verse Forms

Alexandriner English: Alexandrine. Iambic hexameter line of 12-13 syllables with a caesura after the sixth syllable and accents on the sixth and twelfth syllables.

> Du síehst, | wohín | du síehst, ‖ nur Eí- | telkéit | auf Érden.
> (Gryphius)

Blankvers English: Blank verse. Unrimed verses in iambic pentameter.

> Sie wár- | en meín, | im Án- | gesícht | der Wélt.
> (Schiller)

Distichon English: Distich. Also known in English as the Elegaic Couplet, the distich is formed by a hexameter line followed by a (classical) pentameter.

> Ím Hex- | ámeter | stéigt des | Spríngquells | flússige | Sáule,
> Ím Pent- | ámeter | dráuf ‖ fállt sie me- | lódisch her- | áb.
> (Schiller)

Endecasillabo An Italian verse form of 11 (German, 10-11) syllables based upon the French *vers commun*. German imitations of the form usually have feminine rimes.

> Ihr náht | euch wíe- | der, schwánk- | endé | Gestálten,
> die früh | sich éinst | dem trú- | ben Blíck | gezéigt.
> (Goethe)

Freie Rhythmen Form developed by Klopstock in which the length of the lines and the grouping of the stresses are determined not by a metrical scheme but by the surge and flow of the emotion conveyed.

Freie Verse

English: Free verse. Similar to *Freie Rhythmen* in that the length of the line and the number of stresses may vary, but here the metrical feet must be identical, e.g., all iambic or all trochaic.

Hexameter

Six-footed meter (used already by Homer) in which the accented syllable may be followed by one unaccented syllable (i. e., a trochaic foot) or two unaccented syllables (i.e., a dactyl), except in the fifth foot which must *always* be a dactyl. May have a caesura after the second, third, or fourth accented syllable.

Ságet, | Steíne, mir | án, ‖ o | sprécht, ihr | *hóhen Pa-* | láste!
(Goethe)

Knittelvers

German tetrameter (four-footed) line in which the number of unaccented syllables in a metrical foot may vary from one to two. Considered a vulgar form since the sixteenth century, but often used later for comic effect.

Wo sól ich hín, wo kómm ich hér?
Ich sínne bey mír die lánge und quér
Mein gántzes Hértze im Leíbe brícht,
Vertúnkelt íst mein Ángesícht.
(Gryphius)

Pentameter

In modern verse, a five-footed metrical line (the basis for *Blankvers*). The classical pentameter, however, despite its name, has to us the appearance of a **six-footed** meter. The unaccented syllable is omitted after the third and sixth accented syllables, with a caesura after the third. Before the caesura, dactyls may be substituted for trochaic feet; after the caesura, there are usually dactyls.

Éwige | Róma; nur | mír ‖ schweíget noch | álles so | stíll.
(Goethe)

Vers commun

Iambic pentameter line of 10-11 syllables with a caesura after the fourth syllable (second foot).

Auff, áuff, | mein Géist, ‖ und dú | mein gán- | tzer Sínn,
Wirff áll- | es dás ‖ was Wélt | ist vón | dir hín.
(Opitz)

Strophic forms

Ballade

English: Ballad. A narrative poem in stanzas, usually characterized by its simple language, the repetition of phrases or epithets, and "dramatic" elements, like dialogue. The folk ballad (*Volksballade*) was transmitted by oral tradition; the art ballad (*Kunstballade*) is the composition of a known author in the ballad style. The form often consists of alternating verses of four and three stresses with (usually) the rime scheme: *a b a b*.

> Ich hört ein Sichelein rauschen,
> Wohl rauschen durch das Korn,
> Ich hört ein feine Magd klagen,
> Sie hätt ihr Lieb verlorn.
>
> (*Volkslied*)

Lutherstrophe

Verse form common to early Protestant hymns and derived from elements common to other forms: from medieval love poetry, the division into *Aufgesang* and *Abgesang*; from the madrigal, the use of the unrimed *Waise* (see Luther's "Der 46. Psalm," p. 1).

Aufgesang 1st *Stollen* *a* 8 syllables /4 stresses / masc. rime
                       b 7 syllables / 3 stresses / fem. rime
        2nd *Stollen a* 8 syllables /4 stresses / masc. rime
                       b 7 syllables / 3 stresses / fem. rime
Abgesang   *c* 8 syllables /4 stresses / masc. rime
                       c 8 syllables /4 stresses / masc. rime
                       x 7 syllables / 3 stresses / rimeless

Madrigal

Originally an Italian stanzaic form of from 3 to 20 verses, in which the verses are of varied length and metrical form. The rime scheme was free, with occasional *Waisen* interspersed; however, the end of the stanza was usually marked by a rhyming couplet.

Ode

To the Greeks the ode was a form combining choral chant and movement, performed on important public occasions. The strophes were arranged in groups of three: the *strophe* was sung while the chorus moved in one direction; the *antistrophe* (in the same metrical form), while the chorus moved in another direction; and the *epode*, which had a different metrical form, while the chorus stood still. Odes are usually characterized by a lofty and thoughtful tone.

Alkäische (Alchaic) *Ode:*

```
⏑ — ⏑ — ⏑ — ⏑ ⏑ — ⏑ —
⏑ — ⏑ — ⏑ — ⏑ ⏑ — ⏑ —
⏑ — ⏑ — ⏑ — ⏑ — ⏑
— ⏑ ⏑ — ⏑ ⏑ — ⏑ — ⏑
```

> Ihr Freúnde hánget, wánn ich gestórben bín,
> Die kleíne Hárfe hínter dem Áltar auf,
> Wo án der Wánd die Tótenkränze
> Mánches verstórbenen Mádchens schímmern.
>
> (Hölty)

Asklepiadeische (Asclepidean) *Ode*:

— ˘ — ˘ ˘ — ‖ — ˘ ˘ — ˘ —
— ˘ — ˘ ˘ — ‖ — ˘ ˘ — ˘ —
— ˘ — ˘ ˘ — ˘
— ˘ — ˘ ˘ — ˘ —

Wénn der sílberne Mónd dúrch die Gestraúche blíckt
Únd sein schlúmmerndes Lícht úber den Rásen geúßt
Únd die Náchtigall flótet,
Wándl ich tráurig von Búsch zu Búsch.

(Hölty)

Sapphische (Sapphic) *Ode*:

— ˘ — ˘ — ˘ ˘ — ˘ — ˘
— ˘ — ˘ — ˘ ˘ — ˘ — ˘
— ˘ — ˘ — ˘ ˘ — ˘ — ˘
— ˘ ˘ — ˘

Schón und glánzreich íst des bewégten Meéres
Wéllenschlág, wann tóbenden Lárms es ánbraust;
Dóch dem Feúr ist keín Elemént vergleíchbar,
Wéder an Állmacht....

(Platen)

Some poets, like Klopstock, varied the placement of the dactylic foot in the Sapphic ode for effect.

Sonett	English: Sonnet. Originally an Italian form, the sonnet consists of 14 lines made up of two quatrains (i.e., an octet) and two tercets (i.e., a sestet) with a logical and linguistic break between them. The rime scheme is often a b b a / a b b a / c c d / e e d (for example, Rilke's "Der Tod der Geliebten," p. 363), but variation is permitted.
Terzarima	A series of interlocking tercets in iambic pentameter in which the second line of the first tercet rimes with the first and third of the next tercet: a b a | b c b | c d c [...]. Strophic form of Dante's *Divine Comedy*.

Und süße Früchte werden aus den herben   *a*
Und fallen nachts wie tote Vögel nieder   *b*
Und liegen wenig Tage und verderben.   *a*

Und immer weht der Wind, und immer wieder   *b*
Vernehmen wir und reden viele Worte   *c*
Und spüren Lust und Müdigkeit der Glieder....   *b*

(Hofmannsthal)

Volksliedstrophe	A four-line strophe consisting of three or four stressed syllables (i.e., trimiter or pentameter) which may end with either a *männliche* (˘ —) or *weibliche* (— ˘) *Kadenz*.

Zu Koblenz auf der Brücken	*w*
Da lag ein tiefer Schnee,	*m*
Der Schnee, der ist verschmolzen,	*w*
Das Wasser fließt in See.	*m*

(*Volkslied*)

Rhetorical figures

Anadiplosis Repetition of the last word of one line or clause to begin the next.

Lichtlein, schwimmet! Spielt, ihr *Kinder*!
Kinder-Chor, o singe, singe!
(Goethe)

Anapher English: Anaphora. One or more words repeated at the beginning of successive verses.

Mit dir nun muß ich kosen,
Mit dir, o Joseph mein.
(Spee)

Apostrophe A digression in the discourse to address directly some person or thing either present or absent.

Ich genoß einst, o ihr Todten, es mit euch!
(Hölty)

Asyndeton Omission of conjunctions between words, phrases, or clauses. (The *polysyndeton* does the opposite, placing conjuctions between each element.)

Gott schafft, erzeugt, trägt, speist, tränkt, labt, stärkt, nährt ...
(Logau)

Chiasmus English: Chiasm. A passage with two balanced parts which have their elements reversed, forming an X (Greek *chi*).

O *Wonne* der *Sonne*,
O *Sonne* der *Wonne*!
(Fleming)

Epanalepse English: Epanalepsis. The repetition of a word or phrase within the same verse.

Laß ab, Laß ab, zu klopfen
(Platen)

Epanadiplose or *Kyklos*. English: Epanadiplosis. A specific form of epanalepsis, in which the end of a verse or clause repeats the word(s) with which it began.

Wohin? Ach, *wohin*?
(Goethe)

Epiphora Repetition of a word or phrase at the end of several successive clauses or verses. The opposite of anaphora.

> Lichtlein *schwinden*, Sterne *schwinden*
> (Goethe)

Figura etymologica The juxtaposition of words in different parts of speech with a common etymological ancestor.

> Unser Haupt mit *Laub umlaubt*.
> (Klaj)

Metapher English: Metaphor. Substitution of one concept for another, e.g., world=grave.

> Was ist die Welt und ihr berühmtes Glänzen? ...
> Ein faules *Grab*, so Alabaster deckt.
> (Hofmannswaldau)

Metonymie English: Metonymy. Substitution of cause for effect or effect for cause, a proper name for one of its qualities or vice versa, e.g., Adonis=handsome boy who dies young.

> Hier fiel im Frühling Gott gelebter Tage,
> Ein kriegrischer Adon!
> (Karschin)

Oxymoron A paradoxical saying, where the adjective often semantically contradicts the noun.

> Der Schultern *warmer Schnee* wird werden kalter Sand.
> (Hofmannswaldau)

Paradoxon English: Paradox. A seemingly self-contradictory statement, which is shown (often in a surprising way) to be true.

> Zeit ist wie Ewigkeit, und Ewigkeit wie Zeit.
> (Angelus Silesius)

Personifikation English: Personification. Addressing an animal or inanimate object as if it were human. When the speaker's own emotions are projected upon upon these objects, one speaks of the *poetic* or *pathetic fallacy*.

> Der Mond von einem Wolkenhügel
> Sah *schläfrig* aus dem Duft hervor ...
> (Goethe)

Synekdoche English: Synecdoche. Susbstitution of the part for the whole, genus for species, or vice versa, e.g., bread= food.

> Nimmer *Brot* im Sacke,
> Nimmer Geld im Packe ...
> (Logau)

Copyrights and Permissions

List of Illustrations*

---

*Unless otherwise noted, all illustrations come from the collection of the Ward Melville, Jr., Library, State University of New York at Stony Brook.

Index

Poems discussed in the text are indicated by an asterisk (*). Footnotes provide commentary on a number of poems not starred.